Gree

4

ALONSO DE ZORITA

ALONSO DE ZORITA

Royal Judge and
Christian Humanist
1512–1585

Ralph H. Vigil

University of OKLAHOMA Press : Norman and London

*Alonso de Zorita: Royal Judge and Christian Humanist,
1512–1585*

was awarded the second

Spain and America in the Quincentennial of
the Discovery Prize

for 1987

Sponsored by the

Spanish Ministry of Culture

and the

University of the United States

Library of Congress Cataloging-in-Publication Data
Vigil Ralph H. (Ralph Harold), 1932–
    Alonso de Zorita: royal judge and Christian humanist 1512–1585.
    Bibliography: p. 345
    Includes index.
    1. Zorita, Alonso de, 1512–1585. 2. Judges—Dominican Republic—
Biography. 3. Judges—Spain—Colonies—Biography. 4. Indians of Central
America—Legal status, laws, etc.—History. I. Title.
KGQ304.Z67V54   1987   347.7293′014 [B]   86–40531
                                         347.2930714 [B]
    ISBN 0-8061-2061-4 (alk. paper)

Publication of this work has been made possible in part by grants from the
Andrew W. Mellon Foundation and the University of Nebraska, Lincoln.

The paper in this book meets the guidelines for permanence and durability of
the Committee on Production Guidelines for Book Longevity of the Council on
Library Resources, Inc.

For Barbara, Frank, and Rafael

Contents

Illustrations

Preface

ALONSO DE ZORITA—a royal judge of great moral integrity who wrote a book—left this world four centuries ago. But the program of justice for the Indian for which he fought endures, and his virtues have not been forgotten. The worthy Zorita left no descendants, but his family includes all those men and women of good will who continue the struggle against oppression in Latin America today. Zorita, who was especially fond of chapter forty-four of the book of Ecclesiasticus, would have praised the work of the late Monsignor Oscar Romero, the archbishop of San Salvador assassinated in 1980 for promoting land reform and human rights.

My intention in this book is to increase understanding and appreciation of Zorita as jurist, author, and social reformer. In my attempt to capture the significance of Zorita's life and works, I have taken into account the historical-social setting that helped shape his cast of mind. This study therefore opens with an account of Zorita's familial and social background, and his intellectual formation at the University of Salamanca. Subsequent chapters deal with Zorita's career as a royal judge in the high courts of Española, Guatemala, and Mexico. Zorita's last years are placed within the context of Spain's economic problems, and the plight of those Castilian subjects reduced to poverty by a ruinous Hapsburg foreign policy. The work ends with an appraisal of Zorita as historian and anthropologist.

As is apparent, I have focused on Zorita's years of service in the Indies (1548–1566) and the variety of his duties in the royal tribunals and colonies. My reason for this is obvious; Zorita's works, which delineate the issues of the Indian problem and the political and socioeconomic factors underlying the conflict between the crown and Spanish settlers over Indian tribute and labor, were largely based upon what he experienced and observed during these years. For his description of the nature of Indian society in pre-Conquest times, Zorita largely relied on written and oral accounts provided him by members of the regular clergy and aged Indian *principales*.

Zorita is known primarily as the author of *The Brief and*

Summary Relation of the Lords of New Spain. This work, written in retirement, remained in manuscript form until the nineteenth century. But as Benjamin Keen observes in his insightful introduction to his English translation of this work, various copies of the original manuscript made by students of ancient and colonial Mexico show that they "recognized the book's worth and importance long before its first publication."[1]

Scholars of diverse backgrounds have attested to the value of the *Brief Relation* ever since its publication in 1840. The nineteenth-century American historian William H. Prescott approved Zorita's "sound and discriminating judgment." Mexican scholar Miguel Orozco y Berra used Zorita's work for his detailed survey of Aztec social organization and notes Zorita's "scrupulous investigations." More recently, French historian François Chevalier described the work as "indispensable." In his study of the evolution of Aztec society, German writer Friedrich Katz commended Zorita's "true ethnological sense." English historian J. H. Elliott observed that "the reports of the more intelligent and inquiring ... officials, like Alonso de Zorita in New Spain, were in effect exercises in applied anthropology, capable of yielding a vast amount of information about native customs and society." American art historian George Kubler also has used the works of "the learned and experienced Alonso de Zorita" in his study of Mexican architecture.[2]

Granted the importance of the book, one appreciates it more by learning about its creator and the world in which he acted. In this study, I have attempted to approach Zorita and his age from "the position of sympathetic introspection and understanding." Hence I have sought objectivity, but have not been impartial.[3]

Like his contemporary Cervantes, Zorita was a loyal servant of church and crown and "that very rare thing, a Christian."[4] His life confirms Cervantes's statement that true chivalry consists in protecting and defending "the humble and the weak from the powerful and the proud."[5] Like the aged Cervantes, Zorita was constrained by poverty in his last years, and throughout his life saw hardships and misfortunes. But he was never dismayed.

Lincoln, Nebraska   RALPH H. VIGIL

Acknowledgments

MORE years ago than I care to remember, Professors France V. Scholes and Benjamin Keen suggested the topic of this study. Time and chance prevented its completion until now. I owe special thanks for assistance to Benjamin Keen. My colleague William L. Sherman has been a good friend and shared much information. Research in Spain was made possible by a Fulbright grant and was aided by the staffs of various archives and libraries. I should also like to acknowledge the help given me by friends Vicenta Cortés Alonso, Miguel Maticorena, Santiago Montero, Francisco Sánchez Rico, and Antonio Muro Orejón. Any faults to be found in the book are mine. What is good was shaped by the influence of many persons, not the least of whom was Ysabel Córdova, my cousin and first teacher of Spanish, who saw some promise. This potential was later encouraged by Sabine Ulibarrí, Rubén Cobos, and Marshall Nason at the University of New Mexico. Finally, I should like to thank my wife for her patience and good humor.

R.H.V.

ALONSO DE ZORITA

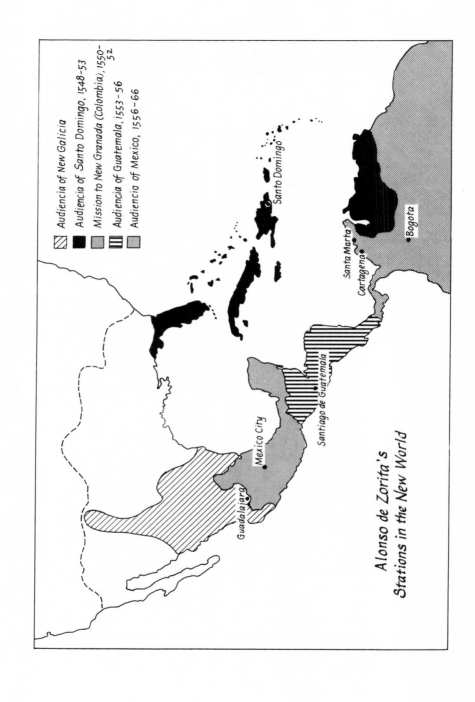

Audiencia of New Galicia
Audiencia of Santo Domingo, 1548–53
Mission to New Granada (Colombia), 1550–52
Audiencia of Guatemala, 1553–56
Audiencia of Mexico, 1556–66

Santo Domingo

Santa Marta
Cartagena
Bogota

Santiago de Guatemala

Mexico City

Guadalajara

*Alonso de Zorita's
Stations in the New World*

CHAPTER 1

The Making of a Judge

ALONSO DE ZORITA's life began in the glorious summer of Spain's rise to power in the Old World and the New. It ended in the melancholy autumn of Philip II's reign, a period characterized by indecision and a failure of nerve. Born in either 1511 or 1512, Zorita lived in an age of transition from the medieval to the modern world, a time in which traditional ways of thought and action were steadily undermined by the immense expansion of Western geographical and mental horizons, the growth of overseas commerce, and the rise of the nation-state and absolute monarchy.

As is true of all other human beings, Zorita's world view was shaped by the social and intellectual conditions of his time and place. A study of this Castilian writer and judge reveals that Zorita shared with other distinguished Spaniards of his generation a distinct attitude toward the world. This attitude was fundamentally and inevitably religious—given the decisive role of religion in the expression of ideology in the sixteenth century—and represented the fusion of classical forms of thought with the deeply felt, traditional Catholic spirituality of an age still rooted in scholastic theology.

Zorita's world view most clearly emerges from his account of life and labor in pre- and post-Conquest Mexico. His inquiry into ancient Indian culture makes frequent comparative and didactic allusions to the history and culture of the Greco-Roman world; in this sense Zorita may be called a humanist. Humanists spoke with several voices, but all were influenced by the secular, urban culture of antiquity, and most became ardent defenders of the nation-state united under an absolute monarch.[1] But if Zorita shared the humanist enthusiasm for the Greco-Roman heritage and sought in the typical humanist manner to educate and guide the steps of the king and his counselors, his views on society, man, and nature are rooted in medieval scholasticism; they reflect a Christian piety unknown to Aristotle and the ancients. Zorita thus represents what has been called the neo-Scholasticism of the Counter-Reformation, which not only sought "with the aid of the Divine Grace the salvation of one's soul, but with the aid of

3

the same earnestly to labor for the salvation and perfection of one's neighbor."[2]

I explore Zorita's social background and intellectual formation in the following pages for obvious reasons. Religion still greatly influenced men's outlook in society, and one's particular place in the distinct estates composing the society of the *Siglo de Oro* still largely determined a man's opportunities for advancement. Social theory lagged behind political and economic reality in the age of Zorita and the antihero of the novel *Lazarillo de Tormes*; the prevailing ideology still regarded plebeians as inferior to nobles and manual labor, merchants, and trade as necessary evils. But because Philip II mistrusted the great lords, lesser nobles and gentry who were graduates of the universities were preferred in appointments to the service of the king. Hidalgos and caballeros were also victorious in their effort to appropriate municipal offices in the sixteenth century.[3] As a royal judge in the tribunals of Spain and the New World, Zorita was a member of the legal hierarchy charged with dispensing the king's justice. Because social standing largely determined occupations and professions in this quasi-feudal world, a review of Zorita's class status and educational background will help to explain his career as bureaucrat and legist.

The late Middle Ages are often viewed as a time marked by the rise of new modes of expression in art and religion and new forms of political, economic, and social life. Consequently there is a tendency to regard the static and hierarchical conception of society held by the nobility in this age "as little more than a remnant of a superannuated order already crumbling into insignificance," a vestige hardly worthy of study for an understanding of the epoch.[4]

There is much truth to the idea that the decline of the nobility and feudalism between the fourteenth and seventeenth centuries and its replacement by a money economy, an infinite variety of religious beliefs, and national states with centralized governments was a major qualitative change. Huizinga is correct, however, in asserting that "long after nobility and feudalism had ceased to be really essential factors in the state and in society, they continued to impress the mind as dominant forms of life."[5]

The Setting

This was especially true in sixteenth-century Spain. Military and religious ideals shaped by the long crusade against the infidel found expression in the concept of the inimitable warrior-noble. The hidalgo of ballads and literature was a knight who lived for war, who lived by a strict code of honor, who won fame and fortune by force of arms. Military leaders, whether in life or literature, admired the virtues of bravery, fortitude, tenacity, and loyalty; they viewed men who won wealth by other than force of arms as lesser men.[6] In contrast, the Spanish bourgeoisie had no distinctive class ideology, and many aspired to become nobles. Those who grew rich by trade often hastened to buy land— ownership of an estate being an essential characteristic of noble status. Others saw in the king's service a direct path to nobility. As Braudel observes, the *letrados* (men of middling condition trained in Roman law) habitually prefixed their names with Don, and were lesser nobles or aspirant nobles far more than bourgeois civil servants.[7]

The essentially aristocratic idea of *hidalguía*, containing the virtues of honor, courage, and the lust for glory, pervaded sixteenth-century Spanish society. Adventurers like Lope de Aguirre, Gonzalo Pizarro, and Hernán Cortés in the Indies sought through military exploits "to be worth more" (*valer más*). The sacred character of the institution of nobility was never compromised by unworthy persons in Spain, and as late as 1781 nobles who were arrested as vagabonds were sent to the army with the rank of "distinguished soldiers."[8] The minor nobility's world view also set the standards for colonial society in the Indies, called by Cervantes the refuge and sanctuary of the hopeless, the bankrupt, the criminal, and the delinquent of Spain.[9] Military and spiritual ideals were joined in the quest of utopia, and glory, adventure, wealth, honor and fame were to be found in the pursuit of gold, subjects, and souls.[10] Even native rulers in the Indies were considered to be lords (*señores naturales*) each of whom, "by inherent nature of superior qualities, goodness, and virtue, and by birth of superior station, attains power legitimately and exercises dominion over all within his land [*señorío natural*] justly and in accord with divine, natural and human law and reason."[11] Although the number of magnates serving as courtiers clearly declined during the reign of the Catholic Kings,[12] most of the military commands, important diplomatic posts, church offices, and positions in the government bureaucracy were filled from the ranks of the lesser nobility composed of *militares, caballeros, gentileshombres, ciudadanos honrados*, and *hijosdalgo*.

From the terms for nobility listed above, it is clear that the lines of division between the urban patriciate (*caballeros de*

Deposition of Alonso de Zorita, written in Córdoba, October 25, 1572.
An unusually clear example of sixteenth-century script.

Deposition of Alonso de Zorita, Córdoba, October 25, 1572.
(Archivo Histórico de Protocolos, Córdoba, Oficio 37, tomo 40,
between folios numbered 1,249 and 1,250).

Sepan cuantos esta carta vieren como yo
el doctor Alonso de Zurita, vecino desta ciudad
de Granada de la collación de la iglesia mayor,
oidor que fuí de Su Majestad en el Audiencia Real
de la Nueva España que reside en la ciudad de México por
mi y en nombre de Juan Pérez de Zurita, capitán general y
teniente de governador en las Indias por Su Majestad, mi hermano
y por virtud del poder que dél tengo ante Gonzalo Madaleno
Castroverde, escribano público de la ciudad de Córdova, su fecha
a cuatro días del mes de julio de mil y quinientos y sesenta y dos
años, y usando del dicho poder digo que por cuanto habemos tratado
y tratamos pleito en esta real audiencia con el señor Miguel Díaz de Zurita, vecino y jurado de la ciudad de Córdova,
por sí y por Francisco de Zurita y con la señora doña Mencia
de Zurita, mujer del señor Alonso de Aguilera y con la señora
doña María de Zurita, mujer del señor Pedro de Olmos de Aguilera y con la señora doña Elvira de Zurita Villavicencio,
mujer que fué del señor capitán Pedro de Arroyo Valdivia que sea en gloria y con el monasterio de la señora
Santa Inés de Córdova en nombre y por cabeza de las seño-
ras doña Inés de Zurita y doña Ana de Zurita Villavicencio, monjas profesas en el dicho monasterio, todos nueve
hijos y herederos de Alonso de Zurita mi señor y padre
que sea en gloria, jurado que fué de la dicha ciudad de
Córdova, sobre la herencia y legítima que cada uno
pretende y sobre las demás causas y razones en el dicho
pleito contenidas que pasa ante Diego de la Fuente,
secretario desta real audiencia, y ahora por nos
quitar y apartar de pleitos y diferencias, costas
y gastos y por saber que son largos y dudosos y no
saber el fin dellos son convenidos con la señora aba-
desa y convento del dicho monasterio de Santa Inés
en que por todo y cualquier de derecho que le puede per-
tenecer por la dicha herencia del dicho Alonso de Zurita mi señor se les den por todos los herederos seiscien-
tos ducados y con esto se contentan y renuncian el derecho
que tenían y les pertenecían y podían perte-
necer a la dicha herencia por razón de la ilegítima herencia.

ciudad) and the nobility of the sword (*nobleza militar*) were no longer clear. In many cases younger sons of urban patriciate became nobility of the sword while the entailed estate (*mayorazgo*) of the family continued to be held by the oldest son, who remained a member of the urban patriciate.[13] In many cities the two groups were closely related and constituted in fact, and sometimes in law, a single class.[14] On the other hand, although caballeros and hidalgos were closely related by marriage and privilege, one who was a caballero was not necessarily a hidalgo, though he well might be as is demonstrated in the term *caballero hijodalgo*. The difference between the two ranks (and the superior social and economic position of the caballero) is pointed out in *Don Quixote* when the niece stresses that the folly of her uncle is to imagine that he is a caballero, not being one, "for although hidalgos can be [caballeros], those who are poor cannot."[15] Nevertheless, as Tomás Thayer Ojeda has observed, it was the general opinion in the Golden Age that nobility consisted principally in *hidalguía* and that the rest was only a difference in social position—subject to change—that did not affect the fundamental fact of noble birth.

The relationship between economic structure and the social system in Spain was especially evident in the system of land holding. Figures differ slightly for the nobility, but this group represented less than 2 percent of the population, or 125,000 persons. Divided into 5,000 magnates, 60,000 knights or hidalgos, and 60,000 urban patricians, nobles directly owned or held jurisdiction of 97 percent of the land by 1500.[16]

In addition to controlling the wealth of Spain, the aristocracy also determined the ideology of the period through its spokesmen. Religion stressed the correctness and maintenance of the static society, and social prestige was accorded only to the achievements of those who maintained the existing order by arms and letters. Chivalry was a virtue attributed to the nobility; as an ethical conception it only followed religion in its domination of noble behavior.[17] Learning was also accorded respect, and nobles and men of learning were considered equals.[18]

Chivalry and learning embodied in the hero and the sage sustained the order of divine and human laws. Conversely, to commoners were attributed only inferior virtues such as humility, diligence, and obedience to their betters. Commoners were the taxpayers, or *pecheros*, of the realm, and peasants and the city proletariat, at least, were still destined to labor as the sparks flew upward.

Sixteenth-Century Spanish Society

At the time of Zorita's birth Spain's population numbered approximately 8,375,000. Of these, 7 million, or about 83 percent, were campesinos. Most rural dwellers were farm laborers and tenant farmers, but some peasants in central and northern Spain were small farmers sharing in that 3 percent of the land not controlled by the nobles. In southern Spain the greater part of the rural population lived on the great estates owned by lay and ecclesiastical lords, and were subject to various taxes, services, and abuses. Poverty was a basic condition of peasant life, and its visible sign was frugality. Hunger was common in the villages, and is captured in the proverb: "If the lark flies over Castile, she must take her grain of corn with her."[19] The hunger that came up from Andalusia met the plague that came down from Castile in the sixteenth and seventeenth centuries. When the right of serfs to leave their lords was confirmed in Castile in 1481, landless and undernourished peasants frequently moved to the towns and cities. Moreover, the importance of the wool trade to the Castilian economy made for royal encouragement of sheep farming. Emigration to urban areas and the growth of the sheep industry made for deserted villages and agrarian decline.[20] Those who depopulated the countryside frequently joined the army, became domestic servants or urban manual workers, went to the New World, or swelled the ranks of the unemployed in the cities. In other instances, peasants became bandits along with impoverished gentlemen.

Apart from the nobility and the peasants were one million *menestrales*, artisans of various sorts, and a small middle class. The workers, who formed 12 percent of the population and included 150,000 Moors (Moriscos), were victims of inflation throughout the sixteenth century. Wages lagged behind prices, and it appears that living standards for this group deteriorated.[21] The middle class represented 3 percent of the population and included 70,000 priests; 155,000 urban dwellers (40,000 of these proceeding from Jewish families); and 25,000 well-to-do peasant farmers.[22] Braudel concludes that it is doubtful whether the middle class of Spain "was aware of itself as a class." Not only was it "always on the verge of disappearing," but "what was vanishing had hardly existed in the first place." Perhaps because the middle class was numerically so small, it unconsciously "turned class traitor." In any case, "rich bourgeois of every origin were irresistibly drawn towards the aristocracy as if towards the sun."[23]

It is characteristic of lower classes that they mirror both the strengths and the weaknesses of the elite, and Spanish society in the sixteenth century was no exception to this tendency. Only the rich could aspire to patents of nobility (or marriage with the aristocracy), but the ideals were prevalent in all social classes and ethnic groups. Dreams of grandeur clouded the minds of most Spaniards and are especially evident in two representative Spanish literary characters of the Golden Age: Don Quixote and Sancho Panza. Don Quixote states in a revealing passage that while it is true that he is a hidalgo with an ancestral house and estate, "the sage who may write my history will perhaps clear up my relationship and ancestry, and find me to be the descendant, fifth or sixth in line, of a king." The good Sancho Panza cannot boast that he is a noble like the mad knight he follows, but he does declare that he is an "old Christian," and that in itself is enough to make a count. "And more than enough," replies Don Quixote.[24]

Zorita's Ancestry

It is apparent that if we wish to understand Zorita we must attempt to define his position in the Spanish estate system of sixteenth-century Castile. To begin with, there is the problem of his name and title. Alonso de Zorita, as Serrano y Sanz observes, always signed his name *Çorita* or *Zorita*. However, the form *Zurita*—termed erroneous by Serrano y Sanz—was used by García Icazbalceta in the preface to his edition of the *Brief and Summary Relation*[25] and also in his collection of documents for the history of Mexico.[26] Serrano y Sanz, a severe critic of Zorita, claims that Zorita's ancestry may have been Arabic and that García Icazbalceta capriciously and for the sake of courtesy gave Zorita the honorific title Don, "which he never used, nor had the right to use."[27]

The confusion between the two patronymic family names *Zorita* and *Zurita* makes for bibliographical confusion, but otherwise is of no importance. The names were recognized as interchangeable in the sixteenth century, and the subject of this study was occasionally referred to as Alonso de Zurita,[28] the form used by his father and those Zuritas of Aragonese descent such as Jerónimo de Zurita, the chronicler of Aragon and a distant relation of our protagonist.[29] Moreover, the name Zorita is probably of Basque origin and not Arabic, as Serrano y Sanz would have us believe.[30]

Alonso de Zorita's ancestors can be traced back to 1267 when
Alfonso X repopulated Jerez de la Frontera with 300 *caballeros
hijosdalgo* from Castile. Among these crusading nobles seeking
fortune and glory was a certain Don Fagut from Zorita de los
Canes, presently in the province of Guadalajara. Don Fagut was
related to the Castilian *rico-hombre* Don Alvaro Fernández de
Zorita, *confirmador de privilegios* in Castile. Another Zorita was
an *adelantado*, while still another was appointed ambassador to
Granada by Juan II in 1441. Zoritas were represented as *regidores*
and *alcaldes mayores* in the governing body of Jerez de la Frontera from its earliest date. A Zorita had won the family a new coat
of arms for his bravery in the Battle of the Salado against the
Marinids in 1340. Alonso de Zorita was thus aware that his
forebears had been knights in quest of adventure and wealth.
Some had gained riches and power following the path of arms.
Others had followed the path of letters and had gained honor and
increased worth as provincial administrators in the service of
Castilian monarchs.[31]

Part of the Zorita family moved from Jerez to Córdoba, and it
is from this branch of the extended family that Alonso de Zorita
descends. The Zoritas of Jerez married into various of the noble
families of southern Spain, and Zorita on both his father's and
mother's sides belonged to the great house of Fernández de
Córdoba. Awareness of one's ancestry was preeminently a Castilian trait, and at an early date Zorita was undoubtedly aware of
the Italian campaigns and victories of his relative Gonzalo de
Córdoba, "the Great Captain." He learned also that members of
this branch of his family owned a great part of Andalusia and
held numerous titles. Because Zorita was born into a family of the
lesser nobility proceeding from the old feudal aristocracy and was
also a member of one of the great families of Castile "made by
God and time," he inherited a frame of reference peculiar to the
Castilian nobility, which by the time of his birth had become a
state of mind. The hidalgo, as Harold Livermore remarks, "was
not only the knight-errant of literature; he was also the soldier
and the functionary on whom the Castilian state depended; his
was the voice of command in a hundred battles, of decision in a
thousand administrative matters, and of morality and tradition in
a million sermons and lawsuits."[32]

Alonso Díaz de Zurita, Zorita's father, was a native of Cañete
de las Torres, today a small municipality of fewer than 5,000
inhabitants about thirty-five miles from Córdoba. When he
moved to Córdoba is not known, but documents in the Archivo

de Protocolos show that he was a *jurado*, or municipal officer, in
the precinct of Santo Domingo de Silos and in that capacity
defended the economic interests of the municipality. He and the
other *jurados* also investigated and reviewed the actions of local
magistrates and members of the city council. *Jurados* or *fieles*
took their name from the oath to defend the interests of the
community and were elected each year by the members of the
municipal assembly (*concejo*). Generally, two *jurados* were elected
from each precinct, or district, of the city. They met periodically
in an assembly, or cabildo, for the determination of local affairs.[33]

Jurados and other city officials were normally part of the urban
patriciate of the towns, and twenty-four in Seville held bachelor's
degrees and were legists in 1480.[34] It is possible that Zorita's
father may have been a university graduate, but in any case he
clearly knew something about city government and bureaucratic
matters. He evidently knew all the *letrados* of Córdoba and was
well aware that Ferdinand and Isabella had "placed the administration of justice and power in the hands of legists," discreet
agents of the Crown "who quietly and systematically overcame
every resistance as they won Spain for the sovereigns over the
feudalism of the lords and towns and over the medieval
Church."[35]

In addition to his civic duties, Alonso Díaz de Zurita and his
wife, Doña Inés Fernández de Valdelomar y Córdoba, owned
considerable property, and he managed this joint estate at the
same time that he acted as *mayordomo*, or chief administrator, for
the estate of his relative, Doña Catalina Fernández de Córdoba,
second Marchioness of Priego and Countess of Feria. Alonso
Díaz was thus in charge of a vast *latifundio*, for Doña Catalina's
annual income from the villas of Aguilar, Priego, Villafranca,
Montilla, Castroreal, the grange of Montalbán and other properties came to 40,000 ducats.[36]

Córdoba: Zorita's City of Origin

The city that Alonso Díaz de Zurita helped administer had a rich
past and still remains in appearance a synthesis of its Roman and
Moorish inheritance. Under Roman rule Córdoba was fought
over by Caesar and Pompey; the two Senecas and Lucan were
born in the city. Under Arab and Berber conquerors, Córdoba
became the capital of Moslem Spain and rivaled Damascus and
Baghdad in wealth and learning. Scholarship and science thrived
in Islamic Spain, and a nun, "writing in distant Germany in the

late tenth century, refers to Córdoba as a 'fair ornament' of culture, renowned for its seven streams of knowledge."[37]

Moslems, Jews, and Christians lived harmoniously in Córdoba until the fourteenth century, and coexistence made for race mixture and the fusion of cultures. European scholars like Gerbert of Aurillac, the future Pope Sylvester II, studied in Islamic Spain, and Jewish scholars who lived in Córdoba included Maimonides, author of a *Guide for the Perplexed*, and Jehuda Halevy, prince of poets.

Christian domination of Córdoba began in 1236 when Saint Ferdinand III captured the city. Under the rule of Castile the open society of the three "peoples of the Book" gradually came to a close. Economic recession and religious intolerance combined to produce a spirit of antagonism against the Jews, many of whom were financiers, money lenders, rich merchants, tax farmers, fiscal officials of the crown, *mayordomos* of great estates, and municipal artisans. Jewish wealth and influence was resented by the clergy, and their propaganda aroused the always latent ill will of the Christian population towards a wealthy, religiously distinct, self-governing community that was subject to the crown and free from control by urban oligarchies. Pogroms and repressive legislation forced many Jews to convert to the Catholic faith, and this divided the Jewish community of Spain. New Christians or *conversos* often resented the Jews, and many became informers and persecutors of those who chose to stay within the Synagogue.[38]

Old Christians also came to resent and hate the wealthy and powerful *conversos*, for this new social class and its abilities appeared to threaten the traditional social order of Castile. Decrees of *limpieza de sangre*, or purity of blood, were introduced in the second decade of the fifteenth century at the *colegio mayor* of San Bartolomé in Salamanca and in 1449 at Toledo; by 1550 these statutes were almost universal and excluded persons of Jewish ancestry from municipal offices, membership in certain religious orders and confraternities, and admission to the *colegios mayores* at the universities.[39]

By 1480 the Holy Office of the Inquisition began its investigation of alleged apostates in Seville, and in 1482 a tribunal was set up in Córdoba. Supported by the common people and most of the nobility, this tribunal inspired fear and promoted the formation of a closed society. In addition to taking action against New Christians, the inquisitors also arrested and confiscated the property of a number of leading citizens on various pretexts.[40]

   The tribunal never investigated Alonso de Zorita's father, but a
document relating the sale of land to the Holy Office by the elder
Zurita proves he had dealings with that much-feared agency.[41]
The climate of fear, mistrust, and suspicion created by the Inquisition was reflected in the tendency of authors to practice a
sort of self-censorship.[42] An example is a passage in Zorita's
History of New Spain, in which he informs the reader that he has
cited several authors whose works were later prohibited by the
Holy Office. He states, however, that nothing in these forbidden
books "has been mentioned that is offensive to pious ears."[43]
   New Christian descendants of Moslems also formed a small
percentage of Córdoba's population in the early sixteenth century, but the greater part of the Moslem population located in
urban centers took refuge in the Kingdom of Granada when
Córdoba and other Andalusian cities fell to the Christians. The
repopulation of Córdoba by settlers from León and other parts
was accomplished within a few months after its conquest in 1236.
So many people from the north arrived in the city that many
people lacked housing; surrounding lands were quickly overrun,
and by 1240 the municipal council was organized and buildings
and lands were allotted to settlers, the Orders of Calatrava and
Santiago, and some magnates.[44]
   Córdoba, situated in the Guadalquivir valley, lies 325 feet
above sea level, and is protected from north winds by the Sierra
of Córdoba, a spur of the Sierra Morena. Deep, narrow valleys
cut the mountains, and above them "scroll-like clouds constantly
rise to fill the vast expanse of sky."[45] South of the city and the
Guadalquivir lies the *campiña*, flat arable land where various
crops, notably grapes and olives, are cultivated. Cattle and horses
graze on the vast and level plains. South of the *campiña* is another
barren mountain region cut by fertile valleys watered by springs.
Towns like Priego and Rute are surrounded by orchards and
cultivated land. Here it is hot in summer and cool in winter, and
spring is the loveliest season. Then the smell and sight of orange
blossoms and other flowers abound, and the city is "luminous
with light and whitewash."[46] Bandits once lived in the surrounding mountains, but today houses perch like white doves on the
summits about the city.
   Córdoba and its province in Alonso Díaz de Zurita's time was
dedicated to agriculture, livestock raising, and the textile industry.
Like the rest of Andalusia, it was the stable, granary, orchard, and
winecellar of Spain.[47] Córdoba's textile industry was particularly

vigorous and supplied both the home market and the New World colonies with woolen cloth. The silk industry also saw its beginnings in the early sixteenth century. Because production was minimal in the province, silk for spinning, weaving, and dyeing was imported from Murcia and Valencia. Velvet, damask, satin, serge, and taffeta cloth was of high quality, and the woven fabrics of the city were justly famous.[48]

In 1541 Córdoba's population was 33,066. There were 31,735 taxpayers in the province, and it was estimated that the hidalgos numbered 2,644.[49] If we use the standard multiplication figure of five to arrive at the total population of the province, we find that it was approximately 172,000. The nobility represented one-twelfth, a much higher figure than that estimated by present-day historians for the whole of Spain at that time.

Córdoba in the second decade of the sixteenth century was a relatively peaceful city, but this was a recent phenomenon. As in the rest of Andalusia prior to the reign of the Catholic Kings, the city's aristocracy was divided into factions. One group was led by Don Diego Fernández de Córdoba, Count of Cabra, and the other band was headed by Don Alonso Fernández de Aguilar y de Córdoba. Zorita's grandfather, another Alonso Díaz de Zurita, undoubtedly belonged to the Aguilar band, for his son, as has been noted, was the *mayordomo* of Don Alonso de Aguilar's granddaughter Doña Catalina. Bloody struggles between the hostile bands occasionally took place on the city's streets, endangering the lives of citizens.[50]

Because the *conversos* of Córdoba were protected by Don Alonso de Aguilar, the Old Christians sided with the Count of Cabra and Bishop Pedro de Córdoba y Solier. When a city mob rioted in 1474 and began to kill *conversos* in God's name, Don Alonso de Aguilar, his brother Gonzalo, and those of his band attempted to quell the mob, but were forced to take shelter in the Alcázar, where the tribunal of the Inquisition was located. Then followed two days of rioting; *conversos* were robbed and killed and their women were raped.[51] Warfare between the two branches of the Fernández de Córdoba family, and between the *conversos* and the Old Christians, continued until 1478, when Ferdinand and Isabella arrived in Córdoba to restore peace. The lord of Aguilar and the Count of Cabra were temporarily forbidden the city. Shortly thereafter the war against the Moors of Granada was declared, and this crusade against the infidel allowed the two clans to close ranks and make common cause against the Moslems.

Following the conquest of Granada, Don Alonso de Aguilar, "the mirror of Andalusian chivalry," was killed in battle against insurgent Moors in the Sierra Bermeja in 1501. His son Don Pedro now became Marquis of Priego, lord of Aguilar, and the leading citizen of Córdoba.[52] Don Pedro was on his mother's side a grandson of Don Juan Pacheco, Marquis of Villena, and Don Juan was on both sides a descendant of the Jewish tax-collector Ruy Capón.[53] Like his father and uncle before him, Don Pedro protected the *conversos* of Córdoba.

Historian Paulus Jovius writes of the protection afforded the *conversos* and the needy by Don Pedro's uncle, Gonzalo de Córdoba:

Many individuals constrained by poverty, confused by lawsuits, or placed in other dangers asked for the Great Captain's help and he favored many. By these acts his reputation was maintained throughout the province, and he gained singular favor and good will everywhere, especially among the *confesos* and the Moors. Those of Jewish lineage who are made Christians and then return to practice the ceremonies of the Judaic law are called *marranos* by the Spaniards. And in order to catch them in this capital crime, it is necessary to set spies on them. Those who are suspect are accused before the Inquisition. Gonzalo Fernández sought to prove the justice of religion by helping them whenever he could, so that these fearful people might not leave Spain and wander through the world and reach Turkey, where they had certain asylum because they are ingenious men and master craftsmen, especially in the manufacture of cloth.[54]

Don Gonzalo was the only protection against Diego Rodríguez Lucero, the Inquisitor of Córdoba. When, however, Lucero invented the myth of a vast Jewish conspiracy in order to denounce both *conversos* and Old Christians, the town's citizens became alarmed, for he spared no rank or dignity. Seeking to stop the persecutions, both Gonzalo's nephew Don Pedro, the Marquis of Priego, and the Count of Cabra wrote to the archbishop of Seville, Fray Diego Deza, the Inquisitor General, complaining against the zealous minister's actions. Although Deza was of *converso* origin, he would not curb the evil Lucero. Because redress was refused Córdoba's chief family, the town council, and the cathedral chapter, the Marquis of Priego and the bishop of Córdoba liberated Lucero's prisoners and forced him to leave the city. Then Lucero complained to the Crown; King Ferdinand sent royal officials to investigate the matter. He also sent an order commanding Don Pedro to stay out of Córdoba. After tearing up

the king's order, the marquis jailed the king's men in the dungeon
of his castle at Montilla.

Ferdinand immediately declared the Marquis of Priego a rebel
and marched on Córdoba with several thousand troops. Don
Pedro was imprisoned, prosecuted, and sentenced to death.
However, because he had submitted to the king, the sentence was
commuted to a fine of 20 million *maravedís*, the demolition of
the castle of Montilla, the royal keeping of the marquis's other
fortresses, and banishment from the district of Córdoba. Other
nobles and lesser persons were not as fortunate as Don Pedro;
some were executed for treason, while others lost a foot or a
thumb.[55] By these and other measures, the Catholic Kings curtailed the power of the nobles in Castile and brought an end to
baronial anarchy.

Restoration of royal power in the towns and countryside by
the Catholic sovereigns brought internal peace to the kingdom
and assured the successful foreign policy of their reign. Domestic
order in the towns also promoted prosperity and helped to com-
pensate for the loss of regional and municipal autonomy. Prosperity, in turn, made for an increasing interest in education and
the rise of the nobility of the robe in the united and expanding
kingdom of Castile.

Family Structure

Although little is known about Zorita's early years, Richard L.
Kagan's excellent study of Spanish education offers some idea of
domestic life in the sixteenth century. Families of the elite and the
rich were patriarchal; the father made the important decisions
about education, marriage, and career. The father's authority was
most evident in the case of the oldest son, for the first-born male
usually inherited the family's entailed estate and bore the responsibility of continuing and elevating the family's good name and
prestige. A father controlled the life of his oldest child, symbol
and object of the family's lineage and its aspirations, from birth to
marriage. Younger children, in contrast, lived under the watchful
eye of the father but had a greater choice of careers.[56]

Ángel Valbuena Prat in his discussion of childhood in the
Golden Age observes that the paintings of that period reveal a
difference between the attitudes and manner of children of the
upper nobility and royalty—portrayed as melancholy miniatures
of their fathers, already weighed down by consciousness of their

exalted positions—and the sons of the common people, who display a winning good humor and candor.[57] As literary sources suggest, children belonging to the urban patriciate or prosperous commoners were greatly indulged by mothers and servants. They had pets, played at various games, enjoyed festivals of the church, and stole fruit at the market. Little ones carried sacred relics, or thin wax cakes with the figure of a lamb that had been blessed, in small purses suspended from their necks to protect them from evil and danger. Mothers sang to them, and they soon learned to repeat these little songs, which often gave a moral lesson.

Play began to mingle with more serious pursuits at the age of five or six. With systematic instruction in literacy and religion, the child began preparation for entry into the adult world.[58] Reading, writing, and arithmetic were usually taught to privileged boys and girls in private and religious schools. Cost of instruction was six *reales* a month. Since this expense was beyond the reach of most working families, Kagan estimates that no more than 15 percent of the population learned basic skills.[59]

Once a child had mastered the skills of literacy, he was ready to enter grammar school. The *escuela de gramática* might be civil, private, or conventual, but the chief subject was Latin. The literary arts of grammar, dialectic, and rhetoric were also taught (the *trivium*), as well as geometry, arithmetic, astronomy, and music (the *quadrivium*). Instruction also included Christian doctrine.[60] The use of Antonio de Nebrija's Latin grammar was almost universal in the secondary schools, and readings from classical authors such as Caesar, Cicero, Horace, Livy, and Virgil were common. As Kagan observes, Latin training might be put off after primary education; thus in Zorita's day students between the ages of sixteen and twenty might be found in the secondary schools, their education having been interrupted by military, clerical, or vocational training. Secondary school instruction lasted from four to six years, and "was mandatory for students seeking to enter the church or to pursue studies in one of the higher disciplines of law, medicine, philosophy, or theology at the universities."[61]

The Zurita Family

Doña Inés de Córdoba and Alonso Díaz de Zurita had nine children. The eldest son was Alonso, our protagonist, born either in 1511 or 1512.[62] The other children were Juan Pérez de Zorita,

Francisco de Zorita, Miguel Díaz de Zorita, Lucía de Zorita, María Zorita de Villavicencio, Elvira Zorita de Villavicencio, Inés de Zorita, and Ana de Zorita Villavicencio.[63]

By reason of birth into a relatively affluent noble family located in a metropolitan center, Zorita and his brothers and sisters easily acquired the skills of literacy. Moreover, their later careers (although the record is incomplete and fragmentary) indicate that their father was well aware of the proverb "Iglesia, o mar, o casa real" ("Church or sea or royal house"). He reared his children to aspire "to be direct administrators of the faith, or to undertake adventure that would lead to lordship, or to serve the king in some way, comfortable in the realization that they were nobles and not plebeians."[64] Zorita's brothers' and sisters' careers seem to typify those of children of a landed and prosperous minor noble of the early sixteenth century.

Juan Pérez de Zorita, born perhaps in 1519, aspired to win lordship by arms. He began in 1539 in the galleys commanded by Don Bernardino de Mendoza and distinguished himself on October 1, 1540, when the Spanish ships made contact with the Moslem fleet led by the Sardinian renegade Ali Hamet and a certain Caramani, formerly a Spanish galley slave. In a battle that took place off the island of Alborán, 125 miles east of the strait of Gibraltar, most of the infidel captains, including Caramani, were killed, and Ali Hamet was captured with more than 400 of his men.[65]

After this great naval victory Charles V was determined to attack and capture Algiers, chief headquarters for pirate fleets in the western Mediterranean. In 1541, Juan Pérez, along with the greatest soldiers of Spain—among them the Duke of Alba and Hernán Cortés—took part in the unsuccessful expedition to Algiers. As is well known, capture of the city was prevented by a tremendous storm in which some 12,000 men and 150 ships were lost.[66]

Three years later Juan Pérez, in North Africa, at his own cost furnished horses, arms, and men in the capture of Tlemcen and the expedition to Mostaganem. Although not yet twenty-four years old, he served as a captain of light cavalry and won the admiration of Don Alvaro de Villaroel, caballero of Ubeda and *maestre de campo* for Don Martín de Córdoba y Velasco, Count of Alcaudete.[67]

In March, 1548, Juan Pérez was in Granada, and shortly thereafter he sailed for the New World with his brother Alonso. When he arrived in Peru in 1553, he learned that Francisco Hernández Girón, the last great rebel against the crown in those kingdoms, had raised the standard of revolt in Cuzco and offered freedom to those slaves who joined his cause. Juan Pérez defended the royal cause by volunteering his services and furnishing arms, horses, and maintenance for four other men from the time of Girón's defeat at Pucara until his imprisonment and execution in Lima in December, 1554.[68]

When Don Andrés Hurtado de Mendoza, Marquis of Cañete and Viceroy of Peru, appointed his son, Don García Hurtado de Mendoza, to the governorship of Chile in 1557, Juan Pérez was commissioned to lead part of the expedition of 700 men from Lima to Chile. Once in Chile, he was appointed *teniente de governador* and *justicia mayor* in the province comprising Tucumán, Juries, and Diaguitas. Lieutenant Governor Juan Pérez de Zorita peacefully won over the Indians of the region and between 1558 and 1560 founded the settlements of Londres, in the valley of Quinmivil; Córdoba, in the valley of Calchaquí; and Cañete, between Copiapó and Londres.[69] During the time he governed Tucumán (also known as New England in celebration of Philip II's marriage to Mary Tudor in 1554) cloth, horses, cows, goats, sheep, seeds, and plants were brought into the territory and were exchanged for honey, beeswax, cotton cloth, and cochineal. That the territory was not yet self-supporting, however, is indicated by Juan Pérez's later claim that he sustained the settlements he founded at his own cost, an amount exceeding 35,000 *pesos de hacienda*.[70]

Back in Chile, Juan Pérez served Governor Don Pedro de Villagrán as *maestre de campo general*, and in 1565 Licentiate Lope García de Castro (who removed Villagrán from office) appointed Juan Pérez governor, captain general, chief justice, and high sheriff (*alguacil mayor*) of the legendary provinces of Trapalanda, the land of the Caesars, and La Sal (Patagonia).[71] The journey to Trapalanda was never undertaken, but in 1571, Francisco de Toledo, Viceroy of Peru, appointed Juan Pérez to the governorship of Santa Cruz de la Sierra.[72] In 1583 the Audiencia of Charcas directed Juan Pérez to take the *residencia* of Captain Luis de Fuentes and other public officials in the villa of San Bernardo de Tarija and made him *visitador* of the Chiriguanos Indian area bordering the settlement. His last letter to the crown was written in 1584, and it is likely that he died in La Plata that year.[73]

Juan Pérez de Zorita, in addition to being a valiant captain, had been a considerate and enterprising governor. He treated his Indian and Spanish subjects with honesty and fairness, and was considered "a noble man of authority, good reputation, and esteem."[74] He served the royal cause selflessly throughout his life, was a *caballero hijodalgo*, and belonged to the Military Order of Calatrava. The coat of arms he displayed was the second one granted the family by the crown after the Battle of the Salado.[75]

Although Alonso de Zorita's other brothers and sisters did not have such distinguished careers, all seem to have maintained their original noble status well. This was rare in a century that saw many nobles beset by financial difficulties and others reduced to poverty by the decrease of old feudal revenues and the price revolution.

Francisco de Zorita became a priest and came to the New World in 1562, where he died in the 1580s. Another brother, Miguel Díaz de Zorita, was a *vecino* of Córdoba and, like his father before him, a municipal officer of the city. His son married into the noble and distinguished Góngora family,[76] and his daughter entered the convent of Santa Inés in Córdoba in 1574.

Lucía de Zorita married Don Alonso de Aguilera about 1540. Aguilera was a *caballero hijodalgo*, served with his relative Pedro de Valdivia in Chile, and in 1550 was one of Valdivia's *procuradores*.[77] In 1551 he and his wife returned to Córdoba. The family moved in 1572 to Villa del Rio, just north of Cañete de las Torres.[78] Another sister, María, married Don Pedro de Olmos, the brother of Alonso de Aguilera, in 1541. Don Pedro de Olmos and his wife helped to colonize Chile, and he was *corregidor* of Valdivia, *alcalde* and *corregidor* of Imperial, and *corregidor* of Angol. He died fighting the Araucanians at the battle of Damas in early 1599. Descendants of Don Pedro de Olmos and Doña María de Zorita resided in Chile in the seventeenth century and belonged to the Orders of Calatrava and Alcántara.[79] Elvira Zorita de Villavicencio married Captain Pedro de Arroyo Valdivia and was living as a widow in 1572. Two other sisters, Inés de Zorita and Ana de Zorita, became nuns in the same convent of Santa Inés, Córdoba. Sister Inés was abbess of the convent for many years.

The Consolidation of Modern Spain

Alonso de Zorita was born into a nation that had in the Emperor Charles V and his son and successor Philip II perhaps the greatest monarchs in Christendom during the sixteenth century. In 1512,

Ferdinand II of Aragon, also Ferdinand V of Castile (1474–1504).
Known as Ferdinand the Catholic, though he was part Jewish, he
supported the Inquisition in Aragon and Castile. (Convento de Madrigal
de las Altas Torres; courtesy of Marqués de Lozoya, *Historia de
España*)

Ferdinand, the wily regent of Castile, became master of Spanish
Navarre. Ferdinand's consolidation of what is today modern
Spain climaxed the rise of the royal supremacy under the Catholic

Kings, Ferdinand and Isabella, and helped liquidate the tradition of separatism and disunion so evident during the reign of Henry IV (1454–74).

For a brief but brilliant period the united Spain that Charles V and Philip II inherited would be feared and respected as the greatest power on earth; the problems of governing their vast possessions in Europe and overseas compelled Spain's rulers to devise a governmental system that administered the largest and most dispersed empire the European world had yet seen.

As is well known, the Catholic Sovereigns transferred to America the government institutions they had created and developed in Castile; they controlled all the dominions in the New World through royal agents acting in the name of an absolute, patrimonial monarchy. But if Spain of the sixteenth century can be called "a Renaissance state" of early modern Europe, the consolidation of power by the crown had its origins in medieval moral principles rather than in the Machiavellian idea that politics has its own laws of existence and the state operates on a purely secular level.[80] The concept of kingship under Charles and Philip had its basis in the reign of the Catholic Kings, who believed that good kingship and royal justice cannot be divorced from religion and exists to defend the weak and subdue the proud.[81] The Crown in creating a well-ordered state merely followed the typical mentality of the late fifteenth century, aptly expressed by Diego de Valera, the contemporary chronicler, who advised the Crown that it must be served by *letrados* in matters of science and justice, by religious and clerics in matters of conscience, and by experienced caballeros in that which pertained to war.[82]

Ferdinand and Isabella followed this advice and founded their royal absolutism on the legists, the clergy, and the military.[83] The ideas advocated by legists and clerics were advanced by devout soldiers, eager warriors in a crusade for the end of heresy, whose prowess in the 1540s was already legendary.[84] For a century and a half, Spaniards like Juan Pérez de Zorita fought engagements in such widely separated places as Lepanto and Chile, seldom losing a pitched battle. The crusading ardor of the Spanish will to power, as well as the religious and political unification that had taken place in the Peninsula just prior to the discovery of America, led Spanish society to think of a universal empire and a universal church. This dream of a universal Christian empire in the sixteenth century was best expressed by Hernando de Acuña in a poem addressed to the Emperor Charles V:

The time draws near, or seems at length fulfilled—
The age of glory promised us by Heaven—
When on this earth one shepherd of one flock
Shall rule in singleness our destinies.

Your Majesty's true zeal, your victories
Mark the beginning of the happy age
And to the expectant world at length foretell
One King, one Empire, and a single sword.[85]

The increasing importance of the legists in sixteenth-century Spain resulted, in part, from the Catholic Kings' desire to grant each subject the opportunity "to freely enjoy the rights that belonged to him by virtue of his station."[86] In order to bring this about, the judicial system had to be unified and regulated, and corrupt and incompetent judges had to be curbed or replaced by faithful and able men of law representing the sovereign, who was the supreme judge: "The judicial organization which served their absolutist political design was in large measure the work of the Catholic Sovereigns."[87] However, their work in this sphere of government also had its roots in the medieval past.

The influence of the Roman law, revived in Italy in the twelfth century, had been eagerly received from the middle of the thirteenth century by Spanish kings and lawyers.[88] Knowledge of Roman law was gained both at Bologna and at the University of Salamanca and "came to exercise a powerful influence upon Spanish legislation and Spanish legal training."[89] In addition to its technical advantage over local law by reason of its uniformity, completeness, coherence, rationality, and equity, Roman law greatly favored royal absolutism and the power of the judge as the representative of the king.[90]

Before the Catholic Kings, the great representatives of absolutism opposed to the progressive fragmentation of the law were Saint Ferdinand III (1199–1252), Alfonso X the Learned (1221–84), and Alfonso XI (1311–50), all three of whom desired better and more uniform law. The influence of the canon law and Roman law is most evident in Alfonso X's *Libro de las Leyes*, which, from its division into seven parts, came to be known as *Las Siete Partidas*. This influential guide was raised to the position of a code by Alfonso XI, who declared its authority whenever new laws found in his *Ordenamiento de Alcalá* and traditional law could furnish no rules for a judicial decision.[91]

With the restoration of royal authority and the reestablishment of unity in the reign of Ferdinand and Isabella, a corresponding codification of the laws became necessary. Accordingly Queen Isabella commissioned Alonso Díaz de Montalvo, a former student of Civil and Canon law at the universities of Salamanca and Lérida, to compile those laws enacted after the death of Alfonso the Learned but not mentioned in the *Ordenamiento de Alcalá*. Montalvo's collection, the *Ordenanzas Reales de Castilla*, was published in 1484. When it became evident that this last collection had become just one among many sources of Spanish law, the Cortes of Toledo recommended another compilation. The result was the *Leyes de Toro* of 1505. This law code reconciled the old with the new and was the culmination of a process that had taken more than two centuries. As was true in former compilations, the preamble to the *Leyes de Toro* stated that to the king belonged the power to make, interpret, and amend *fueros* and laws.[92]

The rise of the professional lawyer in this period was also reflected in changes in the central governing body of Castile. In 1385 Castilian affairs of state were entrusted to a royal council consisting of twelve persons: four prelates, four caballeros, and four *ciudadanos*. From the time of its creation a number of *letrados*, or jurists, formed part of the Royal Council of Castile, but in 1406 the crown specifically decreed that the councilors of the third estate should be *doctores en leyes*.[93] In 1459 the Royal Council was reorganized by Henry IV, and it was ordered that it be composed of eight *letrados*, two caballeros, and two prelates. In spite of this decree, civil war made for the predominance of the great lords of the realm in the Royal Council by 1476. In 1480 the Catholic Kings once again refashioned this chief governing body and decreed that it "should consist of a prelate, three caballeros and eight or nine jurists". Although prelates and magnates of the realm might sit in the Royal Council by virtue of their offices, they could not vote and so enjoyed no political power. As is evident, the king and the *letrados* were now predominant at the highest level of state.[94]

The Spanish conquest of the New World also created a need for trained bureaucratic officials who could administer the lands won for Castile. From the first, the Spanish monarchs made plain their intention of curbing the power of the great expeditionary leaders of the Conquest. As soon as the work of conquest was completed and settlements were established, legists appointed by the crown came to assert the rights of the monarchy. As Cantor observes, "The rise of secular administrative governments in western Europe and the emergence of a new class of civil lawyers are thus contemporaneous and intimately related developments."

Cantor also notes that members of the legal profession trained in the Roman law had devoted many years to formal academic study. Their training under a very exacting regimen helps account for the fact that young lawyers in the service of the nation-state "tended to be cut from the same cloth: they were all well educated and zealous, but also generally impecunious, somewhat inhuman, and eager to sell their services to the highest bidder. They made ideal bureaucrats."[95]

Preparation for Judgeship

Unfortunately, we know little about Alonso de Zorita's life from boyhood to manhood. We do know that he became familiar with the use of arms and the equestrian arts. His fervent piety and admiration for the friars' missionary activities in the New World suggest that he received thorough instruction in the principles of the Roman Catholic faith and could easily have become a member of the reformed Franciscan Order. We can gain some idea of what his education might have been from the study of two contemporaries of similar social status.

Don Martín Pérez de Ayala, born about 1504 and later archbishop of Valencia, tells us that when he was five years old he was taught to read and write at the parish church. A son of poor commoners, he read Latin before he read Spanish and became so proficient that the priest arranged contests between him and others. He demonstrated more ability than his companions and contemporaries because, in the opinion of everyone, God had given him "a keen and discerning mind, fit for learning." In school he "learned to read Spanish with the same ability and quickness I had demonstrated in Latin, but I could not write as well because I was a bit slow in the use of my hands." At the age of ten he began studying the rudiments of grammar with a certain pious and learned *bachiller* Mercado. Had it not been for the "gross and barbarous" method of teaching Nebrija's Latin textbook by memorization, which frustrated the more talented students, "I would have mastered grammar in two years; but I studied what was taught with such facility and continuity that my teachers praised me above the other students."[96]

Like the archbishop of Valencia, Don Diego de Simancas, bishop of Zamora, completed his study of grammar at the age of fourteen, but his circumstances and training may have more closely resembled those of Alonso de Zorita. He tells us that he was born in Córdoba of noble parents. His brother was appointed to the office of archdeacon by his uncle, who held that office, and his mother inherited from the same archdeacon, her brother, the principal houses he had built, "which are of the best to be found in Córdoba." Diego de Simancas learned to read and write and studied Latin grammar in Córdoba until the age of fourteen. He was an able student, and

one day, when the possibility of a canonship for me was being discussed, my mother stated it would weigh upon her conscience if I did not continue my studies and become a great doctor. I never forgot her words and always worked to make them come true, at the least to become a doctor, which I became in her lifetime. And because in Córdoba there were no schools for the study of laws, nor was good Latin in use, I was sent to Valladolid with my brother, Don Juan de Simancas (who later studied at Bologna, became bishop of Cartagena in the Indies, and is now archdean and canon of Córdoba).

At Valladolid Diego de Simancas studied Latin for one more year and also attended lectures in laws. "After a year I went to Salamanca and remained there for nine years, attending lectures for five years and studying for another four, all of this with great care and benefit. Once when I disputed conclusions before many doctors, Fray Domingo de Soto was heard to say in a loud voice: 'Students such as this one should be made doctors after three years of study, and others should not be granted the title after twenty.'"[97]

These and similar sources suggest that bright children of Old Christian stock (or held to be such) studied in their native surroundings until the age of fourteen or fifteen. Then, because their parents had means or because their relatives were priests or magistrates, or because they were aided by some prelate or dignitary, they might be sent to the university. There they competed and perfected their talents for ten or more years in what Julio Caro Baroja has called a "school of intellectual violence."[98] Students learned to debate, to dispute conclusions, to qualify concepts, and to sharpen their ears. They also studied Latin, heard lectures in law, and competed for scholarships. The ultimate aim was to obtain letters of recommendation to a good position.

Since a career in law was one of the quickest ways to achieve economic and political success, and the young Zorita no doubt already displayed the love of books and learning manifested in his later writings, his teachers probably recommended to his father that he be sent to the university for further study. Zurita was wealthy and influential and could afford to enroll his son in an elitist establishment, such as the University of Salamanca. Many

of the distinguished scholars, clerics, and administrators of the
New World colonies were taught there, and although the total
years of Zorita's attendance are unknown, we do know that he
was there from 1537 to 1540.[99]

The University of Salamanca, founded in the early thirteenth
century, was the oldest Spanish university and from an early date
ranked with those of Bologna, Paris, and Oxford. In the sixteenth
century it enjoyed the reputation of being the mother of the
sciences and the "nurse of scholars and gentlemen." In Zorita's
day the university combined the spirit of medieval scholasticism
with the new learning of the Renaissance, and there were between
sixty and seventy chairs. Professors taught a variety of subjects,
but doctors of law were paid higher salaries and appear to have
enjoyed a higher status. One law professor declared that the
faculty consisted of "learned jurisconsults, greasy theologians,
and that rabble of physicians and philosophers."[100]

From its first extant matriculation list, in 1530, which shows a
total of 5,150 doctors, colegiales, friars, and students, it is apparent that the university dominated the town of 13,110.[101] Students
were between fourteen and thirty years of age and represented all
classes, but literary sources indicate that the poor students were
in the majority. These students lived in abject housing and suffered the region's bitter winter cold; their shabby clothing may
have included hobnailed boots and short capes. Known for their
plain caps and poor mantles as capigorrones (cloaks-and-cappers),
they often served as attendants of the wealthier students.

More affluent students, wishing to present the most noble
appearance possible, often spent more than they should on costly
apparel. Their living quarters had large beds, rich tapestries, writing desks, and walnut tables and chairs. This ostentation ran
counter to university statutes, which conceived of the university
as "a small republic, without difference of rank or privilege."[102]
Moreover, distinctions of wealth and rank were commented on
by Judge Diego de Simancas of the tribunal of Valladolid in 1556.
He recommended that the students shed their extravagant academic caps, costly cassocks, and long capes for vestments made
of the black cloth of Andalusia and Albuquerque, "which costs
little and wears well." The Royal Council agreed that the students
should dress more discreetly but decided that the ordinary wear
of undergraduates should consist of plain brown cloth. Professors
and those who were licenciados might wear silk or other cloth, in
different colors for the various colleges. Collegiates of San Bartolomé wore traditional brown cassocks with brown stoles; those of

the College of Cuenca wore purple cloaks and stoles.

Students came from all parts of Spain, Europe, and even from the New World. In *La tía fingida*, attributed by some critics to Cervantes, Claudia describes to Esperanza the distinguishing traits of students from the various regions of Spain. They are all generally

youthful, capricious, unrestrained, without experience but fanciful, wasteful, discreet, diabolical and witty. But in the particular, as most are from different parts, not all have the same traits. The Basques, though few, are short-tempered but spend lavishly if they pursue a woman. Those of La Mancha are swaggering bullies who love to fight. Here are also many Aragonese, Valencians, and Catalans. Consider them polished, perfumed, well-bred and well-dressed; but ask them for nothing. Moreover, one can't play tricks on them, and when angry with a woman, they are somewhat cruel and ill-disposed. Those from New Castile are high-minded. If they have they give, and if they do not give they do not solicit. Those from Extremadura are like pharmacists who have some of everything. They are also like alchemy, which uniting with silver becomes transmuted into silver, and mingled with copper remains copper. For Andalucians, my dear, one needs fifteen senses, much less five. They possess keen and perspicacious minds, and are crafty, astute, and not at all hapless.[103]

Zorita went up to the University of Salamanca perhaps as early as 1527. But he may have attended another university as an undergraduate, or his education may have been interrupted in his teens, and he may have matriculated at a later date. In any case, as a freshman he could not be admitted to a *colegio mayor* since each of these establishments had a minimum age of entrance and only admitted *bachilleres*. San Bartolomé would not admit students under eighteen years of age, and Santa Cruz refused admittance to students under twenty-one.

If Zorita entered Salamanca as an undergraduate, he paid the customary initiation fee and was subjected to the cruel and un-sanitary hazing described so well by Quevedo in *El buscón*.[104] In the lecture rooms Zorita completed the first course of the re-quired curriculum. It included Nebrija's grammar, the study of Latin authors, and Greek classics such as Homer and Aris-tophanes.

The arts curriculum of the early sixteenth century was flexible, but regular courses largely consisted of daily lectures based on Aristotelian philosophy. The degree of bachelor of arts took four years; students who were nobles might receive the degree in three

years. As Caro Lynn notes, "The arts course was not a prere-
quisite for the law, but the course in canon or civil law required
six years."[105]

Through his study of liberal arts, Zorita came to admire the
Greek and Roman past and began to believe, like many other
humanists, that history, even pagan history, provided a basis for
moral criticism and taught moral and political truths.[106] Because
it was also commonly believed that God intervened in human
affairs, Zorita later fused secular and sacred history in his narra-
tives. But like Erasmus and the early Christian fathers, he thought
that sacred history was superior to profane history and that every
man "that is rational, however unusual to us may be the shape of
his body, or the color of his skin, or the way he walks, or the
sound of his voice, and whatever the strength, portion or quality
of his natural endowments is descended from the single first-
created man."[107]

At Salamanca, Zorita undoubtedly imbibed the pro-Indian
ideology of his later career from Fray Francisco de Vitoria, who
held the Prima Chair of Theology until his death in 1546. In his
history of New Spain, Zorita states that this holy and learned
Dominican of clear and profound intellect was "one of the best
theologians of his time. He wrote, among other things, two
Relecciones: one entitled *De Indis insulanis* and the other *De jure
belli*, in which he treats of the conquest, instruction, and conversion of the natives of the Indies."[108]

In its original form, Father Vitoria's *De Indis insulanis* may
have been three separate lectures heard by Zorita at Salamanca in
the 1530s.[109] The first lecture questioned "the right of the Spaniards to bring the heathen foreigners under their control." The
second and third lectures examined "the authority of the Spanish
monarchs over the Indians in temporal and spiritual affairs," and
"whether the monarch or the Church has authority over them in
spiritual matters."[110]

Francisco de Vitoria's lectures at Salamanca must have inspired
much discussion of the question of the crown's rights to the
Indies, for in 1539 "he was the target of a silencing order from
the Crown for lectures on the same topic."[111] Vitoria claimed that
Christians could not occupy the lands of infidels if the latter were
the true owners of those lands. Because the Indians held their
lands as true proprietors, these lands could not be occupied or
held by Spaniards if the Indians did not choose to cede them.
This was so because no Christian prince ruled the Indians nor
did the pope have temporal power over them, since he had

jurisdiction only over Christians or heretics. Vitoria also declared however, perhaps to placate Charles V, that the Spaniards could preach and if the Indians impeded the diffusion of the doctrine of Christ, they could be brought to obedience by the law of war in order to propagate the Gospel. In the same fashion, should Christians find themselves in imminent peril, they were permitted for safety's sake to take the infidels' goods in accordance with the law of nations.[112]

As is apparent, on the one hand "Vitoria wished to destroy the concept of the supremacy of any spiritual or temporal authority in the West over regions and people not de facto under that authority." On the other hand, he seems not to have been opposed to the Spanish colonization itself "but to have been against the worst abuses of Spanish colonial policy."[113] He thus eventually assumes the right of Spaniards to settle in the New World, but attempts "to raise the level of his country's colonial policy and ground it firmly on the twin bases of international law and Christian humanitarianism."[114]

As a student in the law faculty, Zorita acquired basic texts of civil and canon law, including legal manuals that explained first rules and nomenclature. Civil law was based upon the study of Justinian's *Corpus Juris Civilis* and its glossators, the most famous of whom was Bartolus of Sassoferrato (1314–57). Canon law was based on Gratian's *Decretum* and its glossators, the *Decretals* of Pope Gregory IX published in 1234, and other papal pronouncements. The *Siete Partidas* and other Spanish texts of law were studied, "but far less thoroughly."[115] Lectures from the early sixteenth century included historical and philological interpretations of the law, and the task of mastering these "scarce left one time to breathe."[116]

Law students attended both morning and afternoon lectures. Ordinary lectures given in the morning by salaried professors were often reviewed and interpreted later in the day in extraordinary lectures by instructors and advanced students. Because study was rigorous, and time-consuming, Zorita must have often left school exhausted, but the promise of rewards no doubt sustained him. Like the peasant who thought Sancho and Don Quixote were traveling to Salamanca so that they might soon become judges of the royal tribunal, Zorita must have often thought that "everything is foolishness and vanity, except that a man studies and studies and has favor and good luck. And one day, when he least expects it, he'll find himself with a judge's staff in his hand or a bishop's mitre on his head."[117]

A good memory was required, but students also learned that not all the circumstances of a legal action are contained in the laws. Memory only aided the good lawyer or judge to determine fundamental principles. The good lawyer was thus like a tailor who has scissors in hand and the piece of cloth at home. On being asked for a coat, he takes the person's measure and then cuts the cloth to shape. The scissors of the good lawyer are the keen understanding with which he judges the case and clothes it with the law that determines it. And if he does not find a law that specifically fits the case, he makes a vesture with which to defend it from patches and pieces of law.[118]

Once Zorita had completed his undergraduate studies and taken his baccalaureate, he entered one of the four *colegios mayores*. Here he studied in an atmosphere that contained members of the leading Spanish houses and gained further knowledge of the law and the art of legal argument by teaching extraordinary classes. Because orthodoxy in the faith and purity of ancestry had become officially associated after 1449 to exclude *conversos* from high office in church and state, Zorita was undoubtedly required to submit written proof of his lineage, education, and noble virtues before entering one of these honorable hospices. Miguel Díez de Armendáriz, describing his university studies in an attempt to impress the uneducated Sebastián de Benalcázar, wrote in 1547:

I was a student in Salamanca, in the *colegio mayor* of San Bartolomé, as was the *Señor Licenciado* Gasca. Whoever enters that house must submit to three inquiries (*informaciones*): first, in letters; second, in lineage, and the *probanza* must prove beyond doubt that he is not a Jew nor has Jewish ancestors, but that he is of good caste if considered qualified for entry; third, in virtues (*costumbres*), very rigorous.[119]

As a collegiate of San Bartolomé or Cuenca, Zorita was required to take communion once a year and might not carry arms or go into the city without his gown. The speaking of Spanish within the walls of the college was prohibited, and students were subject to some disciplinary regulations "not so much because they were *in statu pupillari* as because they were secular clerks living in community." San Bartolomé had a barber and a cook, and students were provided with fruit, wine, wood, and one pound of meat daily or its equivalent in milk, fish, and eggs. Students enjoyed separate bedrooms, and the young scholars had the privilege of eating in the kitchen instead of in the hall in the winter months.[120]

The purpose of the four major colleges was to produce an aristocracy of talent. San Bartolomé, founded in 1401 by Diego de Anaya Maldonado, archbishop of Seville, was the earliest and most famous of these elite institutions. In the reign of the Catholic Kings it was said that the government was in the hands of the *Bartolomeos*. This was an exaggeration, but the college did produce many distinguished officials, including six bishops and eight royal councilors. The College of Cuenca was also illustrious; its graduates included six cardinals, twenty archbishops, and eight viceroys.[121]

Because *letrados* were required by law to study a minimum of ten years in a university before receiving a Crown appointment, Zorita probably did not take the degree of *licenciado* until 1540. We know that Diego de Simancas and Miguel Díez de Armendáriz remained at Salamanca for nine and ten years respectively, and because of the fierce competition for teaching posts and government offices it was not unusual for a *colegial* to remain at the university fifteen or twenty years. An example is Juan López de Palacios Rubios, the author of the famous (or infamous) *Requerimiento*. He took the degree of licentiate at Salamanca in 1471; thirteen years later, at the age of thirty-seven, he received a fellowship in San Bartolomé. Even after taking a higher degree, graduates frequently resided at a major college and left this semi-monastic life only when they obtained a suitable position.[122]

The distinction between the degrees of licentiate and doctor of law was mainly ceremonial, but in fact doctors of Salamanca were given the same privilege as hidalgos. Because of the high cost of advanced degrees, poorer students studied at Salamanca and then went on to cheaper universities. Since Zorita was already a noble and belonged to a well-to-do family, he may have seen no particular advantage in taking the degree of doctor. Even so, his graduation ceremony was a solemn and expensive affair.

The ceremony began with a procession headed by drums and trumpets; Zorita and his sponsor marched through the streets from his house to the schools. After a preliminary examination he went to the cathedral, where the degrees were conferred. His

final examination was held in the Chapel of St. Barbara in the cloister of the Old Cathedral, and at the door of this chapel on the previous day the texts for the candidate's examination were chosen (*se le daban puntos*), the candidate choosing from a book opened in three places at random. Each examining professor received two beans or counters marked A (*Aprobado*) and R (*Reprobado*). The "approved" candidate

went out by the principal door of the Cathedral, where a richly capari-
soned horse awaited him for his procession through the city; the
"reprobated" found themselves ejected through the Puerta de los Carros
into an obscure side-street.[123]

The chief expense of the advanced degree at Salamanca was the
banquet and fees for the fifty or sixty professors who attended
the ceremony. Each received two gold *castellanos*, "a torch, a box
of preserved lemon-peel, a pound of sugar-plums, and three pairs
of chickens." To avoid great extravagance the menu for the banquet was prescribed and consisted of "one partridge or chicken or
two turtle doves and a bowl of pudding and a fruit before and
another after the wine and bread." The student also paid for the
refreshments "served in the house from which the professors
watched the bullfights held in honour of the degree." Bell
observes that "Luis de León received five hundred ducats from
his father for his degrees, and Dr. Sandoval had spent the whole
of his wife's dowry in obtaining his Prima Chair of Canon Law
and in taking his degrees."[124]

When Zorita took his degree, he was twenty-eight years old
and still single. He depended on his father for living expenses; the
elder Zurita would have frowned upon a marriage while Zorita
attended the "fair of letters" preparing him for the legal profession.

We have no portrait or description of the appearance of the
man Zorita save for two illustrations, probably stylized sketches
of a Spanish functionary, drawn by an Indian draftsman in the
late 1550s.[125] Antonio Domínguez Ortiz, admitting the difficulty
of visualizing what the typical hidalgo of the period looked like,
writes that sources suggest a distinctive noble physical type,
perhaps arising from the different ways of life of the noble and
the peasant, or perhaps from genetic difference of remote origin
reinforced by social barriers. "When Cervantes delineated with
immortal verbal sketches the external appearance of Don Quixote
and Sancho, did he wish to delimit two biological or social
types?" Domínguez Ortiz does not venture to decide the question, but remarks upon an odd coincidence. "When the Knight of
the Greencolored Greatcoat contemplates Don Quixote he 'mar-
veled at the length of his neck.' Well, one of the proverbs collected by Martínez Kleiser says: 'Nobles and greyhounds, lean
and long-necked' ['Hidalgos y galgos, secos y cuellilargos']."[126]
Cervantes was probably following literary tradition in his de-

Gonzalo
Fernández
de Córdoba
(1453–1515)
revolutionized the
Spanish army in
the Italian wars
through use of the
tercios, supported
by cavalry and
artillery, which
established Spain's
military supremacy
in the sixteenth
century. Known as
the Great Captain,
Córdoba was a
kinsman of Alonso
de Zorita.
(Courtesy of
Marqués de
Lozoya, *Historia
de España*)

scription of Don Quixote and the nobility, but it is interesting to
note that he also mentions that the Knight of the Mournful
Countenance has long limbs, little flesh on his bones, and a lean,
gaunt, and sallow face.[127] Because Zorita tells us he was a man of
sparing taste, and from representations of his relative Gonzalo de
Córdoba, the Great Captain, it is more than probable that Zorita
was a slender and handsome individual of polite and affable
manners.

Unlike Don Quixote, however, Alonso de Zorita had taken up
letters rather than arms. He therefore may have had, like the
hidalgo natural of the Greencolored Greatcoat, some six dozen
books or more, some in Spanish and others in Latin. From his
works it is apparent that he enjoyed histories and devotional
works, as well as Marcus Tullius Cicero, "prince of orators";
Bartolus of Sassoferrato, "who said he had never known a corpu-
lent man, excepting Cyrus, who was learned"; Pliny, who, "having written the history of the world, reprimanded authors who
omitted the names of writers who had helped them in what they
wrote"; Varius Geminus, who respected Caesar's greatness; and
contemporary authors such as Thomas More, the author of the
Utopia,[128] and Erasmus, the author of the *Adages*.[129]

In his admiration for More and Erasmus, Zorita was not
unique. Both authors were highly regarded in the Spain of
Charles V. Fray Juan de Zumárraga, first bishop of Mexico, was
inspired by the *Utopia* and was also an Erasmian. Vasco de
Quiroga drew on elements of More's work in his organization of
model Indian communities in New Spain. Spanish translations of
Erasmus's *Enchiridion* and the *Colloquies* were popular in the
1520s. Martín de Azpilcueta praised Erasmus in 1545, "and as late
as 1553 García Matamoros calls him divine."[130] The fact that in
1585 Zorita cited only Erasmus's *Adages*, used by More for his
work, may reflect his cautious awareness that Erasmus's other
publications were included in the Inquisitorial Indices of 1559
and 1582.[131]

A royal decree gave Zorita, a licentiate of Salamanca, preference
over doctors and masters graduated in other universities should
he seek a *letrado* appointment in government or a profes-
sorship.[132] Zorita may have considered competing for a university
chair but probably recognized that the teaching profession was a
means and not an end. Professors frequently left their university
chairs for the king's service; Palacios Rubios left Salamanca to
become a royal judge in the Audiencia of Valladolid and later

became a member of the Royal Council, where he enjoyed the
confidence of the Catholic Kings and the praise of Bartolomé de
Las Casas.[133] Diego de Simancas left his teaching position in the
colegio mayor of Santa Cruz at Valladolid after graduating as a
licenciado and doctor in laws. He became a counsel to the Inquisition, served as rector of the University of Valladolid for a
year, and then held the chair of Víspera de Leyes. Still unsatisfied,
he met with Don Fernando Niño, patriarch and president of the
Royal Council, and told him that he had always wanted to be
employed in the royal government. He left the university after
being appointed *oidor* in the Audiencia of Valladolid.[134]

Lineage and patronage helped as much as merit and achievement in securing a *letrado* appointment; Zorita was thus an ideal
candidate for the appointment. He was not only a member of
the distinguished Fernández de Córdoba family but also related
by ancestral marriages to other powerful Castilian families, including the Suárez de Figueroa, illustrious forebears of Don Hernando de Vega y Fonseca, a graduate of San Bartolomé and
president of the Council of the Indies in the 1580s.[135] Members of
the *colegios mayores* favored their own, and *colegiales* came to
dominate the royal tribunals of Spain. "Their practice was to
maintain at court former pupils known as *hacedores*—men of
rank and influence who would back members of their own colleges for official posts, on the understanding that the colleges
would in turn reserve places for their own friends and
relatives."[136]

Zorita's first legal experience was acquired as an *abogado de
pobres* in the Audiencia of Granada. Spanish barristers who did
not receive a fixed salary for defending the poor in inferior
tribunals were required by royal decree to defend them for
nothing more than "the love of God."[137] All appellate courts,
however, had solicitors for the poor. As a lesser official in the
audiencia, Zorita was paid approximately 15 per cent of a judge's
salary. Still, as public defender, Zorita acquired valuable experience, and this position may be considered an important stepping-
stone on the way to a judgeship.[138] Lawyers, moreover, were
members of a "noble" profession and, like college professors,
belonged to a guild (*colegio*) and were entitled to ride on capari-
soned mules.

Zorita's skill and dedication on behalf of the poor won recogni-
tion by the royal judges of the Chancery of Granada; more than
one probably encouraged the young lawyer to aspire to the office

of *oidor*. In any case, he soon knew all the judges of the tribunal, including Lope de León, the father of Luis de León. It is likely that Zorita more than once conversed with the judge. Aware that Zorita was a graduate of Salamanca, "the mother of those who depart to be in charge of the spiritual and temporal government of these kingdoms,"[139] the judge may have mentioned his oldest son, who had gone to Salamanca University and formally professed in the Augustinian order in early 1544.

The city of Granada, situated between the Darro and Genil rivers, aroused Zorita's admiration. Under a blue sky filled with clouds sometimes resembling white mules, the city built in tiers resembled Fez in color and atmosphere: "... the tawny, bare mountains in the distance, quite African in their ruggedness and nakedness; and, sloping down the ridge in which the river is swallowed up, the white and mauve tones of the buildings, the burning red of the roofs, and the pale green of the porcelain which armours the campaniles of the churches and the *koubas* of the old Moorish pavilion."[140]

In Granada, it appears, Zorita met and courted Doña Catarina de Cárdenas. Andalusian women like Catarina wore high combs in their hair, and the standard of beauty included firm calves and slender feet in neat little shoes.[141] Custom dictated that after Zorita proposed marriage to Catarina and she accepted his offer he was required to discuss the matter with his parents in Córdoba. After Zorita obtained permission to marry Catarina, he would send word to her parents through an intermediary and ask that she be given to him as his wife.

Of Doña Catarina we know very little except that she would suffer greatly from ill health in the New World and that she owned some houses in Granada, undoubtedly part of the marriage dowry provided by her parents.[142] Catarina was probably younger than the young lawyer and like him was of good family. In conformity with patriarchal-religious medieval tradition, upper-class Spanish women like Catarina were educated to respect the family and to revere Mary, Queen of Heaven and Virgin and Mother. The jealously guarded darling of her father and brothers, she was no doubt taught by her mother to be a good and self-respecting woman destined to enjoy the peaceful contentment of matrimony and its blessings and purpose: motherhood. The couple, however, remained childless. In later years Zorita briefly observed that, although he had been married for more than twenty years, he had never sought to accumulate wealth "nor to leave commemorations or an estate, for Our Lord has not been pleased to give me children."[143]

Despite the absence of children, Zorita's "family" would not be small. The family in the sixteenth century "was not one society only but three societies fused together; the society of man and wife, of parents and children, and of master and servants" and dependents.[144] Social custom and economic necessity required that nobles provide for servants and relatives, and Zorita did not deviate from this tradition. In 1564 the royal commissioner Jerónimo de Valderrama wrote the crown from Mexico City that Viceroy Luis de Velasco, contrary to royal decree, had ordered that various sums be given to his friends, relations, and dependents in acquittances and vacation pay. On the list of so-called minions and table-fellows is "Melchor de Adarve, who was paid from his Majesty's strongbox two hundred *pesos de oro común*, being an unmarried lad recently come to this land and the nephew of Doña Catarina de Cárdenas, the wife of Doctor Zorita." Luis de Velasco had also granted one of Zorita's relatives, Gabriel de Aguilera, an *estancia de ganado mayor* (6.76 square miles) and a *caballería y media de tierra* (150 acres). Bartolomé del Corro, one of Zorita's dependents, was granted an *estancia de ganado menor* (3 square miles) and 100 acres of agricultural land. Zorita's *familia* of dependents and servants was never as large as that of a great noble like Don Luis de Velasco, but it is evident that among the upper and lower nobility social custom, ties of blood, and economic dependency made for a larger household than the nuclear family of the lower classes.[145]

When one examines the documents that Alonso de Zorita has left us, it is immediately apparent that he is singularly silent about his ancestry. This is probably because he, like Fray Luis de León, did not consider lineage very important. Works and faith were what counted. On the other hand, Zorita, like Luis de León, may have been aware that he "did not have full knowledge of his ancestors' lineage, but had heard it said that certain rivals of his father had insulted his nobility by claiming that he came from the *converso* caste."[146]

In summary, it can be said that Alonso de Zorita was born into the ranks of the old nobility. However, his ancestry included the Fernández de Córdoba family who were of Jewish ancestry on the Pacheco side. His mother was Doña Inés Fernández de Valdelomar y Córdoba; his grandmother on the maternal side was Ana de Córdoba; and his grandmother on the paternal side was Bea-

triz Moyano de Figueroa y Córdoba, *hija natural* of a certain
Diego Fernández de Córdoba and niece of the Count of Priego,
according to one authority. If his grandmother was of the house
of the Count of Priego, she was a Hurtado de Mendoza as well as
a Fernández de Córdoba.[147]

The name of his great-grandfather, Diego Fernández de Córdoba, was carried by more than one member of this family. An
example is the Count of Cabra, the head of the house of Baena,
who died in 1487. Another Diego Fernández de Córdoba was a
nephew of the Count of Cabra and the Master of the King's
Pages in the reign of the Catholic Kings; he lived in Estepa and
was an ally of the house of Aguilar in its feud with the Count of
Cabra. In 1560, Cardinal Mendoza y Bobadilla noted that Doña
Catalina Fernández de Córdoba's grandson was the father of
the Marquesa de Estepa, "who is today Doña Juana, the wife of
Don Diego de Córdoba, Alcaide de los Donceles." Still another
member of this family was Diego Fernández de Córdoba y
Hurtado de Mendoza, Count of Cabra in 1523; in this year
Charles V asked him and Doña Juana de Cárdenas, the wife of
Don Pedro Portocarrero, for loans of 12,000 and 8,000 ducats,
respectively.[148]

It is apparent that Zorita's wife, Catarina de Cárdenas, if she
belonged to the noble house of Cárdenas, was also a descendant
of the *converso* Don Juan Pacheco, Grand Master of Santiago and
Marquis of Villena.[149]

In spite of the fact that Spain had a discriminatory society in
which "purity of the blood," religious orthodoxy, and "pride of
lineage" were very important concepts, intermarriage between
Old Christians and Jews and Moors had created a multiethnic
society; Zorita is an example. In sixteenth-century Andalusia,
children of hidalgos and Moorish women were considered Old
Christians. Furthermore, at the end of the fifteenth century, it
appears, the *colegio* of San Bartolomé was full of *conversos* and
sons of *conversos*, and Francisco de Mendoza y Bobadilla's *Tizón
de la nobleza* states that most of the caballeros of Navarre descended from Don Juan de Autec, *judío confeso*. "Many of them
are officers of the Inquisition and *colegiales* in San Bartolomé of
Salamanca, and there have been many *confesos* in this college." As
is evident, both the Navarrese Miguel Díez de Armendáriz and
the Andalusian Zorita were not necessarily of "pure ancestry."[150]

CHAPTER 2
Maintaining Law and Order in Española

On May 21, 1547, Licentiate Alonso de Zorita was appointed judge in the Royal Chancellery of Santo Domingo. Established in 1511 to curb the powers and claims of Viceroy Diego Columbus, it was initially staffed with three judges. In 1520, a fourth *oidor* was added to this first American tribunal, and the crown provided for a president who would combine the offices of senior judge and governor. The high court of justice thus became the model for the conventional membership of a smaller appellate court in the New World—four high functionaries assisted by lesser officials.

The royal order elevating the thirty-five-year-old lawyer to a royal judge of the Audiencia of Española cited Zorita's ability, education, and virtuous life and assigned him all "the honors, favors, exemptions, liberties, preeminence, prerogatives, and immunities" enjoyed by the other judges of the tribunal, an annual salary of 1,000 ducats (375,000 *maravedís*), and the general responsibility of the king's magistrates to expedite all legal instruments, petitions, and lawsuits coming before royal courts of justice.[1]

Because his legal practice had not enriched him financially, Zorita asked for and received an advance of 400 ducats from the crown to cover the cost of the voyage to Española. He also received exemption from the payment of export duties in the amount of 1,000 pesos for himself and 500 pesos for his wife on household goods and merchandise; for the service of his household Zorita was granted permission to take four black slaves to America without having to pay the two ducats per license customarily assessed on each slave transported to the Indies.[2]

Four years before Zorita received his commission as *oidor*, the crown issued a decree ordering vessels to sail to the New World in yearly, protected fleets because of the war between Spain and France and the danger of corsairs.[3] Since the spring fleet had already departed when Zorita received his appointment, he was forced to wait for the next convoy and thus had ample time to prepare for the voyage. Before leaving for Española, Zorita and Doña Catarina visited the young lawyer's family in Córdoba;

41

there his father gave Zorita 1,300 pesos in money and goods to help cover the costs of the trip. Zorita in Córdoba also authorized his brother and a certain Licentiate Turiel on March 11, 1548, to collect money owed him by the municipal council of Granada for his services on behalf of the poor.[4]

At his parents' home Zorita's appointment and the forthcoming trip to the New World were doubtless frequent subjects of discussion. Local events touching on Castilian and New World affairs also came to the notice of the Zoritas. Locusts had damaged Spain's crops in this decade, and the year 1548 was "dry, lean, and dear." Foodstuffs were high, and many articles of consumption sold for prices never before seen in the kingdom.[5]

Francisco de los Cobos had died in Ubeda, not far from Córdoba. An able but venal man, Cobos had risen from minor secretary to all-powerful royal counselor, controlling almost every office of Castile and the Indies that depended on the royal secretariat. Ambassador Martín de Salinas said that Cobos had the power of Saint Peter: he absolved those whom he favored and condemned others. Because Don Pedro Fernández de Córdoba, Doña Catalina's son, arranged the marriage of Cobos's daughter to Don Gonzalo Fernández de Córdoba, the Duke of Sessa, in late 1538, Cobos granted Don Pedro the control of the *contaduría mayor de cuentas*, a sort of court of accounts in the Council of Finance; this post was worth over 1,000 ducats and might be sold for 15,000.[6] The friendship Cobos felt for Don Pedro Fernández de Córdoba and his family may have been a factor in Zorita's appointment to the office of *oidor* in the Indies.

Zorita was not entirely unfamiliar with aspects of the New World and its inhabitants; he had formed some image of the Indies by 1547. Having met Alvar Núñez Cabeza de Vaca in Salamanca ten years before, he knew of this explorer's remarkable journey through many and strange lands. An avid reader and collector of books, Zorita had probably read such published chronicles or geographical works as those of Peter Martyr and Gonzalo Fernández de Oviedo. He also knew that various *cordobeses*—including Gonzalo Jiménez de Quesada, a lawyer and graduate of the University of Salamanca—had "gone west" to seek their fortunes in the New World. The Kingdom of New Granada and its capital, Santa Fe de Bogotá, founded by Quesada—the grandson of a linen dealer and a master dyer—was less than a decade old.[7] On the other hand, the island of Española was a long-established colony, and printed versions of Hernando

Cortés's letters on the conquest of the wealthy Aztec empire were published in Seville and Toledo by 1525.

In the spring of 1548, Zorita and Doña Catarina took a coach to Seville. Vehicles were then pulled by mules, but because it was alleged that this practice would hinder the breeding of horses in Castile, the *cortes* of 1578 decreed that all coaches must be pulled by horses, four in number and the property of the owner of the coach. Mules after this date might be used for trips shorter than five leagues.[8]

Travelers ate and lodged in roadside inns called *ventas*. Until 1560 most *ventas* provided only bed, salt, oil, and vinegar, and guests brought their own food and drink. The term innkeeper (*mesonero*) was synonymous with pickpocket like the one portrayed in *Don Quixote*: light-footed and light-fingered men who provided guests with girls "of the district." They also often sold cat meat under the guise of baked rabbit.[9]

Zorita and his traveling companions may have seen at first hand the result of Charles V's foreign policies. By the 1540s the crown's expenses exceeded revenues, and the emperor had mortgaged American treasure and Castilian taxes to various bankers. Deficit financing had become an established practice, and in 1545 Prince Philip wrote his father of the effects of taxation on the common people: They "are reduced to such utter misery that many of them walk naked. And the misery is so universal that it is even greater among the vassals of nobles than it is among Your Majesty's vassals, for they are unable to pay their rents, lacking the wherewithal, and the prisons are full."[10]

Inns of the better sort in the cities were called *fondas*; Zorita and his party may have lodged at one of these hostels before leaving Seville. Seville in 1548 had perhaps 65,000 permanent inhabitants[11] and "stood very fitly and commodiously seated for point of profit." Merchants dealt in all commodities; some years later the novelist Mateo Alemán called Seville "the mother of orphans" and "shelter for sinners; where all cry out of want, and yet no man wants."[12] Cervantes called this Spanish "Babylonia" an asylum and refuge for the poor and outcasts.[13] Seville, like Madrid, had "the savor of a city, another I know not what, other greatness, though not in the same quality." But if it lacked a king and court, silver was more common than copper money in other parts, and people spent freely. In addition, much wax was spent on taper lights during Lent, and alms were bestowed liberally on the poor.[14]

Seville in the late sixteenth
century. The Casa de
Contratación (House of
Trade), established in Seville
in 1503, controlled the Indies
trade. Rich merchants of
Seville and Cádiz kept the
American colonies
understocked and charged
exorbitant prices for goods.
(Courtesy of Marqués de
Lozoya, *Historia de España*)

The city was a mirror of Andalusian society. Cardinal Francisco Mendoza y Bobadilla observed that

the Duke of Arcos, Don Juan [Ponce de León] had a concubine named Leonor Martínez, a woman of low quality but of Old Christian stock. He married her and called her Doña Leonor, from whom descend the following houses: the Dukes of Arcos, the Dukes of Alcalá, of Feria, of Osuna, the Count of Bailén, of Castelar, of Alcaudete, of Villar, of Santisteban del Puerto, the Marqués of Alba, Marqués of Priego, of la Guardia, of Aldales, those of Comares, Don Sancho de Cardona, of Málaga, and all the Téllez of Seville.

By another woman, named Catalina González, the Duke of Arcos had Don Enrique, "from whom there is a great number of descendants in Jerez by Moors, Jews, and mulattoes; and a great number of the caballeros of Córdoba, Seville, Jerez and all of Andalucía can trace their lineage from these many sons and daughters. So that is was said of this caballero that he delibe-

rately had children by all sorts of persons, least of all by noble women."[15]

Not only was the nobility of Seville "of mixed social and racial origins," but it and the clergy of Seville were active in the Indies trade. Great magnates like the Duke of Arcos were engaged in the wholesale trade. Another magnate, Don Alvaro de Bazán, was appointed "captain general in the India navigation," and his armadas transported merchandise and the crown's treasure across the Atlantic. Lesser nobles also owned ships, participated in the slave trade, granted credit and loans, invested in New World enterprises, and maintained business agents in America. As Ruth Pike notes, by 1550 the Sevillian nobility in cooperation with *converso* merchant-commoners "to whom they were often related through blood or marriage" dominated New World trade. Among these *converso* families were the wealthy, prominent, and numerous Caballeros of Seville, related to the secretary of the Audiencia of Santo Domingo, Diego Caballero de la Rosa.[16]

On April 28, 1548, Zorita and Doña Catarina departed for the island of Española in a ship commanded by Cristóbal Romero. They were accompanied by Zorita's brother Juan Pérez and his wife, Doña Jerónima de Mena y Saldaña, and several dependents.[17] Also on board were Zorita's four slaves and six slaves for whom Juan Pérez had requested license for the service of his person and household in the Indies.[18] The ship was accompanied by several *naos* for mutual safety. The square-rigged *naos*, clumsier and slower than the graceful, seaworthy caravels of the period, carried members of the newly created Audiencia of New Galicia. These judges, subordinate to the *oidores* of the Audiencia of Mexico, were Dr. Juan Meléndez de Sepúlveda and Licentiates Lorenzo Lebrón de Quiñones and Miguel de Contreras y Ladrón, the last the son-in-law of Alonso López de Cerrato, president of the Audiencia of Guatemala. Judge Contreras and Zorita were friends and they had practiced law before the Audiencia of Granada before they were appointed royal judges.

The journey across the Atlantic began on the Guadalquivir, filled with white sails and green branches. Working the tides down the river, the ships finally reached the river mouth, anchoring for the last time off Sanlúcar de Barrameda. After lifting anchors and spreading sails, the swaying ships left the roadstead, the passengers and crew praying for an uneventful voyage and fair winds as the beach and dangerous sandbars were lost in the distance.[19]

We do not know whether Zorita's westerly course was eased by white tradewind clouds and bright blue sea and sky—weather like April in Andalucía—but all Atlantic voyages were dangerous and uncomfortable in the days of the galleons. Zorita was silent concerning his passage to the Indies, but Fray Tomás de la Torre, provincial of the Dominican friars in Guatemala, vividly described the trials of the sea road to America in the 1540s.

Because of the war with France, passengers "departed in great fear of the enemy," and the secure and terrible prison of the ship was indiscriminately cruel. All "inmates" roasted in the burning sun or boiled below deck, most becoming sick and vomiting their scanty meals:

The heat, the stuffiness, and the sense of confinement are sometimes overpowering. The bed is ordinarily the floor. . . . There is an incredible thirst, sharpened by a diet of hardtack and salt beef. The water ration is half a liter daily; if you want wine you must bring your own. There are infinite numbers of lice, which eat men alive, and you cannot wash clothing because the sea water shrinks it. There is an evil stink, especially below deck, that becomes intolerable throughout the ship when the pump is working—and it is going more or less constantly, depending on how the ship sails.[20]

More horrible than these common hardships was that of "death constantly staring you in the face; you are separated from it by only the thickness of one board joined to another with pitch." That "even the most uneventful crossing was filled with trials" is attested to by the death of Dr. Meléndez within three days of the arrival of the fleet in Santo Domingo on June 10, 1548.[21]

Once in Española, Zorita was recognized as judge of the tribunal by Alonso de Grajeda, the acting president and only judge in the audiencia when Zorita arrived. Grajeda and Zorita were joined the following year by Juan Hurtado de Salcedo y Mendoza. Juan Hurtado obtained this position when a certain Bermúdez, appointed with Zorita, declined the office.[22]

Unlike the audiencias of Spain, which were purely judicial bodies, New World royal courts had executive and legislative functions. The audiencia, "the most important and interesting institution in the government of the Spanish Indies,"[23] had judicial primacy as the highest court of appeal in its district. It also served as a council of state to the chief civil and military official of a division of government. Moreover, the audiencia provided administrative continuity from one change of government to another, had provisional legislative powers, and assumed full governmental powers in the absence or incapacity of the viceroy or captain general. Zorita, as *oidor* of a corporate entity charged with many responsibilities, assumed a wide variety of duties.

As a judge he aided in hearing and deciding civil, criminal, and ecclesiastical cases of a secular nature in a tribunal that until 1549 had jurisdiction over all the Antilles and the provinces of the northern coast of South America, (today Venezuela and Colombia). As administrators, Zorita and Juan Hurtado formed part of a council of state that met with Alonso de Grajeda, the senior judge, and advised him in all administrative matters. These included the execution of royal orders; administration of the property of individuals who died intestate; inspection and censorship of books; questions of financial administration both secular and ecclesiastical; and the drafting of various reports and letters to the Council of the Indies covering every aspect of colonial life and government. In addition, royal judges occasionally inspected fleets and armadas, acted as probate judges, and made judicial investigations into the conduct of political office. Judges also made triennial tours of inspection within the audiencia district. On these *visitaciones* matters for investigation might range from the condition of roads to the sale of drugs in apothecary shops.

Santo Domingo

A survey of Zorita's day-to-day activities in Santo Domingo gives some idea of his success or failure in maintaining peace and order in the colony; it also contributes to a better understanding of Spanish society in Española during these years. The city and society of Santo Domingo in many ways resembled Seville in the same period. Like Seville, Santo Domingo was a port city and attracted "all kinds of diverse elements." The secular clergy was active in mercantile affairs, clerical concubinage was widespread, and the prebends in the cathedral chapter were sinecures for favored individuals. Finally, Santo Domingo, like Seville, "provided a haven for social outcasts and the unassimilated and a favorable environment for the enrichment and rise of *conversos.*"[24]

Española had changed considerably since the days of its chaotic beginnings under the rule of Christopher Columbus. The admiral's grandson, Don Luis Colón, lived in a magnificent house in the port. This palace, built by his father, had "many fine rooms" and commanded "a beautiful view of both land and sea." First married in 1542, Don Luis married again in 1546 while the first wife was still legally his spouse. He continued in his bigamous ways; when he married for the fourth time in Spain (all three former wives were still living), he was exiled to Oran, in North Africa, "where such manners were understood." Don Luis had lawsuits pending before the audiencia and had attempted to win Alonso de Grajeda's favor by giving him four *caballerías* of land on which to construct a sugar mill. The admiral's younger brother, Don Cristóbal, also had lawsuits before the court and had given Grajeda 180 cartloads of sugarcane plants, certain carts, a teamster, and a slave so that Grajeda might grow cane for the mill being constructed.[25]

Santo Domingo, capital of the island, was a beautiful city, well constructed with many fine stone houses for the prominent men of the island. Situated on the banks of the Ozama river and "as level as a table," the city's port was deep enough for ships of all types to unload their goods and passengers. Dwellings extended to the water's edge and ships anchored "under the very windows of the houses."

Streets were wide, and well planned and afforded a fine view of the principal buildings, which consisted of the cathedral and a school of theology, three monasteries, various churches, a hospital, a fortress, and the royal buildings housing the audiencia. According to Gonzalo Fernández de Oviedo, Santo Domingo's fortress commander and the official chronicler of the Indies, "No town in Spain—unless it is Barcelona, which I have seen many times—is superior in general," and "Santo Domingo is better planned than any town I have seen."[26]

Numerous festivals enhanced the magnificence of the city. The carnival days before Ash Wednesday provided a special opportunity for fun making and the display of women's beauty. The men winding their way through the streets lobbed oranges at the women viewing the procession from windows of the houses lining the boulevards; the ladies hurled oranges back at them. In the evening a masked ball was given by the president of the audiencia. The next day another Shrovetide parade was held, and citizens would pause before the royal building to throw oranges and eggshells filled with perfumed water at the president and his wife and assembled couples. In this and other ways the social distance between the governors and the governed was momentarily bridged, and a feeling of community was created in what may be described as an essentially medieval, highly stratified society.[27]

Santo Domingo's orange-throwing customs during carnival finally came to the attention of the crown. In 1579 participation in this diversion was expressly prohibited to members of the royal tribunal, "because although it may be an occasion for rejoicing and fiesta, it is not seemly that lettered men charged with the government and the administration of justice, should be so familiar with the public." This order expressed the royal wish that its high judicial and administrative authorities live circumspectly, maintaining social relations only with those of their own rank.[28]

Although royal judges were told that they "might not even legally exchange hospitalities, act as godfathers in families outside their own official circle, or be present at marriages or funerals," this rule was not observed in Española.[29] The members of the town council wrote the crown on June 20, 1555, describing an accusation made by a citizen that the *oidores* had on various occasions attended banquets and festivals and mingled with the members of the cabildo and principal citizens as malicious in intent. These practices, they stressed, had begun under Don Sebastián Ramírez de Fuenleal, bishop of Cuenca and president of the audiencia in the late 1520s, and other judges had merely followed his precedent. Judges had always attended marriages or funerals and had been friendly with the principal citizens. In addition, they had often become godfathers and served as best men at weddings, their presence at such functions dignifying them and pleasing the general public.[30]

In spite of its beauty and comfort, Santo Domingo had a smaller population in Zorita's day than it had had in 1525. Oviedo, who lived in Santo Domingo, attributed the population loss to emigration to Spain by those who had become rich and the departure of others to seek greater wealth on nearby islands and the mainland.[31]

Gold production, an important source of revenue in the first two decades of the century, had declined from a maximum annual yield of perhaps 450,000 pesos to less than 3,000 *pesos de oro*.[32] The colony had achieved an economic order in which farming and stock raising were the principal sources of wealth, and the typical Spaniard of means devoted most of his time to the raising of crops and stock. Horses, hogs, sheep, burros, goats, and cattle imported from Spain had multiplied rapidly and were exported. Fruits, green vegetables, and spices were cultivated, and the fare of the citizens and residents was complemented by hens, domestic pigeons, and ducks.

The most lucrative industry of the island in the 1540s was cattle raising. Cattle had increased to such an extent that all residents could afford meat, the interior valleys west of Santo Domingo and the immense plains east of the capital contained the principal stock-raising areas. Some cattlemen owned as many as 10,000 head, and much greater herds were not unusual. Great numbers of cattle ran wild and were hunted for their hides, which were prepared for shipment to Spain. Hunters left the meat to rot or be eaten by the wild dogs common to the island.[33]

Planters grew ginger, anotta, indigo, *Cassia fistula*, and cotton, but the chief money crop produced for shipment to Spain was sugar, which compared favorably with stock raising as an industry. More than twenty sugar mills returned an excellent profit on the large initial capital investment of 10,000 to 15,000 ducats required to build a mill.[34]

The People

The Indian population, so large when Columbus arrived, had practically disappeared from Española. The last Indian uprising—led by the cacique Enriquillo—ended in 1533; seventeen years later only 150 to 500 Indians were left on the island. In 1549 the royal judges reported that there was not a single allotment of Indians held in *encomienda* either privately or under the crown. These figures represent a loss of between 200,000 and 300,000 natives in the space of two generations—if the reckonings of Las Casas, who estimated the Indian population of Española at three million, and S. F. Cook and Woodrow Borah, who estimate the native population at seven to eight million, are discounted. As Carl Sauer observes, most contemporary scholars have asserted that the islands were sparsely inhabited when Columbus arrived. But in the sixteenth century it was commonly accepted that Española at the time of the European discovery had over a million inhabitants.[35]

Immediately after the Europeans arrived in Española, Indians began dying from Old World diseases to which they had no acquired immunity. However, many Indians who died of influenza, smallpox, typhus, measles, yellow fever, and malaria were first weakened physically and psychologically by malnutrition, cruel and merciless treatment, social dislocation, and unremitting labor. Intolerable oppression and overwork caused those Indians still in good health to flee their foreign masters and hang themselves

after having killed their children, saying it was far better to die than to live so miserably, serving such and so many ferocious tyrants and wicked thieves. The women, with the juice of a certain herb, dissipated their pregnancy, in order not to produce children, and then following the example of their husbands, hung themselves. Some threw themselves from high cliffs down precipices; others jumped into the sea; others again into rivers; and others starved themselves to death. Sometimes they killed themselves with their flint knives; others pierced their bosoms or their sides with pointed stakes.[36]

By 1550 most or all of the Indians left on the island had come from other regions. In 1545 the audiencia reported that two caravels had brought more than 250 branded Indians to the port of Santo Domingo. After confiscating these victims of slave hunters, captured on the islands of Margarita and Cubagua in contravention of Article 26 of the New Laws, the judges had deposited them with accredited citizens until the crown decided what to do with them.[37] Among those given Indians were the judges, who had put ten of them to work in their homes as domestic servants. The judges had justified this by claiming that the Indians had been placed in their care to save them from evil treatment and probable death at the hands of various settlers. In addition to being treated well, the Indians served as an example to the citizens of the island entrusted with servants; given wages for cultivating land, sewing, and serving as pages, they were free to leave if they became discontented with their lot. Moreover, the judges said, if the royal decree recently received meant that the Indians might no longer work for the judges, "their [the Indians'] condition will change much for the worse."[38]

The judicial inquiry of Alonso de Cerrato, Grajeda, and Zorita in 1553 confirmed the claims in the judges' letter of 1549 regarding the small number of surviving Indians and their good treatment. To the general charge that the judges had been remiss in converting and instructing the natives of Española and the islands and mainland under the court's jurisdiction, the judges replied that Cerrato had freed all the Indians of the island in accordance with the New Laws of 1542–43.[39] Further, Grajeda, after learning of the plight of the scattered Indians who wandered in the mountains and open country without physical and spiritual care, had personally reduced a small band of Indians under a chieftain named Murcia to the service of the crown and the faith.[40] Zorita stated that the few Indians remaining on the island were Christians; they and the blacks were taken to church on Sundays and feast days for celebration of the mass and religious instruction. He also observed that the audiencia had ordered all governors, bishops, prelates, and friars of monasteries within the court's jurisdiction to take special care in instructing the Indians in Christian doctrine. In 1561, Zorita, recalling his period of service in Santo Domingo, stated that he had dealt out justice to the great satisfaction of the whole island, for there were "no cases involving Indians, which cause Spaniards to hate the honest judge who does his duty."[41]

Because of the rapid decline of the Indian population, and because the natives were not accustomed to the labor required for the production of sugar, non-Christian slaves (*bozales*) were imported from Guinea as early as 1510. The desire of plantation owners and ranchers to establish a slave economy in the Greater Antilles was supported by the religious, who wished to save the rapidly disappearing aborigines. In this fashion Christian humanitarianism and incipient capitalism joined hands in beginning the trading of African slaves in 1518. By the 1540s so many blacks had been brought to Española that Oviedo in his remarks on the island's slave population wrote that the land appeared to be "a replica of Ethiopia."[42]

At the time that Zorita arrived in Santo Domingo, the island's black population may have numbered as many as 30,000. Most blacks worked for their Spanish masters on the sugar mills and farms, but some were domestic servants who occasionally escaped slave status through manumission or marriage with whites. However, Magnus Mörner's observation that "the Crown [and its representatives in the Indies] opposed intermarriage with the African element" holds true for the royal judges of Española. This is suggested by the scornful comment of Zorita and Juan Hurtado de Mendoza that a fisherman named Rueda (found guilty of aggravated assault against *bachiller* Lorenzo Bernáldez, the tribunal's legal secretary) was a man of little worth who had married a black woman.[43]

Many slaves had been illegally introduced into the colony. As early as 1538 the treasury inspector Gaspar de Astudillo, acting as attorney for the crown, had requested that the books of the treasury officials be examined for the years 1526–38 and that a copy be made of the records of blacks brought to the island in this period. Astudillo and Captain Juan de Miranda claimed that Spaniards who had received limited licenses for the importation of 100 slaves had illegally imported at least twice that number to Española, other islands, and the mainland. The slaves had not been registered in Seville but had been brought directly from Cape Verde and São Tomé. Astudillo and Miranda alleged that Diego Caballero de Cazalla, auditor of the exchequer, and his brother Alonso were the most prominent figures among those who dealt in the illegal slave trade.[44]

According to President Alonso de Cerrato, the exchequer officials bent the law by allowing individuals without licenses to purchase those granted to Portuguese factors and other persons in the first instance. The officials also exempted Portuguese and Spanish shipmasters from paying import duties on slaves. This was done by allowing shipmasters to list slaves as ship's boys. After entering port as members of the crew, the blacks were sold as slaves.[45]

In spite of the large number of African slaves brought to Española legally and illegally, there was a constant demand for more *piezas de Indias*. Need arose, in part, because of slave trade

with the mainland. Slaves commanded a much higher price on the
continent, and even President Alonso de Fuenmayor and the
judges under him had sold a great many slaves prior to Cerrato's
presidency. The slave trade with the mainland hurt the island's
economy, but Cerrato had continued to condone the trade by
private citizens because no decree prohibited it.[46]

Slaves frequently escaped into the rugged highlands and mountains, and in 1545 as many as 7,000 runaways (negros cimarrones,
or maroons) may have threatened the island's security. The fugitives, divided into various large tribes and several hundred small
bands, inspired great fear by their raids. Spaniards had begun
moving into Santo Domingo from the small towns; mines and
plantations had been abandoned; the search for new gold-
producing areas had ceased; and black rebels were so shameless
and bold that they had frequently assaulted Spaniards on the
island roads, robbing and killing citizens within three leagues of
Santo Domingo. When peace overtures failed to win over the
rebels, the royal judges financed a general war by emergency
taxation on exports and imports (the avería) and an excise tax on
food and alcoholic beverages (the sisa). By 1546 the situation was
under control, and the crown acknowledged Cerrato's forceful
leadership, congratulating him for restoring the island's sugar
economy.

Cerrato's victory over the maroons was not entirely successful,
for more than 100 rebels continued their raids during the first
months that Zorita was on the island, and settlers remained fearful that plantation slaves might join the renegades. A Spanish
force finally hunted down the warlike band headed by Sebastián
Lemba, killing 140 rebels and capturing others in battle. The
twenty rebels who remained at large then took to horses and
began engaging in banditry on the main roads. To counter this
threat, the audiencia directed a troop of Spaniards and a flying
squad of blacks (negros ligeros) to keep them constantly on the
run. This move proved successful, and the exhausted rebels were
brought to bay in September, 1548. In the ensuing battle Sebastián Lemba and four of his principal lieutenants were killed, but
six or seven members of the band managed to escape. During the
following month the rebels were pursued by soldiers who had been
ordered not to cease in their search until the maroons were either
captured or killed. Meanwhile, another band of runaways had
risen up in the province of Concepción de la Vega. These fifteen
cimarrones had killed a plantation owner and two of his slaves

and were robbing travelers on the main highroad. Eight or ten rebels were still operating in 1549 and had joined a group of twenty-five natives led by an Indian who had been in the band of the black captain Diego del Campo before he was captured in 1546. Two captains with soldiers and trackers had been sent in pursuit of the rebels, who had done some damage near the towns of Concepción de la Vega and Santiago de los Caballeros.[47]

The white population of Española consisted of roughly 5,000 persons living in less than 1,200 households in 1542.[48] White *vecinos* and residents were almost exclusively Spaniards or Portuguese, but more than 100 Berber slaves and freedmen formed part of Santo Domingo's population. Most of the Berbers were carpenters, masons, or skilled craftsmen, but some Berber slave women may have been exploited as prostitutes in the city's brothel, established in the 1520s by Juan Sánchez Sarmientos.[49] A small number of Genoese also had settled on the island. In contrast to the Berbers, who were "plebs," the Genoese formed part of the island's aristocracy and acted as merchants and capitalists. One of these was Valián de Forne, who farmed the *avería* tax, traded in slaves, and bought urban real estate and cattle.[50]

Although the Genoese were important in the transatlantic trade and invested large sums in the sugar industry, the *converso* residents of Española controlled the economy. The *converso* oligarchy also controlled the municipal government as late as 1554, and its members in 1553 included Licentiate Carmona, Cristóbal de Tapia, Francisco Dávila, Diego Caballero, Alonso Caballero, Alonso de la Peña, Juan de Junco, and Francisco de Pineda.

The most prominent *converso* settler in Santo Domingo in these years was Diego Caballero de la Rosa, the perpetual secretary of the audiencia, *regidor* in the cabildo, and sometimes treasurer of the royal exchequer. He combined economic opportunism with political power, and the Caballero clan with its five members was the most numerous of the powerful New Christian families on the island, controlling the office of auditor in the exchequer from 1514 to 1556. Other members of the family resided in Seville; Diego Caballero el Mozo became factor of the Casa de Contratación and ended his life with the honorary title Marshal of Española and the ownership of a magnificent tomb in Seville's grandiose cathedral.

Although Enrique Otte states that Diego Caballero el Mozo was the uncle of Diego Caballero de la Rosa, this is not confirmed by Giménez Fernández. Diego Caballero el Mozo, who

later called himself Caballero de Cazalla, had three brothers,
Pedro, Fernando, and Alonso; Giménez Fernández does not
identify Diego Caballero de la Rosa's father, Juan, as a brother.
Both Giménez Fernández and Oviedo mention that Alonso
Caballero de Cazalla, the auditor of Española's exchequer, was
the nephew of Diego Caballero el Mozo.[51]

Diego Caballero de la Rosa was a native of San Lúcar de
Barrameda and the son of the *converso* Juan Caballero. Despite
the crown's knowledge that both of Caballero's parents had been
punished and reconciled by the Inquisition, this son of judaizers
condemned by the Holy Office had enough influence with the
Council of the Indies to maintain public office until his death in
1554.

Diego Caballero, a wealthy and important merchant and
bureaucrat, began his career in Española as an employee of the
treasury in 1514, acting at the same time as agent for the brothers
Grimaldo, members of the Genoese colony in Seville and active in
the slave trade. By 1520, Diego had made enough money to buy
the office of secretary of the audiencia; shortly thereafter he held
an interest in the best sugar mill on Española and the monopoly
to settle Spaniards and trade on the coast of Maracaibo. From
the time of his arrival in Santo Domingo until his death, Diego
Caballero played an important part in the slave trade. He and the
other Caballeros were also involved in moneylending, enslavement of Indians on the mainland, shipping, and the control of
public offices in Española.[52] On September 30, 1556, the Royal
Council of the Indies found Judges Grajeda and Zorita guilty of
allowing Diego Caballero to hold two offices in the audiencia,
escribano de cámara and *registrador*.[53]

Old Christians in Española resented the economic and political power of the *conversos*. As early as 1537, Oviedo wrote the
crown that many sons, grandsons, and brothers of relapsed heretics condemned by the Holy Office in Spain had arrived in
Española and achieved positions in the government.[54] In 1554,
Oviedo declared that most of the cabildo's aldermen (*regidores*)
were of Jewish descent.[55]

Oviedo also alludes in *Las Quincuagenas de la nobleza de
España* to judaizing members of Saint Teresa's family who had
departed for the Indies to hide their character:

Everyone knows that *sanbenitos*, painted with two crosses, one in front
and the other in the back, are worn for repentance. These penitential

Portrait of Alonso and Diego Caballero de Cazalla, with Diego's son, painted by Pedro de Campaña for the altarpiece of Diego Cazalla's chapel. (Courtesy of Publicaciones de la Escuela de Estudios Hispano-Americanos de Sevilla)

garments are not worn willingly, nor for the devotion the penitent has for these crosses. See what devotion he had, who sentenced in Castile and reconciled, took his habit and threw it in a well; he then came to the Indies with an escutcheon engraved with a rampant purple-colored royal lion on a white field, and a silver sail bordered with eight crosses on a red field, like that of the Cepedas, who are widely known as hidalgos: and this other person was notoriously of the cast of Jews newly received in the Christian faith, who along with others like him, are not always absolved because they departed by the gate of the pardoned, nor more Christians than heretofore, but marked for the persons they are.

Saint Teresa of Jesus, born in Ávila on March 28, 1515, was the daughter of Alonso Sánchez de Cepeda, a wealthy merchant; her grandfather was Juan Sánchez de Toledo, reconciled for apostasy in 1485. Her brothers (Hernando, Rodrigo, Lorenzo, Antonio, Pedro, Jerónimo, and Agustín) had different surnames and emigrated to the Indies; various of their descendants were given patents of nobility or became knights in military orders.[56]

Judge Alonso de Grajeda, like Oviedo, considered the New Christians a dangerous minority in the colony. In 1553, Grajeda wrote the crown that all or most of the band led by the *caudillo* Francisco de Ávila, *regidor* in the municipal council, were New Christians residing in Santo Domingo illegally. Grajeda was intensely resentful of these aliens and requested that the crown authorize a very secret investigation in the manner of an inquisition throughout the city and district of Santo Domingo and the island. Those ten or twelve individuals led by Francisco de Ávila should have no part in the gathering of evidence, "for many of them or almost all are second generation New Christians [*hijos de cristianos nuevos de judíos*] prohibited from passing to these parts. They hate me greatly for two reasons. First, they understand that I was a friend of Licentiate Cerrato who came here with a commission as Apostolic Inquisitor; second, I have not cared to acquire a relative among these people through the marriage of my children." Grajeda also claimed that a witness named Alonso Rodríguez who had testified against him in the judicial inquiry (*residencia*) conducted by Alonso Maldonado was in the Indies illegally. After being referred to the Inquisition of Llerena, a report had been received that Rodríguez was indeed the son and grandson of New Christians and Jews.[57]

The slavocracy of the island, headed by the Caballeros, had entrenched itself in power as early as 1520, and after that date Española had ceased to be a land of opportunity for newcomers. The oligarchy owned most of the best agricultural and pastureland and controlled commerce. Among the owners of the largest sugar mills figured the sons and heirs of the treasury officials (Pasamonte, Ampiés, and Dávila), the *alcaide* Tapia, the secretaries of the audiencia (Caballero, Ledesma, and Tostado), the judges Ayllón and Lebrón, and many others who had benefited almost exclusively from crown loans authorized in the early years of the colony to develop the island. These loans remained outstanding when Licentiate Alonso de Cerrato arrived in 1544.[58]

That various Spaniards desired to leave Española for greener pastures is apparent from a charge that Zorita had granted licenses to petitioners without consulting the other judges in administrative sessions. Zorita pleaded guilty to the charge in the case of a Gaspar de la Torre, who had left for Mexico. Zorita excused his action by noting that the other judges always referred individuals desiring licenses to him; Grajeda and Hurtado de Mendoza were aware of Zorita's speed, diligence, and fairness in his treatment of men who wished to emigrate or wanted a license to retrieve gold and silver bars from vessels that had been wrecked off the island coast.[59]

The crown attempted to arrest Española's population decline in 1550 by authorizing Ochoa de Luyando, of the Council of the Indies, to sell permits for the transportation of 1,000 slaves to Española at 8 ducats per license. Half of the 8,000 ducats collected was to be used to promote the colonization of Española by farmers and their families and to help pay for the cost of the war against the maroons.[60] This and other efforts to increase Española's white farming population failed to halt the movement of people to the mainland. To remedy Española's sad state, Licentiate Alonso Estévez, attorney for the audiencia, suggested to the crown that anyone owning rural property should be prohibited from emigrating to the mainland. He also desired a better sort of colonist from Spain. Estévez stated in 1552 that those settlers brought to Española as *labradores* (farmers) had not helped the island's economy: "They were barbers, tailors, and useless people who very quickly sold the 12 cows and the bull given them by Your Majesty. They could not work and settled only hospitals and graves. Settlers of this kind arrive in abundant numbers without Your Majesty having to pay their passage."[61]

The island's forlorn state continued. In 1555 the dean of the cathedral and the municipal council of Santo Domingo wrote the crown that Spaniards continued to desert the island, and Negroes needed to work the land were lacking: "And because ships only come in convoy, years pass without provisions coming to Española. We lack bread, wine, soap, oil, woolens, and linen. Prices are exorbitant whenever these goods do arrive, and if we wish to establish a fixed price the merchandise is hidden."[62] In 1574, Juan López de Velasco, cosmographer and historian to the Council of the Indies, noted that Santo Domingo had once had a thousand *vecinos* and that "only a few years ago it had 700, so that each day its population diminishes, like the rest of the island's settlements, because ships do not go there to trade."[63]

It is doubtful whether an influx of peasant farmers and laborers and their families would in fact have given Española the better sort of laboring class desired by Licentiate Estévez. Farm laborers and artisans often deserted their trades in the Indies because conditions in the New World tended to transform the traditional social structure of Spanish society. Cultural interchange and interbreeding among Europeans, Africans, and Indians are obvious examples of a Hispanic-American society in the process of formation. Less conspicuous but as important was a tendency toward the leveling of Spanish colonial society.[64]

Those Spanish farmers and artisans who arrived in Española undoubtedly soon learned that economic prosperity was limited in the colony. Española had a declining Spanish population, an oligarchy that controlled the best lands and commerce, and a large group of slaves who performed the tasks traditionally done in Spain by peasants and artisans. For farmers and gardeners, an already low social position became even lower when it was associated with slave labor. Skilled and dedicated white farmers probably tended to become supervisors of black laborers on Spanish plantations. Those settlers who arrived in Española with the intention of becoming farmers soon changed their minds and resumed their former trades or way of life either in Española or in Mexico or Peru, regions with an expanding Spanish population and greater possibilities.[65]

Leveling of Society

A feature of the leveling process in the Indies was the possibility of vertical social mobility in a society that was relatively open when compared to the estate-based, corporative society of Spain. Spanish colonial society was a bit more fluid than society in Spain for a number of reasons.

First, life on the New World frontier put men on their own, and if a commoner made a good soldier, he might attain high military rank. In battle with the enemy and the elements a sense of the inherent equality of all men arose and blurred social distinctions. Moreover, when conquerors of distinct social strata began lording it over Indians and imported black slaves they all became members of the dominant caste, and even commoners came to view agricultural labor as altogether servile. Thus arose the Spanish immigrants' refusal to be identified with Indian or black agricultural laborers and the constant presumption of nobility or a right to higher social status by conquerors or first settlers, a tendency that became even more apparent in their Creole descendants.

Second, the distance between the attitudes and values of nobles and commoners and between formal Spanish and the popular language had never been great. Although there was in various instances a notable difference between the two groups in living standards, clothes, and education—for example, the use of Latin by university graduates in this period—the lower classes of Spain often assumed attitudes and manners that foreign observers connect with the upper levels of society. The reverse is true in Spanish literature, for Spanish authors like Cervantes, Luis de Góngora, and Lope de Vega often drew on the language and poetic images of popular songs, proverbs, and folk imagery. Because the "ideals of the nobility were not confined to them as a class, but instead permeated the whole of Spanish society," sixteenth-century Spanish commoners, "lacking any true revolutionary consciousness," sought to live "nobly" by emulating their declared enemies.[66] Fernand Braudel describes this tendency in "civil servants": "In Spain, where we are better acquainted with the government employee, he would typically come from the urban lower classes, or even of peasant stock, which did not prevent him (far from it) from claiming descent from a hidalgo family (as who did not in Spain?)."[67]

The social aspirations of commoners in the Indies are apparent in the comments of disgruntled aristocrats and individuals who accepted the idea that between classes "there must be inequality; for otherwise a class cannot perform its function, or—a strange thought to us—enjoy its rights."[68] In 1550, Licentiate Hurtado de Mendoza wrote the crown that Negroes in the New World were absolutely necessary "because Spaniards do not work in the Indies since they all consider themselves caballeros. But because of their poverty they cannot purchase Negroes, presently worth 150 pesos per head, and every settlement becomes depopulated."[69] In 1565, Fray Gerónimo de Mendieta declared that all Spaniards in Mexico, even the most contemptible and wretched, wanted to be lords and live as such, serving no one, but being served.[70] When Philip II asked the viceroys of Mexico and Peru whether it would be advantageous to sell patents of nobility in America, the viceroy of Peru answered on August 6, 1582, that "there would not be three persons who would buy them, because in the Indies all are caballeros, and this is one of the reasons why these regions are populated." On October 28 of the same year the viceroy of Mexico wrote: "All are descendants of conquerors and consider themselves noble and reputable."[71]

Although all Spanish commoners in the Indies had seigneurial ambitions, those holding low status found it almost impossible to advance to the highest ranks of New World society. It is also probable that most commoners, whether of low or intermediate rank, made no claim to be hidalgos, much less "*dons*." Still, for those who lived on the fringes of a higher class, rising in status was a real possibility. "Wealthy merchants in Spain," writes James Lockhart, "often were able to marry the daughters of hidalgos, and their sons, while still merchants, could claim hidalgo status."[72] That this was also attempted in the New World is evident in the case of Licentiate Grajeda who spurned at least one offer from a merchant *converso* family seeking a marriage alliance with his family. Grajeda refused the offer, but had he been a marginal hidalgo, a poor gentleman with "much linen but little food" seeking to improve his fortune, he might have accepted a *converso* son-in-law.

It is also apparent that merchants in the Indies were often wealthier than many nobles. Zorita himself was friendly with merchants and acknowledged the aid they had given him. Among the charges listed in Zorita's *residencia* for his period of service in Española is one made by Francisco Bravo, the tribunal's *relator*, that Zorita had favored and been extremely friendly to the merchant Martín García, a former citizen of Seville and the first cousin of Bravo's two sisters-in-law.

Bravo resented García's desire to marry his two sisters-in-law to García's nephew Luis de Ayala and another poor relative. Bravo, the girls' guardian, alleged that García had enlisted Zorita's aid in his scheme to marry the girls to his poor relations. To win Zorita over, García supposedly had various of his relatives give the newly appointed judge many presents in Seville as well as loans of money prior to Zorita's departure for Española. After taking up his duties as *oidor* in Santo Domingo, Zorita was befriended by García and the two ate and drank together frequently, discussing in public and in private the feud that existed between García and Bravo.

Zorita's rebuttal of this charge acknowledged that Martín García had extended him credit many times in the purchase of household goods, but so had the merchants Pedro Díaz Vásquez, Luis Alonso, and Luis Ramírez. Zorita also noted that although he had helped García in one instance to collect a legal claim of 240 pesos against the estate of a deceased individual, he had ruled against García in two lawsuits the merchant had filed against other persons.[73]

Further evidence that there was no clear line of social demarcation between merchants and hidalgo professionals is Zorita's admission that he had accepted lodging and food for himself and his household from the merchant Juan de Villoria upon his arrival in Santo Domingo. After staying at Villoria's home for three and a half days, Zorita rented a place of his own.[74] During his period of service in Española, Zorita's wife was also a guest of Doña María de Villoria at the sugar mills she and the auditor, Alvaro Caballero, owned. Although the relationship between Juan de Villoria and Doña María is not explicitly defined it is reasonable to assume that they were related. In any case, Zorita and his wife were friendly with educated, wealthy merchant entrepreneurs such as Alvaro Caballero, his son Pedro Serrano, shipmaster Tomás Vasallo, and other buyers and sellers of goods.[75]

Just as commoners frequently accepted the minor nobility's world view and standards of conduct, so nobles often displayed the materialism and covetousness of the merchants who came to the New World in disproportionate numbers. Although merchants in medieval Europe were considered "alien and parasite," and merchants in sixteenth-century Peru "had a reputation as cowardly moneygrubbers," trade became increasingly respectable with the expansion of Europe.[76] Following the discovery of America, social morality came more and more to accept commerce and its profits. This tendency is reflected in a comment by the man who discovered America for Spain. Columbus affirmed that all things have their price when he wrote: "Gold constitutes treasure, and he who possesses it has all the needs in this world, as also the means of rescuing souls from Purgatory, and restoring them to the enjoyment of Paradise."[77]

As already noted, the clergy and nobility of Seville were connected with the Indies trade "despite the prevailing Castilian ideas that trade and nobility were incompatible."[78] The power of gold prevailed and by the early seventeenth century, Cervantes remarked upon the new attitude in his gloss of a medieval adage:

We have here in Spain a proverb which to my mind is a very true one, as indeed they all are, being wise maxims drawn from long experience. This one runs, "The Church, the sea, or the Royal Household," which in plainer language is equivalent to saying, "He who would make the most of himself and become a rich man, let him become a churchman, *or go to sea and be a merchant*, or enter the service of kings in their palaces."[79]

New World society in this period, like Spanish society of the Old World, was marked by paradox and contrast. Generally speaking, Spaniards in the overseas dominions aspired to nobility, believed in pride of birth, class, and caste distinctions, and desired a great estate worked by a servile laboring population. However, it is also true that New World hidalgos and caballeros became wholesale and retail merchants and rentiers from an early date. Perhaps the best example of the Spanish conqueror-*encomendero* as an entrepreneur, active in textiles, sugar, cattle raising, mining, agriculture, and real estate, is Fernando Cortés. This transplanted Spaniard of "very ancient, noble, and honorable" lineage did not descend to petty commerce, for he operated through stewards and other intermediaries. His agents, however, appear to have been guilty of collusion in marketing his tributes in textiles in Mexico City. Other first conquerors of New Spain built their houses with shops facing streets, which they rented for profit. As nobles became businessmen and merchants bought *hidalguías* from the Crown, daughters of wealthy commoners married sons of landed aristocrats. One famous example of a celebrated soldier, poet, and caballero belonging to the Military Order of Santiago, who engaged in commerce and lent money at interest, is Alonso de Ercilla y Zúñiga.[80] Another noble soldier-turned-merchant in the Indies is Juan Pérez de Zorita.

Hidalguía and Trade

According to Zorita, he and his younger brother and their families idyllically shared one household until Juan Pérez decided to become a merchant. In fact, it seems that Zorita could forgive his brother's other indiscretions but not his decision to adopt the values of ignoble merchants.

After arriving in Santo Domingo, Juan Pérez, an unemployed warrior without an official post, killed time in the downtown section of the city, becoming acquainted with various merchants and disreputable Spaniards. When one of his servants attacked and slashed the face of a certain Diego González Navarro, Juan Pérez intervened and used threats to induce Navarro not to report the assault to the *alguacil major*, the municipal officer chosen by the audiencia to maintain public order. Francisco Bravo, Zorita's bitter enemy, claimed that when the incident became known to the audiencia, Zorita and Grajeda conventiently ignored this infraction of the peace.

Juan Pérez also had negotiated with the procuress Catalina de Valencia, who had "taken care of him" (*había tenido cuenta con Juan Pérez*) in various unspecified relations. She had been sentenced to wear a cone-shaped cap (*coroza*) as a mark of infamy and was exiled for two years from the island. Because of her relationship with Juan Pérez, however, it appears that the sentence was reduced on appeal to one year's exile and even then was not enforced.[81]

Zorita ignored these incidents of violence and moral laxity so alien to his own rigid ethical norms. He did, however, initiate a *probanza* in 1554 attempting to prove that Juan Pérez had greatly embarrassed him by buying cheap in order to sell dear.[82]

In his report to the Council of the Indies, Zorita stated that in February of 1553 a ship belonging to Don Alvaro Bazán, captain general in the India navigation, entered the port of Santo Domingo. The ship's destination was Vera Cruz in New Spain, but it was so badly damaged that the audiencia allowed the cargo to be sold at public auction by a resident named Melgarejo. Because the merchant Melgarejo and Juan Pérez were friends, they struck an agreement whereby Juan Pérez agreed to take part of the goods for resale in Honduras.

After Melgarejo assured Juan Pérez that the goods might be paid for after they were sold on the mainland, he took "different kinds of cloth, casks of wine, soap, and other things from the auction, part of what Juan Pérez selected being taken by the merchant Melgarejo for his own use." Having shipped the greater part of the cargo to Puerto de Caballos, Juan Pérez was about to embark for Guatemala when Melgarejo went back on his word and demanded immediate payment. Juan Pérez borrowed blacks, wine, and cloth from the merchants Pedro Díaz Vázquez and Esteban Pérez; after selling these "goods" in Santo Domingo, Zorita's brother paid Melgarejo in hard money and slaves, the human chattels being credited to Juan Pérez's account for a lesser sum than he had contracted for with Vázquez and Pérez.

Meanwhile, Zorita, having learned of the business venture,

angrily berated Juan Pérez. Saying that he knew nothing about trade, Zorita initially refused to travel with Juan Pérez to Guatemala where Zorita had been appointed judge in the audiencia. This threat failed to stop Juan Pérez from persisting in his project. After stubbornly rejecting his brother's advice, Juan Pérez continued to quarrel, finally becoming so angry that he left Zorita's house for a place of his own. After Juan Pérez bought a third part of a caravel to transport his merchandise to Honduras, Zorita relented and decided to travel to Guatemala with him. Once on board, however, the brothers again quarreled and refused to speak to each other on the voyage to Puerto de Caballos. At the port, the silence was broken by another heated argument; it ended when Juan Pérez found lodging in other quarters than those occupied by Zorita and his household. From Puerto de Caballos, Juan Pérez left for Golfo Dulce, on the coast of Guatemala; a pack-train service run by Hernando de Ajuria and Hernando de Madrid conveyed his goods from that point to Santiago de Guatemala. There a servant of Pedro Díaz Vázquez named Juanes de Vidoy sold the cloth and other goods in the city's central square, and a division of profits to all parties having an interest in the merchandise was made.

Zorita's professed disapproval of his brother's merchant activities had its origins in the medieval distinction between power, on the one hand, and riches, on the other. According to King Sancho IV of Castile (1284–95), riches not joined to civil power and nobility tended to make a man mean rather than fortunate, "although he recognized that, joined to nobility and power, they were honey poured on pancakes."[83]

Medieval social theory held that an aristocracy of nobles and those holding great ecclesiastical offices should occupy the top rung of the social scale. Social theory corresponded to social reality in the first centuries of the *Reconquista*, for the Castilian-Leonese nobility directing society consisted of an old nobility claiming Visigothic ancestry and a new aristocracy based on service to the king. Members of the new aristocracy occupied high administrative offices and were given vast tracts of land in recompense for service. Still, the number of high public offices was limited and the characteristic quality of the Castilian nobility was its professional dedication to arms and equestrian skills. The exigency of sufficient patrimonial wealth to pay for a knight's equipment explains the crown's assignment of land and other benefactions to these warrior-nobles; possession of real property also determined the essential quality of nobility: the economic freedom to train oneself to be competent as a warrior. Caballeros of the *Reconquista* followed the Cross, believed in the military virtues of courage, loyalty, and honor, plundered the enemy and sought the king's favor, and regarded manual labor and commerce with contempt.[84]

But as the Middle Ages waned, the political and military power of the nobility declined. Warrior-nobles, for example, went to war with a class known as *caballeros villanos* or *caballeros ciudadanos*. This intermediate class between the nobility and those free commoners of the towns called burghers marked a society in transition. Status was still the primary determining factor in how a man lived, but money became increasingly important. In short, status without wealth made for an unhappy and insecure life.[85] Still medieval at heart, the era of the later Middle Ages and the age of the Renaissance nevertheless produced individuals who claimed that wealth by itself was a positive good. In 1475, Sabina de Santángel, the mother of the first Duke of Villahermosa's wife, declared that there were only two types of lineages, those who have and those who have not. In the sixteenth century, Juan Huarte de San Juan placed wealth before birth among the attributes of an honorable man and stated that men were basically the product of their works. By the end of Philip II's reign, Mateo Alemán's *Guzmán de Alfarache* expressed the contrast between the ideal and the real: "Tell me, what gives honor to some and takes it away from others? Wealth or its absence."[86]

Formally, at least, Zorita adhered to the traditional Spanish attitude that nobility and commerce or manual labor were incompatible. Work on the land, income from rents, or public service did not demean nobility, but the militarist and aristocratic ideals of the age still relegated trade, usury, and labor "to a dishonourable position, despite the efforts of statesmen and writers to denounce such an attitude as evil."[87] Juan Pérez, in contrast, was willing to engage in commerce because he had not attained a post and income commensurate with his nobility and previous service to the crown as a warrior. Zorita's brother, in effect, had adopted the "modern" bourgeois attitude that wealth, regardless of how acquired, was honorable.

Zorita's opinion concerning nobility and small-scale commerce did not, however, make him scornful of merchants. Although he professed to disapprove of his brother's commercial activity, it appears that he was on friendly terms with several merchants; he dined frequently with his friend and creditor Martín García, was the guest of another when he arrived in Española, and was indebted to several others. Zorita also undoubtedly tolerated his brother's offenses. There is abundant evidence, however, that he was a judge of great integrity who administered justice "with all the probity and rectitude of which he was capable."[88]

Maintaining Public Order in Española

An important duty of the royal judges was the maintenance of public order. One of Zorita's many duties was to help maintain the peace in Santo Domingo by patrolling the city at night. He quickly became such a terror to rowdies, boozers, and ne'er-do-wells that these turbulent wrongdoers made a point of remaining safely indoors when Zorita made his nocturnal rounds.

Sailors in port, transient soldiers bound for Peru or Mexico, chronic tavern brawlers, and some criminal elements created many problems, but the most notorious wrongdoers in Española were various members of the secular clergy holding benefices in the cathedral chapter. The worst of these offenders was prebendary Juan de Medrano, an arrogant bully and the acknowledged leader of the delinquent clerics. He caused a great deal of trouble in Española. Before assuming charge of the other clerics' allowances in the cathedral chapter as *racionero*, Medrano had been a parish priest in Santiago de los Caballeros and Concepción de la Vega. He had been dismissed from both churches because of his terrible language and scandalous behavior. In Santiago, Medrano offended his parishioners by openly attempting to seduce many women; the town's citizens ordered him to leave when he set fire to a married woman's cottage in a fit of jealousy.

At the time of Zorita's arrival in Santo Domingo, Medrano's mistress was Juana de Alegría; she had recently been exiled for two years from Santo Domingo and the area surrounding the city for a distance of five leagues for the practice of witchcraft. The thirty-five-year-old cleric had taken this New World Circe from her husband, the *bachiller* Tinoco, who departed the city in shame after being dishonored by his wife. Though Juana had not yet completed her period of exile in January, 1549, Medrano kept his pregnant concubine in his house and beat her in moments of anger.

After Medrano's neighbors reported that the cleric had whipped Juana so severely that her screams alarmed them, Zorita sent Constable Casaverde and the collector of evidence (*receptor*) Diego de Herrera to search Medrano's house. Meanwhile, the prebendary, informed of Zorita's investigation, immediately moved Juana to his hacienda in the country. When Casaverde and Herrera arrived at Medrano's house, they learned that Juana had already left Santo Domingo. Consequently Zorita's attempt to arrest Medrano for moral turpitude and housing a person banished from Santo Domingo by the audiencia failed.

In addition to being a great fornicator and woman chaser, Medrano was a very acquisitive type. Medrano, an exporter of cattle hides from his hacienda and sugar from a mill he and other clerics owned, once told Captain Alonso de Peña, the treasurer of the exchequer, that he had accumulated over 70,000 pesos during the twelve years he had been in Española, despite his large gambling losses during these years.[89] Medrano also sold wine in Española and his cronies, Canons Tarifeñe and Monsalve, had become wealthy as merchants and vendors of eggs, soap, and figs to the public. Clerical greed found perfect expression in a remark of Monsalve's. While dressing for divine service on a Holy Thursday, he told other clerics of the cathedral chapter that money had divine attributes; he added that he would willingly suffer 200 lashes for 200 pesos.[90]

The lewd and lawless behavior of Medrano and other clerics of the cathedral chapter made for much public scandal and gossip; it is confirmed by several witnesses, including chronicler and fortress commander Gonzalo Fernández de Oviedo. Medrano, Archdean Antonio de Salinas, and Canons Monsalve and Roca, as well as other clerics, had lived in concubinage with single and married women. They had fathered children by these women and made over property to their offspring. Oviedo declared that the clerics had many weaknesses but their licentiousness was such that it "could not be described in many pages." He then singled out Medrano as the most immoral of the clerics. "Of him there is so much to say that Your Highness, if he knew this, would be amazed! A special report containing charges against him was sent to Spain by Licentiate Zorita, but he was never punished, nor is it believed that it has been seen, because certainly he would have been deported from here had the matter been looked into."[91]

Oviedo's observation that Zorita had made an investigation of Medrano's many crimes referred to an inquiry by the audiencia into the conduct of the cathedral chapter in 1549. Zorita began the *información* after Medrano disrupted a Sunday morning pro-

cession returning to the cathedral from the church of Santa Bár-
bola on January 20. When Doctor Díez Montaño, the dean of the
chapter, saw that the customary route by way of Pedro Ortiz
street was muddy, he told the sacristan leading the cavalcade to
return to the cathedral by the same street the column had used on
departing. Medrano countermanded the order and began a violent
argument with the dean. Only Zorita's timely appearance saved
Díez Montaño from being assaulted. When Zorita ordered Medrano to return to his position in the column, the prebendary
refused and was joined in his verbal attack on the dean by his
crony, Canon Pedro Díaz de Fuenmayor. Fuenmayor grabbed
the dean's surplice and threatened to tear all the dean's hair from
his head. When the dean demanded that the canon unhand him,
Fuenmayor "told the dean to kiss his ass!"[92] Zorita again ordered
Medrano and Fuenmayor to return to their places in the column;
when they refused he commanded *Provisor* Antonio de Mendoza,
the ecclesiastical judge, to remove them from the procession.
Mendoza, a frail elderly man of little spirit whose salary was
dependent upon Medrano's good will, begged Medrano and
Fuenmayor to leave, but they remained in the column until the
procession arrived back at the cathedral.

   After the procession dispersed and its members left for their
homes, Zorita summoned Mendoza to appear before an assembly
of the city's magistrates and principal citizens. Mendoza was
accused and found guilty of neglecting his duties as ecclesiastical
judge and attempting to cover up what had taken place between
the dean and his unruly clerics. The *alcaldes* then ordered Mendoza to place Medrano and Fuenmayor in the ecclesiastical jail while
Zorita and the other royal judges completed an investigation of
the cathedral chapter.

   The audiencia's judicial inquiry and other related material confirmed Oviedo's statement that a significant number of the cathedral chapter's clerics were idle, violent, acquisitive, immoral individuals who refused to obey Dean Díez Montaño, considered by
the judges to be a good theologian, an excellent preacher, and an
upright man, but totally incapable of controlling the delinquent
priests dominated by Juan de Medrano.

   As Oviedo was aware, the worst of the clerics was their leader.
Medrano refused to remove his dagger when celebrating mass; he
had also quarreled with and threatened to kill many principal
citizens and priests in Santo Domingo. The prebendary's dress by
night included a coat of mail and helmet, a broadsword, and the

dagger he was prone to use on the slightest provocation. Two of his many assaults will serve to illustrate the temper of this thuggish priest. Quarreling with Gonzalo Fernández de Oviedo, Medrano struck the seventy-one-year-old chronicler of the Indies, threatened to kill him, and had his servants remove the coat of arms sculptured over Oviedo's tomb in the cathedral.[93] In another quarrel with Fray Gerónimo de Toledo, a Mercedarian friar, Medrano told his servant Benito Carrasco to stab the priest. Carrasco attacked the helpless friar, severely damaged Toledo's upper jawbone and two teeth, and cut the priest's face so badly that thirty-five stitches were required to close the wound.

Zorita's *información* of 1549 appears to have been completely ignored by the Council of the Indies. Other judicial inquiries followed, but Medrano and the clerics he led continued to defy the dean, who we are told was so vexed by their evil ways that he died of grief and rage. Influence in high places contributed to the immunity these malefactors enjoyed. Medrano had the protection of Rodrigo de Bastidas, the bishop of San Juan, whose estate he administered, while Canon Díaz de Fuenmayor was a relative of Archbishop Alonso de Fuenmayor; thus they had never been arrested and tried for their many crimes. In fact, prior to Zorita's judicial investigation, ecclesiastical judge Mendoza had either ignored all charges against the prebendary and his followers, or Medrano and his band had threatened in their persons any witnesses to their crimes. Intimidated by the threat of physical violence or worse, these citizens refused to testify against the delinquent clerics.[94]

The corruption, worldliness, moral disorder, and general defiance of the laws in Española by the secular clergy is perhaps attributable to the fact that "the moral worth of the clergy is always proportional to the moral worth of the people in whose midst it lives."[95] However, the situation may not have been much better in Spain. In the late fifteenth century, the Spanish clergy in general was wealthy, ignorant, and immoral. Many of the high clergy "had worldly tastes and passions," and some were better warriors than priests. Although Isabella reformed the regular clergy and improved the manners of the secular clergy, anticlericalism "was very much alive at the opening of the sixteenth century" and proverbs still reflected the evil reputation of clerics. Moreover, priests were frequently found among the condemned in the autos-da-fé of the period.[96]

Although it is impossible to compare the spiritual worth of the

secular clergy of Spanish America with the secular clergy of
Spain, given the fact that men of learning and high character and
idle and corrupt priests were found in both groups, Juan López
de Velasco believed that New World Spaniards in general were
less restrained by conventions of morality. This he attributed to
the fact that Spanish emigrants represented less than a full cross
section of the Iberian population in the first half of the sixteenth
century. The first cosmographer and chronicler of the Indies
noted that Spaniards who emigrated to America were as a rule
greedy, turbulent individuals who wished to enrich themselves
quickly and move on. Heedless and petulant, New World Spaniards spent their time seeking offices and *encomiendas*. Their
Creole descendants were usually bigger than their parents, and
the violence of their spirits matched the size of their bodies.
López de Velasco could not altogether explain the change in
Spanish character, but reported that men's conduct had degener-
ated. A tendency to defame one's neighbors and engage in turbulent behavior characterized the more aggressive men of the
Indies.[97]

Public disorder in Española and the inability of the royal
judges to bring to justice some of the more unsavory characters
belonging to or related to the elite is also explained by the fact
that from an early date the legal staff employed by the audiencia
and the *oidores* frequently were either incompetent or dishonest,
or both. Magistrates often quarreled with each other, and not a
few judges were immoral, completely at home in a materialistic
and violent milieu. An excellent example of a man suffering from
these afflictions in a society undergoing social and economic
transformation is Don Alonso de Fuenmayor.

Appointed president of the audiencia in 1532 and archbishop of
Santo Domingo in 1547, Fuenmayor was an incompetent judge,
governor, and captain-general, and a licentious cleric. Until he
was suspended from office on January 2, 1544, by Alonso de
Cerrato, President Fuenmayor had constantly quarreled with *oidores* Juan de Vadillo and Iñigo López de Cervantes de Loaisa.
Passion and prejudice aroused by the conflict motivated decisions
in lawsuits. Refusing to recognize Fuenmayor's authority, the
judges tried cases in their homes rather than in court and addressed Fuenmayor as *tú*, a term used only in talking to small
children, animals, intimate friends, or near relations. Fuenmayor
became so incensed by the judges' insults that on one occasion he
ordered his servants to kill Vadillo after quarreling with the latter

about a case before the audiencia. The order was not carried out, but Vadillo was arrested, imprisoned, and placed in the stocks without cause.[98]

Other charges confirmed by the Royal Council of the Indies give evidence of Fuenmayor's greed and immorality. After being bribed by Juan de Medrano, Fuenmayor favored the prebendary in several lawsuits. He also accepted 600 *marcos de plata* from Don Francisco Pizarro. Diego de Fuenmayor, the president's brother sent by the audiencia with a commission as captain of Spanish arquebusiers to aid the Pizarros in their battle with Diego de Almagro's men of Chile, had delivered this inducement upon returning from Peru. Circumstantial evidence indicates that the Pizarros bribed Fuenmayor to allow the passage of men and arms to Peru; after suspending Fuenmayor and assuming the presidency of the audiencia, Alonso de Cerrato reported to the crown that following the Pizarros' revolt more than 3,000 men had passed to Peru, and a ship carrying coats of mail and breastplates for the rebels had been detained in the port of Santo Domingo.[99] Another charge found Fuenmayor guilty of concubinage; he had kept a Spanish woman named Doña Inés de Zúñiga as a "dueña" and a mestiza surnamed Alvarado in his house and had fornicated with both women. In addition, Fuenmayor had ruled unjustly in lawsuits Doña Inés had before the audiencia; e.g., in one case she was absolved of paying 500 *pesos de oro* she legally owed a creditor. During the time that Fuenmayor was president, the audiencia also allowed free Indians in Venezuela to be enslaved and brought to Santo Domingo for sale to plantation owners, permitted debasement of the coinage minted in Española, and let various public officials hold more than one office—the most flagrant example being Diego Caballero de la Rosa, secretary and recorder (*registrador*) of the audiencia and councilman in the cabildo.[100]

The departure of Fuenmayor and Juan de Vadillo for Spain to plead their suspensions was quickly followed by the death of Judge Iñigo de Guevara. Licentiate Cervantes remained in Española but was relieved of judicial duties; in 1548 he was ordered to hand over the salary he had been paid from January 2, 1544, until April 27, 1548, within four months, to the person who had replaced him as judge.[101] Fuenmayor's successor was Alonso de Cerrato, said by Oviedo to be a native of the village of Mengabril in the province of Medellín.[102] Cerrato and Judge Alonso de Grajeda arrived in Santo Domingo on January 1, 1544. The new president of the audiencia was empowered to hold the judicial inquiry of Fuenmayor and his subordinates, reform the audiencia, and audit the accounts of the treasury officials.[103] Cerrato and Grajeda were aided in their duties by Francisco Bravo, the secretary of the *residencia* held by Cerrato, who was given the post of court reporter (*relator*).[104]

Cerrato, an honest, intractable man of great ability, proved to be a reforming judge and able governor. But his arrogant, austere manner and extreme rudeness when provoked offended many citizens.[105] When Cerrato appointed Bartolomé de Monesterio, his son-in-law, treasurer of the exchequer, angry plantation owners became his principal detractors. Cerrato had determined that the *sisa* and *avería* taxes were insufficient to pay the costs of the war against the Negro rebels endangering the island's sugar economy; he accordingly authorized Monesterio to levy a tax on all citizens who owned haciendas based on the value of their property.[106]

Disgruntled *hacendados* and *vecinos* who resented Cerrato's impartial enforcement of the laws exerted pressure on the cabildo to send representatives to Spain to petition for Cerrato's removal. One of the municipal council's *procuradores* appointed for this mission was Gonzalo Fernández de Oviedo, a bitter enemy of the reforming judge. A feud began when Cerrato found Oviedo, the garrison commander of Santo Domingo's fortress, guilty of misusing the 90,000 *maravedís* granted annually by the Crown for the expense of seven soldiers and a gunner. Oviedo failed to hire sufficient troops and never held a review of the soldiers on the day they were paid as was required by law.[107] Because Cerrato found Oviedo guilty of malfeasance, the chronicler of the Indies initially confirmed in his *Historia general* the low opinion of Cerrato held by many citizens of Santo Domingo.[108]

Following Cerrato's departure for the Audiencia of Guatemala, Oviedo, now a permanent alderman in the cabildo, lamented the "total ruin" of the city under the unofficial rule of Diego Caballero de la Rosa and wrote the crown that the only remedy for the reform of Española was to recall Cerrato as president. In 1554, Oviedo recalled that when he had gone to Spain in 1546 with Captain Alonso de Peña to complain of Cerrato's government, he had been deceived about the character and motives of Diego Caballero (the audiencia secretary), Alvaro Caballero (auditor of the exchequer), and other public officials, and for this reason had participated in the plan to have Cerrato removed from office. As soon as Cerrato left Santo Domingo to take possession of the Audiencia of Guatemala, the government had been corrupted by the Caballeros; this cunning, hypocritical, and deceitful family, allied and related to Marshall Diego Caballero of Seville, had become the virtual owner of the island.[109] Oviedo claimed that because of their common interests Diego Caballero and other citizens were one and the same person, undoubtedly hinting that the *conversos* led by the Caballeros aided each other for their mutual benefit. The Caballeros of Seville and the Caballeros of Española all had common interests; they resembled Lope de Conchillos at court and Miguel de Pasamonte in the Indies.[110] Oviedo concluded his lament with the words: "God in his mercy defend your king and thee, Santo Domingo. The only thing that I have gained from all this is that all the *regidores* are angry with me because I do not agree with them, and will not conceal the many and diverse larcenies perpetrated by Francisco de Ávila, Diego Caballero, Peña, and Alvaro Caballero, so that Your Highness can see in what condition justice exists here."[111]

Oviedo's contention that justice was not administered impartially after Cerrato left for Guatemala on April 20, 1548, was confirmed by Alonso Maldonado's judicial inquiry of the judges. Alonso de Grajeda, provisional president until the arrival of Maldonado in 1552, was a greedy and dishonest judge favored by the Columbus family and hated by the *converso* oligarchy. He was unable to work with his fellow judges and especially hated Licentiate Hurtado de Mendoza. The Council of the Indies found him gravely guilty (*culpa grave*) of personally insulting Zorita and Hurtado de Mendoza and spreading evil rumors about them by words and letters because they would not agree with him in various judicial cases.[112] Grajeda also became a bitter enemy of Alonso Maldonado when the latter charged him with many offenses in the *residencia*. President Maldonado concluded that Grajeda's chief defect was his inability to judge cases objectively; he recommended that Grajeda be transferred to another audiencia.[113]

Grajeda's frequent quarrels with his fellow judges began when Licentiate Juan Hurtado de Salcedo y Mendoza arrived in Santo Domingo in 1549. Because Hurtado and Zorita were natives of Córdoba and old friends, Zorita was drawn into the incessant disputes between the two judges and sided with Hurtado. Francisco Díaz de Pernia, one of Grajeda's partisans, even claimed that after a heated argument, Hurtado and Zorita had armed themselves and threatened to kill Grajeda. Díaz also alleged that citizens of Santo Domingo had been drawn into the conflict;

choosing sides, they had divided into factions and created such an uproar that it appeared a pitched battle was about to take place in the city's streets. Fearing the destruction of the city, Archbishop Alonso de Fuenmayor and the bishop of San Juan, Don Rodrigo de Bastidas, intervened and managed to end the disturbance. Aware that Díaz had written to the crown about the matter, the Cabildo of Santo Domingo refuted the allegation, pointing out that Díaz was a man of evil character who had killed his son-in-law in Santo Domingo. Councilmen Juan Caballero de Bazán, Admiral Luis Columbus, Diego de Iliesca, Diego Caballero, Luis de Santa Clara, Juan de Junco, and Gonzalo Fernández de Oviedo unanimously agreed in their letter to the king that Díaz had blown the differences between the judges out of proportion. Because they praised the conduct of Zorita and Hurtado and made no mention of Grajeda, the inference is obvious that the latter was to blame for any quarrels between the judges.[114]

The best example of the division between the royal judges is the criminal investigation of Francisco Bravo, the court reporter accused by Zorita and Hurtado of murdering his wife Catalina Tinoco. On June 24, 1549, Zorita and Hurtado in the company of audiencia notary Nicolás López inspected Catalina Tinoco's corpse. Her throat and windpipe had been severed by repeated slashes of a dagger, and she had been stabbed twice in the left breast. Zorita and Hurtado accused her husband Bravo of the murder when they were told by the female slaves of the household that he had fled the city with all his money and jewels after killing his wife for having a love affair with a citizen of Santo Domingo named Lázaro López de Salazar. Bravo remained absent from the city for two months; he then returned secretly to Santo Domingo and consulted privately with his friend Grajeda before presenting an accusation to the court charging López de Salazar with the killing.

Francisco Bravo's case was delayed for three years, and his guilt or innocence was still undetermined when Maldonado took the judges' *residencia* in 1553. Maldonado found all the judges guilty of obstructing justice in their handling of the case. Zorita and Hurtado, on the one hand, had not investigated Francisco Bravo's accusation that López de Salazar had murdered his wife and had refused to withdraw from the case after Bravo objected to them as hostile judges.[115] Grajeda, on the other hand, had continued to gather evidence against López de Salazar after he was accused of prejudice by Pedro Rodríguez, López's friend.

The Council of the Indies also found Grajeda and Zorita guilty of compelling the lawyer Juan Rodríguez to become prosecuting attorney against Bravo after Rodríguez conferred with the accused and agreed to defend him in the trial.[116]

Although the judges of Santo Domingo had many personal differences and allowed those differences to influence their treatment of friends and enemies, they united in defense of the island against foreigners. The first foreign intruder to threaten Española was an English vessel that entered the port of Santo Domingo in 1527. In the 1530s French corsairs sacked several coastal towns. When French corsairs attacked and captured Chagres on the Isthmus of Panama, La Yaguana (Port-au-Prince), and nine ships of the fleet bearing Peruvian treasure to Spain in 1537, Santo Domingo's citizens and public officials fearfully awaited an attack. Although the truce of Nice in 1538 ended French attacks in American waters for a short period, the West Indian colonists were aware that chronic warfare between Spain and her Protestant rivals would continue and they sought to protect territory and trade more effectively "beyond the line."[117] The idea of "no peace beyond the line" arose when France, rationalizing her attacks on Spain's New World possessions, established the principle that warfare in American waters was permissible even though peace prevailed in Europe.

French and English pirates continued to challenge Spain in the Indies in the next decade. In July, 1540, a ship that had left Azua loaded with 6,000 *arrobas* of sugar, 2,000 cattle hides, *cañafístulas*, and other fruit and merchandise was captured by a heavily armed English ship of 400 tons. When the loaded pirate ship's bilge began to fill with water, the captain and his crew abandoned the vessel at Cape Tiburón. After setting the Spanish prisoners free on the coast, the corsairs left in the direction of England in the captured Spanish *nao*.[118]

On April 24, 1545, the Audiencia of Santo Domingo wrote the crown that several ships of France had committed depredations in the West Indies the year before; the French corsairs had then left for Honduras where the tender attending the squadron had been captured with twenty-two Frenchmen; another French ship that had taken on too much water had gone to the port of Matanzas in Cuba, been repaired, and then left and captured a *nao* coming from New Spain. To defend Santo Domingo, the audiencia was supervising work on the bastion ordered by the crown to be built below Santo Domingo's fortress. Located on the river's edge at the port's entrance, the bastion, to be completed within four months, would be reinforced by positioning the heavy artillery the city possessed on the bulwark. The judges also reported that work continued on the wall that would eventually surround the city; work had begun six months before and the part of the enclosure that had been completed appeared to be very strong.[119]

In June, 1548, the crown wrote the audiencia that French corsairs had left for the West Indies. After receiving this dispatch in late September, Judges Grajeda and Zorita visited Santo Domingo's fortress and inspected the artillery and powder, as well as other arms and munitions. The people of the city were alerted to prepare arms and horses for the town's defense; immediately thereafter messengers were sent to the ports of the island to inform the people there to prepare for combat. The judges ordered citizens to wage an offensive against pirates attempting to enter any port town and to have no business dealings with them. They must not be allowed to take on water, wood, and provisions as in the past.[120]

With the aim of enforcing Spain's restricted commerce with the Indies, and to give protection from corsairs to merchant ships, the Casa de Contratación (House of Trade) finally perfected a fleet system supplemented by coast guard ships for policework. The various modifications between 1543 and 1564 affected Española's defense efforts and occupied much of the judges' time while Zorita was on the island.

An audiencia report to the crown dated January 23, 1549, illustrates the danger from foreign raiders and the judges' concern for the protection of trade. The high court reported that five ships had recently left Santo Domingo's port and sailed into a fierce tempest. Four of the vessels had managed to return to the harbor, but one badly damaged ship with a cargo of hides, sugar, gold, and other goods worth 20,000 ducats had been captured by French corsairs off Mona island. The pirates had also captured another Spanish ship that had left Santo Domingo for Puerto de la Plata, while two French sails had been seen off Cabo de la Vela and two others had been reported to be near Jamaica. The three French ships sighted in December at the mouth of the Ozama River had recently entered the port of La Yaguana where they had taken several prizes and sought to trade French wines and linens for meat and water. When the town's *vecinos* refused to agree to the exchange, the corsairs had landed and forced the colonists to trade with them. The report concluded that future attacks by the pirates were imminent; to meet this threat the officials of the Casa de Contratación should dispatch two armed *zabras* to the island with munitions, especially powder, for the arming of ships moored in Santo Domingo's port.[121]

On May 13, 1549, the audiencia once again mentioned the French privateering offensive. The judges now asked the crown to provide a squadron of four vessels for the defense of the island and surrounding waters. After being armed, the four might be joined by other large ships in Española's ports to pursue and destroy the corsairs.[122]

Adverse political and economic conditions seem to have caused a delay in meeting the French challenge in the Caribbean. In any case, the audiencia's request for help against French adventurers was delayed for almost three years. On April 11, 1552, the judges wrote the Crown that they had received a royal decree authorizing the formation of an armada for the defense of the island in the renewal of the war with France. The squadron would number four vessels, two *naos* and two caravels, manned by 300 persons. The Casa de Contratación should send necessary munitions for the arming of the fleet, as well as fifty sailors and ships' boys and an equal number of arquebusiers to complete the armada's force. The judges also noted that they had reviewed decrees ordering the construction of fortresses received ten years before by the audiencia; because these orders had been ignored by former members of the court, the judges now requested confimation so that construction of fortifications at Puerto de la Plata and La Yaguana might proceed. A fort at La Yaguana was urgently needed because French pirates were attracted to that settlement by the many ships from Nombre de Dios and Mexico that deposited gold and silver at its port.[123]

Late July of 1552 saw the armada patrolling the sea passages off San Germán, Mona, Cabo del Engaño, and Saona, where pirates had attacked merchant vessels in the past. The fleet was provisioned with artillery, arms, and powder and consisted of a large *nao* of 360 tons, a caravel of 206 tons, a smaller caravel, and a *patache*.[124] The armada's captain-general was Don Cristóbal Colón, granted a salary of six ducats daily by the audiencia. Captains like Luis de Bazán, the twenty-year-old son of Diego Caballero, received two ducats daily; approximately three hundred soldiers, sailors, and gunners were paid monthly wages of four, five, and eight pesos, respectively.[125]

The proud armada met with disaster when it ran into a hurri-

cane on August 29, 1552. The small caravel commanded by Captain Juan de Zárate was almost destroyed in the giant swells
before it was beached on the sands of the island of Saona; its men
and artillery were saved, but the ship commanded by Luis de
Bazán was engulfed by great waves, and 130 men were drowned.
The flagship carrying Don Cristóbal and the large caravel commanded by Juan de Berrio ran aground on Española's coast, but
were "so broken up and ruined that they were left without masts,
sails, and rudders." The hurricane destroyed other ships in Santo
Domingo's harbor, including a caravel that Zorita had freighted
with goods in Puerto Rico. Not a tree was left standing on the
island, and damage to the stock farms and plantations was estimated at 400,000 *pesos de oro*.[126]

Following the loss of the armada, Captain Alonso de Peña
alarmed the town's citizens by proclaiming that Santo Domingo
was defenseless against an attack by the enemy. Terror increased
when French corsairs arrived off the port. Fearing that the pirates
might land and attempt to capture the city, the audiencia
appointed Judge Zorita captain of the cavalry. After changing his
somber robe for the warrior's sword and armor, Captain Zorita
readied all of the citizens of Santo Domingo and the surrounding
area for battle. He then

divided the men into patrols to guard the city and looked to its defense
with the horsemen, riding along the coast vigilantly by day and night
because there were many places close to the city where the corsairs
could easily debark. He had the artillery cleaned and the gunpowder
purified, and when the corsairs were sighted off the harbor he ordered
many shots fired. As was learned later from several Spaniards the pirates
had on board their ships, the corsairs lost their courage once they heard
the shots and did not return to the port.[127]

On December 6, 1552, the colony's treasury officials wrote the
crown that eight months had passed since ships from Spain had
brought commodities. This delay and the damage caused by the
recent hurricane made for a great scarcity of necessities.[128] The
tempest had only made more acute the chronic shortage of goods
like wine, bread, and flour, for the wealthy merchants of Seville
and Cádiz, enjoying a monopoly of trade with Spain's New
World possessions, kept the American colonies chronically
understocked, charging exorbitant prices for those goods that
passed to the Indies.[129]

The audiencia repeatedly mentioned the excessive cost of goods in Española. Even prior to Zorita's arrival the high court had asked the crown either to raise the judges' salaries or order that they be paid in good currency. Bad coinage (*vellón*) accounted for half of the magistrates' salaries, and it was impossible to live on a salary of 300,000 *maravedís* (800 ducats), given the style of life the *oidores'* position demanded.[130] Conditions failed to improve; in another letter Zorita and his fellow judges wrote that the crown had raised the judges' annual salaries to 1,000 ducats at the same time that another decree cut annual salaries to 900 ducats and ordered them to make a yearly inspection of the towns, sugar mills, and stock farms of the island. The judges were to alternate tours of inspection, and the *oidor* making the *visitación* was to receive 300 ducats more than his reduced salary of 900 ducats. The judges pointed out that what appeared to benefit the inspecting judge actually deprived all of the *oidores* of part of their salaries, for the extra 300 ducats to be paid the judge making the inquiry were to be taken from the stipend of each *oidor's* previous salary of 1,000 ducats, thus giving the judge conducting the tour of inspection 1,200 ducats yearly while the other two judges occupied with audiencia matters in Santo Domingo only received 900 ducats. The judges correctly observed that this decree added to their economic plight in a colony where prices were 500 percent higher than those in Spain.[131]

President Alonso Maldonado's arrival on February 1, 1555, was followed shortly by the judicial review of the island's royal officials. As judge of residence, Maldonado recognized Zorita's honest performance of his duties. None of the specific charges against Zorita were serious enough to warrant suspension from office during the period of the *residencia*. After Maldonado completed his review of Zorita's conduct on May 20, he fined Zorita ten pesos for granting licenses to individuals going to New Spain without consulting with the other *oidores*. All other charges reviewed by the Council of the Indies have the words *remitele* or *remitido* (pardoned) added to them.[132]

As a judge in Española, Zorita cracked down on lawbreakers and denounced the vices of various officials and priests. However, most citizens of Santo Domingo seem to have appreciated his efforts to help create the ideal Christian Commonwealth where justice was accessible to all. A letter written by the Cabildo of Santo Domingo when it learned in early 1553 that Zorita had been appointed *oidor* in the Audiencia of Guatemala suggests the confidence he enjoyed:

Sacred, Caesarian, Catholic, Royal Majesties—the city, magistracy and government of Santo Domingo of the island of Española kiss the royal feet and hands of Your Caesarian and Catholic Majesties for the care and regard you have always had in granting favors to this republic in all that affects its sustenance and growth. And because past favors have led us to believe we shall always receive such from the royal hand, we request that Your Majesty order Licentiate Alonso de Zorita to reside and stay in this your royal Audiencia where he is presently one of the judges, for in truth he is a person of good conscience and letters and has always seen to the royal service with that zeal and rectitude which all judges must have in the administration of justice. By reason of these qualities, all those of this city who live justly and love the truth admire him, and because we have learned that Your Majesty is not informed of the need here for his person and has ordered him to serve in another province of the mainland this city and the government in its name humbly requests that Licentiate Zorita remain here and not move from the royal Audiencia. In this way the good government and service of Your Majesty and the good of this republic will be served, which is the principal cause that moves us in this petition; and in the same manner God Our Lord will be served, who may always prosper the Caesarian and Catholic Majesties of Your Royal Persons with the growth of more kingdoms and dominions as Your Majesty desires. From this city of Santo Domingo of the island of Española, February 17, 1553.

The humble servants and vassals of Your Sacred, Caesarian, Majesties who kiss their royal feet and hands.

Licentiate Carmona. Cristóbal de Tapia. Francisco Dávila. Diego Caballero. Alonso Caballero. Alonso de la Peña. Juan de Junco.

By order of the said *señores*, magistracy and government.

> Francisco de Pineda,
> Notary of His Majesty and of
> the Municipal Council
> (signatures and rubrics)[133]

CHAPTER 3

Enforcing the New Laws in New Granada, 1550–1552

ZORITA was still practicing before the Audiencia of Granada when another graduate of Salamanca, Miguel Díez de Armendáriz, was commissioned to enforce the New Laws of 1542–1543 in Tierra Firme. This body of legislation contained fifty-four articles, twenty-three of which were concerned with good treatment and preservation of the Indians. The New Laws declared that the Indians were free persons and decreed fundamental reforms in the regulation of Indian labor, tribute, and the *encomienda* system. Enslavement of Indians was forbidden, and Indian slaves held without legitimate title were to be freed. Compulsory personal services were ended, and tribute and services were to be fairly assessed and regulated by the audiencias. *Encomiendas* were to be of moderate size, new grants of *encomiendas* were prohibited, existing ones were to be vested in the crown upon the death of the holders, and all those held by public officials and ecclesiastics were to be transferred to the crown.

As is evident, the New Laws were a direct attack upon the system of *encomienda* and hence bitterly opposed by those colonists who benefited from the labor and tribute of the Indians. The crown, as Lesley Byrd Simpson notes, "did not entrust the execution of these unpopular laws to the existing authorities" in America.[1] Four new officials were commissioned to begin, in the New World, the work of vesting Indian vassals in the royal crown; of the four, only Alonso López de Cerrato proved to be a reforming judge. Francisco Tello de Sandoval allowed a temporary suspension of the New Laws in Mexico. Blasco Núñez Vela, an overbearing and tactless man, lost his life at the hands of rebellious Peruvian colonists. The selection of Miguel Díez de Armendáriz proved to be an unmitigated disaster for the Indians of New Granada.

On March 22, 1543, Licentiate Miguel Díez was given various *cédulas* and letters in Valladolid. Named governor of Santa Marta, the New Kingdom of Granada, Cartagena, Popayán, and Río de San Juan,[2] he was instructed to take the *residencias* of previous governors and their lieutenants in these provinces. In addition to taking the judicial inquiries of Alonso Luis de Lugo, Pedro de Heredia, Sebastián Benalcázar, Pascual de Andagoya, and their subordinates, he was to proclaim the New Laws,[3] inspect the settlements in the provinces, and decree "whatever laws agreed with the service of God and His Majesty." Armed with ample powers, he was ordered to punish those individuals who had "killed, maimed, tortured, and robbed the Indians since the discovery and conquest of the region."[4]

Accompanied by his first cousin Pedro de Ursúa, Miguel Díez departed from Spain for New Granada on July 10, 1544. Both men belonged to important Navarrese families and thus were not representative of Spanish emigrants to the Indies in the sixteenth century, since few overseas migrants came from Navarre. They were typically Spanish, however, in their primary loyalty to family and region, and an account of their backgrounds may help to explain the character of their rule in New Granada.

A native of Valtierra in the Kingdom of Navarre, Miguel Díez de Aux de Armendáriz was the illegitimate son of Martín Díez and María de Abenza. Nothing is known about the mother's ancestry, but his father's lineage is said to have its origin in the French city of Auch, near the Spanish border. Miguel Díez's ancestors can be traced back to a Juan Díez de Aux; in about 1250 this French caballero was in the service of the king of Aragon and was given the lordship of the villa of Bielsa in the province of Huesca. In the last decades of the fourteenth century, another ancestor, Martín Díez de Aux, had been the *justicia* of Aragon. He was a most important figure, for his primary duty as *justicia* was to defend the ancient privileges of the kingdom against any infringement by officials of the king or the nobility. During the time he served as interpreter of Aragon's traditional laws for the protection of all classes, the venal Martín Díez sided with the aristocracy in their oppression of the Aragonese peasantry.[5]

Although Miguel Díez's mother later married an individual named Pedro de Garmendi, her son identified with his father's family and was acknowledged by these relatives. In 1547 he wrote the king: "One of my uncles, Luis Díez Armendáriz, lord of Cadereyta in the kingdom of Navarre, has been more than a father to me for 28 years." Yet Miguel Díez's letters convey a sense of insecurity and ambivalence masked by an exaggerated arrogance, perhaps due to the circumstances of his birth and childhood. As is evident from a letter he wrote to Sebastián

Benalcázar, also in 1547, he believed in the concept of purity of blood (*limpieza de sangre*) and in statutes that excluded descendants of Jews and Moors from higher education, public office, and positions in the Church. After exalting his own education and worth by a scornful reference to the racial dichotomy between Old and New Christians, Miguel Díez mentioned that twenty-seven of his forty years had been spent outside his native land. He had pursued letters for ten years at Salamanca, and for another four years he had lived in France near Navarre. Although he wrote that the best years of his life had been spent in France, he qualified this remark by stating categorically: "I am not French, I am a Beaumont."[6]

In claiming Beaumont status, Miguel Díez reminded himself and Benalcázar that early in the sixteenth century the Navarrese had been divided into a French party led by the Agramonts and by a Spanish party headed by the Beaumonts, counts of Lerín. Miguel Díez thus claimed to be a loyal subject of the Spanish monarch despite having lived in France and being aware that French people and French ways were important elements in Navarre.

Miguel Díez's claim of allegiance to the Spanish party of the Beaumonts, loyal to Ferdinand the Catholic and his successor, may be questioned for several reasons. First, various of his relatives had been loyal vassals of the Prince of Viana, Ferdinand's halfbrother. Second, Miguel Díez's grandmother was a member of the Agramont family. In about 1504, Jaime Díez de Armendáriz, lord of Cadereyta and captain-general of Don Alonso de Aragón, archbishop of Saragossa and the illegitimate son of Ferdinand the Catholic, married Doña Leonor Veraiz, the daughter of Pedro Veraiz and Doña Isabel de Vergara y Agramont. Pedro Veraiz was the *mayordomo mayor* of Jean d'Albret, king of Navarre (1484–1516) by his marriage with Catherine de Foix. The forces of Jean d'Albret defeated the Beaumont party in 1507.[7] Third, Zorita and other Spaniards took Miguel Díez for a Francophile in New Granada.

Various witnesses in New Granada told Zorita that Miguel Díez had given his lieutenant Jorge Robledo a standard for the expedition to Antioquia and Popayán, which had for its coat of arms fleurs-de-lis on a white field and other escutcheons of France. Nicolás Beltrán, *regidor* and citizen of Cartagena, stated that Luis de Manjarres, Francisco de Lidueña, Francisco Arias, Luis Lanchero, and other enemies of Miguel Díez had insulted the judge in Santa Marta, "saying that he was a Frenchman and if he were to come downriver from the kingdom they would kill him." Citizens in Cartagena told Zorita that when news was received that Princess María had died, "Miguel Díez never mourned her death in the slightest or ordered funeral honors for her, as was proper. Instead, he appeared on the following day dressed in purple silk. However, when news was received of the armistice agreed to by His Majesty and the king of France, he put on mourning clothes."[8] From what is known about Pedro de Ursúa's ancestry, it appears that Miguel Díez's love of France was strengthened through the family's tie with the Ursúa family and their relatives in the Basque country of Labourd.

Pedro de Ursúa's historical image, as Caro Baroja observes, has been formed mainly from the circumstances surrounding his death. When this Basque-Navarrese captain was killed at Machifaro on January 1, 1561, he became the first and most distinguished victim of the "monster" and "traitor" Lope de Aguirre, the Wrath of God, Prince of Liberty, and terrible *caudillo* of those adventurers who journeyed down the Marañon and Amazon rivers in search of El Dorado, dubbed by Aguirre the "invincible *marañones*, companions until death."

Following his assassination, various chroniclers created the legend of Pedro de Ursúa. Toribio de Ortiguera wrote about the expedition to Omagua in the 1580s. He described the somewhat effeminate but well-proportioned, handsome, red-bearded, affable Ursúa as a gallant Spanish commander. Pedro de Ursúa, dead before his thirty-sixth year, was symbolically transfigured into a Knight of El Dorado, a glory of Navarre gilded by martyrdom and a cavalier of singular virtue. As is apparent, Ortiguera and other chroniclers were unaware of Alonso de Zorita's assessment of Ursúa. Zorita compared this villainous conqueror to a "fallen angel" who enjoyed killing Indians.[9] His monstrous deeds soon forgotten, the selfish, ungrateful, dissembling Ursúa became a man who would found colonies, a legend of Spanish chivalry.

In his analysis of the personalities of Pedro de Ursúa and Lope de Aguirre, Caro Baroja demonstrates how the heraldic animals that appear on their blazons define, in part, the characters of these two men. The sinister black doves on Ursúa's coat of arms, birds "consecrated to Venus and to those considered amorous in essence," symbolize a major defect in the personality of the governor of El Dorado and Omagua. In like manner, Aguirre's heraldic animal, a black she wolf with red claws and extended tongue, symbolizes the uncommon character of the fearsome and bloody tyrant who desired to burn in hell with Alexander, Caesar, and Pompey: "In any case, there they remain, face to face for centuries, the refined, genteel, diplomatic and astute Basque, and the hot-headed, sardonic, humorous and dreadful Basque: the one honored, accursed the other."[10]

Because Ursúa may have been less than twenty years old when he came to the Indies, one might suppose that his personality was largely shaped by the savage American environment—rebellious colonists, "bloodthirsty" Indians, guerrilla warfare, cruel deeds, dysentery, hunger, fevers, and sleepless nights. Caro Baroja, however, largely discounts these factors, suggesting that Ursúa's familial antecedents "sufficiently explain his psychological profile and his personality as warrior and 'diplomat.'"[11]

On the paternal side, Pedro de Ursúa was the eldest son of Tristán de Ursúa, lord of the tower or "palace" of Ursúa in Arizcun located in the Baztán Valley close to the French border. The tower of Ursúa in the fifteenth and sixteenth centuries was typical of fortresses built by great noble houses. It had "embrasures, tower, barbican, and walls at a distance from the palace, with a moat and drawbridge, which defends its entrance."[12] As is apparent from the names given Pedro de Ursúa's father and other nobles of Navarre—Tristán, Perceval—books of chivalry or novels of knight-errants were read avidly by the Navarrese aristocracy.

Pedro de Ursúa's mother, Leonor, was a Díez de Aux de Armendáriz. Members of this family were granted various properties by kings of French origin; the original estate was located in the district of San Juan de Pie de Puerto near the French border. The family spread throughout Navarre, and theirs is a more common surname than Ursúa. Although Pedro de Aguado and other historians, including Sir Clements Robert Markham,[13] write that Pedro de Ursúa was Miguel Díez's nephew, the latter called Ursúa his cousin.[14] Legal testimony confirms that Ursúa was indeed the judge's first cousin; Miguel Díez's only nephews were Pedro and Juana, children of his half-brother Pedro de Garmendi, and Ursúa's mother was Miguel Díez's aunt rather than his sister.

Various members of the house of Ursúa acquired lands and titles in Navarre during the years it was under the rule of the French crown or the French feudal house of Evreux. In the fifteenth century, the Ursúas and the Beaumonts backed Charles,

Prince of Viana, against his father, John of Aragon. When John II
died in 1479, his daughter Leonor, married to the Count of Foix,
inherited the kingdom, and the Ursúas and the Beaumonts became partisans of the Spanish party in Navarre. In the Castilian
conquest of Navarre (1512–1521), the last stronghold that fell to
the forces of Ferdinand the Catholic was the Castle of Maya,
initially sieged by troops led by Don Tristán de Ursúa and the
governor of San Juan Pie de Puerto.

The fact that Tristán de Ursúa chose to join the winning side in
the contest for Navarre between Louis XII and Ferdinand of
Aragon helps explain the honors granted the family when the
kingdom was incorporated into the Crown of Castile. However,
the house of Ursúa also remained on good terms with the defeated house of Albret in French Navarre and its successor, Antonio de Borbón. "Perhaps the knowledge which he had from
conversations with Pedro de Ursúa himself of the latter's relations
with families in French Navarre (Ultrapuertos) led Lope de
Aguirre to call his victim on a memorable occasion 'Navarrese, or
more properly speaking, French.'"[15]

Long before Pedro de Ursúa was suspected of being a Frenchman by Lope de Aguirre, an ancient ballad of the Basque country
dealing with incest and murder confirmed the house of Ursúa's
French connections. Caro Baroja also believes that the ballad
draws a profile of many traits to be found in Ursúa's basic
personality. Whether or not one agrees with Caro Baroja, it
seems that the history of medieval Navarre was a troubled one
"full of violence and intrigue, treachery, sedition and murder."[16]

The regionalism and violence of the Basque—Navarrese region
appears reflected in the careers of Miguel Díez and Pedro de
Ursúa, two Basques of "arbitrary temper" who arrived in the
Indies with other family members from the Baztán Valley and
Base Navarre.[17] When Miguel Díez arrived in Cartagena de Indias
in 1544, he brought relatives and dependents like Martín Díez de
Armendáriz and Francisco Díaz de Arles, the latter another
Navarrese with a name that suggests French origins.[18] The governor also brought the trappings of civilization to Santa Fé de
Bogotá: ". . . a barber, a surgeon, a blacksmith, two tailors, a
hosier, tilers, scribes, two carpenters, six Negroes, three married
men with their wives, and two widows to be married, each with
daughters."[19]

In Cartagena, Miguel Díez quickly became aware that New
Granada's colonists were divided into several factions. Powerful

caudillos like Don Pedro de Heredia, the governor of Cartagena, disputed governmental jurisdictions with equally powerful rivals. Another problem had to do with disputed rights to *encomiendas*. Following the conquest of the interior provinces by Gonzalo Jiménez de Quesada in 1538, Alonso Luis de Lugo was appointed governor of the country discovered by Quesada. This worthless official annulled or appropriated Indian allotments previously granted by the first conquerors. In Vélez, Lugo voided *encomiendas* given to settlers by founder Captain Martín Galiano. In Bogotá and Tunja, Lugo collected the tribute from Indians granted to colonists by Quesada. Described by Bartolomé de Las Casas as "a most irrational and bestial man," Lugo, who was married to the sister of the king's secretary Francisco de los Cobos, used his influence at court and was cleared of all charges brought against him by Crown officials and various settlers.[20]

Greedy, cruel, and contentious colonists quarreled with each other and exploited the Indians unmercifully; their actions were unrestrained because no central authority had been established in New Granada. Judges in Santo Domingo received contradictory and incomplete reports from provincial governors and their officials and partisans. Government by remote control had failed to create a stable society in any of the sparsely populated towns that dotted the vast territory, and crown decrees for the good government of the region were either laughed at or ignored. Miguel Díez and his fellow adventurers would only add to the misery and inequities of the land.

Several citizens of Santa Fe de Bogotá gave the new governor a royal welcome in Cartagena. These enemies of Alonso Luis de Lugo persuaded Miguel Díez to send Pedro de Ursúa to represent him in Santa Fe while he took the *residencia* of Governor Pedro de Heredia and his officials in the coastal settlement. After being granted authority from his cousin to act as his deputy and captain-general in New Granada, Ursúa and enemies of the Lugo family left Cartagena for Santa Fe. When the party arrived in the highland city on May 14, 1545, Ursúa proclaimed himself governor of the New Kingdom in the name of Miguel Díez, but his right to the government was immediately challenged by Lope Montalvo de Lugo, acting as lieutenant governor and captain-general for his relative Alonso Luis. When Montalvo de Lugo refused to relinquish his *vara de justicia* (rod of justice), Ursúa seized the official's symbol of jurisdiction and arrested him; he also confiscated the prisoner's estate without proclaiming his *re-*

sidencia. Montalvo de Lugo was eventually shipped downriver to
Cartagena, where Miguel Díez delayed his judicial inquiry so that
his cousin in Santa Fe might enjoy the captive's property and
encomienda as long as possible. On June 26, 1547, Montalvo de
Lugo wrote Charles V that he had been a prisoner for twenty-
seven months. During that time he had been badly treated, and
his estate had been destroyed.[21]

In Cartagena, Miguel Díez began the *residencia* of Don Pedro
de Heredia and his officials, made several appointments, and
proclaimed the New Laws. In his letters to the crown he declared
himself an honest and faithful servant in the fashion of his relatives, royal vassals all to their "King and Lord." His actions as
governor and judge do not confirm this claim.

The royal commissioner's despotic and arbitrary ways naturally
aroused resentment by Governor Pedro de Heredia and his
brother and lieutenant, Alonso de Heredia. When the governor
challenged Miguel Díez's authority by the legal process of
recusation,[22] accusing him of personal enmity, he provoked the
judge's wrath. Realizing he could not expect justice from Miguel
Díez, Don Pedro attempted to flee Cartagena but the judge's
vigilant henchmen prevented his escape: Miguel Díez then spent
fifteen leisurely months taking the governor's *residencia*, after
which he sent Heredia to Spain as a prisoner.

Having proclaimed the New Laws, Miguel Díez vested Indians
held by Pedro de Heredia and the treasury officials in the crown.
However, in contravention of the New Laws, the exchequer
officials continued to extort corn, clothes, and other goods from
the Indians. Miguel Díez granted Indians he had taken from
Heredia to relatives and friends, except in the pueblos of Tubará
and Mahates, which he reserved for his own profit. Fearing what
he might do to them, none of the treasury officials dared complain to the crown that Miguel Díez had awarded new Indian
allotments, expressly forbidden by the New Laws. Miguel Díez
also seized the stamps used by the treasury officials to show that
the king's fifth had been paid; this allowed him to defraud the
crown. That he stole from the crown is more than likely, for
Captain Francisco de Arias wrote the Royal Council of the Indies
in 1546 that Licentiate Miguel Díez used money he collected in
fines to buy goods for shipment upriver instead of placing the
money in the royal strongbox.

Captain Arias further noted that Miguel Díez in Cartagena
punished severely those individuals he disliked, but ignored

crimes committed by his friends and servants, or by persons who had the good sense to bribe him. He favored his countrymen and relatives in appointments and granted them *encomiendas* at the expense of his enemies. Things had come to such a pass that captive Moriscos in Granada had greater freedom and more control of their estates than the crown's subjects under Miguel Díez.[23]

Equally unwise, according to Arias, was his choice of friends and appointments, for Miguel Díez chose the worst. In violation of crown decrees, Miguel Díez in Cartagena authorized expeditions into Indian country by Captain Luis de Manjarres, Juan Ortiz de Zárate, Alonso López de Ayala, and other Indian haters. Horrible crimes were committed by these adventurers on their *jornadas*; an example was the charge that López de Ayala had dogs trained to hunt down and kill Indians. After confirming this charge, the Council of the Indies ordered that the dogs be killed and forbade any Spaniard to raise or own dogs of this type in New Granada.[24]

Miguel Díez's most disastrous appointment was the commission he gave to the hidalgo Jorge de Robledo, former captain of Spanish troops in Italy, to act as his lieutenant in Cartago, Antioquia, and Santa Ana de Anserma. Cartago and Anserma belonged to the government of Popayán headed by Sebastián de Benalcázar, described by Don Juan del Valle, the first bishop fo Popayán, as a conscientious protector of the Indians.[25] The settlement of Antioquia, or Nori, was claimed by both Benalcázar and Pedro de Heredia.[26]

Before being appointed Miguel Díez's deputy, Robledo had served under Pedro de Alvarado, Benalcázar, Francisco Pizarro, and Pascual de Andagoya. After extending the Peruvian conquest northward from Quito, Robledo left for Spain in 1544 to petition the crown for the independent government of the provinces he had explored and settled. He left for Spain but not as a free man, for Alonso de Heredia arrested him in San Sebastián de Buenavista for having usurped Pedro de Heredia's jurisdiction in Antioquia. Meanwhile, Benalcázar had discovered Robledo's intention to establish a separate government and pronounced him a traitor to the commission he had received from the government of Popayán to explore and settle the lower reaches of the Cauca Valley.[27]

On his arrival in Spain, Robledo was granted the crown's permission to return to New Granada to have his *residencia* taken by Licentiate Miguel Díez. Should the judicial inquiry confirm that Robledo had served faithfully and well during the time he had been Benalcázar's lieutenant in the "cities" he had founded, Miguel Díez might appoint Robledo his deputy in those settlements until the crown ruled otherwise. Miguel Díez ignored this crown decision on Robledo's return to New Granada, for he commissioned Robledo his lieutenant in Antioquia, Cartago, and Santa Ana de Anserma before taking his *residencia*. When Pedro de Heredia reported his action to the crown, an order was sent to Miguel Díez on April 17, 1547, to immediately revoke Robledo's appointment; the governor might only reinstate Robledo as his deputy if the judicial inquiry previously ordered cleared Robledo of any charges.

Unaware that the crown had revoked the appointment granted him illegally by Miguel Díez, Robledo arrived in Antioquia on April 24, 1546. The town's citizens received him well, but in Arma, Robledo had to imprison the villa's *regidores* and a Captain Soria to assume control of the municipal government. Before being taken captive, Captain Soria ordered one of his black slaves to inform Adelantado Benalcázar in Cali that Arma had fallen to his enemy.

In Arma, Robledo wrote Miguel Díez that he had taken approximately 4,000 pesos from the royal strongbox in the villa "so that the money might not be used to wage war against His Majesty." He also reported that Benalcázar had sent him a letter ordering him to leave the area; he had ignored this threat and urged Miguel Díez to come in person and reinforce him. He was not to come with paper and ink, "for these will not suffice, but with ropes and knives so that the wicked may be punished and the virtuous may fear the king."[28]

After Benalcázar carried out his threat to defeat and capture Miguel Díez's lieutenant, he discovered letters on Robledo's person stating that Benalcázar and his men were friends of the Pizarros and traitors to the royal cause. Had these letters not defamed the *adelantado's* honor, Benalcázar might have spared Robledo's life. Convinced that Robledo was an enemy and a traitor to his former commander, Benalcázar heeded the advice of Francisco Hernández Girón, his chief lieutenant, to call a council of war to decide Robledo's fate. On October 5, 1546, Robledo's execution took place after a crier announced the council's sentence that he be hanged and beheaded.[29]

Aware that he had acted illegally, Miguel Díez wrote the crown attempting to justify his commissions to Ursúa and Robledo.

Although the crown had not authorized him to appoint Ursúa his lieutenant governor in New Granada before his own entry into the kingdom, this "necessary" action had been taken after he sent a *procurador* to Santa Marta so that he might technically be acknowledged the legal representative of the crown by the city's officials. He also asserted that Ursúa had been granted only limited powers, "for he only went to keep the land in peace in the name of Your Majesty." Miguel Díez found it harder to explain Robledo's appointment. After declaring that Benalcázar had treacherously captured and slain this faithful servant of the crown, Miguel Díez wrote that if Robledo had taken the gold from the strongbox of the royal exchequer in Anserma—as Benalcázar asserted—and had used the money to pay debts owed by Robledo and Miguel Díez, both the audit of the treasury officials and Benalcázar's *residencia* should be taken by another official, "since I am a participant in the alleged treason."[30]

Miguel Díez's insatiable greed and injudicious appointments angered many settlers. Others were offended and terrified by his immorality and excessive cruelty. Although Miguel Díez died a priest, he showed himself to be a very worldly man in Cartagena. Citizens testified that he arrived dressed in the somber garb befitting a royal judge; he soon shed this apparel for a short cape, white doublet, and wide linen breeches with the legs showing, armed with a broad sword, and every bit the noble dandy. Dressed in close-fitting mulberry silk or other "unseemly garb," he went through the streets of the city by night to visit single or married women. It was said that married men feared to leave their wives alone after they learned of Miguel Díez's sexual excesses.

Miguel Díez appears to have carried on affairs ("se echava carnalmente y estaba amancebado") with Francisca Pimentel, with her daughter, Ana de Soria; with Doña Ana de Montalvo, the wife of Sebastián de Heredia; and with Doña Ana's sister, Doña Luisa. Sebastián de Heredia's judicial inquiry was not taken with "the necessary diligence" because of the affair with Doña Ana. Friends and relatives were allowed to share his women; thus Juan Bautista Sordela, his *fiscal* and scribe, slept with Ana Díaz. Francisco Díez de Armendáriz, his relative and *alguacil mayor*, slept with Luisa Álvarez. Juan de Pinilla slept with Beatriz Nieta. Unrestrained in his sexual appetites, Miguel Díez tolerated licentiousness in others, and even priests were allowed to keep their concubines.[31]

Spaniards saw Miguel Díez as the chief cock in the henhouse, but the Indians knew him for a hungry fox. When Sebastián Pérez, *encomendero* of the village of Mahates in the province of Cartagena, asked the Indians of the town why they had not killed the fox that ate their chickens, "an Indian called Gonzalillo, a *ladino* versed in our Spanish language, responded: 'That fox eats no more than one or two chickens; that other fox who comes from Castile has eaten many and does much harm.' When Pérez asked Gonzalillo to identify the fox, the Indian said it was Licentiate Miguel Díez who had taken and eaten a great number of the Indians' chickens."[32]

Other charges against Miguel Díez lodged by citizens of Cartagena indicate that he was both a sadist and a fool. He sentenced Christians found guilty to receive excessive lashes in many instances. When they attempted to appeal, he denied them the right. He combined this unnecessary cruelty with ridiculous, frivolous conduct. At various times, he demeaned the dignity of his office by participating in foot and horse races with citizens and soldiers. Wearing a fine scarlet cloak, he rode his horse to the jingle of bells as he raised his arm shouting "Amores! Amores!"[33] Those who accused Miguel Díez of misdeeds he slandered or charged with being capital enemies of the king, vile and despicable men of little worth and quality.

When Juan López de Orozco, a notary of Cartagena commissioned to aid Miguel Díez in his *residencia* of Pedro de Heredia, gave the mate of a merchant ship a letter for delivery to Licentiate Juan de Salmerón, a member of the Royal Council of the Indies, Miguel Díez had the letter confiscated before the ship left the port for Spain. After reading the letter which accused him of various crimes, Miguel Díez discharged Orozco as *escribano de residencia*, called him a Jewish dog, and threatened to have him killed. When Miguel Díez finally decided to deport the terrified notary, Orozco sought sanctuary in the church where he became ill with a fever and died without being able to draw up a will.[34]

Miguel Díez attempted to discredit Pedro de Heredia's accusations against him by impugning the *adelantado's* honor through his wife. He stated that although Don Antonio de Heredia was reputed to be Don Pedro's son, there were doubts about this because his mother Constanza Franco was a dissolute woman. Miguel Díez also observed that "Gonzalo Palometo, the great-grandfather of Don Antonio de Heredia, was burned by the Holy Office of the Inquisition in the villa of Madrid and his *sanbenito* is in the church of Santo Domingo el Real in the said villa." The vindictive judge then declared that it was common knowledge that "Tomás Franco, Don Antonio de Heredia's grandfather, would beat his wife in Madrid with a string of garlic so as to make her consent to use her body in an evil way." As for Don Antonio, "he is a man of little worth who married a vile woman in Santo Domingo. He brought a Negress to this city of Cartagena to be her friend, and gossip has it that the Negress has given birth to his child."[35]

Before leaving Cartagena for Santa Marta in April, 1546, Miguel Díez ordered the *calpixque* (stewards) of the surrounding villages to bring Indians to the city; the natives were used to carry merchandise belonging to Miguel Díez, merchants, and other particular persons like Don Martín de Calatayud, the bishop of Santa Marta. The Indians hauled chests, bundles, and bales containing linen, serge, woolen cloth, and other goods to Malambo, Santa Marta's port on the Magdalena river, thirty leagues distance from Cartagena. Indian porters also carried Miguel Díez and other persons to the port in hammocks.[36]

On his departure from Santa Marta for Santa Fe, Miguel Díez was accompanied by almost 100 Spaniards, various Negro slaves, and Indian women to cook for the party. On the trip upriver, the Negro slaves forced the Indian women to have sexual relations with them but the judge ignored this abusive conduct. He also ignored the plight of the Indians in the New Kingdom after his arrival in Santa Fe on January 17, 1547. Miguel Díez proclaimed the New Laws, but decided not to put them into effect when representatives of the 700 Spaniards in the kingdom persuaded him to suspend their enforcement for two years.[37] After siding with the *encomenderos* of New Granada, Miguel Díez allowed the municipal council of Santa Fe to appoint commissioners to visit Spain to petition for the repeal of the New Laws, "particularly that provision which prevented children and widows from inheriting *repartimientos* or *encomiendas* which had been held by a father or a husband."[38]

Having settled the matter of the New Laws by invoking the solemn formula "Obedezco pero no cumplo" ("I obey but do not carry out"), Miguel Díez reported that he had found the arsonist who had torched the house ordered built by Pedro de Ursúa in the crown's name for his and Ursúa's residence. The captured incendiary had implicated three other individuals in the plot to kill Ursúa. These were Captain Luis Lanchero, a alcalde of the city; Francisco de Belandia, the Crown's *veedor* and *factor* under Don Alonso Luis de Lugo; and an individual named Juan de Coca. Following the arrest and imprisonment of the alleged conspirators, Belandia escaped from jail before being interrogated, but Lanchero and Coca were questioned and tortured without admitting their guilt.[39]

The arrest, imprisonment, and torture of Captain Lanchero and other persons appears to have been without foundation and was probably a calculated act to imprison key individuals capable of rallying the first settlers of the kingdom against the new governor and his lieutenant. This seems apparent for a number of reasons. First, Miguel Díez failed to mention the name of the alleged arsonist who turned in his fellow conspirators. This individual is identified by Juan de Castellanos as Francisco Palomo who confessed to the crime only after being tortured. Sentenced to death for the crime, Palomo was not guilty in the opinion of most citizens of Santa Fe. Just before his execution, Palomo declared that neither he nor any of the persons he had named as accomplices were guilty of any crime. Second, it seems that the house Miguel Díez claimed had been built with Crown funds was owned by Montalvo de Lugo and constructed prior to Ursúa's arrival in Santa Fé.[40] Third, the alleged conspirator Lanchero had initially challenged Ursúa's right to hold the office of *justicia mayor* in Santa Fe and had been arrested with Lope Montalvo de Lugo when Ursúa realized that the captain might head an uprising against the new government.[41]

In the crown's name Miguel Díez bought an adobe house covered with straw for 1,200 *castellanos*. His enemies stated that he ate and drank to the sound of trumpets with friends, his concubine by his side. Meanwhile, various persons whom the judge had offended sent letters accusing him of misdeeds. Miguel Díez was certain that these adverse reports of his conduct charged him with actions "unworthy of a Guinea Negro." However, he was aware that these accusations would undoubtedly influence the crown to appoint someone other than himself to the presidency of the high court soon to be established for New Granada.[42]

In its report to the crown the Audiencia of Santo Domingo informed the king and the Council of the Indies that the accusations against Miguel Díez and other officials were so serious they could hardly be believed. Although the tribunal had the authority to take direct action in matters concerning judges and their officials under its jurisdiction, it had instead transmitted these complaints to Spain because royal judges were directly appointed by the crown and sufficient time had not passed for reports of their excesses to have reached the Council of the Indies.[43]

Letters and personal reports to higher authorities accused Miguel Díez of inexperience in governing people; general dishonesty and extreme greed; stupidity; immorality; failing to furnish bond for himself and his deputies for the *residencia* that would eventually be taken of his office; delaying Lope Montalvo de Lugo's judicial inquiry; excessive use of torture in interrogating persons accused of crimes; sending secretly out of New Granada more than 60,000 pesos illegally obtained; robbing the treasury of the crown and the estates of individuals who had died intestate; hearing cases between Spaniards disputing *encomiendas*, thus usurping the jurisdiction of the Audiencia of Santo Domingo; and transferring Indians held in *encomienda* without allowing appeals to the judges in Santo Domingo.[44]

Following the audiencia's report to the crown, the judges received more grievances concerning Miguel Díez's many injustices and offenses. So many and so serious were the charges that Licentiates Grajeda and Zorita feared that the Indians and Spaniards of Tierra Firme would eventually rise up against Miguel Díez's despotic rule. Accordingly, they wrote the crown on Juanuary 23, 1549, that it had been decided that Zorita should go to New Granada as *juez de residencia* and governor to end the many infractions of the law in that land.[45]

Meanwhile, the Council of the Indies had already determined to end the divided rule brought about under the various governments of New Granada by creating an audiencia in Santa Fe de Bogotá. The new royal tribunal's judges were to be Gutierre de Mercado, Melchor Bravo de Sarabia, a Licentiate Mieres, Juan de Galarza, Beltrán de Góngora, and Pedro de Saavedra.[46]

After learning that the Audiencia of Santo Domingo had commissioned Zorita to take Miguel Díez's *residencia* and appointed him governor of the New Kingdom, the Council revoked Mercado's orders to take Miguel Díez's judicial inquiry at the same time that it "withdrew from Zorita the title of governor and vested governmental powers in the new Audiencia of New Granada." The new tribunal was forbidden to receive appeals from Zorita's verdicts, but the "resulting division of authority between Zorita and the Audiencia of New Granada, so characteristic of Spain's colonial policy, seriously impaired the prospects of success of Zorita's mission."[47]

The Royal Council's assignment of governmental powers to the

newly created tribunal in Santa Fe troubled Zorita, as indicated
by his letter to the crown on October 12, 1549. He wrote that
when news had been received in Santo Domingo of the royal
judges appointed for New Granada, he had supposed his trip to
the mainland was unnecessary. In fact, the municipal council of
Santo Domingo and the city's principal citizens had petitioned
the high court to have Zorita remain in Española, giving as one of
their reasons the establishment of the new audiencia in Santa Fe
which should have powers of judicial inquiry. Although he feared
the governmental authority vested in the new tribunal would
cause endless confusion, Zorita agreed to take Miguel Díez's
residencia. However, the cost of the trip would be great and he
should be paid the salary that Miguel Díez received in Santa Fe as
well as his own salary during the period of the judicial inquiry.[48]
A month later, Zorita repeated his request and explained in some
detail why an increase of salary was justified. He had contracted
debts in Seville before leaving Spain for Española; he needed new
clothes for the trip to New Granada and would have to outfit
himself and his servant at inflated prices; he would have to
support two households, that of his wife in Santo Domingo and
his temporary one in New Granada; finally, the trip upriver to
Santa Fe from the coast, including the hiring and outfitting of
Indian carriers, would cause additional expenditures. Zorita's request for a higher salary included the observation that royal
tribunals in Spain customarily paid a judge's regular salary in
addition to the salary of the official whose residencia he had to
take during his absence from the city where he resided. Not only
was this the usual practice in Spain, but it had been followed
when Judge Juan Hurtado de Mendoza of the Audiencia of Santo
Domingo had gone to Cuba to take the judicial inquiry of Licentiate Antonio de Chávez, governor of that island.[49]

The Council of the Indies partly complied with Zorita's request, for it authorized him to receive 2,100 ducats above his
regular salary of 900 ducats, the equivalent of Miguel Díez's
annual salary. The council also authorized Zorita to use the
notaries Bartolomé González de la Peña and Martín Ramoyn in
the judicial inquiries and decreed that as a person of quality
Zorita was to be treated honorably by the judges of Santa Fe and
aided in his task if required. Finally, the council specifically
charged Zorita with responsibility for investigating and punishing
offenses against Indians in Tierra Firme.[50]

The royal order of June 8, 1549, appointing Zorita investigating judge of Miguel Díez and his lieutenants, was received in Santo Domingo in late September. Because no ship bound for the mainland was available, Zorita did not leave Santo Domingo until January 17, 1550. Legal maneuvers by the newly created audiencia of New Granada filled Zorita's mission with hardships, disappointments, and obstacles. Some years later he recalled that he traveled mostly on foot through that harsh and craggy land, suffering great losses. Because of his investigations into the judicial inquiries and of persons who had mistreated and killed Indians, all involved in these crimes hated him; so did the officials of the royal exchequer who falsely claimed they did not have the funds to pay him. When his salary was not forthcoming, Zorita was forced to sell at reduced prices personal household goods that he had brought. The judicial investigations were so many and the time allotted for their completion so short that he had to work day and night, including Sundays and church feast days. He also visited many Indian villages in empty and mountainous lands, where he found no shelter from the extreme cold. In the lowlands he suffered from the oppressive heat and a plague of mosquitoes that swarmed around him in clouds. His hands were covered with sores, and his feet suffered because he traveled on foot to gather Indians into villages.[51]

Zorita arrived in Nuestra Señora de la Hacha on January 22, 1550. When bad weather forced him to remain there for several days, he spent the time informing himself of conditions on the coast. He then departed for Santa Marta, arriving there on January 28.[52] After Santa Marta's municipal council recognized his credential of authority, Zorita sent for canoes located upriver for the ascent of the Magdalena river. While he waited for transportation to Santa Fe, Zorita wrote the crown about what he had learned in these communities.

Income from the pearl fisheries had diminished, but the production of gold from the mines of Buritacá should soon increase. Black slaves were working the diggings, and the Indians had been won over by gifts of wine, caps, hatchets, and trinkets. A settlement had been established at the mines, and its founders, citizens of Río de la Hacha, had elected a municipal council to govern the town.

Settlers at both Río de la Hacha and Buritacá claimed that Santa Marta had no governmental or legal authority over their settlements. However, Zorita was told in Santa Marta that the right of self-government asserted by Río de la Hacha's citizens was limited by a royal decree to an area extending eight leagues inland from the pearl fisheries. Since Buritacá was about twenty-two leagues from Río de la Hacha, it fell under the jurisdiction of Santa Marta. Unable to determine whether Buritacá's municipal council or a representative of the governor of Santa Marta had ultimate authority in the mining settlement, Zorita referred the matter to the crown for decision; Francisco de Castellanos, the treasurer of the pearl fisheries at Río de la Hacha, had left for Spain to make a full report on the subject. After reviewing Castellano's petition, the crown decreed that Buritacá was independent of Santa Marta. Until 1593, both Río de la Hacha and the mining settlement had legal authority in first instance in civil and criminal cases within their districts with right of appeal by the accused to the Audiencia of Santo Domingo.[53]

Settlers of the coastal area fought with each other and delayed implementation of the crown's writs and orders. Neither in word nor deeds did they give proof of being Christians. In Santa Marta, the priest and notary Domingo Orgóñez de Villaquirán had frequently quarreled with the town council's alcaldes, who had beaten him at the door of the city's church. When the town's magistrates learned that Orgóñez intended to report the assault to the judges in Santo Domingo, his house was set on fire while he lay in bed recovering from his injuries. He escaped from the fire, but his house, clothes, and books were destroyed. The quarrel between the cleric and the alcaldes had not abated when Zorita arrived in Santa Marta; it ended only when Zorita persuaded Orgóñez to leave for Spain to report this ugly episode to the Council of the Indies.

Licentiate Gaspar de Magallanes was investigating a much more serious case of arson in Santa Marta. He had imprisoned those individuals accused of the crime and would shortly send them to Santa Fe for sentencing by the Audiencia of New Granada.

Zorita had also investigated Indian affairs on the coast. He found these vassals of the crown being bought and sold publicly in Río de la Hacha. Settlers in that town and Santa Marta committed many offenses against the Indians and neglected to teach them Christian doctrine. Because the magistrates refused to implement the laws decreed by the crown for the protection of the Indians, *encomenderos* had absolute dominion over the natives. To remedy this situation, Zorita verified all titles to *encomiendas* and freed from tribute payment those Indians who were not legally held by Spaniards. He ordered all Spaniards receiving personal services from Indians to appear before him with their charges. The Indians were told that they might serve their *encomenderos* voluntarily, but could not be forced to perform any services and were to be paid wages for their work. The Spaniards were told that no *encomienda* Indians or those still not under the obedience of the crown could be enslaved; those found guilty of this crime were to be fined 100,000 *maravedís* or, in default of payment, were to suffer 100 whiplashes to be administered before the general public. No longer might Indians be bought or sold, and all Indians were to be treated as vassals of the crown with the same rights as the natives of Castile. Because Zorita could not find one Indian who could recite the Ave María, he ordered the Spaniards to take their charges to church on Sundays and feast days to hear Christian doctrine. He particularly charged priests and sextons of the region to carry out their spiritual responsibilities to the Indians.

Zorita attributed the general poverty of the *encomenderos* in Santa Marta to their neglect of agriculture and their dependence on the meager tribute they obtained from the Indians. Zorita thus approved titles to *encomiendas* with the stipulation that the Spaniards plant fields of maize and cassava immediately and build houses of stone on their land within two years if this was feasible.

In Santa Marta, Zorita also learned that the judges of the Audiencia of New Granada had sided with Miguel Díez and were placing obstacles to Zorita's efforts to obtain canoes for his trip up the Magdalena. Senior Judge Gutierre de Mercado had planned to wait for Zorita in Mompox so that the latter might enter Santa Fe with the members of the new tribunal. But after Mercado's death on January 9, 1550, Licentiate Juan de Galarza, obligated to Miguel Díez for many favors, and Judge Beltrán de Góngora, a relative of Miguel Díez,[54] had conspired to arrive in Santa Fe and be recognized by the municipal government so as to assume the government of the New Kingdom before Zorita's arrival in the capital. Thus they ignored Zorita's request that they secure canoes for him in Mompox and send them to Santa Marta. After insulting messengers that Zorita sent upriver to request transportation, Góngora and Galarza informed Zorita's emissaries that they thought highly of Miguel Díez; they had already told everyone they met on their trip to Santa Fe that Zorita had no governmental powers and had only been commissioned to take Miguel Díez's *pesquisa secreta* within sixty days. After completing this first or secret part of the judicial inquiry, Zorita must transmit the records of the judicial inquest to the Council of the Indies and depart from New Granada without completing the second part of the *residencia*, which was public and for the purpose of substantiating the complaints presented by private persons.[55]

In Santa Fe, Góngora and Galarza wooed the principal citizens and attempted to turn them against Zorita. In addition, after being recognized on April 7, 1550, as judges in the high court with governmental powers, the two magistrates used all their authority to frustrate Zorita's mission and impugn his character.

According to Góngora and Galarza, Zorita arrived in Santa Fe on May 8, 1550. After being recognized as *juez de residencia*, Zorita presented the writ granting him the governorship of the New Kingdom by the Audiencia of Santo Domingo and requested that it be honored. The judges further declared that after the municipality refused to recognize Zorita as governor, he arrested and imprisoned the alcaldes and *regidores* of the city.

Góngora's and Galarza's accusation seems to be a falsehood intended to discredit Zorita, for Miguel Díez did not include this accusation in the charges he made against Zorita. What appears to have happened is that after Zorita's meeting with the town council of Santa Fe he suspended all the cabildo's members because they were appointees and creatures of Miguel Díez. Zorita also suspended Alonso Téllez from his office of secretary, *relator*, and *fiscal* in the audiencia, explaining that Téllez was a former official of Miguel Díez. All of these embittered men were ordered to appear in Tunja on June 1, when the *residencia* of Miguel Díez and his officials would be proclaimed.

When members of the various municipal councils of the kingdom learned that Zorita was to hold the *residencia* in Tunja, they and Alonso Téllez petitioned Góngora and Galarza to change the location of the judicial inquest, giving as their motive the fact that Santa Fe rather than Tunja was the chief city of New Granada and the place where *residencias* were usually held. The judges responded to the petition by ordering Zorita to hear the judicial inquiry in Santa Fe; Miguel Díez and his officials were now in the midst of friends and Zorita was surrounded by enemies.

Góngora and Galarza also sided with the *encomenderos* when the latter banded together, deciding that by acting as one against Zorita "they could cover up their unheard-of-crimes and cruelties against the Indians."[56] When *encomenderos* of Santa Fe and Tunja petitioned the royal tribunal not to allow Zorita to hear cases involving legal title to *encomiendas*, the judges claimed jurisdiction for themselves in deciding rightful titles to Indian grants.[57] Furthermore, when Zorita jailed individuals guilty of crimes against Indians, Góngora and Galarza ordered their release.

On June 1, Zorita began the *residencia* of Miguel Díez, his lieutenants, notaries, and other officials. That same night Zorita's enemies showed their contempt by staging a protest march. As they paraded through the town, the demonstrators insulted and mocked Zorita to the sound of bugles, mule bells, and other instruments. The unruly mob insulted women in the streets and shocked decent citizens with their foul language and the infamies they shouted to demonstrate their disdain for Zorita.[58]

Refusing to be intimidated by the rabble stirred up by the judges and Miguel Díez, Zorita continued the *residencia*. So numerous and serious were the accusations against Miguel Díez that Zorita ordered him confined under guard in the house used as the audiencia building. After Miguel Díez appealed his detention to the judges, they placed him under house arrest in his own residence.[59]

Zorita encountered other problems in taking the *residencia*. To complete the task he had to appoint his enemy Galarza as his assistant in the judicial proceedings because all the municipal officers of Santa Fe were under investigation and other citizens qualified to fill the position were suspected of being partial to Miguel Díez. Proceedings were then delayed for several days because Miguel Díez interfered in the taking of testimony and had the suspended members of the town council challenge Zorita's impartiality as investigating judge. When Zorita refused to remove himself as presiding judge, the accused petitioned Góngora and Galarza to order the judicial inquiry terminated, giving as their reason the fact that sixty days had passed from the day Zorita entered Santa Fe. After Zorita appeared before the audiencia and correctly pointed out that the *residencia* had begun on June 1, the day of its proclamation, the judges were legally obligated to allow the inquiry to continue; they, however, ordered Zorita and his notary not to leave the city under penalty of being fined 500 pesos each.[60] Góngora and Galarza qualified this order by promising Zorita and Bartolomé González de la Peña that they would be allowed to leave Santa Fe if the original of the judicial inquiry and its copy were surrendered to Alonso Téllez and Miguel Díez. Peña's refusal to give up the judicial records led to his arrest by the judges, and only Zorita's intervention kept him out of jail. The notary was thus able to escape the city by night with the original of the judicial inquiry. When after several days the judges called off the search for Peña, they permitted Zorita to leave Santa Fe. His departure, which took place on October 7, was not without incident, for about five leagues from the city an alcalde and a notary opened and inspected the trunks Zorita had packed with books and clothes to take to Los Panches, on the Magdalena.

Zorita made his way to Los Panches by way of Tocaima in heavy rain, and the rough and treacherous mountain passes proved so dangerous that he had to go on foot. As Zorita led his horse across one narrow path, he was kicked in the leg by the frightened animal; for several days he walked with great difficulty on an injured and swollen foot whenever he was forced to dismount.

In Tocaima the exhausted and injured Zorita sent an edict in the crown's name to the city of Santa Fe ordering Miguel Díez and other persons to come to the coast to answer charges against them made by citizens of Cartagena and Santa Marta. Zorita's messenger, a crown notary named Juan Riquelme, personally notified Miguel Díez, Alonso Téllez, and others of the proclamation and then posted it on the door of the city's church. The morning after it was posted, the parish priest and citizens who had, arrived to celebrate mass found the decree hanging from its two lower nails and completely covered on both sides with fresh human excrement. So foul was the odor in the church that the parishioners left in disgust, and the shocked and angry priest cried out that neither Indians nor Moors would think to commit such a vile act before the Blessed Sacrament. When the priest reported this act of knavery to Góngora and Galarza, they refused to order an investigation in spite of the fact that many citizens and residents publicly stated that the defilement of the church had been ordered by Miguel Díez and Alonso Téllez.[61]

On November 20, Zorita began his descent of the Magdalena from Los Panches, only to encounter more problems. For two days Zorita and his men were pursued by hostile Indians, who followed the two boats hired for the voyage and shot poisoned arrows at the crew and passengers from the riverbanks. The party was defenseless, for Zorita had sold his arms and many of his clothes when the treasury officials in Santa Fe refused to pay his salary. Fear and confusion mounted among the oarsmen and steersmen as the boats reached a dangerous passage called the

Salto, filled with many large rocks hidden in the swirling water. After entering the Salto, one barge struck a rock that opened a gap more than six feet long. Water poured in, damaging Zorita's clothes and bed linen and ruining many of his precious books.

On his arrival at Santa Marta on December 20, Zorita proclaimed the *residencia* of Miguel Díez and his officials. As had happened in Santa Fe, the municipal council refused to cooperate with Zorita in holding the judicial inquiry and witnesses were bribed or intimidated. Despite these difficulties, Zorita began the *residencia* on January 13, 1551. His investigation confirmed that some city magistrates and several of Miguel Díez's officials were guilty of very serious crimes against Indians. Among those individuals Zorita arrested and jailed in Santa Marta were the royal *factor* Juan Ortiz de Zárate and Captain Luis de Manjarres, one of the town council's alcaldes and later lieutenant-governor of Santa Marta under the Audiencia of Santa Fe.[62] Zorita charged these two henchmen of Miguel Díez with having killed and tortured many Indians in expeditions illegally authorized by the latter. Juan Ortiz and Manjarres had seized much gold from the Indians in these *entradas* but had failed to pay the royal fifth due in bullion. When Zorita told the prisoners they must furnish him their defense pleas (*descargos*) before being sent to Spain to appear before the Council of the Indies for final sentencing, they laughed and taunted him.

One night, near the end of the *residencia*, a cleric named Juan González entered the jail. After the priest freed Juan Ortiz from his bonds, the *factor* fled the city with the consent of the guards, who had been bribed not to sound a call to arms. In his investigation of the jailbreak, Zorita learned that González was a licentious and avaricious priest who had been exiled from Mompox; he had then appeared in Santa Marta where he became a merchant and made friends with settlers as greedy as himself. Zorita found González guilty of being a party to Ortiz's escape and sentenced him to be deported to Spain because of his evil life.

Meanwhile, other allies of Ortiz attempted to persuade the Indians of the villages surrounding Santa Marta to rise up against Zorita. They told the Indians that Zorita was an evil man who had come to arrest and hang Indians. Had Zorita not been well loved and admired by the natives for his previous attempts to remedy injustices done them by their masters, he would probably have been faced with an Indian revolt. Instead, the Indians daily informed Zorita of what the Spaniards plotted against him.

Not content with these intrigues against Zorita, Luis de Manjarres had those friends who visited him in the city jail order his servants to hide all the canoes and oars used to row through his *encomienda* called the Marsh, the means of entry and departure from Santa Marta. This made it impossible for Zorita to transport his prisoners to Spain for final sentencing. Zorita himself prepared to abandon the city when he learned that the Audiencia of Santa Fe had given writs to his enemies authorizing his and his notary's arrest and the seizure of the judicial inquiries taken in Santa Marta. Four or five days prior to the end of the *residencia*, Zorita had Peña flee the city with the judicial records; the notary was attacked on his way to Cartagena but eluded his pursuers.

On Zorita's arrival in Cartagena on March 20, he immediately asked Pedro de Heredia to aid him in carrying out the sentences he had been prevented from executing in Santa Marta. "Like a good servant and vassal of His Majesty," the governor, who was ill, assumed command of the troops he mobilized for the trip to Santa Marta. At Malambo, Heredia and Zorita learned that one of Heredia's men, sent ahead of the main party to guard the port, had detained several men from Santa Marta who were going to Santa Fe.[63] When these men were searched and interrogated, they told Zorita and Heredia that no sooner had those prisoners confined by the judge in the city jail been freed than they had drawn up a libelous declaration charging Zorita with many shameful crimes. They had then dishonored Zorita and defied God and king by having these accusations proclaimed to the citizens of Santa Marta. Those questioned by Zorita carried copies of the false charges for presentation to the Audiencia of Santa Fe and told Zorita that Góngora and Galarza would soon assume jurisdiction in the *residencia* in Santa Marta. Once the judges in Santa Fe took over the judicial inquiry, they would revoke all of Zorita's sentences.

After sending these prisoners to Cartagena, Zorita and Heredia proceeded to Santa Marta. Entering the city at night, they met no resistance. Zorita once again arrested Juan Ortiz de Zárate and Luis de Manjarres. He also imprisoned Hernán Álvarez de Azevedo, "a completely pernicious and seditious man" who had incited the citizens of Santa Marta to commit injuries against Zorita. Before taking up residence in Santa Marta, Álvarez had been expelled from Venezuela, Cubagua, and Margarita. The municipal authorities had decided to expel Álvarez and his thugs from Santa Marta, but had allowed them to remain when they agreed to defame Zorita by giving false witness to the lies contained in testimonials they had been given for delivery to Góngora and Galarza in Santa Fe.

After returning to Cartagena with the prisoners, Zorita issued a sentence of death by hanging against Luis de Manjarres, who had not confessed his sins in twenty-five years. His many crimes included the theft of part of the estate of Fray Martín de Calatayud, the bishop of Santa Marta, when Manjarres had been made an executor of the estate after the bishop's death in late 1548.[64] Manjarres had also been excommunicated for hunting down Indians with dogs and killing them after robbing them of their gold. Because of the ugly temper of the citizens of Cartagena who thought Zorita's sentence too harsh, he sent Manjarres with Juan Ortiz de Zárate to Spain where the Council of the Indies could review Zorita's sentence.

After the prisoners were placed on board ship, another vessel in which Manjarres's son served as a boatswain docked in the harbor. The son arranged his father's escape and Manjarres reached Santa Marta and safety before an alarm was raised. The son was captured and burned for his crime in Nombre de Dios.[65]

In Santa Marta Luis de Manjarres met with Miguel Díez and Góngora, who allowed him to remain in the city after he obtained Miguel Díez's pardon for having presented before the tribunal in Santo Domingo in 1549 an indictment accusing the latter of various crimes.[66] When Manjarres also promised that he would act as a false witness against Zorita, Góngora granted Manjarres's confiscated *encomienda* to the latter's wife and appointed him lieutenant-governor of Santa Marta.

Góngora befriended and made confederates of other individuals whom Zorita had sentenced to be deported to Spain to answer for their crimes. He allowed Alvaro de Ballesteros, a great slanderer of women exiled from Santa Marta two or three times, to remain in the city; he also revoked Zorita's sentence vesting Ballestero's *encomienda* in the crown and allotted it to several of Góngora's friends. When Hernán Álvarez de Azevedo charged Zorita with various crimes, Góngora granted him asylum in Santa Marta. Iñigo López, an alcalde of Santa Marta, lost his *encomienda* and was suspended from office when Zorita found him guilty of beating a cleric savagely; hunting down Indians with dogs; robbing, mistreating, and killing other Indians; forcing those Indians he held in *encomienda* to pay excessive tribute; and branding and selling many free Indians as slaves. Góngora not only allowed

López to continue acting as a city magistrate but increased his *encomienda*; the judge also chose to ignore a crown decree ordering López's wife, a Moor born and reared in North Africa, to be deported to Spain.

In Cartagena, Zorita completed his judicial inquiry of Miguel Díez and his officials on July 23, 1551. In addition to many other offenses, Miguel Díez was found guilty of allowing his lieutenants and private citizens to exploit Indians in various ways. He had allowed those Spaniards traveling with him in the province of Cartagena and in New Granada to live off the Indians; they had taken the natives' chickens, corn, fruit, and other things without paying for them. *Encomenderos* had been permitted to use and rent Indians as carriers. With Miguel Díez's consent, they had forced the Indians to raise pigs and other livestock for their benefit. Indians had involuntarily rendered personal services, and many had sickened and died from the heavy burdens they had carried to Cartagena, the unremitting labor from dawn to dusk on the Spaniards' farms, and from constant hunger and sleeping on the bare earth in the rain and night dew.

Not only had Miguel Díez used Indians as carriers, but he was accused of allowing Jorge de Robledo to take many Indians as burden bearers, against their will and in violation of the New Laws, from Cartagena, Urabá, Caracuna, and Abibe on the expedition to Antioquia. Tied to each other by chains, all or most of the carriers died on the expedition.[67]

Zorita's report to the crown and the *residencias* he forwarded from New Granada confirm that it was common practice for *encomenderos* to kill and mistreat Indians, make them pay excessive tribute, overburden them with personal service, and deny them justice. *Encomenderos* like Bartolomé Porras, alcalde and merchant, made Indians carry excessive loads, including pigs, for many leagues; many died from being used as pack animals. Indians and Negroes on Porras's hacienda often failed to complete field work assigned them because they were so tired from carrying burdens; this angered Porras, who beat the exhausted workers and loosed dogs against them. Several Indians and at least two blacks died from the beatings and wounds inflicted by the dogs.

So shocked was Zorita by the Spaniards' abuse of the Indians that twenty years later he wrote that he had heard how "one could not lose one's way between that country and the province of Popayán because it was marked with the bones of dead men."[68]

He also noted that in Cartagena and Santa Marta the Spaniards' cattle ate, trampled, and damaged the Indians' crops; when he visited the New Kingdom there "were as yet few cattle there, but since then a very large number of cattle has been brought in, and the same abuses will arise here as elsewhere."[69]

In their mistreatment of Indians, Miguel Díez's officials and the secular clergy were as culpable as the *encomenderos*. Alonso López de Ayala, Miguel Díez's lieutenant in Cartagena, had ordered all Indians over twelve years of age in one provincial district to be branded as slaves; he had also loosed dogs trained to hunt and kill on illegal expeditions into Indian territory.[70] Zorita's inspection of Indian towns on the coast revealed that clerics were held in low repute by the Indians. When Zorita informed the cacique of the pueblos of Pinchorro and Pacueua that a priest would soon be assigned to these towns, the chief told him: "Up to now we have had one lord, the *encomendero*. Now we shall have two." The Indians were spared their second lord because they were "poor and naked folk" and no priest desired the assignment. Clerical abuse was exemplified by the ecclesiastical judge and vicar of Popayán, described by Zorita as "a soul borne by the demon of greed" who spent much of his time, including Sundays and feast days, in search of Indian tombs containing gold and jewels. Because he was lame, the vicar was carried on the shoulders of two Indians in his "plundering" expeditions. His Indian parishioners noted that in church he could not walk, but in search of gold he ran; "other priests buried the dead, but the vicar dug them up."[71]

Zorita's investigation of the settlers' and the secular clergy's exploitation of the Indians and failure to teach them Christian doctrine strengthened his respect for the Franciscan and Dominican friars who supported his efforts to enforce the New Laws. Zorita's subsequent experiences in Guatemala, Mexico, and Granada, Spain, confirmed his low opinion of the secular clergy. In retirement he wrote an "Opinion Concerning the Religious Instruction of the Indians" in which he criticized the work of the secular clergy in Granada and recommended that friars, preferably Franciscans, be placed in charge of Indian parishes.[72]

As Zorita prepared to return to Santo Domingo, French corsairs were sighted off the coast. Zorita aided in the defense of Cartagena by taking command of the cavalry. The French invasion feared by the city's defenders did not take place, but Zorita lost much sleep during the nights he and his men kept a con-

stant watch on the coast. Thoroughly exhausted, Zorita became
seriously ill and almost died because no doctor could be found in
Cartagena.

Not yet recovered, Zorita took ship for Santo Domingo on
May 10, 1552; the long and dangerous homeward voyage did not
help him. Toward the end of the journey, three ships of the
armada of Santo Domingo mistook Zorita's ship and the caravel
that accompanied it for French vessels that had recently raided
the town of San Germán in Puerto Rico. The pursuers fired heavy
shot, harquebuses, crossbows, and stones; they almost succeeded
in sinking the ship before recognizing it as Spanish.[73]

After reaching the port of Santo Domingo on August 28,
Zorita and his people were rowed to the city. As soon as Zorita
reached home, he took to his bed with a high fever. Then arose
high winds that turned into a hurricane; five ships in the harbor
lost their lines and were driven out to sea—one was the caravel
containing cloth and other goods that Zorita had purchased on
credit in Puerto Rico. The hurricane blew the ship on a rocky
coast, where crew and cargo were destroyed; Zorita's loss
amounted to 1,500 ducats.[74]

Doctor Juan de Montaño's Residencia

In Santo Domingo, Licentiate Hurtado de Mendoza and Grajeda
informed Zorita that they had arrested Miguel Díez the summer
before. After being stopped at the port of Yaguana on his way to
Spain, Miguel Díez presented a writ given him on October 3,
1550, by the Audiencia of Santa Fe; it allowed him to ignore the
judicial inquiry held by Zorita and granted him a year's grace to
take his case directly to the Council of the Indies. The judges
refused to allow Miguel Díez to leave for Spain, but did grant him
freedom in Santo Domingo after he furnished bond of 50,000
castellanos; they then wrote the crown asking for further
instructions.[75]

Meanwhile, Zorita's letters and other charges against Miguel
Díez had been read and acted upon in Valladolid, and Bartolomé
González had left for Spain with Zorita's residencia of the judge.
On August 3, 1551, the Council of the Indies recommended that
the residencia of Miguel Díez should again be taken before he was
allowed to leave the New Kingdom. The judge appointed for this
task should also hold a judicial inquiry of oidores Góngora and
Galaraza. It appeared that Zorita had not been given entire liberty

as *juez de residencia* and inspector of Indian affairs because Gón-gora and Galarza were alone in the New Kingdom without a president or a third judge to check their actions.

To correct irregularities in New Granada and the harsh treatment of the Indians, the council asked Charles V to appoint a president of the royal tribunal in Santa Fe as quickly as possible. Because he was a man of parts, the council had nominated Licentiate Alonso Maldonado for this office. However, the council recognized that Maldonado had held Indians in Central America by registering them in the name of his wife and children; it was also apparent that Maldonado's father-in-law was an *encomendero*:

And because the principal thing that needs to be remedied in that kingdom is that which relates to the treatment of the Indians, we believe that those who have or presently hold Indians will not be free from bias in their votes since they are obliged to punish in others what they themselves may be accused of having done or allowed, nor will they have that pious enthusiasm that is needed for this task.[76]

Not until 1554 did the king appoint a permanent president of the Audiencia of Santa Fe, and then he rescinded the appointment. However, he did commission Licentiate Juan de Montaño as the new judge of judicial inquiry. On July 8, 1552, a royal writ ordered Miguel Díez to return to New Granada so that the *residencia* begun by Zorita might be completed. Unless Miguel Díez posted bond of 10,000 ducats, he was forbidden to leave for the mainland on his own recognizance and must be taken to Tierra Firme by a magistrate.

On February 21, 1553, Miguel Díez wrote the king to thank him for delivering him from the oppression and affliction he had undergone in Santo Domingo. Licentiate Montaño had bypassed Santo Domingo on his way to the mainland, and would call Miguel Díez before him shortly to complete his judicial inquest. Miguel Díez was in high spirits in spite of having to sail for the mainland on a small, dangerous boat and face the constant danger of attack by French pirates. He was sure that with God's help he would soon be vindicated; he was also confident that the king would give him a new post once His Majesty was informed that Miguel Díez had done no more than defend the crown's interests in New Granada.[77]

On arrival at Cartagena, Miguel Díez found himself a royal prisoner of Doctor Juan Maldonado, *fiscal* of the Audiencia of Santa Fe and Protector of the Indians. Maldonado told Miguel

Díez that his *residencia* would not be held until Licentiate Juan de Montaño returned to the city after taking the judicial inquiry of Judges Góngora and Galarza in Santa Fe.

In Cartagena, Miguel Díez enjoyed the freedom of the city and undoubtedly learned from the kindly Doctor Maldonado of Montaño's harsh rule in Santa Fe. When other citizens portrayed Montaño as a stern, ill-tempered, and arrogant judge, Miguel Díez probably realized that the chance for a happy outcome and the recovery of his freedom was doubtful. In his letter to the Crown reporting Miguel Díez's arrival in Cartagena, Doctor Maldonado stated that Montaño was a dangerous, shameless, dishonest man who sought to deceive the crown with windy rhetoric.[78]

Miguel Díez had reason to fear Montaño's arrival in Cartagena, for the former had complied with the wishes of the *encomenderos* while the latter chose to curb the power of the colonists. Juan de Montaño, native of Palos and former *relator* of the Audiencia of Valladolid, aroused the wrath of the *encomenderos* when he arrived in Cali and supported Juan del Valle, bishop of Popayán and protector of the Indians. The reason for this friendship is unknown, but according to Juan Friede the hatred the *encomenderos* professed for both men united them against a common foe.[79]

Early chroniclers, according to Friede, characterized Montaño in terms of the general opinion held by the colonists. Because modern Colombian historiography has not attempted to ascertain the roots of the severe criticism, Montaño is still considered to have been "a despicable man and a traitor, even worse than a bandit and thief." Whether Montaño was a pro-Indian reformer is open to question, but it is certain that he was no friend of the *encomenderos*. It is significant that of all those judges investigating cruelties done to Indians, Montaño was the only royal judge who found an *encomendero* guilty of killing Indians without cause, sentenced him to death, and executed the sentence. Judge Alonso de Grajeda, Zorita's bitter enemy, would later hold Montaño's *residencia*, finding him guilty of various offenses, "unjustly beheading" the *encomendero* and hidalgo Pedro de Salcedo, and killing another under torture. The Council of the Indies confirmed Grajeda's charges, on July 29, 1561, and Juan de Montaño was decapitated in Madrid by order of the king.[80]

In Santa Fe, Montaño suspended the judges Góngora and Galarza, placing them in chains and then sending them to Spain for final sentencing. The ship carrying the prisoners and Governor Pedro de Heredia ran into a heavy storm. All those on board the vessel, including Alonso Téllez, Miguel Díez's notary and former secretary of the Audiencia of Santa Fe, went "to the true *residencia* and accounting for the things they had done."[81]

Zorita's letters to the crown mention that Licentiate Góngora had arrived in New Granada without a penny, but within a year and a half the judge had become a man of property, drinking from a gold cup encrusted with emeralds worth 1,000 pesos. Galarza's belongings were worth more than the salary he had received as judge in the New Kingdom. Zorita noted that among Galarza's possession was an ingot of gold worth 1,000 pesos, sent to him by his brother after the judges had authorized the latter to create a settlement in the Valle de las Lanzas. While founding the settlement the judge's brother, Andrés de Galarza, had loosed dogs against the valley Indians and robbed them of their gold.[82]

Montaño's judicial inquiry of Góngora and Galarza confirms the information found in Zorita's letters. Montaño and Licentiate Francisco Briceño found the judges guilty of sixty-one specific offenses, including receiving gifts in kind from many persons; allowing the forced labor of Indians in the mines and as carriers; permitting treasury officials to hold Indians in *encomienda*; neglecting to moderate Indian tribute payments and allowing *encomenderos* to assess excessive tributes; and failing to see that the Indians lived together in villages. Moreover, although they were required to defend the lives and good treatment of the Indians, and obliged inviolably to prohibit expeditions of plunder or settlement because of the great harm and injury resulting to the Indians, Góngora and Galarza had permitted and even ordered many expeditions like the one to Ibagué. In this expedition to the Valle de las Lanzas, Andrés López de Galarza, the judge's brother, had attacked the Indians with horsemen and footmen, harquebuses, crossbows, and dogs. The Spaniards despoiled the Indians of their food, farmlands, and wealth; burned their houses and huts; and killed, impaled, and attacked the Indians with dogs, committing other cruelties against them.[83]

Montaño and Briceño also found the judges guilty of allowing Miguel Díez and his officials to ignore the judicial inquiry proclaimed by Zorita; this confirms Zorita's statement that, although "Miguel Díez and many of his officials were obliged to come and give their *residencia* in this city [Cartagena] and in Santa Marta, they did not do so in spite of being notified of this many times."[84]

Another charge against the judges called attention to Pedro de

Ursúa's expedition to the province of the warlike Muso Indians. Because these Indians had defended their lives and property when Góngora and Galarza had commissioned Captain Melchor de Baldes to invade their territory, the judges appointed Captain Ursúa to punish them and settle their lands. Ursúa entered the Indians' country "powerfully armed with horsemen, footmen, dogs, and other trappings of war. He loosed the dogs against them and killed many Indians. He impaled and hanged a great number of Indians and caciques, committed other cruelties and evil deeds, robbed them of their food and property and burned their huts and houses." The Indians, in defense of their land, "killed many of the captain's men, native carriers, and horses, putting him in so much need that the judges twice sent him provisions and troops for the punishment and pacification" they had ordered.[85]

This count in the indictment agrees with Zorita's declaration that the campaign against the Musos was unjust and unnecessary. Men recruited against their will had gone on this punitive expedition. Eyewitnesses told Zorita that Ursúa had hanged more than fifty *principales*, and on certain days it was not unusual for the Spaniards to kill 300 or more Indians. The Spaniards had killed many Indians at peace with them, and the Musos themselves had simply defended their houses, families, and property from the predatory Spaniards. Zorita further observed that the expedition to El Dorado had been proclaimed in Cartagena; it would shortly be proclaimed in Santa Marta. Pedro de Ursúa, compared to a fallen angel by Zorita because of his atrocities against the Indians, would be the leader. "I have been told that he will depart when he finishes the punishment I have described."[86]

Pedro de Ursúa's Destiny

From the moment he heard of the undiscovered never-never land of El Dorado, Pedro de Ursúa hungered to command an expedition there. Instead, he reluctantly agreed to become captain-general and chief magistrate of Santa Marta when Góngora and Galarza received a royal decree prohibiting all expeditions of discovery. Ordered by the judges to pacify the Indians of the province of Tairona, Ursúa campaigned unsuccessfully against the Indians of the Sierra Nevada with fewer than thirty men when he was not furnished auxiliaries promised him by the treacherous Luis de Manjarres, whom the judges had appointed governor in Santa Marta.

In 1553, Pedro de Ursúa learned that his *residencia* was to be held by Montaño and Briceño. He was also informed that his commission to pacify the Indians had been revoked and that Captain Luis de Villanueva had been sent by the new judges to investigate charges that Ursúa had mistreated the Indians of Tairona.[87] Meanwhile, the bishop of Santa Marta had written to the Council of the Indies and reported that the Indians of Buritacá had rebelled against Spanish rule because of the outrageous treatment they had suffered when Ursúa and his men had attacked their settlement fourteen leagues from Santa Marta.

On May 10, 1554, the council wrote the Audiencia of Santa Fe that it had learned that the Indian rebellion caused by Spanish atrocities in New Granada had spread to 400 pueblos; the judges should investigate and punish those responsible for the revolt. Montaño, needing no directive from the council to punish the cruelties to the Indians, had already ordered Ursúa's arrest when he received this directive. He ordered that should Ursúa and those with him resist being taken into custody to answer for their alleged crimes, they should be given the customary three *requerimientos* afforded fugitives; should they choose to defend themselves after the summons was proclaimed, Montaño declared that Ursúa and his followers should be killed as rebels.[88]

When Ursúa chose not to appear before the royal justices in Santa Fe, Captain Luis Lanchero at the head of a troop sought him throughout the kingdom. Ursúa escaped his old enemy by fleeing to Panama. There Viceroy Andrés Hurtado de Mendoza, on his way to Lima, appointed him captain of an expedition against rebellious maroons in the Chepo region. Unable to defeat the fugitive slaves in battle, Ursúa won their friendship and then poisoned the wine he gave them to drink at a banquet to celebrate the peace. After killing or capturing the escaped slaves, Ursúa departed for Peru, where the viceroy granted him the long-desired command of the expedition to El Dorado and Omagua. On the epic journey down the Amazon Lope de Aguirre rebelled and took over the expedition. According to one chronicler of the expedition, Ursúa, who was killed at three o'clock in the morning on New Year's Day, 1561, died "like a bad Christian and a very genteel heretic."[89]

The Fate of Miguel Díez de Aux de Armendáriz

Miguel Díez did not suffer as tragic or glorious a fate as the one that befell Ursúa, the "Knight of El Dorado." Before proclaiming the *residencia* of the former governor of New Granada, Juan de Montaño in Cartagena angrily admonished Maldonado for not having fettered and imprisoned Miguel Díez. Montaño then ordered Maldonado's *alguacil* to take the prisoner to the local jail and secure him with two pair of leg chains. Miguel Díez remained in jail during the ninety days of the judicial inquiry, then Montaño allowed him to furnish bond and be confined to a house in the city. Fearing that the prisoner might escape, Montaño ordered that the leg chains were not to be removed and had him guarded by two men. Detained in this fashion for approximately two years, Miguel Díez finally obtained permission to leave for Spain and plead his case before the Council of the Indies.[90]

On September 4, 1556, Miguel Díez arrived at Seville's seaport, Sanlúcar de Barrameda. After he was turned over to the officials of the Casa de Contratación (House of Trade), that agency sequestered his estate pending judicial proceedings. Included in the property Miguel Díez turned over to the House of Trade were 38 marks of worked silver, a cross of gold encrusted with emeralds, and 394,854 *maravedís* or about 1,053 ducats.[91]

After taking up a new career as a canon in a church at Sigüenza, Miguel Díez, presbyter and self-styled "timorous servant of God and his commandments," died in Madrid in late January, 1573.[92] Following his death the Council of the Indies ordered that all but 26,250 *maravedís* of his property held by the Casa de Contratación be released to Pedro and Juana de Garmendi, citizens of the villa of Cascante and the legitimate sons of Miguel Díez's half brother Pedro de Garmendi and Juana de Sarria, both deceased.[93]

Montaño's lengthy judicial review of Miguel Díez confirms Zorita's charges and disproves the account of Miguel Díez's government by such respected historians as Bernard Moses and Sir Clements R. Markham. Although Moses and Markham conclude that Miguel Díez's conduct was proper and state that he was exonerated by the Council of the Indies,[94] an examination of the *residencia* charges show that these scholars erred. Not counting the 101 charges drawn up in Santa Fe and the crimes he was accused of in Santa Marta, Zorita's indictment in Cartagena lists 201 offenses. The Council of the Indies found Miguel Díez either guilty or subject to investigation of more than 100 specific offenses in Cartagena.[95]

On July 23, 1551, Zorita had sentenced Miguel Díez to perpetual loss of office as *juez de residencia* and a fine of 4,000 *pesos de oro*, not including the specific sums assessed for particular offenses. The Council of the Indies reduced this sentence to a suspension totaling five years and a fine of 100 ducats. The first three years of the suspension were for hanging three innocent men who had come to Cartagena after being banished from Peru by Pedro de la Gasca. The last two years' suspension and the fine were the sentence imposed for all the other charges.

The council's sentence suspending Miguel Díez for executing three innocent men, one of whom was a minor, also declared his sentence of execution null and void. The council restored these men (Diego Dardo, Sancho de Figueroa, and Alonso de Villadiego) to the honor and good repute they had enjoyed before being hanged; it also released their descendants from any infamy or disablement visited on them by this miscarriage of justice and allowed the relatives of these men to sue Miguel Díez for damages they had suffered.[96]

The council found Miguel Díez guilty of many other cruelties. He had tortured and sentenced individuals without cause and had confiscated other persons' property and ordered them whipped without allowing appeal.[97] In summary, after one dismisses all those charges not proved against Miguel Díez, the specific charges of which he was found guilty demonstrate that he was a greedy, malevolent, licentious man who "won the affection of some by lavish gifts of lands [and] Indians, and ... the enmity of others by stripping them of their spoils."[98] However, when one compares Zorita's original sentence with the one imposed by the Council of the Indies, it is apparent that the lesser punishment decreed by the council is explained by the presence of Miguel Díez at court to plead his case with the aid of powerful friends and relatives.

An example of lesser punishment imposed by the council is the following:

Charges 113, 114, 115, 116, 117, 118, 119, 120, 121, 122, 123 ... that in violation of the laws he ordered certain expeditions, especially the one made by Alonso López de Ayala to the province of Matrina and the expedition of Captain Luis de Manjarres to the province of Tamalameque; and the expedition led by Manjarres to the province of Xegua and another for the punishment of the Indians in the province of Cartagena. Also, concerning the banishment of two caciques of Turipana and Copala and the statement that he made a present of a woman named Carrillo, the daughter of the cacique of Turipana, and promised *encomiendas* to those who went with Manjarres to Tamalameque; and the expedition led by Juan Ortiz de Zárate to settle and pacify the Indians of Cimitarra and the punishment of the caciques sent to him by Licentiate Leonardo de Santisteban, as well as the crimes committed by Baltasar de Parraga and the negligence of Alonso López de Ayala in punishing the said Parraga. For these crimes, Licentiate Zorita condemned him to pay 4,000 pesos. We revoke the sentence and find him gravely guilty [*culpa grave*].[99]

Despite the many hardships Zorita suffered between his departure for the mainland and his return to Santo Domingo, his mission can be considered a success insofar as it led to the removal of Miguel Díez and the completion of the *residencia* by Juan de Montaño, the stern, wrathful judge who replaced Zorita as investigating judge in New Granada.

Zorita's mission to New Granada can be considered a failure because he never completed his judicial investigation, although various factors not of his own making account for this failure. Most important was the crown's decision to send Zorita to New Granada as *juez de residencia* without government powers. The resulting division of authority between Zorita and the newly created royal tribunal of New Granada was taken advantage of by Miguel Díez and his allies and caused Zorita endless problems.

Zorita might have gained the cooperation of the Audiencia of Santa Fe had it differed in composition. Because the senior judge, Gutierre de Mercado, died before reaching Santa Fe, and another judge, Francisco Briceño, was sent to investigate affairs in Popayán, only two judges assumed the government of New Granada. One of these judges (Góngora) was related to Miguel Díez; the other (Galarza) was "obligated to him for many great favors."

Reflecting on the legal maneuvers of the audiencia, the hatred of the settlers, his hazardous and debilitating journeys, his financial plight and material losses, Zorita may have regretted being appointed a royal commissioner in a remote section of America. Despite these obstacles his judicial review and the letters he wrote the crown provided important information to the Council of the Indies. Zorita's efforts in behalf of the Indians of Tierra Firme resulted in royal intervention that eventually brought some order to the colony. Zorita's investigation of Indian affairs and related matters also sheds light on the economy, society, and politics of New Granada in the 1540s.

Because settlers in this period relied excessively on Indian tribute and service, they regarded themselves as feudatories, neglected agriculture, and lived in general poverty. Because no central authority existed in New Granada and the distance separating the mainland from the Audiencia of Santo Domingo made for government by remote control, power devolved upon provincial governors and private individuals who ignored the New Laws.

When the crown attempted to eliminate frontier disorder by centralizing the administration of New Granada in the hands of Miguel Díez, it made a poor choice and only added to the politics of conflict. The crown made an equally bad choice of judges when it replaced Miguel Díez as governor by creating the Audiencia of Bogotá.

Scandals, thefts, and other disorders were common in New Granada before and after Zorita's mission to the mainland. Zorita's replacement, Montaño, enforced the New Laws, but his excessive zeal and total assumption of power in New Granada eventually cost him his life. Judge Francisco Briceño, investigating affairs in Popayán, authorized new expeditions into Indian territory and even took part in them. According to Bishop Juan del Valle's ecclesiastical judge, many Indians were killed on these plundering expeditions, and unheard-of cruelties were committed against the Indians. Briceño also allowed *encomenderos* to assess excessive tribute and assign Indians to work in the mines. After sentencing Sebastián de Benalcázar to death for killing Marshall Jorge de Robledo, Briceño married Robledo's widow and offered to resign his office to keep the *encomienda* she had inherited. Having acted like "a first conqueror in everything he did" while in Popayán, Briceño in Santa Fe was so servile to Montaño "that throughout the kingdom he was known as Montaño's woman."[100] Doctor Juan Maldonado, so friendly to Miguel Díez, proved to be a bitter enemy of Don Pedro de Heredia when he took the governor's *residencia*.[101]

In form and character government in New Granada resembled that of other frontier areas in the colonial period. Local rule prevailed until the 1540s; town magistrates and provincial governors acted without supervision from a representative of the crown. Local and provincial offices were monopolized by *encomenderos* who looked after their own interests and disputed over Indians, lands, and titles. Lack of restraints created a social environment that allowed ambitious settlers to "cast the conventional moralities to the four winds and live in a world more in accord with their own sweet but selfish desires."[102]

In its desire to replace local tyranny and anarchy with peace and order, the crown sent royal agents to end civil strife in New Granada. The powers given a royal official like Miguel Díez, combining as they did supreme judicial and political authority of the kingdom, made it possible for this self-seeking man to become an absolute tyrant. The powers given the honest and energetic Zorita were more limited and conflicted with those given the Audiencia of New Granada, thus limiting his prospects of success.

The crown not only granted greater or lesser powers to royal judges like Miguel Díez and Zorita but punished the offenses of its royal agents in different ways. The crown suspended Miguel Díez from office for three years for hanging three innocent men; it beheaded Juan de Montaño for executing two men, one of whom was clearly guilty of killing several Panches Indians. Apparently royal agents like Alonso Luis de Lugo and Miguel Díez were cleared of all charges or received significantly less severe punishment for offenses because they were men of wealth and members of great houses and had friends at court.

It is also clear that in the eyes of the crown offenses of the sort committed by a royal official like Miguel Díez did not detract from the honor and esteem of other members of a great house. In 1578, Miguel Díez's first cousin Doctor Lope Díez Aux de Armendáriz assumed the presidency of the Audiencia of New Granada. This son of the lord of Cadereyta, Don Luis Díez Aux de Armendáriz, was suspended from office within two years. Another of Miguel Díez's relatives, Don Lope Díez de Armendáriz, Marqués de Cadereyta, was viceroy of New Spain in the years 1635–40.[103]

CHAPTER 4

Alonso de Zorita: Protector of the Guatemalan Indians

THE NEW LAWS of 1542–43 established the Audiencia of Guatemala. Originally situated on the boundary of Nicaragua and Guatemala, it had political and legal jurisdiction over all of Central America and the provinces of Chiapas and Yucatán in modern Mexico. Alonso Maldonado, the court's first president and a native of Salamanca, was recommended for the office by Fray Bartolomé de Las Casas. Maldonado set up the royal tribunal in the Honduran town of Valladolid in the Valley of Comayagua. Finding the town's facilities inadequate and the distance from Guatemala, Chiapas, and other provinces inconvenient, the judges moved to Gracias a Dios, about thirty leagues from Valladolid. On May 15, 1544, the audiencia convened formally; two days later the judges proclaimed the New Laws.[1]

The judges failed to enforce the New Laws. Las Casas, bishop of Chiapas since 1543, and Bishop Antonio de Valdivieso of Nicaragua wrote the crown that greater crimes were committed under the audiencia than under the rule of former tyrants. The devil had filled the judges with ambition and greed, they believed, and the land would soon be ruined if the enforcement of the New Laws were not entrusted to the bishops.[2]

Other prelates and settlers stated that Maldonado and the judges looked after their personal interests and neglected the welfare of the Indians. Cristóbal de Pedraza, bishop of Honduras and Protector of the Indians, asserted that President Maldonado had the best *encomiendas* in the province. Rented out as carriers, Maldonado's Indians labored incessantly and were virtual slaves; a black overseer whipped them as they carried loads of merchandise from the highlands to the sea.[3] Other persons declared that Maldonado granted *encomiendas* to relatives, servants, and friends; he and those he favored exploited anywhere from one-third to one-half of all the Indians in Honduras. Meanwhile, Maldonado, whose assets may have been worth 300,000 pesos, had written the crown that "the New Laws seemed very harsh." Having received news of the Pizarro revolt in Peru and the many protests against the New Laws in Mexico, he and the judges had decided not to implement the new code pending the crown's instruction.[4]

The reform of the audiencia began with Maldonado's removal and replacement by Alonso López de Cerrato. After taking the judges' *residencias* in 1548, Cerrato reported to the crown that the judges had been the first to disregard the New Laws and other royal decrees. The new president fined and refused to reinstate Judge Diego de Herrera, "a troublesome and greedy" man. *Oidores* Juan Rogel and Pedro Ramírez de Quiñones continued to serve in their offices, but Cerrato was well aware of their faults. The crown rewarded Maldonado—no reformer and the most important *encomendero* in Honduras—with Cerrato's former post, the presidency of the Audiencia of Santo Domingo.[5]

Soon after assuming the government of Guatemala, Cerrato sought a new location for the royal tribunal. In Gracias a Dios the judges lodged in private houses, and the president lived in the parish priest's house, where court sessions were also held. Moreover, this isolated, shabby mountain community of eighteen settlers lacked adequate food supplies and fodder, the climate was unhealthy, and no physician was available.[6] In contrast, Santiago de Guatemala was more centrally located in a fertile, level valley where all the fruits and edible plants of Spain except grapes gave good yields.[7]

Following the crown's approval that the audiencia be moved, Cerrato accepted Bishop Marroquín's offer that the judges use his episcopal palace as a court and place of residence. In 1550, a year after Cerrato moved the audiencia to Santiago, the crown approved the purchase of Marroquín's houses.

Santiago de Guatemala

Santiago de Guatemala probably had no more than 100 *vecinos* when it became the seat of the audiencia. It witnessed rapid population growth, however, and by 1572–73 the city housed 500 settlers, 70 of whom were *encomenderos*. The Spaniards lived in houses that were solidly constructed and attractive because of the abundance of building materials: lumber from pine, oak, and cypress groves, and sufficient stone, lime, gypsum, roof-tile and brick.[8]

Founded in 1534 by Bishop Marroquín, the cathedral was the most imposing building in the city. Completed in 1680, it even-

Fray Bartolomé de Las Casas (1484–1566). This missionary to the New World and champion of the Indians was a major source of Zorita's ideas and writings. (Courtesy of Marqués de Lozoya, *Historia de España*)

tually had fifty windows, eight chapels, and seven great doors. An image of the Virgen de Piedad stood on the high altar and was popularly known as Nuestra Señora del Socorro; it was believed that she warded off public disasters and brought rain.[9] In the 1570s the regular clergy consisted of fewer than sixty Dominican, Franciscan, and Mercedarian friars. The Indian hospital built by the Dominicans enjoyed an income of 400 ducats a year; the hospital founded by Bishop Marroquín to care for Spaniards had an annual income of 2,000 ducats.

The center of the city was the *plaza mayor*. Facing this square was the building in which the audiencia and the treasury officials conducted business. Along the sides of the large plaza also stood the bishop's residence, the cathedral, and the city hall. The main plaza was filled by day with people shopping at the local market, watching bullfights, participating in festivals, or hearing the town crier proclaim the news. Local color was enhanced by a fountain, a gallows, and a whipping post. Public executions and floggings aroused excitement and compassion and also served as morality plays teaching the uncertainty of life. Given the legalist temper of the times, the spectators undoubtedly felt that a reminder of these harsh penalties deterred potential criminals.

In 1550 conquerors and first settlers monopolized the offices of Santiago's municipal council. Town magistrates and aldermen were invariably also *encomenderos*. Don Francisco de la Cueva, a relative of the duke of Albuquerque and son-in-law of Pedro de Alvarado, had an *encomienda* of 2,100 Indians. Juan Pérez Dardón's *encomienda* had 1,150 Indians; Bernal Díaz del Castillo had 370.[10]

Like other members of the city council, Bernal Díaz held Indian slaves and resented the "instigator" of the New Laws, Fray Bartolomé de Las Casas. He and other city officials in 1543 wrote the king that Las Casas was an "unlettered, unholy, envious, vainglorious, hateful, and factious friar."[11] In 1551, Bernal Díaz was the town council's representative before the Royal Council of the Indies. On orders of the cabildo and the *encomenderos* he petitioned for the perpetuity of the *encomienda* and against the freeing of the Indian slaves. Like other settlers, Bernal Díaz lived with an Indian woman but refused to marry her. Although he treated his Indians well, his view was typical of the conquerors' intolerance of the natives.[12] Bernal Díaz, however, differed from other conquerors turned city officials in Santiago in two ways: he had literary ambitions, and he was friendly to Zorita.

Bernal Díaz, the author of the *True History of the Conquest of New Spain*, "found that Zorita was often fair and certainly incorruptible at a time when most government officials were interested only in enriching themselves." Bernal thought enough of Zorita to consult him, and, as far as we know, Zorita was the first man other than Bernal's family members and closest friends to read the beginning of his manuscript.[13]

City council members (called an exclusive, aristocratic group by Ernesto Chinchilla) guarded their prestige and resented favors to more recent arrivals.[14] According to Severo Martínez Peláez, relations between the cabildo and the Indians who provided goods and services to the city were typical of a society composed of masters and servants.[15] Mestizos were also denied access to the economic and political strata occupied by Spaniards and Creoles; members of this group labored as artisans, shopkeepers, apothecaries, tanners, and millers. All occupations were organized into guilds controlled by the cabildo, but craftsmen and artisans had no representation in the city council.[16]

The settlers of Santiago had an abundance of cheap labor; within the district the jurisdiction of the city were some 140 Indian villages with 22,000 tribute payers. Indian slaves freed by Cerrato inhabited the settlement of Santa Fe, next to the city. In the early 1570s, this village had approximately 800 households. All the inhabitants worked as journeymen in various crafts, lived like Spaniards, and were considered "useful and profitable for the commonwealth." Santa Fe's Indians remembered their emancipator after his death by founding a chaplaincy in the monastery of Santo Domingo, where Cerrato was buried; each year they honored him with solemn funeral rites.

Zorita's "Relation of the Things of New Spain," completed in 1585, describes the fertile and productive land of Guatemala, its abundance of cacao and balsam, and the nobility of the city of Santiago. His description is derivative, for Zorita uses as his source Fray Toribio de Motolinía's comments on Guatemala found in the latter's *Memoriales*.[18]

Being the seat of government, Santiago was well provisioned, and its merchants and officials directed a lively trade. The city had an ample tract of level, fertile ground with many fruit trees. Motolinía claimed that on this land the citizens harvested more than 600 *fanegas* of corn from one *fanega* of seed.[19]

Zorita also noted that on September 10, 1541, water contained in the crater of the Volcán de Agua rushed down its slope (either from an earthquake or from heavy rains) and destroyed the first

Santiago (Ciudad Vieja).[20] To avert a future deluge, the new city of Santiago (Antigua) was founded half a league from the old city and built by Indian laborers.

The royal order of July 11, 1552, appointing Zorita judge in the Audiencia of Guatemala stated that he was to replace Licentiate Juan Rogel. Judge Rogel, in his forties, was regarded as a passionate man whose conduct was the subject of gossip in Santiago. He had told Cerrato that he was quitting his post to go to Spain and marry; he departed for the Peninsula with no intention of returning to the New World.[21] On the same day that the crown appointed Zorita judge in Guatemala, a similar order was sent to Juan de Galarza, who was to replace Judge Tomás López. Zorita was spared from serving in the same court with this bitter enemy by Galarza's judicial inquiry and subsequent death at sea.[22]

Alonso López de Cerrato was undoubtedly pleased when he learned that Zorita was replacing Rogel. Although the Dominican chronicler Antonio de Remesal considered Rogel "a wise and educated man" and "a friend of peace and justice," Bishop Marroquín and President Cerrato did not share this opinion. Marroquín stated that Rogel was a licentious, opportunistic judge who had tarnished the reputation of the royal tribunal.[23] Cerrato had reappointed Rogel after taking his *residencia* in 1548; shortly thereafter he wrote the crown that Rogel was so vengeful with those who had testified against him that Cerrato could not trust his legal decisions.[24]

Before leaving Santo Domingo for his new post, Zorita contracted new debts to pay for the move. After failing to find a ship bound for Puerto de Caballos, on the coast of Honduras, he, his brother, and a certain Diego Ramos bought a small caravel. On this small boat Zorita, Juan Pérez, and their wives and households sailed for the mainland in the summer of 1553.[25]

Having reached the tropical pesthole of Puerto de Caballos, the prudent Zorita sought to recoup his investment of 200 *pesos de minas* by selling his share in the caravel. This sum and the money he had spent to caulk and repair the vessel were lost when he could find no buyer with ready cash; he finally bartered his share in the boat to a sailor for a cask of island wine worth thirty pesos.

Another ship took Zorita and his party to Golfo Dulce, on the coast of Guatemala. This hot, humid, unhealthy point of disembarkation of passengers and goods bound for the Central American interior consisted of a few warehouses. There Zorita met a friend he had known in New Granada who was packmaster of a mule train operating between the coast and Santiago. After arranging to have his baggage transported in the pack train, Zorita hired horses for the long trip to the capital. He and his party made their way under the steady fall of rain across some fifty leagues of wild uninhabited country before reaching Santiago de Guatemala.[26]

The Audiencia of Guatemala officially recognized Zorita on September 20, 1553.[27] During the thirty-one months he served in Guatemala, Zorita visited most of the province; his three tours of inspections included one *visita* of two months, another of three months, and one lasting eight months. Traveling where no Spanish judge had ever been, Zorita inspected Indian villages never seen except by their *encomenderos*. He corrected abuses, made head counts, and moderated tributes. He gathered isolated Indians into towns. Zorita met with opposition from the corrupt secular clergy, his fellow judges, the *encomenderos*, and the Franciscan order, rivals of the Dominicans in Guatemala, but won the support of President Cerrato whose principal aim was implementation of the New Laws.

Although reformers like Cerrato and Bartolomé de Las Casas lauded Zorita for enforcing the provisions of the New Laws, his efforts on behalf of the Indians did not markedly ameliorate their condition. Unfortunately for the pro-Indian cause, honest judges were rare in Guatemala; they ultimately departed while the *encomenderos* remained. When Alonso de Cerrato's death was followed by Zorita's transfer to the Audiencia of Mexico, the colonists met with little opposition from the judges who replaced them and thus eventually gained most of their objectives.[28]

Reforms and Rebellions

Before Zorita's arrival in Santiago, President Cerrato had successfully implemented many of the New Laws. He had freed all slaves held by persons who could not show title of legitimate possession. He had done so despite the cabildo's insistence that the colonists had treated Indian slaves as their own children. Cerrato also ended slave traffic in the province of Guatemala, moderated tributes, limited the use of Indian carriers, and punished gross infringements brought to his attention. The improvement in the natives' condition by 1550 is largely attributable to his courageous reform efforts. A measure of Cerrato's success was the hostile reaction of the Spanish settlers.[29]

In his study of the early economic history of Central America, Murdo J. MacLeod has attempted to assess the importance of

Cerrato's reforms. He concludes that Cerrato's success in elimi-
nating the Indian slave trade in Guatemala was based on several
factors, the most important being the gradual disappearance of
the slave trade between Guatemala and Panama and Peru. Mac-
Leod notes that following the end of the first Peruvian conquests
and civil wars Spaniards in that region employed local Indians to
work in fields and mines. Meanwhile, Panama's black population
had grown, and Indian porters and laborers were being replaced
by them and by locally bred mules and horses.[30]
Another factor in the end of the slave trade was according to
MacLeod, increased local demand for labor at a time of rapidly
declining Indian population:

About 1545 the *encomenderos* of the coastal province of Izalcos were
beginning to cultivate the large plantations of cacao, which were to give
them such prosperity in the following two or three decades. One can
assume that their reaction to the export of the local servile populations
was the same as that of the *encomenderos* in Nicaragua and Honduras;
they did not want to lose their work force.[31]

MacLeod also points out that by the time Cerrato arrived in
Central America, slavery "had already fallen to a minor position,
far surpassed as a method of controlling labor by the now
flourishing *encomienda*." Spanish slave owners in Chiapas complained bitterly when Cerrato liberated their charges, "but others
in the Spanish community enthusiastically helped local friars to
settle the newly 'freed' slaves in *encomienda* villages. One man's
poison was thus another man's meat."[32]
Cerrato's reform of the *encomienda* system was, in MacLeod's
opinion, "superficial" in that it did not alter the colony's
economic structure: "There is evidence that he applied the New
Laws only to those who lacked power in the community and that
he completely ignored his other charge, that of breaking up the
large *encomiendas* and distributing them among the poorer
Spaniards."[33]
In Cerrato's defense it must be said that as president of the
audiencia he had to administer a vast area controlled by *encomenderos* who acted as one in defense of their interests. Other members of the audiencia were for the most part not interested in
reform, and Cerrato himself lacked the physical stamina needed
to bring about all the changes he desired. Approximately sixty
years old in 1550, Cerrato had lost all his teeth and was frequent-

ly bedridden with a kidney stone that caused him great pain. With "insufficient strength for so much work," Cerrato desired only to return to Spain "to die as a Christian."[34] Further, Cerrato had attempted reform in a colony where cruelty to Indians may have been far worse than elsewhere. Historian Hubert Howe Bancroft, still a formidable authority for students of Central America, believed that, in comparison with other regions, "nowhere was oppression carried to such an extreme as in Guatemala."[35] Finally, if Cerrato's reforms were essentially superficial, the Cabildo of Santiago, spokesman for the *encomenderos*, would not have attacked them so fiercely.[36]

Cerrato certainly had his failings. Blunt of speech and lacking in charm, he was "as stern and humorless a man as the master who sent him, Philip II."[37] He was also excessively loyal to family and friends and unquestionably practiced nepotism. Various critics, including Bartolomé de Las Casas, denounced Cerrato for granting *encomiendas* and official posts to his relatives, friends, and retainers.[38] Still, as William L. Sherman observes, there is no evidence that Cerrato took "advantage of his position for personal gain."[39]

Zorita, well aware of Cerrato's shortcomings, wrote the crown in 1560 that Cerrato had served the king so well in the Indies that "none has surpassed him and few have equaled him." Zorita also noted that Cerrato had died poor.[40] Another contemporary, Fray Tomás de la Torre, wrote the king in 1553 that Cerrato had his faults

both in matters pertaining to the government as well as in being very friendly to his relatives, as Your Highness will have learned. But we have never seen anyone in these parts who equals him in his help to the Indians and in carrying out the orders of Your Majesty. I believe it would be much easier to correct his faults than to find another who has the good that is in him.[41]

When Zorita arrived in Santiago de Guatemala, Cerrato was under attack by virtually the whole Spanish community. Zorita, as zealous as Cerrato in enforcing the New Laws, inherited Cerrato's enemies and suffered the same recriminations.

The town council of Santiago resented the reform efforts of Cerrato and Zorita. Municipal officers angrily defended the *encomendero* cause and had considerable power in spite of the audiencia's formal supremacy. In his study of Santiago de Guatemala, Christopher Lutz observes that the presence of the royal

tribunal in the city gives one the impression that from 1549 the
city council, dominated by conquerors and their sons, relinquished power over Indians in the Valley of Guatemala to the
audiencia, which had superior jurisdiction in regulating Indian
labor and tribute. This was not the case, for the town council's
alcaldes ordinarios also served as district governors (*corregidores*)
of the valley. These two town magistrates alternated the position
of governor every six months and had civil and criminal jurisdiction in the towns of the *corregimiento*.[42]

Even before the removal of the audiencia to Santiago, the town
council had condemned Las Casas and the New Laws and defended Indian slavery. After the move of the royal tribunal, the
cabildo filed a protest with Cerrato regarding the commission
given him to free the slaves. When Cerrato ignored this letter, the
town council sent Bernal Díaz del Castillo to Spain to lobby
before the Royal Council of the Indies. The cabildo's petition for
the perpetual *encomienda* and the continuation of Indian slavery
was denied. The settlers now began to "spread rumors of rebellion and other alarming reports out of Peru and Mexico."[43]

By late 1554 the feud between the city council and the audiencia had become so intense that Cerrato claimed that the magistrates plotted to kill or imprison him and Zorita to prevent their
visitas and the reduced tribute assessments His Majesty had
ordered. Figures in the plot, according to Cerrato, included the
alcaldes Santos de Figueroa and Juan Pérez Dardón; *regidores*
Don Francisco (de la Cueva), Francisco López, Alonso Gutiérrez,
Cristóbal Lobo, Bernal Díaz del Castillo; *factor* (Francisco de)
Ovalle; and *procurador* Juan Vázquez.[44]

City council members felt that Cerrato and Zorita did not
understand their problems. Before the arrival of these two reforming judges they had enjoyed a free hand with the Indians;
now their slaves had been freed, and the income from their
encomiendas was threatened.

Francisco de la Cueva, according to Bartolomé de Las Casas,
had an income of 4,000 *pesos de oro* a year from his large *encomiendas*. The holdings of other municipal officials were not as
large, but none was poverty-stricken. Juan Pérez Dardón's *encomienda* had 1,150 Indians, but the 107 slaves he held in 1549
were taken from him. Francisco López, with an *encomienda* of
123 Indians, felt that Indians should be terrified of their betters,
for otherwise they would not obey. Cristóbal Lobo, who held
526 Indians, bitterly resented Cerrato's actions; in 1551 he com-

plained that when he had written the Council of the Indies about Cerrato's nepotism the president had deprived him of forty Indian slaves he used to mine some 1,000 *pesos de oro* a year.[45]

City officials may have talked of killing Cerrato and Zorita, but most likely the alleged murder plot was no more than threats reflecting local bitterness toward the judges. Cerrato was undoubtedly correct, however, when he stated that the conspirators had sworn "to prosecute me in this *residencia* and destroy me so that other judges appointed to the Audiencia will not dare to do anything against them from now on."[46]

No attempt to kill Cerrato or Zorita was made, but the judges, recalling the murder of Bishop Antonio de Valdivieso, may well have feared for their lives. Valdivieso, appointed to the bishopric of Nicaragua in 1544, soon denounced the government of Don Rodrigo de Contreras. In letters to the crown and from the pulpit, Valdivieso, a Dominican friar and great admirer of Bartolomé de Las Casas, castigated the greed and cruelty of the colonists, opposed the governor, and called for the enforcement of the New Laws.

Valdivieso and the Dominicans asserted that Contreras and his family owned as much as one-third of Nicaragua; it is certain that the governor had transferred his *encomiendas* to his wife and one of his sons to evade the clause in the New Laws forbidding royal agents and clerics from possessing Indians. Moreover, as late as 1548 Contreras had allowed slave exporters to brand free Indians and ship them out of the province. Valdivieso's reform efforts and his recommendation to the crown that the Indians be placed under the control of missionaries met with firm opposition from the governor. Settlers, fearing for their property, backed the governor, stating that "they wanted no prelate except to say Mass, and preach to suit their fancy."[47]

Valdivieso's complaints against Contreras, Indian slaveholders, and *encomenderos* had a solid factual basis. In the 1520s, Spanish conquerors estimated that Nicaragua had 600,000 Indians. In 1544 only 150,000 Indians, or 30,000 tributaries, remained. Nine years later, Fray Tomás de la Torre, the Dominican provincial in Guatemala, stated that the 7,000 tributaries still alive in the province would soon die out because they were worn down with excessive payments and labor.[48]

Alonso de Maldonado, ignoring Valdivieso's complaints, allowed Contreras to keep his *encomiendas*. The situation changed when Cerrato replaced Maldonado as president of the audiencia. One of Cerrato's first acts in Gracias a Dios was the judicial inquiry of Contreras. The new president confiscated Contreras's Indians when he found that transfer of the governor's *encomiendas* had been made after passage of the New Laws. Don Rodrigo left for Spain to seek redress.

During Contreras's absence news came to Nicaragua that the Council of the Indies had upheld Cerrato's sentence. To avenge the family's loss and the insult to their father, Contreras's two sons enlisted more than 300 disgruntled Spaniards, including exiles from Peru. After murdering Bishop Valdivieso in León, the rebels plundered the episcopal treasury and the royal exchequer. They then sailed for Panama; after taking possession of Nombre de Dios and the province, they planned to make their way to Peru. The rebels briefly threatened Panama before being defeated by its loyal citizens in April, 1550.[49]

The Contreras revolt, Bancroft observed, rid Nicaragua of many dissatisfied vagrants and adventurers, most of whom found graves in Panama. A problem with which Cerrato and Zorita had to contend was the "residuum of floating ruffianism" remaining in the audiencia district. This motley mass included many mestizos, mulattoes, and blacks who wandered from village to village exploiting the Indians. Moreover, these vagabonds and runaways living among the Indians incited them against their parish priests. "All those who are scattered throughout the land," wrote Zorita, "come to join those in rebellion, as was seen when Juan Gaitán rebelled, gathering people from San Salvador to Nicaragua and committing great robberies and offenses in the Indian villages, encouraging them to rise up."[50]

Four years after the Contreras revolt the audiencia ordered Zorita to lead troops against the rebel Juan Gaitán. The rebellion began when various Spanish settlers of Honduras and Guatemala —aware that the bulk of the royal forces were committed to maintaining order in recently pacified Peru—saw an opportunity to throw off their allegiance to the crown "and live in liberty, ridding themselves of the obligation to pay their many debts."[51] Approximately forty Spaniards, joined by blacks and runaways who chose to become highwaymen, were led by Juan Gaitán, a Spaniard expelled from León by Licentiate Juan Caballón, the city's *alcalde mayor*.

On Wednesday night before Pentecost the rebels attacked the Spanish settlement of San Miguel.[52] They seized all the citizens' arms and horses, plundered the town, and proceeded to the villa of Jerez de la Frontera, where they did the same. The bandits then decided to capture the gold mines of the district, but changed their plans after learning that they would meet stout resistance. Instead they went to the city of León to kill Caballón.[53]

News of the outbreak reached Zorita in Los Izalcos, where he was taking the *residencia* of the *alcalde mayor* of Sonsonate. The audiencia sent word that he should immediately take command of all the horsemen he could summon and proceed to Nicaragua to put down the insurgents. In less than eight days Zorita had iron lances made and summoned all the Spaniards of the region to horse and arms. He was about to lead his force into Nicaragua when he learned that the "tyrants" led by Gaitán had been routed.[54]

On September 6, 1554, the audiencia wrote the crown that Licentiate Caballón had had sufficient warning of Gaitán's intention to attack León to be able to call the town's citizens to arms before the rebels entered the capital. Caballón suffered two serious wounds in the furious battle that took place in the central square, but he defeated the rebels. Among those captured and hanged were Juan Gaitán, two other leaders, and some dozen rebels. Caballón's forces eventually caught most of those not immediately apprehended, but some made their way back to Indian villages.[55]

Although the rebels were few, the Gaitán insurrection had caused great alarm throughout Guatemala. The audiencia's investigation of the uprising revealed that many of the participants had come from Mexico. Expecting that disorderly elements would continue to come to Guatemala to cause trouble, the royal tribunal established a watch at the border so that all unidentified persons might be turned back. The judges also ordered the district magistrates to eject all suspicious persons and vagabonds from their jurisdiction.

The violent tenor of life in Guatemala was not solely attributable to frustrated rogues and rebels. The arbitrary conduct of upper-class individuals also caused injury and struck fear in the hearts of government officials and law-abiding citizens. The career of Diego de Robledo, the audiencia secretary, offers an example of such conduct. As royal notary, Robledo "prepared the pleas [*procesos*] with the supporting evidence in writing, in due form for presentation before the court." Because he did the routine legal work, Robledo was aware of all cases pending before the court and had the opportunity to manipulate evidence supplied by litigants and their witnesses. Motivated by vengeance, passion, and greed, Robledo enriched and protected himself and his relatives and ruined various *vecinos*.[56]

Robledo was related through marriage to many influential citizens. His brother-in-law Luis de Estrada had an income of 3,000 pesos from the *encomienda* of Anacantlan [Zinacantlán?] in Chiapas. Robledo's mother-in-law and her husband, Gonzalo de Ovalle, held various *encomiendas*, including two in Chiapas granted them by Cerrato and the godfather of Robledo's child, Judge Pedro Ramírez de Quiñones. Other relatives of Robledo included Juan Vásquez de Coronado, Carlos Bonifaz, Gaspar Arias de Ávila, Gaspar Arias Hurtado, and Juan Pérez de Dardón.

In a letter to the crown, Francisco de Morales, who had worked closely with Robledo as *relator* of the audiencia, noted that the notary's relatives held the best and largest *encomiendas* in Guatemala and did whatever they wished, "as was confirmed by Doctor Zorita in the *visitas* he made of the land." In addition to exploiting Indians, Robledo's relatives oppressed, threatened, and even murdered their enemies with impunity.[57]

In Chiapas, Luis de Estrada and a retainer killed one Francisco Ramírez. Although Estrada and his servant were clearly guilty of murder, Robledo, acting as notary in the case, prepared the defense pleas for the accused, and the defendants went free after being given a light sentence. Robledo's brothers-in-law had killed another man, one Alonso Enríquez; they had also severely wounded *regidor* Francisco Girón, but had never been brought to justice for these crimes.[58]

Robledo usually ruined his enemies through the power of his office or had his wife's brothers avenge him, but Morales declared that Robledo had personally attempted to kill him. Morales, who had served as *escribano mayor* of the Cabildo of Santo Domingo before coming to Guatemala with Cerrato, was left without defenders when Cerrato died and Zorita was transferred to the Audiencia of Mexico. Harassed and fearing for his life, Morales accepted Zorita's invitation to become *relator* of the court in Mexico City.

In 1563, Morales observed that, although he had lived in Mexico for the past eight years, Robledo continued to hound him. "Seeking to have me returned to Guatemala so that he and his relatives can kill me, as they have done to others," Robledo had sent a number of summonses to Mexico falsely charging Morales with various crimes. Morales asked the crown to allow him to rebut these charges before the Audiencia of Mexico.[59]

The secular clergy, headed by Bishop Francisco Marroquín, also opposed the reform efforts of Cerrato and Zorita. Cerrato resented the priests' exploitation of the Indians and allegedly called them "scoundrels, thieves, robbers and similar names."[60] The Dominicans and Zorita shared this opinion. Yet, as William Sherman notes, "Marroquín, backed by the secular clergy and most of the *vecinos*, was an opponent Cerrato could ill afford."[61]

Bishop Marroquín was at best a moderate reformer, opposed in principle to Indian slavery and the use of Indian carriers. Brought to Guatemala by Pedro de Alvarado, the bishop recommended to the crown that the Indians be given in perpetuity to married *encomenderos* who would live and die in grace and comfort in Guatemala.[62] The bishop of Guatemala was at worst an opportunistic, venal, scheming politician.[63]

On his arrival in Guatemala, Marroquín supported Las Casas and his movement; later Marroquín became severely critical of him. When Las Casas threatened to excommunicate settlers who refused to give up their slaves, Marroquín assured them that he would grant them absolution. Although Marroquín had been appointed Protector of the Indians, he sympathized with the *encomendero's* alleged plight. In 1548, Cerrato wrote the king that the tribute assessments made by President Alonso Maldonado and Marroquín were so heavy that they could not be met even if the Indian population were doubled.[64]

Marroquín was also unwilling or unable to correct or punish those clerics who mistreated and exploited the Indians. When an Indian woman bleeding profusely from her bruised mouth complained to Cerrato and the bishop, Marroquín refused to punish her assailant, the dean of the cathedral chapter.[65] On another occasion Zorita inspected a large village of Indians in the coastal province of Izalcos, where he learned that the cleric placed in charge of the Indians by Marroquín had sold them wine from a room filled with jugs. Zorita sent the bishop a report after ordering the culprit to appear before Marroquín for correction. On arrival at Santiago after completing the inspection, Zorita discovered that the "punishment the bishop gave the priest was to press me urgently to be kind enough to allow the cleric to return to the village." Ignoring Zorita's objections, Marroquín permitted his return. Zorita noted that his inspection report was disregarded

by both the bishop and the audiencia and that the priest remained
in the village.[66]

Dominican provincial Tomás de la Torre was also very troubled by the conduct of the priests. Declaring that they "taught no
doctrine other than public drunkenness," he complained to the
king that neither Bishop Marroquín nor the audiencia corrected
them. The friar had been "exceedingly importunate" with Cerrato about the matter, but the president, who was "almost desperate about the situation at times," had told Fray Tomás that he
could not correct the clerics' faults and even feared to write to
His Majesty about the problem.[67] His complaints of inaction were
confirmed by Zorita; he wrote that his colleagues referred to the
priests as "fathers of the country, because they always favored the
clerics and held the religious and Indians in low esteem. And
because I was of the opposite opinion, they called me a destroyer
of the land."[68]

The faults of the secular clergy, tools of the *encomenderos*,
were many. Fray Tomás was of the opinion that the Indians
would lose nothing if the priests left Guatemala. Ignorant of their
languages, the clerics preached to them through young Indian
pages (*pagezillos*); rare was the priest who confessed his
parishioners and did more than celebrate Sunday Mass and bap-
tize children.

The poorest villages gave their parish priests more than 1,000
pesos de minas yearly. The clerics could save this amount and all
the crown or the *encomenderos* gave them, because the Indians
also provided the food and services needed for their persons,
servants, and horses. Fray Tomás alluded to the fleshly appetites
of the secular clergy by noting that some priests refused to accept
the women assigned to their houses to bake bread if they were
old. A bishop's tax required each village to give its priest a
chicken and a turkey daily, but many Indians had told Fray
Tomás that they were ordered to give four turkeys daily. The
priests struck them in the face with any turkey found to be not of
the proper weight.

Some priests had grown so wealthy that they owned up to
eight horses apiece; exploitation of Indians was so profitable that
many canons and other high church officials had left their
assigned bishoprics and illegally entered Guatemala to plunder
the Indians. Other Guatemalan church officials had left offices to
become village priests, presumably to make more money. Some
Indian villages had been divided between two or more *encomen-*

deros, and Fray Tomás knew of one village containing forty households that had three churches to support. None of the three priests celebrated mass or preached; each claimed to be the principal curate and attempted to get the other priests' parishioners to attend his church.

A major obstacle to solution of the Indian problem in Guatemala was the ambivalent posture of the crown. On the one hand, the crown professed to seek justice for the Indians and accepted advice in this search from the mendicant orders. On the other, it was very sensitive to the material needs and interests of the Spaniards.

Cerrato, backed by the Dominicans, was aware that giving the Spaniards a free hand meant oppression and destruction of the Indians. Early in 1548 he wrote to the king that he had yet to find a Spaniard in Guatemala who did not have five or six Indian men and women in his house. The Indians had to render personal service in addition to paying tribute. Although they were called house servants (*naborías*), they were actually slaves; their masters parted parents from children and wives from husbands. Conditions in Chiapas were especially bad. In that province *encomenderos* hired out their Indians to owners of sugar mills; one mill easily consumed 2,000 lives yearly.[69] Cerrato also quickly realized that the Indians of Guatemala gave far too much in tribute payments. When he learned that they were usually at least a year behind in their payments to their *encomenderos*, Cerrato abolished the payment of delinquent taxes and ordered the judges to inspect all Indian villages to moderate excessive tribute assessments.[70]

In his letters to Cerrato the king instructed him to enforce the crown's decrees abolishing slavery and praised him for forbidding *encomenderos* of Chiapas to rent their Indians to the sugar planters. But in specific disputes over Indian tribute payments and the treatment of Indians by their *encomenderos*, the contradictory stand of the crown became apparent.

Although the king desired that Indians be treated as free men, in 1552 he said that he had been informed that a large number of Mexican Indians in Guatemala paid no tribute. Natives had joined the Mexicans to enjoy the same freedom—a freedom that made them lazy and vicious. The judges should investigate the matter immediately. The order also stated that, because native Indians had departed to join the Mexicans, excessive tribute payments were being made by the remaining Guatemalan Indians. According to Bancroft, on July 20, 1532, the crown had exempted Mexican Indian auxiliaries in Guatemala from paying other than a nominal tribute of two *reales*. The order was ignored, and the Mexican Indians were so badly treated that there were barely 100 survivors in 1547.[71]

In 1553 the crown noted that Francisco Girón, *regidor* and *procurador general* of Santiago de Guatemala, claimed that the colonists had suffered great injury when Cerrato and the judges forgave delinquent tribute payments. After consulting with the Royal Council of the Indies, the king ordered the audiencia to resolve the matter quickly in such a way that the litigants should not suffer injury. An addendum noted that *encomenderos* accused of mistreating their Indians had been immediately deprived of their charges. The king, in agreement with the Council of the Indies, recommended that "those found guilty of committing excesses against the Indians for the first time should be punished but not deprived of their Indians."[72]

Before Zorita's arrival in Guatemala, the crown had ordered the audiencia to ensure that every Indian in its jurisdiction work at a trade. Farmers should sow and work the soil so that there would be an abundance of food supplies in the colony. Idle or landless Indians should be put to work in the fields or at city trades. In 1554 the audiencia wrote the crown that an *oidor* had recently been dispatched to the Indian villages to compel the Indians to cultivate the soil. Furthermore, because the crown had ordered that tribute payments be more justly assessed, many of the villages in the audiencia district had been inspected. After the Indians were counted and their lands appraised, this report was used to fix the new tribute. The judges also noted that His Majesty had sent many letters and decrees to the audiencia informing the tribunal of his great desire to gather the Indians into villages. Once the scattered Indians were congregated into pueblos, they could be more easily instructed in the doctrine and civilization of the Holy Catholic Faith.[73]

Zorita as Reformer

Zorita, as William L. Sherman observes, "held views on Indian labor similar to those of Cerrato." His vigorous prosecution of Spanish lawbreakers soon made him a marked man. Soon after he began implementing the New Laws, Zorita was accused of using Indian carriers illegally on his journey from Golfo Dulce to

Santiago. Aware of the seriousness of the charge, he immediately prepared a report for the Council of the Indies. His witnesses before the audiencia all agreed that his baggage had been carried to Santiago by mule train.[74]

Zorita's *probanza* of August 6, 1554, was supported by Cerrato in a letter to the crown. Cerrato praised Zorita, declaring that "in all the Indies there is not another judge who compares with him in desiring to serve Your Majesty." Zorita's great zeal in completing the crown's decrees had aroused the settlers' hostility; they had accused him of being rude and of giving *repartimientos* to his favorites, and "they now rejoice about a legal summons sent him by the Crown's *fiscal* concerning some emeralds, because they already forsee his banishment and destruction."[75]

Cerrato's last comment about a summons concerned a charge made by Miguel Díez and the town council of Santa Marta. They claimed that when Zorita went as *juez de residencia* to New Granada, he had pressed treasury officials in Santa Marta to sell at public auction some 190 emeralds in the king's strongbox. When these emeralds, which belonged to the crown as its share of the royal fifth on treasure, were put up for sale, Alonso de Torrijos, a citizen of Santa Marta acting as Zorita's agent, offered seventy-five pesos for the lot. It was alleged that no one at the auction dared bid higher because they knew that Zorita wanted the jewels. Although the emeralds were worth 6,000 *castellanos*, they were sold to Torrijos; he gave them to Zorita, who sent them to his wife in Santo Domingo.[76]

Zorita refuted this accusation when his *residencia* was taken in Santo Domingo by President Alonso Maldonado. He was found innocent of the charge, but Maldonado referred it to the Royal Council of the Indies at Zorita's request. Zorita stated that even before his judicial inquiry in Santo Domingo he had become aware of Miguel Díez's attempt to excuse his own crimes in New Granada by vilifying Zorita's character before the council. In his correspondence with the crown and in other depositions Zorita observed that Juan Ortiz de Zárate, the crown's *factor* in New Granada, had allowed Miguel Díez to take the emeralds and 25,000 pesos worth 9,000 pesos in fine gold he had brought to Santa Marta from the New Kingdom. Miguel Díez and Zárate had spent the gold illegally and would have done the same with the emeralds if they had been worth anything. Moreover, Zárate had priced the emeralds before depositing them and found them to be worth very little. Zorita confirmed the poor quality of the jewels after purchasing them by having three crown notaries estimate their worth. He also pointed out that the emeralds were of such low value that they had been in the king's strongbox for five years before being sold to Torrijos. When Zorita had inspected the contents of the strongbox, the treasury officials had offered to sell him the emeralds for forty pesos. Zorita had declined the offer and had also refused to give permission for their sale. He did, however, buy the jewels from Torrijos when the latter repented having bought them.[77]

In his defense of Zorita, Cerrato wrote the crown that he had seen the emeralds and would not give thirty ducats for them. The charge was obviously false, an example of the stream of false accusations against pro-Indian officials flowing from the colonies to the king and the Council of the Indies. Cerrato observed that he had suffered a thousand blasphemies from his enemies, and they hated him as though he were Mohammed and thirsted for his blood like hungry lions. Were his enemies correct, he said, he would deserve to be drawn and quartered, but, he added, "I assure Your Majesty that they complain more about Zorita than they do about me." Condemning Zorita's critics, Cerrato equated their accusations with "wickedness, treason, and insurrection." None of the accusations had any substance; they stemmed only from Zorita's "great zeal in carrying out Your Majesty's decrees."[78]

Uncertain whether he would be acquitted of the charge relating to the emeralds, Zorita also felt keenly the enmity of the Spaniards in Guatemala. He considered asking for permission to leave for Spain, but Cerrato finally dissuaded him. In Santiago, Zorita lived for a long time under the shadow of Miguel Díez's allegation, for the Council of the Indies did not dismiss the charge until April 29, 1557, some time after Zorita was appointed *oidor* in the Audiencia of Mexico.[79]

Despite the burden of his worries, Zorita proved a capable and devoted agent of Cerrato. His defense of the Indians inevitably caused the cabildo to complain of his overbearing ways. "One case," says Sherman, "concerned a 'poor *conquistador*' who used an Indian on a two-day journey from Santiago to carry a six- or eight-pound package of hardtack, which was consumed along the road. Zorita proceeded against him in such a way that the *conquistador* died saying the *oidor* was killing him."[80] The affair reminds one of Cerrato's statement, "Your Majesty and his Council know that people in the Indies have little more to do than think up accusations [against Cerrato and other pro-Indian officials]."[81]

Zorita lost his only friend and protector in the audiencia when Cerrato died on May 5, 1555, a few days before the completion of his *residencia* by the new president, Antonio Rodríguez de Quesada.[82] The latter has been given credit for planning Indian reforms and completing "the organization of Indian towns, hoping thus to compel the natives to adopt a civilized mode of life and establishing in them a municipal government similar to that of Spanish settlements, the offices being confided to their hereditary chiefs according to rank." Bancroft, however, notes that "the carrying into effect of Quesada's plans was in great part due to the efforts of Zorita."[83] Quesada's own role in resolving the Indian question in Guatemala was probably minimal for a number of reasons. He had little time to implement Indian plans, for he did not assume the office of president until August 13, 1555, and died in October of the same year.[84] Moreover, Zorita and Quesada had many differences, and Zorita had begun gathering the Indians into villages even prior to Cerrato's death.

During Cerrato's presidency, Zorita was initially commissioned to make reports concerning the resources and population of Indian towns held by the crown or the *encomenderos*.[85] Zorita was also to report whether the Indians were being abused or had suffered harm from crown officials, *encomenderos*, friars or clerics assigned to Indian villages, *corregidores de indios*, or other persons. Having made a head count of the Indians, Zorita was to question them with respect to the following points:

1. Had a friar or cleric been assigned to the village for the purpose of teaching the Indians Christian doctrine? Had any Indians died before being confessed or baptized? Had the Indians contributed anything for the ornaments and other things needed for the church and service of mass, or for the maintenance of the cleric or friar? Was the church properly equipped, and had anyone impeded the teaching of the Holy Catholic Faith?

2. Had the Indians of the village been abused physically or verbally? Had the Indians been assigned *calpixque* (overseers)? Were any Spaniards, mestizos, or blacks living among the Indians, and did they abuse them?

3. Had any of the above persons killed or injured any Indians or forced them to flee the village, depriving them of their houses, wives, children, and cultivated fields?

4. Had any crown official, *calpisqui, corregidor, encomendero*, or his children, servants, or blacks or other persons living in the village forcibly taken any woman from an Indian noble or commoner to have sexual relations with her or do her other harm?

5. Had the Indians of the village been sold wine, hatchets, machetes, horses, dogs, or any other thing by any of the above persons or their agents? If so, what were the Indians charged for these goods? Further, had the Indians been coerced by threats to purchase back those items they customarily gave as tribute payments?

6. Had the royal officials or the *encomenderos* forced the Indians to pay them more than the assessed tribute? If the Indians paid only the assessed tribute, had these payments been made before the time set for payment? Also, when the Indians went to Santiago de Guatemala to pay the tribute or for other reasons, did they take gifts to the officials, and had agents been sent to the village to ask for gifts?

7. Had the Indians, in violation of crown decrees, been forced to make tribute payments in years of poor or lean harvests?

8. Could the tribute given to the crown's officials be paid without undue hardship and oppression? If the tribute was excessive, had any Indians fled the village? Did the Indians pay their tribute in what they grew on their own lands, or were they obliged to take their products elsewhere to barter for what they paid in tribute?

9. Had any of the Indians been hired out to merchants or other persons or forced to work in the mines or as burden bearers? Further, did they carry the tribute on their backs to Santiago or elsewhere? When they went to pay their tribute, were they detained and made to carry earth, adobes, wood, hay, and water or forced to perform other services? Had any of them died or become ill from doing work of this kind?

10. Had any *encomendero* ever sold or exchanged his village? If so, had the Indians been obliged to give money or products to complete the transaction? At a later date, had the Indians been made to pay their new master the money he had given for them?

11. Had any of the officials, *encomenderos*, friars or clerics, *calpixque*, or *corregidores* maintained a jail in the village equipped with shackles, stocks, or chains? Had any Indians been told to the prejudice of royal or ecclesiastical jurisdiction not to fear the royal tribunal, magistrate, or bishop, nor to answer to anyone except the above persons in any matter?

12. Had the royal officials or *encomenderos* injured lawful caciques by appointing others in their place?

13. Had the said officials or *encomenderos* appointed alcaldes or *alguaciles* in the village, giving them symbols of authority (*varas*) so that they might arrest or imprison or intimidate the Indians and make them do what they ordered?

14. Had the said officials, *encomenderos*, or other persons taken any of the Indians' ground plots, houses, orchards, or lands used for raising corn or cacao? Had the property of Indians who died without heirs been taken by any of the above individuals?

15. Had the Indians involuntarily sold land or other property to royal agents, *encomenderos*, or other persons?

16. Had royal officials, *encomenderos*, or other persons diverted water used for irrigation by the Indians?

17. Had the Indians involuntarily given alms or been assessed tithes? Had the Indians been made to pay money, cacao, horses, or other things under the pretext that they were contributing to the village church or its adornments or other communal undertaking?

18. Had the royal officials, *encomenderos*, or other persons been given women to act as housekeepers or wet nurses, causing these women to cease caring for their own children and households?

19. Had the Indians been forced to make cloth for royal officials or *encomenderos*? If so, had these Indians been gathered up and confined in a workshop?

20. Had any of the royal officials, *encomenderos*, or other persons used the Indians' land to raise cattle, hogs, sheep, goats, or pigs? Had the Indians been made to act as herdsmen or been obliged to build enclosures or sheds for these animals?

21. Had the Indians been forced to cut and saw wood, furnishing beams, boards, and wood for windows and doors to the royal officials and *encomenderos*? Had the Indians constructed houses for these persons in the village, in Santiago de Guatemala, or in another place? Had the Indians built boats or canoes for these persons? If so, had the Indians been forced to leave their houses, wives, and children, and were they paid anything for their work?[86]

Two years before Zorita took up his duties in the audiencia, the Dominicans serving as missionaries in Guatemala, Honduras, Nicaragua, and Chiapas were organized into the province of San

Vicente de Chiapas. Provincial Tomás de la Torre directed the work of the friars in founding convents adjacent to Vera Paz. (known as Tuzulutlán, or the Land of War, before its peaceful conquest by Las Casas). Zorita supported the Dominican program and did what he could to advance their work. An example is Zorita's letter to the caciques of Chalchutlán, Balamiha, Abebah, Acul, Chaxa, Cuneb, and Balancolob on behalf of the order. Zorita also befriended the Mercedarians; in 1555 he and Judge Pedro Ramírez wrote the crown that these friars had first begun the work of converting the natives in Chiapas and Santiago de Guatemala. They noted that the convent the Mercedarians were building in Santiago was very humble and could not be completed unless the king aided them.[87]

In Guatemala, Zorita sought information from the friars about the history of the Indians and their condition in pre- and post-Conquest times. In his *Brief and Summary Relation* he described the decline of the Indian rulers of Utlatlán, a province bordering on Guatemala:

I made a visit of inspection to this province. With the help of a religious of the Dominican Order, a great servant of Our Lord and very fine interpreter, a most learned and eloquent preacher who is now bishop [probably Fray Tomás Casilla], I learned with the aid of paintings that they had which recorded their history for more than eight hundred years back, and which were interpreted for me by very ancient Indians, that in their pagan days they had three lords. The principal lord had three canopies or mantles adorned with fine featherwork over his seat, the second had two, and the third one.[88]

Zorita

saw their lords ... in the town of Utlatlán. ... They were as poor and miserable as the poorest Indian in the town, and their wives fixed their tortillas for dinner because they had no servants, nor any means of supporting them; they themselves carried fuel and water for their houses. The principal lord was named Don Juan de Rojas, the second, Don Juan Cortés, and the third Domingo. They were all extremely poor; they left sons who were all extremely poor; they left sons who were all penniless, miserable tribute-payers, for the Spaniards do not exempt any Indians from payment of tribute.[89]

Zorita often visited the Dominican convent in Santiago and discussed the work of the friars with Fray Domingo de Vico, a religious "greatly admired by everyone for his devout and exemplary life." This saintly man was constantly ill from doing great penance and because he worked so hard preaching to the Spaniards and instructing and converting Indians not yet under Spanish rule and those Negroes and Indians in the service of the Spaniards.[90] From Father Vico, who had been sent to Tuzulutlán by Las Casas in 1545, Zorita learned that the warlike Indians of this region had been brought to peace by Fray Luis Cáncer.[91]

Bancroft writes:

As early as 1550, attempts at the pacification of the adjacent province of Acalá were begun by the Dominicans of Vera Paz. For a time their efforts were successful, but finally incited by their neighbors and allies, the majority of the natives refused to receive the friars, and in 1555 the combined tribes destroyed the only mission thus far established and murdered Father Vico, the originator of the attempt, together with his companion Father López, and a number of converted Indians from Vera Paz.[92]

Acalá, which was two or three days' travel from Vera Paz, was described by the friars as a tiny, rugged province with a very hot climate. The Dominicans had destroyed many idols in Acalá, instructed Indians, and begun to build churches. But "the Devil was vigilant" and had the native priests bring in the neighboring Lacandón Indians to kill the friars. One morning the Lacandones attacked and burned the friars and their converts out of their rude shelter (*casilla*), killing thirty-three converts. One of the friars was sacrificed before their idols; another was killed in the church. Among those killed was "Fray Domingo de Vico, the prior of Santo Domingo de Cobán in Vera Paz. He was a saintly, learned, zealous man who preached and administered the Sacraments in seven Indian languages. The other friar was Fray Andrés, a virtuous missionary newly arrived in the land."[93]

At the request of Bishop Marroquín and the Dominicans the audiencia commissioned Zorita to gather the Indians into towns. Once in communities they were to be instructed by the friars; the salaries of Indian officials would be fixed; each town was to have a communal strongbox and a jail; lands were to be assigned the Indians; and tributes were to be justly assessed.[94]

Friars Tomás de Cárdenas and Juan de Torres give a description of one of Zorita's tours of inspection to the mountainous country of Sacapulas. In March, 1555, Zorita began working in a region of the sierra so rugged and harsh that no Spaniards other than the Dominicans had ever gone there. For six months Zorita visited Indian settlements hidden in ravines containing no more than "eight, six, or even four houses or hovels."[95] He found people so isolated that it would have been almost impossible to instruct them in the Christian religion. His inspection revealed that they kept a great number of idols, some hidden but others openly displayed in public buildings, as had been the custom before or just after the Indians' baptism.

Now that Zorita had gathered the Indians together, wrote the friars, they had less opportunity to practice idolatry because the friars visited them more often. They could now be instructed in the Holy Catholic Faith and in civilized ways of life.

The friars judged Zorita's work worthy of praise, and they recommended that the work of congregating the Indians should continue. If they continued to be dispersed into small groups in the mountains, "it would be impossible to build churches or to have adornments for the service of the Mass. They would not even have a small bell to gather them to hear the word of God; instead they would use an infernal wooden instrument which they play in their native dances, an indecent, ugly thing to use as a bell."[96]

Zorita's tours of inspection were made

in rain, on foot, without sleeping in a bed, and he toured regions where horses could not ascend with packs. Because he traveled on foot, through country where there are great variations in climate, he lost the skin from his face, hands, and feet. In some places they must build bridges and had to cut rafters to make them, and he helped with his own hands, for he had no Indians to assist him, only his own people, and they even lacked sufficient food.[97]

Because many of the Indians continued to worship their ancient gods, Zorita and his Dominican supporters confiscated and destroyed their idols, in an effort to stop pagan practices. The Indians soon learned to respect and fear Zorita. Told that he would punish them severely if they refused to give up their idols, they turned them in in great numbers. They did the same in places that Zorita did not personally visit when they learned that he was in the vicinity.[98]

To encourage them to adopt a civilized mode of life by establishing municipal governments, patterned on cabildos, Zorita was to tell the Indians that His Majesty desired them to be treated like his sons. The king did not wish them to pay more tribute, "nor as much as they formerly gave their *caciques* and lords." Also, Zorita was to tell them that all tribute payments were to be waived for one year so that the congregated Indians might more easily build their houses.[99]

Learning that the Indians gathered into towns were exempt from tribute for one year, the *encomenderos* immediately condemned the policy. Precisely because Zorita made his *visitas* "with great diligence, observing Your Majesty's decrees favoring and defending the Indians with all his power, endeavoring to have the *encomenderos* punished for their iniquities and tyrannies," the settlers' enmity toward Zorita grew.[100] "Finding him incorruptible they had recourse as usual to false reports. Witnesses for any purpose could be cheaply bought; and since he woud not yield the Spaniards determined to drive him from the province."[101]

Fellow judges would not defend Zorita. Encouraged by the silence of the *oidores*, the *encomenderos* read and displayed their false charges in the streets of Santiago; then they sent them to the crown and the Royal Council of the Indies.[102] "There was much hostility," wrote Fray Juan de Torres, "shown him even in the audiencia, for what he does in his *visitas*—doing justice and not going beyond what Your Majesty has ordered—is hampered by the tribunal. He is disfavored and discouraged in everything, and thus the *encomenderos* have dared to draw up an *información* condemning his actions."[103]

In his report to the crown Fray Tomás de la Torre observed that the *vecinos* of Guatemala had a royal decree allowing them to take affidavits against any royal official, the witnesses' testimony to be taken by anyone they chose:

Although Your Highness issued this decree with the good intention of ensuring that the judges take great care in performing their duties, it has greatly weakened the authority of the Audiencia. Yet a greater injury has resulted from this royal decree, for the citizens now have their foot in the throat of the royal tribunal and the judges are under pressure to avoid doing what they are required to do in order to please those who can greatly injure them.[104]

Zorita also incurred the hostility of the Franciscan friars. The Franciscans in Guatemala considered Zorita a creature of the Dominicans, and he became involved in their disputes. As early as 1537, Franciscans and Dominicans argued over the degree of prebaptismal instruction required by Indian converts. Las Casas criticized wholesale baptism as practiced by Fray Toribio de Motolinía and other Franciscans. Another dispute, which arose as early as 1550, had to do with rights of possession to sites for churches and convents: "These being them determined by the simple act of taking possession, many towns and districts were seized upon by the ecclesiastics which they could not attend to themselves, and would not permit their rivals to control."[105]

In a bitter report to the crown recommending that Zorita be barred from making tours of inspection, the Franciscans stated that for eight years before the judge's *visitas* their order had gathered Indians into towns from mountains and caves to Christianize them, in accordance with a royal decree. But Zorita, lacking experience and ignorant of the Indians' languages, had destroyed the Franciscans' towns on the pretext of improving the natives' lot.

Not satisfied with destroying the Franciscan reductions (*reducciones*), they charged, Zorita had forced many Indians to settle in alien lands: "Because he moved them from *tierras frías* to *tierras calientes*, many Indians died or became ill. The worst part of the move is that it took place in winter under heavy rains." Zorita, according to the Franciscans, had moved the Indians from pleasant and fertile lands to sterile areas. Aware of the injuries they would suffer from resettlement, some refused to leave their homes. Because force was necessary to accomplish their removal, Zorita, the friars charged, "ordered their houses or villages burned." As the fires destroyed the Indians' houses, it seemed to them that the day of the last judgment had come. Husbands escaped to the mountains from fear of being slain; their wives were captured, bound, and marched down the road with their children on their backs. One poor woman, her husband having fled, was raped by the Indian conducting her to a new settlement. Her two small children, witnesses to the attack, died from fear and despair. Another, unwilling to move, hanged herself in desperation. "The worst part is that the aforesaid Zorita has been told by the religious that these evil actions hurt them, but he has not desired to receive advice except from those who incite and counsel him to destroy the land."[106]

In addition to desolating and burning the land "as a perpetual memorial to himself," Zorita, said the Franciscans, had refused to punish the horrible vices of the Indians. "The other day he arrived at some villages where there were sodomites. When their parents and relatives asked him to punish them because they consider sodomy an abominable thing, he would not do it. As a result the Indians give themselves up to this vice with greater vigor than before."[107]

Custodio Antonio Quixada and Friars Pedro de Betanzos, Juan de la Cruz, and Alonso Mella ended their letter by requesting that

Zorita be replaced as *visitador* by another judge who would punish the horrendous vices of the sodomites. Zorita should also be "removed from this land as quickly as possible."[108]

The letter describes Zorita's activities between March and August, 1555, but is dated January 1, 1556, suggesting a tardy awareness of Zorita's offenses. It is also curious that the Franciscans asked the king to send Quesada a decree removing Zorita from Guatemala, for audiencia secretary Diego de Robledo wrote the crown on April 10, 1556, that Quesada had died in the month of October, 1555, leaving only Judges Ramírez and Zorita.[109] In any case, the Franciscans praised Quesada as an impartial, experienced man who had adopted all the measures needful for maintaining the Indians in peace and justice. In contrast, the order considered Zorita (like Cerrato before him) a tool of the Dominicans.

Aware that the settlers, supported by the Franciscans, were intent on ridding themselves of Zorita, the Dominicans wrote several letters justifying the work of this "upright, well-intentioned, and zealous judge." They declared that Zorita, hated by the colonists because he did not favor them, had greatly profited the Indians temporally and spiritually by gathering them into towns. Dominican friars now resided in these communities; the religious knew the Indians' languages and were on friendly terms with the natives, who had recourse to the friars in all things. Although one *encomendero* charged that an Indian had hanged himself when Zorita attempted to move him, the Dominicans residing in the villages had never heard of such a thing. Moreover, all the witnesses supporting this charge lived in Santiago de Guatemala at the time Zorita was gathering the Indians together. Zorita's actions, condemned by the *encomenderos*, were instead praiseworthy, for he had "opened the road and gate allowing the friars to uproot the tares and plant the word of God." In these *visitas*, Zorita had not killed or dismembered anyone, "nor ordered any punishment except that which a father uses to correct his son." If force had been used by Zorita, it had been necessary, for "to a sick man all medicines have a bad taste":

It is true as a rule that the things that are best for us offend us most. If everything had to depend on the consent and pleasure of [the Indians] ..., neither we nor our predecessors could do anything for their betterment; nor could Your Majesty do anything good here or in Spain if he had to await the approval of each individual. None of the Indians want to leave their pestilential hollows and inaccessible crags and the huts their fathers left them, for there they bury the bones of their grand-fathers, or worse yet, they place their household gods in the foundations of their huts, calling these penates the hearts of their houses.[110]

The settlers' complaints, dismissed by the Dominicans as false and capricious, were believed by Quesada, who supported the Cabildo of Santiago in a legal deposition they brought before the audiencia. After Quesada's death, Zorita had difficulties with Pedro Ramírez de Quiñones, who as senior judge acted as president of the royal tribunal. On November 5, 1555, Zorita formally requested that he be excused from serving in suits pending before the court. He asked that Licentiate Ramírez appoint a person in his stead until His Majesty should decide whether he should continue in office.[111]

In a letter to the crown Ramírez noted that his differences with Zorita had been cleared up quickly and had not disturbed the court. He attributed their difficulties to the support Quesada had given the town council of Santiago in their attempts to drive Zorita from the province. After Quesada's death, Zorita felt that Ramírez had also encouraged his foes to attack him. Seeking to end their quarrel and maintain the unity needed in the court, Ramírez convinced Zorita that he was not his enemy; they remained on good terms up to the time the king favored Zorita by promoting him to the Audiencia of Mexico.[112]

The Audiencia After Cerrato's Death

In his letter to the crown, Pedro Ramírez, who acted as president of the audiencia until the arrival of Juan Martínez de Landecho in 1559, complained of the disfavor shown him by the crown. He noted that when President Cerrato had asked for permission to retire the request had been granted. Then the crown had favored Judge Tomás López with a better appointment after he had served only four years in Guatemala. Now Judge Zorita had improved his position by being appointed to the Audiencia of Mexico. The crown, wrote Ramírez, had shown him no such consideration. It had merely decreed that at Quesada's discretion he might be suspended from office without leaving it; if he were to be found innocent of the charges listed against him in his *residencia*, he might be reinstated. Was this his reward for thirteen years of faithful service to the king? During his period of service he had complied with the provisions, decrees, and letters of His Majesty, giving liberty to more than 5,000 slaves, moderating tributes, forbidding personal services, punishing many other excesses, and executing reforms that no other audiencia had done as well. Although Cerrato had received credit for these reforms, Ramírez had completed the work. "While my companions gained profits and increased their estates, I was pacifying the land and punishing disturbances."[113]

Diego de Robledo also mentioned the quarrel between Ramírez and Zorita, but this *encomendero* and enemy of Fray Bartolomé de Las Casas used it to discredit Zorita.[114] Claiming that the quarrel between the judges was Zorita's fault, the secretary of the audiencia wrote that Zorita's new assignment to the Audiencia of Mexico appeared to be a very good thing, "for the majority of the people here hate him." Zorita, said Robledo, had become very angry when various individuals sent a report against him to the Council of the Indies. He also wrote that, although Zorita wanted to favor the Indians, the judge had little experience or knowledge needed for this task, and the audiencia had received many complaints from the natives concerning things that Zorita had done during his *visita* of the districts of Santiago.[115]

Robledo also claimed that Zorita and the tribunal's public prosecutor Juan Márquez had quarreled bitterly. This man, said Robledo, had won Zorita's bitter enmity when he notified the judge of the royal inquiry concerning the emeralds Zorita had purchased in New Granada. Cerrato and Zorita, Robledo asserted, had abused Márquez,

as appears in the *residencia* taken of Cerrato, and they finally sent him to Nicaragua where he died. Licentiate Márquez left his wife and three small children in this city, the eldest being seven years old, poor, and in want. It would be a great act of charity for Your Majesty to remember them. Because Zorita and his friends are so supreme here, justice cannot be done in anything that touches them.[116]

In Guatemala, Zorita had won Robledo's bitter enmity and had been subjected, according to Francisco de Morales, to the secretary's false reports; these were so "shameless and audacious" that they deserved great punishment.[117] After moving to Mexico, Zorita became aware that Robledo still sought to blacken his name and wrote the king refuting the charges.

Before Cerrato's death Zorita learned that a royal *cédula* had been sent to the audiencia ordering that Robledo's *encomienda*, "not the worst of those held there," should be vested in the crown. Zorita did not mention how Robledo, an official of the royal court, had acquired the Indians he held. However, Francisco de Morales and Bartolomé de Las Casas wrote the crown that President Cerrato, in violation of the New Laws, had favored the secretary with this *encomienda*.[118]

Although the royal order forbidding crown officials to hold *encomiendas* had been in the court's possession for almost two years, it had not been executed, "nor did anyone dare to discuss it or bring it forth." Convinced that the New Laws' provision requiring crown officials to give up their Indians, reinforced by a specific order, should be implemented, Zorita attempted to carry it out. President Cerrato and the judges "stated they were not commissioned to act as crown attorneys, and because it was not their responsibility they would not investigate the matter."

When the judges informed Robledo of Zorita's attempt to have the decree enforced, the secretary began to show his enmity for the judge. Made aware that his colleagues refused to obey the decree, Zorita did not bring the matter up until the presidency passed to Quesada, who, although he vacillated when Zorita told him that it was not right that Robledo should hold Indians and receive tribute in violation of the king's will, finally permitted Zorita to present the royal *cédula* to the audiencia. Robledo attempted to block the hearing by declaring Zorita a hostile judge whose prejudiced evidence should not be admitted. The other judges, however, found Robledo's legal arguments without foundation and refused to halt the proceeding. After the evidence was presented, the court took Robledo's *encomienda* but only pro forma, for the judges allowed the secretary to continue to receive tribute payments after he posted a surety bond. Robledo must have appealed the audiencia's decision, for Zorita noted in 1558 that Robledo "believes that Your Majesty will return the Indians to him and he does not want them to forget their home."[119]

Robledo subsequently attempted to have Zorita dismissed from the bench as a prejudiced judge in other matters, with no other basis than the charge that Zorita had caused the loss of his *encomienda*. Robledo also organized "alliances, groups of gossip mongers, and *juntas*" against Zorita and formed part of the band of *encomenderos* seeking to drive him from the province. Zorita noted that false witnesses and notaries were plentiful for whatever the secretary planned against him for two reasons: Zorita had angered the *encomenderos* because he had assessed the tributes of a good part of the province and executed the king's decrees, and Robledo, as the secretary of the royal tribunal, had all the notaries in his power.[120]

The audiencia's efforts on behalf of the Indians suffered a setback, first by the death of Cerrato in 1555, second by Zorita's move to Mexico in 1556, third by the appointment of Licentiate Juan Martínez de Landecho as president of the tribunal in 1558.[121]

Landecho, a native of Biscay, assumed the presidency in 1559; he lacked two qualities assigned by the Dominican chronicler Antonio de Remesal to his predecessor's government: Christianity and justice.[122] Landecho, described by Remesal as opinionated, haughty, and unscrupulous, took bribes from litigants and stole from the exchequer. He despised friars, clerics, and the Indians; showed little respect for the bishops; afflicted the Indians with new taxes and tributes; and rewarded his relatives and favorites.[123]

The Cabildo of Santiago enthusiastically welcomed Landecho, a gentleman by birth and education, and he satisfied their expectations. Members of the town council petitioned the crown to order that the political administration of the Indians be vested exclusively in the president. The granting of this petition eliminated the need of the settlers to control a majority of the judges: "The colonists were jubilant that the humane measures of Cerrato and of Zorita, which their constant efforts had hitherto failed to accomplish, were now certain of defeat."[124]

Antonio Mejía, a native of San Martín de Valdeiglesias, arrived in Guatemala in midsummer, 1556. He was transferred from the Audiencia of Mexico to replace Zorita after he and another judge, Francisco de Herrera, had disturbed the peace of that tribunal by engaging in constant quarrels.[125] Mejía allegedly arrived in Guatemala with a human pack train of fifty to seventy Indians carrying excessive burdens. Unlike Zorita, he used Indian porters on his tours of inspection to carry his bed, clothing, and food; his *residencia* revealed that he had not paid them anything for their work. According to William Sherman, Mejía "was involved in scandalous love affairs with various women" and had sexual relations with indias, mestizas, and mulatas.[126]

One of Mejía's first duties in Guatemala was the *visita* of San Salvador. He found the Indians of this region so overburdened that one village of about twenty inhabitants was paying 600 *pesos de maravedís* a year in tribute. He moderated payments by halving them, but asserted that this still left the Indians overtaxed, for the smallest tribute amounted to ten or twelve *tostones de a cuatro reales de plata*, or five or six silver pesos.

Mejía claimed, however, that *encomienda* Indians paid very little to their Spanish masters in comparison to what they paid the friars, especially the Dominicans. The Dominicans, said he, had asserted their lordship so thoroughly over the land that the judges had to be compliant. They used the royal jurisdiction freely, for they had their own courts and had appointed Indian sacristans (*fiscales*) in each town. The *fiscales* had been given *varas de justicia* and had authority to whip and punish the Indians publicly. These agents of the friars collected great quantities of tribute in money, *mantas*, and other goods. The friars also required the Indians to plant fields of corn, which, after harvest, the Dominicans sold for their own profit.

When Mejía forbade the Dominicans to exercise royal justice or to levy tributes and exactions he considered excessive, the friars lodged a complaint before the audiencia. The two friars who appeared before the court were accompanied by many Spaniards who protested that Mejía had unreasonably reduced tribute payments and appraisals of what the Indians were able to pay. The other judges had suspended Mejía's reductions and told him to quit annoying the friars.

In a long report to the crown justifying his actions, Mejía singled out the Dominicans and the *encomenderos* as the chief obstacles preventing reform in Guatemala. Having castigated the friars, Mejía stated that among the many examples of excessive tribute demands by *encomenderos* were the two Izalco pueblos held by Juan de Guzmán and Francisco Girón. Efforts by other judges—including Zorita—had failed to remedy the crimes committed against the Indians of Los Izalcos by their master, their masters' relatives and black overseers. Each village had between 150 and 200 Indians; each was taxed at the rate of 4,000 *pesos de maravedís* a year. "Although the assessments are very excessive, they are minor in comparison with the evil treatment and oppressions the Indians receive from Juan de Guzmán and others." Mejía noted that the audiencia had ordered Guzmán to correct the situation, but he had ignored the command because he was so powerful and enjoyed the protection of numerous relatives and servants at Los Izalcos, some thirty leagues from Santiago.[127]

Mejía's estimate of payments by Indians of Izalcos is confirmed by Fray Tomás de la Torre. In 1553 he wrote the crown that Izalcos and Tacurcalos (Tacuxcalco) had each been divided into two pueblos. These four villages were worth 8,000 pesos in tribute. Although under the care of clerics, the Indians had no polity (*lustre de policía*) or Christianity. He recommended that a Franciscan or Dominican monastery be built there, for "if there were friars to teach them politeness and reason tempered with charity, six Medinas del Campo would arise there in six years, since it is the richest cacao-producing land in the Indies."[128]

Juan de Guzmán, first cousin of the former audiencia president Alonso Maldonado,[129] exercised justice in the fashion of a feudal lord over his Indians. In violation of royal ordinances, he resided with his household, relatives, and intimates in the pueblo of Izalco and assessed payments on an individual basis. When asked by Mejía to explain how he fixed tributes, Guzmán refused, stating only that assessments had been done by his command. Because no witnesses were present, Guzmán could collect whatever amount he wanted. Mejía attributed the failure of the Indians to complain about their exploitation to the fact that Guzmán so thoroughly intimidated them.

Guzmán's fields, planted in cacao and other crops, were scattered among the Indians' cultivated fields. In violation of the New Laws, the Indians were forced to work in Guzmán's cacao fields. At harvest Guzmán's servants and black slaves picked the fruit belonging both to Guzmán and to the Indians in the adjacent fields. Mejía, who questioned whether Guzmán had legal title to any of the land he cultivated, estimated that his income from cacao and other crops was in excess of 5,000 *pesos de maravedís* a year. The *oidor* also noted that Guzmán held another *encomienda*; this was the town of Macholoa, "which because of the many *tamemes* (Indian porters) it provided was worth 2,000 *pesos* a year."[130] President Alonso Maldonado had given Macholoa to Guzmán in violation of royal decrees forbidding an individual to hold two *encomiendas* at the same time.[131]

Mejía believed that Mexican Indians were treated better than were those of Guatemala. Irregularities of the type he described to the crown were, said Mejía, absent from Mexico because *corregidores* in that audiencia district resided in the Indian towns, and the friars and clerics were paid a salary. In contrast, no *corregidores* or magistrates lived in the villages of Guatemala, a land much more extensive and less populated than Mexico. Indians in Guatemala never saw "another king or lord except their friar or cleric," and excesses went unchecked. To improve conditions in Guatemala, Mejía recommended that at least two or three judges should make tours of inspection on a regular basis throughout the land; they should be paid a decent salary because prices in the land were six or eight times greater than those in Castile.[132]

Mejía reported that the Indians, in addition to being whipped by order of the Dominicans, were forced to construct huge buildings and do other work without being paid for either the labor or the materials used. The Indians did this work during the growing season, to the detriment of good harvests, and the friars provided neither food nor water during the workday. Many Indians had died from overwork, and Mejía claimed to have seen a number killed or injured during construction of a chapel in the patio of a church. He was shocked by this inhumane exploitation because he had recently arrived from the Audiencia of Mexico, where it was not the custom "to allow the religious to build so many great works with Indian labor without permission and payment."[133]

Mejía may have exaggerated the misdeeds of the Dominicans. Bancroft notes that this order was "the object of Mejía's special dislike, and he subjected them to such annoyance and persecution that they were on the point of abandoning the province of Guatemala."[134] However, one cannot ignore his claim that tribute payments in Guatemala were generally excessive,

at least in comparison to New Spain, for there I cannot recall having known a married Indian to pay above eight or ten *reales* a year. I know that some tributary Indians in this district pay more than 70 *pesos de maravedís* in tribute to their *encomenderos*, equivalent to 800 *reales de Castilla*. Although Your Majesty may find this incredible, I testify to this as an eyewitness.[135]

Fray Bartolomé de Las Casas confirms Mejía's remarks on this subject. Indians of Guatemala, Honduras, and Nicaragua were greatly burdened with tributes which daily grew more intolerable. Zorita, "a just man who feared God," had moderated tributes, but other judges, "partisans and friends of the *encomenderos*," had revoked all his humane measures.[136]

Other statements by Las Casas in the same document serve to confirm Mejía's charges against the *encomenderos*. However, it appears that Mejía, if he ever had been a reformer, soon ceased to be one in Guatemala. Las Casas said that in San Salvador Mejía spent more time finding a wife than relieving the poverty of the Indians. The judge quickly became a kinsman and friend of the colonists, leaving the Indians more oppressed than they had been before his arrival. Although they were more than ten leagues from fishing sites, Mejía allegedly commanded the Indians to give a certain number of fish each week to their lords. In some villages Mejía may have ordered half the available Indians to work the fields and *estancias* of their Spanish masters three times during the year. Each laborer was to be paid one *real* in wages for three days of work. To meet this obligation, the Indian had to walk ten or twelve leagues to the *encomendero's* estate. During the time he worked the Spaniard's fields, the Indian's family suffered "because an Indian needs two *pesos* to sustain himself and his family for three days."[137] Moreover, Mejía's order violated legislation prohibiting personal services.[138]

Mejía, wrote Las Casas, had harmed the Indians in other ways. He had entrusted the regulation of tribute to the *encomenderos* and their creatures, the *caciques*, which gave rise to a thousand vexations, aggravations, and robberies. He had ordered the Indians to sell chickens for no more than half their worth and had given the Spaniards permission to take the chickens by force should the Indians refuse to sell them for the set price.

Another intolerable abuse condemned by Las Casas was the system of *repartimiento*—the use of Indians in labor gangs. Indians assigned to work on the Spaniards' estates were required to walk ten leagues or more to a town or village. While waiting to be assigned to employers, they were placed in a corral in the manner of sheep or brute beasts:

There a constable allots a Spaniard so many Indians and others so many more. The Spaniard seizes them violently by the hair and takes them with him, as if he were taking an animal. When the Indian arrives at the Spaniard's house, he takes his mantle brought by the Indian to cover himself, leaving him practically naked, and mockingly asks the Indian why he does not run away. He puts the Indian to work at whatever tasks he wishes without feeding him. The Indian sleeps on the portal in the raw cold and eats only the few maize cakes he brought. He works for a week and is paid two *reales*, returning home with this sum to find his wife and children hungry, sick, or dead. Many of the Indians, unable to endure the work and the cold, naked and hungry, leave their mantles and escape to their homes and lands.[139]

The treasury officials of Guatemala also complained that the audiencia judges had failed to assess crown Indian tributes correctly. They reported that income from crown Indians amounted to less than 8,000 pesos a year when they should have amounted under normal conditions to 20,000 pesos without causing the Indians any harm. The treasury officials attributed the loss of royal income to audiencia assessments and reassessments, which since 1551 had been made without consultations with the exchequer or on-site counts of the Indians. Nor had the judges considered the fertility, quality, or value of the Indians' lands and the amount of products harvested, factors of prime concern for taxing them justly. Because of the judges' indifference, the Indians lived in idleness and failed to cultivate their fertile lands, which were capable of producing abundant harvests. They recommended that the audiencia reassess tributes in the company of a treasury official.[140]

Although the treasury officials' report of this ineptness differs radically from Las Casas's protest, both communications to the crown recommended that head counts be made of the Indians before new assessments were made. Las Casas delcared that villages containing 2,000 tributaries ten years before now had less than 500 but still paid the same amount. Although exchequer officials complained that crown towns were not assessed enough, they did state that when they had learned of one crown village that paid too much they had asked the audiencia to lower these payments.

A number of factors hindered the implementation of the New Laws in Guatemala between 1544, the year of their proclamation, and 1560. Audiencia presidents like Maldonado and Landecho favored the interests of the *encomenderos*. Judges and officials of the royal tribunal like Mejía and Robledo were under the control of the colonists. Dominicans and Franciscans quarreled and failed to unite in solving the Indian question. Both orders despised the secular clergy, creatures of the *encomenderos* who helped exploit the Indians. Cerrato and Bishop Marroquín became enemies, and rivalries existed between the audiencia and the Cabildo of Santiago. Meanwhile, the *encomenderos* either intimidated or sought to destroy anyone threatening their economic well-being.

As Benjamin Keen remarks, "We can only speculate as to whether Zorita's appointment in 1556 as *oidor* of the *Audiencia* of Mexico represented a royal yielding to reactionary pressure or a reward to a loyal servant for his services to the Crown."[141] On the one hand, the crown, as William Sherman notes, "began to waver in its support of Cerrato" before his death.[142] Zorita, who helped maintain Cerrato's reforms, may have been considered too heavy-handed in applying the New Laws, and the crown may have decided to rid the colony of his presence by "promoting" him. It may be, on the other hand, that the crown, ignoring the accusations of the *encomenderos* and the Franciscans, chose to reward

Zorita after reading Cerrato's and the Dominicans' letters of praise.

In any case, the new assignment pleased Zorita. Both he and his wife were in poor health, and Zorita and the other judges complained unanimously that Guatemala was a poor place in which to serve the crown. The audiencia frequently mentioned that prices in Guatemala were at least twice as high as those in Mexico, and the treasury officials agreed. It also appears that Central America at midcentury swarmed with vagabonds, disaffected adventurers, and runaways from other provinces who caused injury to Indians and Spaniards; it undoubtedly contained some of the cruelest and most despicable *encomenderos* to be found in the Indies.

Zorita and his wife left Santiago on April 25, 1556. Because mule trains leaving Guatemala for Mexico carried only cacao, Zorita purchased pack horses, saddles, other equipment, and two black slaves to act as drovers for the journey. To pay for the trip, Zorita borrowed 3,000 *pesos de minas* from friends, thus assuming new debts on top of old ones. The trip of 270 leagues through mountains, forests, and swamps began under heavy rain and took over seventy days to complete. Although extremely ill from the journey and the "great chills" he had endured in his tours of inspection in Guatemala, Zorita assumed the duties of his office in Mexico City on July 9, 1556.[143]

In Guatemala, Zorita found much the same reaction from the settlers that he had experienced in New Granada. Like New Granada, Guatemala was "another battlefield of the tense struggle between the Crown and the settlers over the Indian question." Spanish settlers in both regions treated the Indians harshly, burdened them with excessive tribute; the secular clergy exploited and neglected to teach the Indians Christian doctrine; and local government officials represented and defended the *encomenderos'* interests. Whereas in New Granada Zorita had won the friendship of the Franciscans, in Guatemala he incurred their enmity; they claimed that he refused "advice except from those who incite and counsel him to destroy the land." Moreover, when the *encomenderos* found Zorita incorruptible, they made false charges against him before the audiencia and in reports to the king; these allegations were buttressed by Franciscan complaints and requests that Zorita be replaced by another judge who would punish the horrible vices of the Indians. President Cerrato and the Dominicans praised Zorita's implementation of the New

Laws, but most of Zorita's colleagues in the royal tribunal lacked courage and conscience "and allowed his foes to read and display these charges in public with complete impunity."[144]

Zorita's services in Guatemala burdened him with additional debts, and his tours of inspection over rough trails and mountainous country contributed to his later disabling illness. In retirement he recalled his difficulties with the settlers of Guatemala; he also remembered some defenders of his work. On one tour several "chiefs spoke so warmly to me, thanking me for the hardships I endured for their sake in that rugged land, that it made me happy to hear them and lightened the great hardships I had in fact to bear on that tour."[145]

CHAPTER 5

Troubles in New Spain, 1556–1566: Zorita, the *Visitador*, and the *Encomenderos*

THE TEN YEARS Zorita passed in Mexico were troubled and eventful. Unlike his experience in Guatemala, in New Spain, Zorita had the support of the Franciscan missionaries, and he played a major role in incorporating Franciscan and Dominican ideas in a plan for the spiritual conquest of the borderlands. His initial optimism appeared justified, for in addition to Franciscan support he enjoyed the high regard of Viceroy Velasco, who wished to curb the abuses of the *encomienda*, and moderate tributes in New Spain. As he went about his official tours, Zorita collected material on Indian tribute in pre- and post-Conquest Mexico and questioned Indian lords and elders about their habits and customs. The impressions and materials he gathered in his notebooks during this decade (1556–66) served as the basis for his study of Indian life and labor written after his return to Spain.

Zorita's optimism and renewed energy were, however, short-lived. His chronic deafness took a turn for the worse and impaired his ability to hear cases in the courtroom. Moreover, his efforts on behalf of the Indians, and the support he gave Velasco's reform measures, caused him to be hated by the *encomenderos* led by Don Martín Cortés and the royal commissioner Jerónimo Valderrama. Luis de Velasco's death in 1564 weakened the pro-Indian movement in Mexico and left Zorita without the protection of this powerful friend. After Velasco's death Valderrama assumed charge of the audiencia. Intent on augmenting crown revenues by increasing Indian tribute burdens, Valderrama backed the Creole or *encomendero* party, dismissed royal judges at will, justly gained the title of *afligidor de los indios*, and considered Zorita an ineffective though well-meaning judge who should be removed from office.

The Grandeur of New Spain

Although Zorita's last years in Mexico were filled with disappointment, his major work, completed in retirement in the city of Granada in 1585, is full of praise for the "very great and celebrated city of Mexico." Nostalgia undoubtedly inspired him when he praised the liberality and fertility of New Spain's soil, yielding abundantly both native products and plants and animals brought from Castile. All kinds of metals were to be found in Mexico, and it enjoyed one of the best climates in the world. Cattle and other domestic animals had multiplied exceedingly and filled the countryside. Looking backward, aspiring to return to the viceroyalty as a notary, Zorita grown old in Granada sounded the praises of the New World Byzantium. Hoping to cross the sea again, pressed by poverty, he recalled the birds and beasts of Mexico, attributing the beauty of the small, handsome horses raised in Mexico to the corn on which they fed, maize being a much better fodder than barley.[1]

Surrounded by mountains covered with cedars and cypresses, in 1570 the viceregal capital had 3,000 *vecinos* who lived in the center of the city. The rest of the Mexico City's population consisted of 30,000 Indian households located outside the district occupied by the Spaniards and their Creole neighbors and relatives.[2] Zorita praised the Spanish section's long, wide, very straight streets, most of which were paved with stone. These well-designed thoroughfares lent the city charm and also aided in the defense of the metropolis, a responsibility of the cavalry. Great, squat fortresslike houses lined the streets leading to the main plaza. Because none of the solid houses of the gentry and the merchants exceeded a certain height, all equally admitted the sun and allowed the wind to carry off the pestilential vapors emitted by a neighboring swamp.[3]

Forming part of the hustle and bustle in the crowded streets, Zorita and Doña Catarina met a variety of people when they went shopping. According to Zorita, the city had many rich citizens who owned large estates, mines, and herds, and lived in magnificent houses filled with servants and silver plate; some held Indian villages under the *encomienda* system. A significant number of the elite were caballeros and hidalgos, some belonging to the Military Order of Santiago. There were many skilled artisans, a group formed by both Spaniards and Indians.[4] Spaniards and Creoles isolated themselves geographically and socially from the República de indios, but economically a white artisan probably had more in common with an Indian craftsman in Mexico City than he did with a rich noble like Alonso de Ávila Alvarado or the rich merchants mentioned by Zorita.

Zorita had read Francisco Cervantes de Salazar's vivid and high-flown description of the city[5] and may have compared the university professor's guidebook with the street scenes unfolding before his eyes. The heart of the city was the *plaza mayor*, a level, spacious, beautiful square with a great number of tidy shops filled with valuable merchandise. During business hours shoppers thronged the square, filling the air with a great murmur. All that was desirable or valuable in the entire world was for sale in this one marketplace. Buyers were not lacking in spite of high prices; what copper coins could purchase in Spain sold for triple the price in silver in the stores or at the auctions held in this commercial quarter.[6]

On the east side of the square stood the viceregal palace, bought from Hernando Cortés for 50,000 ducats and enlarged after becoming crown property.[7] This imposing structure, with its four battlemented towers and three great columned doors facing the central square, dominated the plaza. The viceroy and the royal judges entered and departed the castle through one door. The two other doors were used by the staff of the royal prison and the treasury officials, respectively. Those who worked in the mint used another door not facing the central square.

The first of the four large courtyards in the palace housed the audiencia. During the years Zorita resided in Mexico, two to four judges heard cases in one courtroom. The number of judges increased after 1564, and in 1585 Zorita wrote that the tribunal was staffed by eight judges who heard civil cases in two courtrooms; three *alcaldes de corte* judged criminal cases in another courtroom. The other court officials in the 1580s consisted of the attorney general, *relatores* who prepared the summaries from the evidence submitted by litigants, a chancellor and recorder, porters and interpreters, and two lawyers and two solicitors for the poor, all with good salaries.[8]

As he entered the castle, Zorita may have remembered the silence of the empty land of Guatemala on his tours of inspection to isolated hamlets. How strongly the lonely, soundless trips through deserted provinces must have contrasted with the clamor made by the people who filled the palace corridors. In the main hall thronged litigants, business agents, attorneys, notaries, the idle, and the curious. Those who were there to see the judges were appealing cases from the municipal judges, were plaintiffs or defendants in cases of first instance, or had other important business requiring the immediate attention of the audiencia:

"Now they walk slowly, then rapidly, now they pause, then they run, and no sooner do they shout than they lapse into silence, in a manner resembling madmen!"[9]

Upon entering the large and ornate courtroom, litigants were immediately humbled by the presence of the judges seated around the viceroy on a dais. The platform was covered with rich carpets; the benches, with a canopy of damask trimmed with braid. So imposing was the courtroom that Cervantes de Salazar compared it with the royal tribunals of Granada and Valladolid, the most renowned in Spain.[10]

Viceroy Luis de Velasco lived in the second quadrangle. Adjacent to his apartment was the armory, consisting of three rooms filled with weapons: pikes, shields, crossbows, all kinds of military stores, and much powder and artillery. There were also a chapel and a lovely garden within a large corridor spanned by twenty arches; Luis de Velasco usually granted hearings to important negotiants in the garden.

All members of the royal exchequer except the treasurer had their living quarters in the third and largest quadrangle. They had their separate offices, heard fiscal suits, and collected the royal fifth paid on silver and gold by bullion merchants in rooms adjacent to their lodgings. The fourth courtyard had its separate rooms and housed the royal mint and the treasurer's living quarters.[11]

Described by Cervantes de Salazar as a city within a city because of its many rooms, extensive wings, and imposing structure, the palace was also a stronghold, and the government following that of Luis de Velasco appears to have taken further measures to secure the building after the Creole conspiracy allegedly led by Alonso de Ávila was discovered. In Zorita's time the palace, built in the shape of a square, had a moat on one side that was fifteen feet wide and nine feet deep: "It is filled with water to a height of six feet and will eventually extend about the entire building, making it a very strong palace with drawbridges."[12]

The Royal and Pontifical University building faced the *plaza mayor* in these years. Founded on the day of the Conversion of Saint Paul, January 25, 1553, the university had a close connection with the audiencia. The university's first rector was Antonio Rodríguez de Quesada, one of the royal judges. Its first chancellor was another judge, Gómez de Santillán. The chair of canon law was initially held by Pedro de Morones, the audiencia's prosecuting attorney. Two other judges served as rectors in this period, Pedro Sánchez de Paredes (1584) and Eugenio de Salazar (1592).[13]

The first university site was temporary. Pedro Sánchez laid the first stone of the permanent university building on June 29, 1584; the building was on four lots owned by the Marqués del Valle on the small square known as El Volador. After several years of litigation the marqués was paid 8,000 pesos for the lots, and classes began at this new site in late 1592 under the rectorate of Don Eugenio de Salazar. The building was finally completed in 1631.[14]

On November 20, 1556, Judges Alonso de Zorita and Juan Bravo attended a plenary meeting of the university faculty. They accepted Viceroy Luis de Velasco's invitation to become members of the university, and with the unanimous consent of the university government were admitted as doctors in laws, "inasmuch as they were."[15] The history of the university indicates that Zorita was also present at a meeting of the university's governing body on November 11, 1557. He may have also been present on May 2, 1563, when Damián Sedeño, the audiencia's attorney general, presented a petition to Velasco requesting that he and the royal tribunal's judges be admitted to the university as doctors so that they might enjoy the immunities and privileges which the crown had made to the school, one of these being the right to make caballeros of its graduates. The viceroy honored the request, stipulating that the royal judges would be preferred in senority to all the other doctors.[16]

Zorita's comments on the remarkable things to be found in Mexico City include informative and interesting remarks on the many churches, convents, and hospitals. His statements about Christian charity and the state of religion demonstrate his deep interest in the spiritual conquest of Mexico. His remarks also confirm that the stratified social classes and different ethnic groups all shared in the splendor of church ritual and the universal message of Roman Catholicism.

Zorita was impressed by the cathedral, but his description of the main church in Mexico City differs from that found in Cervantes's *Dialogues*. Cervantes wrote that the cathedral, dedicated to the Virgin Mary, was a small, humble, poorly adorned building. Zorita, in agreement with Fray Toribio de Motolinía, who died in 1565, seems to be saying that the cathedral became more impressive as its revenues and gifts from rich donors increased. In his chapter on the notable things of Mexico City, he wrote that the cathedral was well administered and equipped with ornaments, musical instruments, and singers. Three priests baptized and administered the sacraments during the week; they were joined by the sacristans and other clergy when the dead were buried. Because the large, heavy cross on the main altar was entirely gilded, it was not covered with a case of silk. One elaborately designed silver tabernacle was reputed to have cost more than 20,000 ducats.[17]

Most of the city's *vecinos*, Zorita wrote, gave generously to the church. Their piety was demonstrated by the several confraternities formed to celebrate particular feast days with splendid ceremonies. The Confraternity of the Blessed Sacrament and Charity was the most important religious guild. It provided the oil and wax used by the cathedral; supplied the torches and candles on the feast days of Holy Thursday, Corpus Christi, the Visitation of Our Lady with Saint Elizabeth, and Advent; supported a school for orphan girls; and helped the poor, many of whom were indigent prisoners and penniless Spanish immigrants brought by every arriving fleet.[18]

The Confraternity of the True Cross was a flagellant order. More than 400 of its disciples made up its penitential procession on Holy Thursday. The brotherhood carried thirty or more crucifixes, each the size of a man but so light that the Christ on each one weighed no more than twelve pounds. The society used up two casks of wine, each worth 100 *pesos de minas*, in washing the feet of the poor on this holy day.[19]

Members of the brotherhood of Jesus held their meetings in the Convent of Saint Augustine; they married off three or four orphan girls each year, providing each of the brides-to-be with dowries of more than 500 pesos. Another confraternity under the rule of the Dominicans met each Saturday to celebrate a very solemn mass; members of a branch of this lay order did penance each time they blasphemed by giving a certain sum to the society.

Zorita's brief mention of the black confraternities supports Frank Tannenbaum's thesis that Spanish law, reinforced by the "Catholic doctrine of the equality of all men in the sight of God, was biased in favor of freedom for the slave."[20] The blacks had two brotherhoods, one in the Dominican monastery and the other in the main church, and met on feast days to be instructed in the faith. They gave many offerings at their baptisms and marriages, each of those present giving a *real* or more. This was a considerable sum in light of their humble circumstances, and Zorita in writing this may have been thinking of that certain poor widow praised by Jesus who, out of her want, gave all she had: two mites, "even all her living." The Negro brotherhoods used the alms they received from their members to purchase the freedom of their fellows in bondage.[21]

As is apparent, Zorita was delighted by the sight of resplendent churches and admired acts of charity and ritual, outward expressions for him of a higher spiritual reality. He, however, was more than a mere admirer and participant in the rituals of the church; he was an intelligent and zealous Catholic deeply interested in the war fought by the ministers of the gospel against the "demons" who had held Mexico in their sway. Through God's favor, with valorous spirit and ceaseless work, the Franciscan missionaries had opposed "those princes of darkness" and extirpated the idolatry in which the Indians had lived for so many years.[22]

Class Structure

Sixteenth-century Mexican society from an early date was separated into four broad categories: Spaniards (Europeans and Creoles), Indians, mestizos, and mixed bloods and Negroes. However, individuals were classed in the caste system according to their wealth and sociocultural status, in addition to their physical appearance. The designation *español* was synonymous with the terms *blanco*, *gente de razón*, and *vecino*, but never implied absolute purity of blood. Mestizos born in wedlock or recognized by their Spanish fathers were accepted as Creoles in post-Conquest society; the best example of this in Zorita's day is Don Martín Cortés, the son of the Conqueror and Doña Marina. He was acknowledged as a Spaniard and received the habit of the Military Order of Santiago. As the Society of Castes developed, racial lines became more stratified, but vertical social mobility always existed. In eighteenth-century New Spain a person who was genetically one-eighth Indian was considered to be white, as was an individual who was one-sixteenth black. In the opinion of Angel Rosenblat, the system of castes was free from an exaggerated racist bias, and the term "white" or "Spaniard" was flexible to an extreme degree.[23]

Zorita's comments on the white ruling class of Mexico confirm that racial lines were not very strictly drawn. In discussing Hernando Cortés's relations with Doña Marina, Zorita pointed out that the Conqueror married Marina to Juan Jaramillo and gave him the province of Xilotepec, which was one of the best in New Spain. Jaramillo's daughter by this marriage was named Doña María; she married Don Luis de Quesada, a native of Ubeda. After Doña Marina's death, Juan Jaramillo married Doña Beatriz de Andrada. No issue resulted from this second marriage. After Jaramillo's death, the province of Xilotepec was divided between his daughter Doña María and his second wife. Doña Beatriz then married Don Francisco de Velasco, *comendador* of the Military Order of Santiago and brother of Viceroy Don Luis de Velasco. The viceroy's brother "died without issue and Doña Beatriz remained with half of Xilotepec in *encomienda*. The other half is held by Don Pedro de Quesada, son of Don Luis de Quesada and Doña María, the daughter of Juan Jaramillo and his first wife Marina. He is married to the daughter of Doctor Vasco de Puga, native of Galicia and former *oidor* in the Royal Audiencia of Mexico." The tribute from each one of the Xilotepec *encomiendas* were said to be worth more than 12,000 pesos.[24]

This kind of information furnished by Zorita gives us a view of the racial intermixing common in the first decades following the Conquest. It also demonstrates that it was not unusual for children of "mixed blood" to be absorbed into the white ruling class of Mexico. Thus Pedro de Quesada, *encomendero* of Xilotepec and a captain in quest of New Mexico in the 1560s, was the grandson and heir of Doña Marina, Cortés' Indian interpreter, and of Juan Jaramillo, a native of Villanueva de Balcarrota (Barcarrota?) and the son of Alonso Jaramillo and Mençia de Matos.[25] Redeemed by wealth and social position, this Creole aristocrat was also related by marriage and family ties to the viceroy's family and to an audiencia judge. Consequently, despite genetically belonging to that group classified as mestizo, Pedro de Quesada—like his blood relative Don Martín Cortés—belonged to the class of rich, privileged whites making up the nobility of the viceroyalty.

Although all members of the white ruling class were theoretically equal, by the second half of the sixteenth century Spaniards of this group were divided into sons and grandsons of conquerors, and first settlers and more recent arrivals from Spain. Peninsular Spaniards and Creoles competed for government posts and land grants, preference usually being given to the Peninsulars.

Zorita alluded to this cleavage in the white upper class. He observed that many students had received the degree of master and doctor and that not a few were *bachilleres* and *licenciados*. He claimed that all graduates of the various branches of learning at the University of Mexico were praiseworthy and had excellent command of Latin. Some were able rhetoricians and scribes, as well as good horsemen skilled in arms. In short, they could perform well in all fields. They had ability for everything, and almost all knew "the language of the Indians." Zorita then pointed out that Creole youths would give themselves to study in greater numbers and more willingly "if the prebends of the Cathedral chapter were given to sons of *vecinos*." He also recommended the establishment of patrimonial benefices, to be filled by competitive examinations. With more incentive all the sons of conquerors would be learned and would use their education for the benefit of Spaniards and Indians.[26]

Given his interest in religious confraternities and the work of the friars in Mexico, it is curious that Zorita chose to remain silent about a sermon he probably heard on the idolatry underlying the new Creole cult of Guadalupe. At a high mass celebrated in honor of the Nativity of the Blessed Virgin on September 8, 1556, at the Church of Saint Francis, Fray Francisco de Bustamante addressed a large gathering assembled in Saint Joseph's Chapel. Those present included members of the clergy, Viceroy Luis de Velasco, the royal judges, and the principal citizens of Mexico City.

Father Bustamante, the Franciscan minister provincial and a gifted orator, lived up to his reputation in his eloquent praise of the Mother of God and her birthday. He had finished with his eulogy when suddenly he paused, and his countenance changed, turning pallid and full of dread. Declaring that he did not intend to destroy the faith of the least of his hearers, he told his audience that the observance of religious duties by the city's *vecinos* at a hermitage of Our Lady, "to which they have given the name Guadalupe," represented a great danger to the Indians.

Situated half a league from Mexico City, this sanctuary on the hill of Tepeyac had an image painted "the other day" by an Indian. Spanish devotees of the Marian cult told the Indians that the image worked miracles, "and so was God." This directly contradicted what the Franciscans had made the Indians understand from the time of their arrival in New Spain, for the missionaries had taught the neophytes not to adore images, only what they represented, "which is in Heaven."[27]

Stating that the cult had arisen "without the least foundation," the pious Franciscan declared that he had been informed that those who went to the shrine had committed various sins offensive to God Our Lord. He also questioned the motives of Archbishop Alonso de Montúfar in encouraging the veneration of the image, pointing out that the alms given at the shrine would be better spent on the city's poor. After implying that the archbishop promoted the cult for monetary profit, Bustamante asserted that the first person who had said the image worked miracles should have been given a hundred lashes. He ended his condemnation of the new cult by urgently requesting the viceroy and the royal judges to make an official investigation of the matter to correct this "great evil," and recommending that the founders of the cult be given two hundred lashes. Should the archbishop declare otherwise, he would be told that, although he was the prelate of the church, the king was its patron and its temporal and spiritual head. The viceroy and the audiencia judges, as the king's representatives, thus had ultimate jurisdiction in ecclesiastical matters.[28]

Don Luis de Velasco and the judges may have considered the cult of Guadalupe relatively harmless, for no evidence exists that he and the *oidores* investigated the cult's origins or its potential harm to the Indians. Indeed, Archbishop Montúfar built a church to replace the humble hermitage where the Indians had once sacrificed to the goddess Tonantzin-Cihuacóatl, the mother of the gods and the wife of the Serpent, the latter always associated in the Christian mind with "the Devil, and Satan, which deceiveth the whole world" (*Revelation* 12:9).

Constructed in the year 1556, the "very fair church" of Our Lady of Guadalupe soon had an income of seven or eight thousand pesos a year and a confraternity of 400 members.[29] Indian devotees soon joined the Creoles in worship at the church, but the Franciscan friar Bernardino de Sahagún considered their devotion suspect, "for there are everywhere numerous churches consecrated to Our Lady, but they do not go there, preferring to come from afar to this Tonantzin, as in the past."[30] In his study of the formation of Mexican national consciousness, Jacques Lafaye observes that this Creole cult eventually triumphed over the Erasmian purity of the Franciscans. In his foreword to Lafaye's work, Octavio Paz ironically remarks that Mexicans, "after more than two centuries of experiments and defeats, have faith only in the Virgin of Guadalupe and the National Lottery."[31]

Zorita's silence concerning the new cult of Guadalupe and its condemnation by Fray Francisco de Bustamante may perhaps be explained by his low opinion of the secular clergy and his affection for the friars. Because he supported the Franciscan cause in Mexico and desired that Indian parishes should be entrusted to the regular clergy, Zorita may have had grave doubts about the cult, which in the sixteenth century was under the exclusive patronage of the bishops. Zorita's attitude toward this form of worship by the Creoles may have been similar to that of Gerónimo de Mendieta; so distrustful was the latter of the cult that "he did not mention it once in his voluminous writings."[32] Mendieta, Bustamante, and Sahagún knew Zorita, and it is likely that they privately discussed with him their hostility to the cult. In any case, Zorita probably heard Bustamante denounce the pernicious effects of venerating this image and may therefore have chosen to ignore this confraternity in his *Historia*.

Although Zorita failed to mention the image of Tepeyac and did not say whether he believed the Indians worshiped an ancient mother goddess under a new name, he did state that the Indians of Yucatán and Mexico thought that a Christian missionary had visited them in ancient times. This pioneer missionary was later identified by the Creole intellectual Carlos Sigüenza y Góngora and by the Dominican friar José Servando Teresa de Mier as the apostle Saint Thomas, known to the Indians as Kukulcán and Quetzalcóatl.

Zorita's source for this pious legend was Fray Estevan de Salazar, an Augustinian doctor of theology in Mexico who eventually returned to Spain and became a Carthusian monk so that he could have more time for letters and study. Zorita believed that had Salazar's Latin history of the Conquest not been lost in a shipwreck in 1564 its publication "would have silenced those who have desired to write on this subject."[33]

Citing Fray Bartolomé de Las Casas as his authority, Father Salazar had written that in the province of Chiapas the native nobility and caballeros had received news of the blessed Trinity. And in Cozumel (Acuçamye) ancient traditions of the Indians related that a very handsome man had passed through that land and taught them the sign of the Cross so that they might always remember him:

Others say that they were told that one more resplendent than the sun had died in that land, as is mentioned by Peter Martyr in his *Decades*. Martyr states that if this is true there is no doubt that our Holy Faith and religion was preached and proclaimed throughout that land, as is indicated by certain buildings and letters of characters found in the province of Chiapas.[34]

An Indian of Cholula had also told Father Salazar that the
histories of the Indians, written "in the manner of the Ethiopian
and Egyptian priests who drew pictures and figures of diverse
things on chamois," confirmed that in ancient times there had
come to New Spain a white man with a beard who had taught a
certain doctrine, "already forgotten with the passage of time."
This virtuous man had been killed at Cholula because he forbade
idolatries, "after which they built a great temple over his body."[35]

In his study of the myths of Tonantzin-Guadalupe and Quetzalcóatl–Saint Thomas, Lafaye has shown how these syncretic
religious beliefs were used by revolutionaries in the nineteenth
century to express "the Mexican claim of supernatural equality
with Spain." Lafaye also examines the genesis of the Creole
myths, observing that, when Hernando Cortés arrived in Tenochtitlán, Montezuma II supposedly told the Conqueror about one
of their kings (the Toltec ruler Ce Acatl Topiltzin, who assumed
the name of Quetzalcóatl) of earlier times who had left the land
and whose descendants would one day return "to subjugate this
country and take us as their vassals." Montezuma then recognized Cortés as Quetzalcóatl's representative, giving the Spanish
adventurer command of all his dominions.[36]

Lafaye does not discuss whether there is a relationship between
the myths of Quetzalcóatl-Guadalupe and the Cortés-Ávila Conspiracy of the 1560s. He does state, however, that the conflict
between Spaniards and American-born descendants of the conquerors arose about 1550.[37] Is it only coincidental that the roots
of religious Creole consciousness and Creole discontent arose in
the same period? Did Creole conspirators like Alonso de Ávila
Alvarado recognize Don Martín Cortés, the Conqueror's heir
born in Mexico, as Cortés-Quetzalcóatl?

The divisiveness between Spaniards and Creoles that arose in
the sixteenth century never abated, and the hostility may have
been the fundamental cause of the independence movement in
Mexico. In any case, there are similarities between the abortive
Cortés-Ávila conspiracy and the insurgents who led the independence movement. In the sixteenth century not only did members of the secular clergy led by Dominican Archbishop Montúfar promote the cult of Guadalupe, but the audiencia charged
various clerics with conspiring to overthrow the viceregal government. Those accused of being rebels included Dean Alonso Chico
de Molina and Prebendary Cristóbal Ayala de Espinosa of the
cathedral chapter; the former Dominican friar Rodrigo de Car-

vajal, parish priest of the villa of San Miguel de los Chichimecas;[38] and the cleric Pedro de Aguilar. Also, while Franciscans like Sahagún "openly rejected the hypothesis of an ancient evangelization,"[39] the Dominican Las Casas "concluded that a merciful God had announced the coming of the Spanish missionaries to the misguided pagans through the lips of a demon, Quetzalcóatl."[40] In the independence movement secular priests once again conspired to overthrow the Spanish-dominated government. Miguel Hidalgo y Costilla and José María Morelos raised the banner of Guadalupe in their mobilization of the Indian and mixed-blood proletariat. The revolutionary Dominican friar Servando Teresa de Mier expressed doubts about the apparition of the Virgin of Guadalupe but believed that Saint Thomas of Mylapore had preached the Gospel in Mexico about the sixth century.[41]

In spite of the antipathy between Creoles and Peninsulars at midsixteenth century, socioeconomic and other differences between individuals in both groups worked to the benefit of the crown by preventing separatist tendencies. Spaniards in Mexico brought their regional rivalries with them. Older settlers were resentful of more recent Spanish arrivals. Old Christians looked down on New Christians and Europeans of other nations. Spanish royal officials quarreled with each other as well as with Creole municipal officials. In addition, whites, whether born in Mexico or in Spain, were socially and economically divided into major and minor bureaucrats, *encomenderos*, merchants, miners, a large number of skilled workers, recently arrived poor immigrants, and perhaps 3,000 to 4,000 vagrants.[42]

Rich and powerful Creoles lived with their equally important Spanish neighbors and relatives in the great houses in the heart of the city. In contrast, most of those whites who lived by their wits consisted of lower-class Spaniards who had left Spain to avoid work and taxes. In the countryside, renegade whites often lived with and exploited Indians. In the villages and towns many poor whites and mestizos avoided useful work and sold pulque, the native wine, to the Indians. Ne'er-do-wells of both sexes, wrote Zorita, lured Indians into their homes and got them drunk, for Indians paid whatever price was asked for the wine.[43]

Although the antagonism between Spaniard and Creole was evident in New Spain by the 1550s, it is apparent that Creoles were not a united group or a new people with a distinct identity. Creole graduates of the university undoubtedly resented being denied important government and church offices; sons and grand-sons of conquerors and first settlers complained to the crown about the royal judges, the friars, and the viceroy; and members of the municipal council protested the cabildo's displacement by the audiencia in the annual Corpus Christi procession. But re-gardless of their frustrations and complaints, upper-class Creoles still considered themselves loyal vassals of the king, sought favors from the crown, and remained loyal to the Spanish government during the years that Don Luis de Velasco governed the colony. Lower-class Creoles might resent their condition, but they lacked class consciousness.

All Creoles in sixteenth-century Mexico were legally equal to Peninsular Spaniards and considered themselves members of the ruling group. To be sure, the distinction between Peninsulars and Creoles might be noted in official correspondence, where the latter group might be called "Spaniards born in this land," or "Spaniards born in this country," but the term *criollo* would not be generally adopted as a term of self-reference by Spaniards born in Mexico until the end of the colonial period.[44]

Hardly distinguishable from their Spanish forebears and differentiated only by their wealth or lack of it within the hier-archic estate system, Creoles did share at least one thing in com-mon. They "were and were not Spaniards; like the Indians, they were born in America and, usually unaware of the fact, shared many of the Indian beliefs."[45] Aware that they belonged to the race of the conquerors, Creoles feared, exploited, and scorned Indians. But, as Zorita observed, most Creole students at the University of Mexico knew Náhuatl. "Spiritual *mestizaje*," the mingling of Indian and white ways and values, "was gaining control of the body and soul of the proud Creole, without his realizing it." In the words of the Creole Juan Suárez de Peralta, "The Indians hold those born in this land as their children, and their wives those whom they have nourished with their milk."[46]

Creoles, besides knowing the Aztec language, Indian foods, and Indian herbs and drugs, were influenced in other ways by Indian servants and wet nurses. Even as adults Creoles played at being Indian, perhaps unconsciously reflecting their attachment to the Mexican landscape, their alienation from the European past, and their hatred of the lawyers who had come to rule them from across the sea.

On one notable occasion Alonso de Ávila and twenty-four companions donned Indian masks and native apparel at his *en-comienda*, Cuauhtitlán. Alonso de Ávila was dressed as an Indian cacique and led the other horsemen to the house of the Marqués del Valle. The make-believe Indians carried rose bouquets (called *suchiles* in Náhuatl), and the food they brought for the banquet in honor of the more recently arrived second Marqués del Valle and his wife consisted of Aztec dishes prepared by the Indians of Cuauhtitlán. After passing out the bouquets, Alonso de Ávila crowned the marchioness with a feather garland. It is said that as it was placed on her head a Creole in the crowd witnessing the masquerade shouted, "Take that crown, Marquesa!"[47]

Another member of the white community who played at being Indian was Licentiate Cristóbal Ayala de Espinosa, cleric and prebendary of the cathedral chapter, administrator of the Indian hospital, and the son of Juan de Espinosa Carrión and Bernarda de Ayala, citizens of Seville and natives of the villa of Carrión de los Condes, in the province of Palencia. Espinosa, allegedly an intimate friend of Viceroy Luis de Velasco, also a native of Carrión de los Condes, frequently left the hospital disguised as an Indian to make his nightly assignations with mestizas and other women.[48]

The sexual proclivities of the prebendary were not unusual in this period of the colony's history. Fray Gerónimo de Mendieta wrote in 1562 that almost all of the 10,000 or 11,000 daughters of Spaniards in Mexico lacked the wherewithal for marriage. In addition to adding to the number of illegitimate children brought into the world by casual intercourse and concubinage, the sexual habits of the colonists promoted the rapid spread of venereal disease. Fray Toribio de Motolinía observed that in Mexico syphilitic pustules were called "las infinitas." His statement is confirmed by Dr. Juan de Cárdenas, a physician and author of *The Problems and Marvelous Secrets of the Indies* (1591). The French disease, Cárdenas wrote, was generally transmitted after one committed "filthy, stupid, and unchaste" acts. This "infernal, pernicious, and malignant" illness was so common in Mexico "that it is said that he is not an upright man who does not have a trace of this ailment. The sight of a velvet patch, black with use, to cover a chancre on a person's face, a swelling at the temple, or a scar with a lack of bone in the forehead, is so common that it passes unnoticed among them."[49]

The Audiencia of Mexico

Four judges served in the audiencia when Don Luis de Velasco took over the government of New Spain in 1550. These were

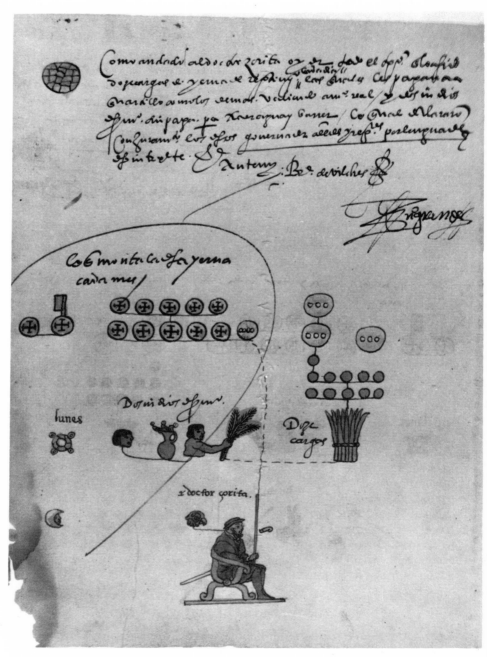

Stylized sketch of Dr. Alonso de Zorita by Indian draftsman in late 1550s. The sketch of Indians and burdens apparently shows what service was performed for Zorita. (Courtesy of *Pintura del gobernador, alcaldes y regidores de México: Códice Osuna*)

Illustration from *Pintura del gobernador, alcaldes y regidores de México: Códice Osuna* (Madrid: Servicio de Publicaciones del Ministerio de Educatión y Ciencia, 1973).

(figure)   Como han dado al doctor Zorita oidor todo el tiempo que lo ha
             sido
             doce cargas de yerba de repartimiento cada día, las cuales les
             pagaba
             a cuartillo como los demás, valiendo a medio real, y dos indios
             de
             servicio sin paga para traer agua y barrer, lo cual declararon
             con juramento los dichos governador, alcaldes y regidores por
             lengua
             de dicho interprete, etc. Ante mi   Br^e de Vilches
                                                 (rúbrica)

                                                            Ju° Grande
                                                            (rúbrica)
Lo que monta la dicha yerba cada mes.

(figures)

                    Dos indios de servicio
lunes   (figure)
(figure)   Doce cargas (figure)

               Doctor Zorita

                  (figure)

Lorenzo de Tejada, Gómez de Santillán, Francisco de Herrera, and Antonio Rodríguez de Quesada. The next year saw the appointments of Antonio de Mejía and a man named Trenado. Mejía arrived in Mexico City in 1552, but Trenado died on board the ship carrying him to New Spain.

Among the letters and reports submitted concerning the fitness of the judges, a letter signed by the municipal council praised Tejada's work. It contrasted strongly with the complaints by Indians of Metztitlán, in modern Hidalgo, who told the *visitador* Diego Ramírez that Tejada had not paid them for six beds they had made for him. It was also charged that Tejada had conspired with the Franciscans, Dominicans, and Augustinians to exploit Indians. In return for allowing the friars to use many Indian laborers in their monasteries, the missionaries allegedly ignored or concealed Tejada's employment of Indians to construct a number of houses and shops in Mexico City.[50]

Tejada was not the only judge charged with excessive greed. Diego Téllez, a seventy-year-old lawyer who had pleaded cases in the audiencia, wrote Prince Philip that in violation of the law *oidores* Santillán and Herrera had married in Mexico and had received excessive dowries. His wife's parents had given Santillán 20,000 pesos, causing great prospective hardship for their unmarried children. Téllez declared that in Herrera's case part of the 16,000 Castilian ducats the judge received with his wife legally belonged to her brothers. But because Herrera served in the audiencia, his brothers-in-law dared not sue him for their portion of the family estate.[51]

Criticism of the judges increased with the arrival of Antonio de Mejía. Isabel de Villegas, a widow and the sister-in-law of Judge Herrera, appeared before the vicar general of the archbishop to complain that Mejía, after marrying her before witnesses one night, refused to acknowledge her as his wife. Because Herrera sided with his sister-in-law in her quarrel with Mejía, the two judges became bitter enemies.

In 1553, Rodríguez de Quesada was reassigned to the Audiencia of Guatemala and commissioned to take the *residencias* of the judges serving in that court. In the same year four new judges were appointed to the Mexican tribunal: Doctor Diego López Montealegre, Doctor Juan Bravo, and Licentiates Pedro de Puertocarrero and a certain Villagar. Only two of these judges served in the audiencia, for Puertocarrero died at sea, and Villagar died shortly after he disembarked. López Montealegre, commissioned to take the *residencias* of the judges, reinstated Mejía and Herrera following their judicial reviews. Hence their incessant quarrels continued to disturb audiencia sessions. The conflict between the two ended only with the transfer of Mejía to Guatemala and the reassignment of Herrera to Santo Domingo in 1556.[52]

Meanwhile, Velasco, constantly preoccupied by the need for more judges to handle the business of the court, suggested that one of the archbishop's ecclesiastical judges be appointed to the court. He also recommended an exchange between judges and members of the Council of the Indies, pointing out that this would give the home government a better idea of New Spain's problems.[53]

The Council of the Indies ignored the viceroy's recommendations, but in 1555 the number of judges was increased with Zorita's appointment to the court. Only two judges (Bravo and López Montealegre) were handling audiencia matters when Zorita began serving in the tribunal. Other judges appointed in the following years were Pedro de Villalobos (1556), Jerónimo de Orozco and Vasco de Puga (1557), Francisco de Ceynos (1558), and Luis de Villanueva Zapata (1560). When Bravo died in 1560, the number of judges was reduced to six: Zorita, Villalobos, Orozco, Vasco de Puga, Ceynos, and Villanueva.

The crown based judges' salaries on the importance of the particular tribunal and local prices. The judges of the Second Audiencia of Mexico, for example, were originally paid an annual salary of 650,000 *maravedís* or 1,733 ducats. Owing perhaps to the decline of inflation, economic conditions improved in the colony, and in 1535 this sum was reduced to 500,000 *maravedís*. Fifteen years later the crown restored the original salary and ordered a supplemental cost-of-living allowance of 400 ducats because of inflation.[54]

When the supplementary amount was not paid, the judges and the court's attorney general sent the crown a deposition. They pointed out that they were in extreme need because prices in New Spain were very high and increased daily. In addition, the cost of maintaining a household in Mexico City was considerably higher than in other places because appearances had to be maintained by judges and their wives in this viceregal center. Was the crown aware that the services of a Spaniard cost a minimum of 150 *pesos de minas* a year and that a judge could not manage without at least a couple of servants?

Those who testified to the financial need of the judges were the bishop of Michoacán and former judge, Don Vasco de Quiroga; the bishop of Tlaxcala, Fray Martín Sarmiento de Ojacastro; the bishop of Chiapas, Fray Tomás Casilla; councilman Andrés de Tapia; and Don Luis de Castilla, knight of the Order of Santiago. Their importance must have impressed the king, for after consulting with the Royal Council of the Indies, Philip II ordered that the judges be paid the additional 400 ducats. However, this salary increase in 1558 did not greatly help the judges, since after 1550 they were obliged to pay for the houses they rented. In 1554 and again in 1555 the judges sought to reduce living expenses by asking to be assigned housing in the viceregal palace. Velasco approved the judges' petition, but in a personal letter to the king he wrote that he had gone along with the proposal only because the majority of the judges had voted in favor of it in consultative session. The judges' petition should be refused because what space was available in the palace was being used by the treasury officials for their strongbox, smelter, auctions, and other business.

Although Velasco stymied the judges when they sought to move to the palace, he did attempt to relieve some economic distress. When Zorita and Doña Catarina arrived in Mexico City, they moved into a house that proved to be damp and infectious. Located next to "an irrigation ditch emanating from a smelly pool discharging evil vapors," the dwelling was so unsuitable that Zorita had to look for another house. In 1560, the viceroy and the other judges wrote the crown that the rent for Zorita's and Vasco de Puga's houses should be paid for from court fines. If money was not forthcoming from this source, their housing costs should be paid for by the treasury officials, as was being done for Judges Pedro de Villalobos and Jerónimo de Orozco, who were living in houses owned by Don Martín Cortés.[55]

The judges were able to present a united front in their complaints about inadequate salaries and the high price of goods and housing, but they often quarreled among themselves about other matters. In his attempt to arbitrate these disputes and restore harmony to the court, Velasco only angered those judges he blamed for beginning these squabbles.

In the 1550s the judges' critics said that their offenses were many. Various *vecinos* stated that because the judges received indefinite appointments, *oidores* soon became corrupt, believed themselves to be gods, and treated other members of the court and Spanish and Indian litigants in a despotic manner. In the opinion of their detractors the judges should be appointed for no more than three or four years. Those who faulted the *oidores* were supported by Don Luis de Velasco; he wrote the crown that the judges should serve in the audiencia a maximum of five or six years. Diego Téllez, one of the court's most severe critics, suggested that just and impartial persons be chosen to take the *residencias* of the audiencia's members; he also advised Prince Philip to order frequent inspections of the tribunal.[56]

Zorita, Quesada, and Herrera generally cooperated with the viceroy. Tejada, Gómez de Santillán, Mejía, and the *relator* Hernando de Herrera opposed him. Extremely critical of the viceroy, these court officials complained that Velasco ignored their counsel in *acuerdo* sessions, abused his power by meddling in judicial affairs, and was unduly influenced by family interests in his actions. They also claimed that the viceroy's brother Francisco lacked respect for the tribunal's members and interfered in matters reserved for the court.

The hostility shown Velasco by these individuals had its origin in the viceroy's efforts to correct their venality and immorality. In the case of Tejada and Gómez de Santillán it began when Velasco commanded these magistrates to sell the *estancias* and houses they held in the jurisdiction of the audiencia. But when the judges contracted to sell their property by receiving installment payments, the purchasers complained to Velasco that Tejada and Gómez de Santillán had attempted to charge more than the original prices agreed upon. Because the viceroy was authorized to act as judge in cases between *oidores* and other persons, he intervened in the disputes and angered the judges.

To settle these and other differences and draw a clear-cut line between his powers and that of the judges, Velasco asked Charles V to give him more power over the court. He specifically wanted the king to forbid appeals to the audiencia of his administrative decisions removing cattle *estancias* endangering Indian villages. As Chevalier notes, Velasco's efforts to protect the harvest lands of the Indians were constantly frustrated by cattlemen, for they "had recourse to the usual delaying tactics: an appeal to the *Audiencia* (where they doubtless had friends.)"[57]

In 1552, the crown ordered the audiencia to execute all of the viceroy's orders in governmental matters even if his decisions were appealed to the court. In addition, all appeals from the viceroy's decisions to the audiencia were to be sent to the king before final determination. Unfortunately for Velasco, this decree failed to end his problems with those judges who opposed him, and he asked the crown to order a *visita general* of the judges. Instead of ordering a general inspection of the audiencia in 1553, the crown once again ordered the judges not to interfere in governmental decisions specifically charged to the viceroy. In turn, Don Luis de Velasco was required to deliberate all important matters of policy with the court's magistrates.[58]

Although the degree to which the viceroy shared power with the audiencia still remained nebulous in 1554, Velasco's battle with the tribunal may be considered a partial victory for him. In a private letter Prince Philip affirmed the crown's confidence in Velasco. Meanwhile, the transfer of those judges who had given Velasco the most trouble allowed him to act with a greater degree of freedom and confidence.[59]

Velasco's peace with the audiencia ended in 1559. Several of the new judges questioned Velasco's centralization of authority, complained they were under duress, and Vasco de Puga wrote Philip II recommending that the viceroy not take part in the *acuerdo* meetings so that justice might be administered more equitably. Other discontented persons wrote the king, informing him that Velasco was old and sick and that matters of government and justice should be discussed and voted on by the audiencia.

In 1560, King Philip (after lamenting Velasco's illness) ordered the viceroy to deliberate on all matters with the judges before any official determination was made. The result of this new arrangement created an even greater backlog of business. It also encouraged the judges to intervene in any and all matters, notably hampering the administration and embittering Velasco's last five years as viceroy.

An idea of how governmental matters stood is given by Fray Gerónimo de Mendieta in a letter to his superior in 1562:

If the viceroy is asked at the top of one's voice why he acquiesces in or ignores many things that he knows are clearly against the service of God and His Majesty and the welfare of the Indians under his government, he pretends to be deaf or makes empty promises. Moreover, when his orders in these matters are not complied with, he does not reproach himself. Instead, he says that he needs to receive more authority from His Majesty, that he is hemmed in by the judges; and because they are many and he is one, he does what he can and not what he wants or believes is right.[60]

The king's decision that Velasco share his executive power with the audiencia was protested by the religious orders and the cabildo. With the viceroy's permission a commission was sent to

Spain. It consisted of *regidores* Jerónimo Ruiz de la Mota and Bernardino de Albornoz and representatives of each of the three religious orders. This body was to inform the king that the division of authority between the viceroy and the audiencia made for an even greater delay of business than formerly, especially in Indian affairs.

Before the departure of these representatives of the religious orders and the municipal council, the viceroy directed them to petition the king to relieve the audiencia of responsibility for settling Indian affairs. Trivial disputes could be resolved by a committee of *alcaldes ordinarios* and *corregidores*. More important issues (such as boundary and property questions) might be judged by two or three persons appointed to handle these matters exclusively. Velasco's choices for this proposed special court were Judge Alonso de Zorita and the lawyer and former crown attorney Sedeño.[61]

Fray Gerónimo de Mendieta supported Velasco's plan for a more efficient way to handle Indian disputes. He also shared the viceroy's admiration of Zorita and was undoubtedly aware of Zorita's antipathy for lawyers and other interested parties who benefited from the many Indian cases appealed to the royal tribunal. On January 1, 1562, Mendieta wrote Franciscan provincial Fray Francisco de Bustamante. Bustamante and the Dominican and Augustinian provincials, with the advice and consent of the fathers of all the Orders, had decided to go to Spain to give an account to His Majesty of the dangerous state in which matters stood in Mexico. Mendieta made several suggestions that Bustamante might relate to the king; among these was the proposal for speeding up judicial procedure in Indian cases presented to the audiencia regarding land claims between Indian towns. A specific tribunal should handle these disputes, which sometimes dragged on for twenty years without being decided. Composed of from one to three persons known for their Christian piety, goodness, wisdom, and affection for the Indians, the tribunal should visit the Indian villages; after hearing cases relating to boundary claims, members of this special court should settle the lawsuits on the spot without right of appeal. One of the three persons in Mexico possessing the necessary qualifications for the proposed tribunal was Zorita.[62]

In his study of the conflict between Indian and European institutions and law, Woodrow Borah observes that the exercise of administrative power by Luis de Velasco in resolving Indian business

stimulated strong opposition from the *Audiencia*, which held that much
of the business handled as administrative was really judicial and should
come before it. Involved also was the rivalry of the two sets of notaries,
secretaries, and other officials in the viceregal secretariat and the *Audiencia*, both avid for business and accompanying fees. Further, the
protection afforded the Indians by use of administrative process in cases
of seizure of land and goods, invasion by livestock, and extortion by
Spaniards (in private and public function) evoked widespread opposition
among the Europeans in the provinces as well as in Mexico City.[63]

Among the many letters to the crown that mentioned the
differences between the viceroy and the audiencia, one written by
the municipal council in 1562 contained requests seeking an end
to the abuse of power in Mexico. After petitioning for a judicial
inquiry of the viceroy and the judges, the cabildo asked the king
to separate the offices of viceroy and president of the audiencia
by appointing different persons to these positions. Also, the provincials of the three orders and some of the judges wrote the king
in support of the viceroy, and Velasco himself once again requested that a visitor general be sent to Mexico to examine his
work before he left office.

These letters of complaint or praise constantly reminded Philip
II of the differences between Velasco and the audiencia. The
intensely suspicious king decided to send an agent to look into
the matter, resolve questions of Indian administration, and verify
allegations of fraud and loss of potential income to the crown. He
therefore commissioned Licentiate Jerónimo Valderrama to make
a general inspection of New Spain. Valderrama was to investigate
the work of the audiencia, the viceroy, the treasury officials, the
alcaldes ordinarios, and other magistrates, in addition to inspecting the university and the mint and generally informing himself of
Mexican affairs.

Visitor General Valderrama's arrival in 1563 further reduced
the power of the viceroy; his *visita* also weakened the audiencia
and caused Zorita great problems. Critical of almost every individual and institution, Valderrama accused Velasco of unjustly
patronizing only his relatives and cronies, of allowing the friars to
exercise temporal administrative jurisdiction over the Indians (a
function not always compatible with the work of conversion),
and of permitting the judges to seek their own gain and to live in
greater liberty than was reasonable.

Valderrama, described by one historian of Mexico as "a figure
of blurred outlines," was essentially a bookkeeper and the polar

opposite of Christian humanists like Luis de Velasco, Zorita, and the brilliant and passionate Bartolomé de Las Casas. Intensely concerned with the increase of crown revenues and partial to the cause of Martín Cortés and the *encomenderos*, he had little sympathy for the Indians and their defenders. In fact, it appears that the reason Valderrama was so highly critical of the Dominican friars and persons like Luis de Velasco and Zorita was because they differed with his opinions on the condition of the Indians and their ability to pay higher tribute assessments.

Indian Head Counts and Tribute Payments

In his study of the *encomienda* in New Spain, Lesley Byrd Simpson points out that the implementation of the New Laws by Viceroy Antonio de Mendoza had purged the system of labor exploitation of its most notorious fault, "the power to coerce labor," making *encomenderos* virtual pensioners of the crown.[64] Simpson's statement needs qualification in light of more recent research. Reform efforts in the 1540s failed to tame the *encomienda* completely since Indians at midcentury continued to pay excessive tribute to *encomenderos*, *corregidores*, and the native aristocracy. In addition, certain towns in the Valley of Mexico had received no *tasaciones* (assessments), local magistrates or *corregidores* used their offices for personal advantage, and *principales* (under various pretexts) made extra and exorbitant demands for money and goods.[65]

These and other abuses were brought to the attention of the crown by reformers, who called for an end to the countless cruelties inflicted upon the Indians. The crown heeded the cries for reform and instructed Viceroy Luis de Velasco in 1550 to protect the Indians fully and see to their religious instruction. Velasco's emancipation of 150,000 male Indian slaves, the regulation of tribute payments, and the suggestion of a lapse of *encomenderos'* rights to the Indians they held in trust angered those holding *encomiendas* in their third generation. So desperate did some Creoles become about the loss of their Indians that they plotted the murder of the viceroy and the audiencia judges. Once they had secured the country, the Creole conspirators intended to make Martín Cortés king of Mexico.[66]

In Mexico (as in New Granada and Guatemala) Zorita assisted in the task of enforcing the amended New Laws. In his *visitas* and *cuentas* he took counts of the Indians held by *encomenderos* and determined the relationship between the resources and the populations of the Indian towns. Among the many inspections was the count of the Indians held by Don Martín Cortés, the greatest *encomendero* in Mexico and the first example of the rich, Europeanized Creole.

The question of how many Indians Mexico's first family held in *encomienda* began shortly after the fall of Tenochtitlán. In 1522, Hernando Cortés informed the crown that he had introduced the *encomienda* system into Mexico. This occurred when he was "almost forced to deliver the chieftains and other natives" of the newly conquered lands to those Spaniards who had accompanied him in search of the marvelous and wealthy dominions held by the great lord Montezuma. Having also assigned himself an enormous number of Indians and not being disposed to give them up, the Conqueror gave various reasons why he was unable to comply with the emperor's order of 1523 forbidding *encomienda* grants in Mexico.

The crown overlooked this first act of defiance by a Mexican *encomendero*, and by 1524 Cortés's income from his grant of Indians amounted to 42,800 pesos.[67] Five years later, Cortés's holdings (and income) were reduced to 23,000 tributary "vassals," but he was given the title Marqués del Valle de Oaxaca and Captain General of New Spain. This grant and title changed Cortés's *encomienda* into a perpetual fief (*señorío jurisdiccional*).[68]

The Cortés estate, "about five times the area of Connecticut," was inherited by Don Martín Cortés, the conqueror's son by Doña Juana Ramírez de Arellano de Zúñiga, the daughter of the second Count of Aguilar. Born in Cuernavaca in 1532, Martín Cortés was reared at court. He became one of Prince Philip's favorites, forming part of his retinue in England and France and returning to Spain in 1563. Before leaving Spain, Don Martín learned that the lawsuit pursued in vain by his father had been settled. At first it appeared that the Royal Council of the Indies' determination that the estate should not exceed 23,000 vassals in twenty-two towns would prevail. The Cortés family appealed this ruling and insisted that each household, which might include several families, be counted as a vassal. The issue was finally decided in favor of Don Martín in 1560, when the crown ruled that all the towns except Tehuantepec granted to the Conqueror in 1529 should form part of the fief.[69] This royal decree allowed Martín Cortés to receive about 86,000 pesos from some 60,000 tributaries in 1560.[70]

An Aztec aristocrat of the sixteenth century. (Miniature from
the Codex of Bernardino de Sahagún held by the Real Academia
de la Historia, Madrid; courtesy of Marqués de Lozoya,
Historia de España)

Zorita began his count of the Indians held by Cortés in Coyoacán, headquarters of the Spaniards in the last days of the siege of Tenochtitlán. The audiencia's assessment of tribute payments based on Zorita's count and appraisal of resources in Coyoacán and Atacubaya greatly displeased Don Martín. In late 1563 he declared that this new assessment was "the greatest aggravation that had been committed in the world."[71]

Zorita's name appears in another complaint by Cortés, but in a different context. In March, 1564, the Marqués wrote the crown that the friars had asserted that Cortés's *alcaldes mayores* and *justicias* would not allow the Indians to appear before the audiencia to present complaints and that Don Martín had given *varas de justicia* (symbols of authority) to his tribute collectors (*calpixque*) and local magistrates. The Marqués denied the allegations and stated that he had submitted an *información* about these accusations to Zorita, who was then counting the Indians held by Cortés.[72]

Zorita appears to have been occupied with the count of Don Martín's *encomienda* Indians during 1563 and 1564, for on April 28, 1564, the audiencia's record of tribute assessments noted the action of the court regarding tribute payments to be made by the capital town of Oaxtepec and its subject towns. Payments to be made by the Indians in these towns held by Don Martín were based on information provided to the high court by Zorita.

Zorita's eager collaboration with the crown "in its efforts to weaken the economic base of its great vassals" did not greatly injure Don Martín. Following Zorita's adverse report to the audiencia, the court ruled that Don Martín was to receive no service or tribute from the Indians of Oaxtepec and its subject towns other than that specified by the tribunal's assessment. However, Don Martín's tributary vassals were not reduced, and in the early nineteenth century "the Cortés holdings, still in possession of the Conqueror's heirs, composed an immense domain occupied by some one hundred fifty thousand inhabitants."[73]

The crown's inability to complete its offensive against the *encomienda* system and its abuses in the "Silver Age" of Philip II is explained, at least in part, by the actions of Charles V in the 1540s. When the New Laws caused a revolt in Peru and a flood of protests in the other Spanish colonies, the emperor retreated and compromised. The partial repeal of the New Laws marked a turning point in crown policy that culminated in the end of the Lascasian movement during the reign of Philip II.[74] Creole "feudalism" finally triumphed at the end of the sixteenth century, to the detriment of the Indians. This development took place because "total or partial retreat followed every major Crown effort to enforce Indian protective legislation."

An example of the redefinition of Indian policy under Philip II can be seen in the conclusion reached concerning tribute payments. When the crown was asked to choose between material gain or Indian betterment, it opted for greater revenues.

Under Charles V, Indian barrios in Mexico City were exempt from paying tribute because they furnished labor for the construction, repair, and maintenance of public works. Under Philip II the exempt status of the capital's Indians was questioned, and the king asked the viceroy, the audiencia, and other royal officials to determine whether tribute burdens should be imposed on this native group.[75]

Both Zorita and Luis de Velasco were convinced that the Aztecs of Mexico City should continue to be exempt from paying tribute, chiefly because these Indians had formed a privileged group exempt from taxation under Montezuma. They also furnished the crown with the following conclusions:

1. No tribute had been imposed on Indian *vecinos* of Mexico City after the Conquest.

2. Mexico City's Indians were mostly native nobility or "gente principal o hidalgos a su modo," and to make them pay tribute would be the same as equating them with commoners or *macehuales*.

3. If tribute were imposed on these Indians, they would be exempt from work customarily done in the city and the repair of bridges, roads, fountains, and streets. Repairs of this sort were necessary in most years, and were the city required to pay for this work "a great deal of money would be needed and the city does not have the wealth (*propios*) for this."

4. Indian *vecinos* of the city had few lands for planting the grain in which tributes were usually paid.

5. Up to now, Mexico City's Indians had paid tribute for the support of their communities. From what was collected, they had built and continued to raise churches, monasteries, and other works, in addition to paying the salaries for governors, alcaldes, *regidores*, and other officials: "What each tributary pays for this purpose is two and a half *reales* a year, paid at the rate of half a *real* every 80 days; widowers pay half this sum." Although the

Indians gave personal service in lieu of tribute, Zorita claimed they preferred to pay, for they considered forced paid labor more onerous than payment of tribute.[76]

In spite of Viceroy Velasco's pro-Indian stance that the natives of Mexico City should be exempt from tribute burdens and Zorita's remarkable argument citing "the Aztec law of war and peace as precedent for exempting the Indian quarters of Mexico City from payment of tribute,"[77] the crown agreed with the opinions of the treasury officials and judges like Vasco de Puga. Treasury officials declared that the 18,000 tributaries of Mexico City and Santiago de Tlatelolco, rather than suffering any inconvenience, would actually benefit by paying the king. As was apparent from the *residencia* of the governor and *principales* of Santiago taken by Zorita, these native officials had obtained imposts and labor services from poor *macehuales* (commoners) in excess of 50,000 pesos, a much larger sum than any the crown might impose. Consequently, the Indians would enjoy paying a certain, single assessment if they were relieved of the unauthorized and excessive personal services and taxes they were paying their Indian lords.

Vasco de Puga, in defense of his opinion, declared that the Indians were greatly oppressed by their governors and lords, who continued to rob and tyrannize them, "as was the custom in the days of their infidelity." Each Indian commoner in the towns inspected by Puga allegedly paid their governor and *principales* three or four pesos, all of which they spent on getting drunk. Puga was also convinced that the crown in the early 1560s was being defrauded of 200,000 ducats yearly in the seven Indian capital towns, Huejotzingo, Cholula, Tlaxcala, Chalco, Texcoco, Xochimilco, and Mexico City.[78]

Zorita and Don Luis de Velasco disagreed with Puga's opinion. Zorita qualified Puga's claim that Indians were ruthlessly exploited by their lords by noting that, although the Indians of Mexico City had paid excessive tribute and labor services to their rulers up to 1562, these abuses had been curbed and were being eliminated. Velasco, for his part, considered Puga's estimate of the Indian tributaries in these towns highly inflated.

After reading contrasting reports by individuals like Puga and Velasco, the crown must have been deeply confused about the true condition of the Indians of Mexico City. It appears, however, that because Puga's opinion coincided with the government's need for additional revenues, it was given greater weight. On January 18, 1564, each married tributary of Mexico City was obliged to pay an annual head tax of one *peso de oro común* (eight silver *reales*) and half a *fanega* (four-fifths of a bushel) of maize. Single and widowed tributaries were to pay half this amount.[79]

In addition to making tributaries of previously exempt Indians, the crown ordered the audiencia to establish a uniform head tax for both *encomienda* and crown Indians. The usual sum in the early 1560s was a payment of between eight and nine and a half *reales* of silver and half a *fanega* of corn. Widowed individuals and single persons not living with their parents were ordered to pay half of this amount.[80]

The effect of the uniform head tax is difficult to assess, for commentators "were divided, as usual, into two mutually contradictory camps."[81] In theory, a uniform tax eliminated the plurality of material and personal requirements demanded by the crown, the caciques, and the *encomenderos* up to 1560.[82] Accordingly, the crown's objective of making "each family head a tribute payer," with each "paying an equal sum," may be considered a worthy aim. But viewed from another perspective, "tribute reform" was sought because additional revenues were desperately needed by Philip II, and the uniform head tax was the method used to increase Indian tribute burdens.

The best example of a crown official who advocated the increase of tribute paid by the Indians under the guise of reform was Visitor General Jerónimo Valderrama. Before Valderrama's arrival in Mexico on July 31, 1563, imposts had been considerably reduced by Philip the Prudent. In fact, Maldonado, attorney for the crown, appeared before the audiencia in 1559 to "complain that the Crown was losing too much revenue from the constant lowering of taxes on the Indians."[83]

Like his father, Philip II initially allowed the audiencia to fix the tributes paid by the Indians in accordance with the New Laws, which stipulated that payments should always be less than that obtained under the native rulers in pre-Conquest times. He also succeeded in moderating many other imposts paid by the Indians; these included taxes paid by Indian commoners to their caciques, governors, and alcaldes; the community fund; and the building, repair, and ornamentation of churches, as well as the support of the clergy. With the arrival of Valderrama, however, the king's reform efforts ended, and tribute burdens became heavier and more oppressive.[84]

In his letters to the crown Valderrama reported that the tribute payments made by the Indians were small and that they were "getting off too easily." Valderrama's attempt to "reform" the tribute system was supported by other royal agents. In 1565 the *oidor* Francisco de Ceynos wrote the Council of the Indies that tribute assessments had been further curtailed with the arrival of the visitor general. These new assessments were based on inspections and counts already commenced by former viceroy Luis de Velasco. The *visitas* and *cuentas* had shed light on the labor and fees demanded of Indian commoners by their *principales* and governors, the costs of the large monasteries built in the land at the expense of the poor, and other excessive services demanded by some priests and clerics. New assessments were being made daily in accordance with the number of Indians counted and the quality of the land they farmed, and it was no longer permissible for any priest, layperson, or Indian to use the services of these poor people without paying the standard wage (*paga moderada*): "So that when they have paid their tribute they are free of all services and unpaid labor."[85] In short, Ceynos concluded, a sound system of support of the *principales*, clergy, and the upkeep of the churches was, in conformity with Christian and human reason, rapidly being achieved.

The uniform head tax system imposed by Valderrama was later supported by Viceroy Martín Enríquez. In 1575, Enríquez wrote that the head tax system, a personal rather than a property tax, did not injure those who had least, while those who could pay more "receive a favor."[86]

There were contrary opinions. As Simpson notes, "Certain members of the mendicant orders cried that the tribute was the cause of the diminution of the Indian population." He also correctly observes that crown officers like Valderrama "do not make a very convincing case" that the Indians were moderately taxed.[87] Although the crown made an effort to have tribute payments adjusted in crown towns in conformity with "the fluctuation of population and crops," there is "no such positive evidence that the tributes collected by the *encomenderos* were subject to the same kind of rigorous adjustment."[88]

There is evidence, however, that the uniform head-tax tribute system made for greater regularity and increased tribute yields. But the assertion by some students of the tribute system "that a uniform payment had been achieved by 1570" is incorrect. Charles Gibson concludes that in the Valley of Mexico "individual payments still varied and would continue to vary from town to town."[89] Gibson's observation is confirmed by José Miranda, and both point out that tribute paid to Spaniards did not include additional payments made by Indians. In addition to the varied payments made by Indian towns to the crown or to *encomenderos*, Indians also made payments to their caciques and were subject to special contributions, extraordinary duties, and in part the *alcabala* (sales tax).[90]

The one definite conclusion that can be made about tribute in the sixteenth century is that it remained "a continuing annual burden for the Indian communities" and greatly benefited the crown. Keen observes that Valderrama's "insistence on squeezing more tribute out of the Indians" made for the steady reduction of "the number of categories of persons exempt from payment." This measure, as well as the progressive raising of the tribute quota "and the gradual escheat of *encomiendas* to the Crown," increased the amount of royal monies collected annually in Mexico. Between 1550 and 1800 the amount increased from "about 100,000 pesos to well over 1 million pesos."[91]

In spite of the weakening of the *encomendero* class resulting from reform legislation and a determined effort by the royal judges to enforce a uniform head tax, evidence from several sources shows that *encomenderos* continued to abuse their Indians. The Diego Ramírez *visita* (1551–55), for instance, "disclosed the fact that in many places the Indians were overtaxed, that personal service was demanded, and that the Indians were forced to deposit their tribute at the residence of the *encomendero*. The evidence demonstrated that the *encomendero* seldom had provided adequate means for converting the Indians to Christianity."[92] This agrees with Augustinian friar Nicolás de Witte's statement of 1554 that there was a "great difference between the old Indian lords and the Spanish *encomenderos*; the appetites of the former were limited, but the greed of the latter was infinite, which was the cause of the destruction of the land."[93]

Zorita himself roundly condemned the *encomenderos*. He stated that "since the introduction of counts and assignments of tributes by heads, the practice has arisen of collecting tributes from cripples, blind and maimed persons, and other wretches who cannot work and even lack food; and they collect from minors and single young women without means of support."[94]

Zorita also believed that the Indians should pay the tribute only in what "the land yields, be that little or much." Great evil arose from making the Indians pay in money, for many Indians had "never seen a *real* in all their lives, and do not even know what a *real* is." Moreover, apart from a few *principales* and merchants, an Indian's entire fortune did "not amount to the value of the tribute that he must pay. Indeed, there are many whose total fortune does not come to a peso." An Indian who found it impossible to pay the money tribute was sent to jail, "and his time at forced labor [was] sold to some Spaniard to cover the tribute and jailer's costs."[95]

To pay their tribute, many Indians hired themselves out. Zorita wrote that they

must quit their towns and homes, leaving their wives and children without means of support, and go 30, 40, and even more leagues to climates different from their own, where they sometimes [lost] their lives. Sometimes in their despair they [preferred] not to return home, or perhaps one would take to living with another woman and lead a depraved life, leaving all the burdens of supporting his family to his poor wife."[96]

Further evidence of the *encomenderos'* exploitation of the Indians in these years is given by the Audiencia of Mexico's *relator* Francisco de Morales. On April 9, 1562, he wrote the crown that, because the president and judges of the Audiencia of Guatemala were related to a number of *encomenderos* in that tribunal's jurisdiction, they should not take part in any lawsuits and judicial decrees that might result should the crown attempt to recover the land and wealth it had lost to the *encomenderos*. Rather, the person chosen for this mission should be one who would make honest *visitas* and reports of the "excesses, despoilments, exorbitant tribute assessments, and evil treatment of the Indians." He should act as a prosecuting attorney, preparing the lawsuits, deciding cases, and executing the sentences notwithstanding that appeals from his decisions might be sent to the king. "And he should collect and review those *visitas* made by various judges, including those of Doctor Zorita who has a great deal of experience in this important matter."[97]

Morales noted that Judge Jofre de Loaysa had married one of his daughters to a Sancho de Barahona, *encomendero* of Atitlán. Another daughter was married to Bartolomé de Molina, *encomendero* of Apaneca. A niece was married to Juan Rodríguez Cabrillo, *encomendero* of Xicalapa. These holdings were described by Morales as "large provinces." Barahona was a brother-in-law of Licentiate Juan Caballón, the audiencia's prosecuting attorney in Mexico. Alonso Hidalgo, stepfather of the Barahonas, was a nephew of former audiencia president Alonso de Cerrato and *encomendero* of Xalapa. Francisco López, Hidalgo's brother-in-law, was *encomendero* of Naolingo. One of Barahona's brothers was married to a sister of Juan Guerrero, grandson of former president Cerrato and a brother-in-law of Manuel Barros de San Millán, an *oidor*. Governor Juan Núñez de Landecho's relatives were also married to *encomenderos*.

In the same letter Morales declared that the Mexican audiencia's *fiscal*, the late Luis Maldonado, had been a violent man who had greatly profited from trade with Spain, mining investments, trade, and other capital ventures. He had died a painful death but had left his wife, children, and brothers rich and in lucrative positions, one relative holding the post of *alcalde mayor* in Zacatecas, "worth more than his weight in money." This official had led expeditions to make war on the Chichimecas, "taking many Indians from their homes as was clearly verified by Doctor Zorita, *oidor* of Mexico."[98]

Morales also claimed that Juan Caballón, Maldonado's replacement as *fiscal*, compromised because he was related by marriage to *encomenderos* in Guatemala and Mexico. This had proved true in the case of Caballón's brother-in-law, Sancho de Barahona the Younger, who illegally held half the town and province of Atitlán in Guatemala. Although Caballón was required by law to ask that a royal decree be executed ordering that this important capital town be placed in the crown, he had failed to do so. Instead, he had protected Barahona, who received excessive tributes by charging the crown, the possessor of the other half of the pueblo and province, all the costs of religious instruction and other things.[99]

Morales recommended that Caballón be given other employment and be replaced as crown prosecutor by Licentiate Zorita, a brave, firm man and a judge with much experience who feared God and his conscience. Zorita lamented the destruction of the Indians and blamed the inaction of the crown's prosecutors for the mischief and depravity of the *encomenderos*.

Morales observed that in New Spain and Guatemala those pueblos of Indians granted as *encomiendas* to individuals or remaining in the crown had never been inspected, nor had investigations been made of the mistreatment of the Indians by *ecomenderos*, *alcaldes mayores*, and other persons. To be sure, some *visitas* had been ordered, one being the inspection of the *alcaldes mayores* of the New Kingdom of Galicia in New Spain. But this and similar *visitas* had been mockeries, for the men who had conducted them had not had the wish nor the knowledge needed to carry out investigations; in particular they had had no desire to discover the truth concerning the compromising personal relations and interests of these officials.

Those *visitas* that had been made had had little effect, for the greater part of the land remained uninspected. Indeed, these inspections had caused more harm than good, as could be quickly verified in Spain from a reading of the *residencias* of the judges making the *visitas*. Morales included among the ineffective *visitas* those made by Diego Ramírez. All or most of these inspections, he claimed, had come to naught thanks to the false allegations and calumnies of the *encomenderos*.

Morales gave another example of *visitas* that had done no good: those made by Licentiate Zorita in Guatemala. Zorita had officially investigated "enormous crimes, cruelties, and prodigious robberies," substantiating them with many witnesses, judicial inquiries, subpoenas, and all else that was needed. These were the best-documented and most thorough *visitas* ever made in the Indies, in the course of which Zorita had seized and burned forty *cargas* of idols the Indians had worshiped during the thirty years they had paid tribute to their *encomenderos*. Yet Zorita's findings were scuttled by a thousand lies after they had been sent to the Audiencia of Guatemala. Zorita had hardly departed for Mexico when *oidores* Pedro Ramírez de Quiñones and Jofre de Loaysa nullified his *visitas* by freeing the guilty parties after decreeing some light punishments.[100]

Morales urged the crown to order new *visitas* for the vindication and protection of the Indians in Guatemala and Mexico. Those in charge of the inspections should be Christians and true servants of the king, knowledgeable and experienced. The crown should order *corregidores*, *alcaldes mayores*, *calpixque*, *mayordomos*, and *tenientes* to give new *residencias*, for these posts were presently held by persons as guilty as the men they replaced after holding their judicial inquiries.

This should be done for the good of the Indians and for the good of the royal conscience and so that the *encomenderos* might know that there was to be a reckoning where truth and justice would prevail. Further, crimes would be punished and it would be known that "we have a God and a king of truth and justice."

Too long had arbitrary will replaced the rule of law, allowing the *encomenderos* to use the Indians worse than if they were beasts, the result being the depopulation and destruction of many kingdoms, once great but now uninhabited.[101]

Other Duties

In spite of his pro-Indian stance and his opposition to the *encomienda* and *repartimiento* systems, Zorita tried to mete out impartial justice to both Indians and Spaniards in Mexico, as exemplified by his conduct at Teotihuacán, where he settled a dispute between the Indians and the Augustinian friars. The Franciscans originally had the duty of instructing the Indians of San Juan Teotihuacán. But when the Augustinians founded a monastery only one league from the town, this religious order was given the *visita* of Teotihuacán as part of its ministry. A *visita* of this sort was quite different from the tours conducted by *oidores* and investigations made by a visitor general.

A monastery, as Lino Gómez Canedo says, was usually built in the ecclesiastical capital and had charge of various towns in the same district. The monastery town was called a *cabecera* and the communities under its jurisdiction were called *visitas*. Unless there was an abundance of friars, the missionaries generally did not reside permanently in the *visita* towns. If the district was extensive or heavily populated, several *visitas* might be grouped into an *asistencia*, or vicarage, with permanent residence by the friars. "All of this in the aggregate formed what was called a *doctrina*, or an organization whose end was to evangelize or to instruct (*doctrinar*) the Indians. Hence the friars occupied in this task were called *doctrineros*. *Doctrinas*, in their definitive phase, were simply Indian parishes."[102]

In 1557 the Augustinians decided to build a monastery in Teotihuacán because they had a surplus of friars and because the town's population, numbering some 2,000 *vecinos*, was able to support the cost of constructing and maintaining the proposed monastery. The Indians, however, were opposed to this project because they feared the expense and work involved in constructing the large buildings that were planned, and because they hoped eventually to be reassigned friars of the Franciscan order.

After rejecting the Augustinian project for their town, the Indians of Teotihuacán visited a Franciscan chapter being held in Mexico City and asked this order to minister to them. Both

Commissary Francisco de Mena and Provincial Francisco de Bustamante discussed the matter with the Indians, telling them that they should be satisfied with the good instruction they were receiving from the Augustinians. Unhappy over the failure of their petition, the Indians left after telling the friars that they would not cease in their efforts to have the Franciscans reassigned to their town.

Meanwhile, the Augustinian provincial assigned two of his religious to the pueblo. When these friars reported that the Indians would have nothing to do with them, the provincial asked the viceroy and the archbishop for help in resolving the problem. The *alcalde mayor* of Texcoco, Jorge Cerón, and the archbishop's ecclesiastical judge were sent to Teotihuacán to investigate and settle the issue. In Teotihuacán, Cerón and the archbishop's representative agreed that the Indians were acting like rebels. Cerón broke one alcalde's *vara*, symbol of his jurisdictional authority, seized another's, and ordered all of the *alguaciles* (Indian police) to be whipped in the town square. The ecclesiastical judge, a certain Licentiate Manjarres, was as harsh as Cerón. After ordering all the Indians of the church stripped and beaten, he preached a mass to the naked and fettered Indians.

The *provisor* and the *alcalde mayor* having departed, the Augustinians in charge of the monastery ordered the Indians to paint the images of various saints, including that of their patron, on the main door of the building the friars occupied. This was done, but one night the images, symbols of Augustinian possession, were obliterated. The friars failed to identify the person or persons responsible for this insolent act but did order the whipping of several Indians who they thought knew something about the matter. When the sentence was carried out and the Indians refused to reveal the names of the culprits, Licentiate Manjarres was again sent to bring peace to Teotihuacán.

Manjarres ordered several Indians punished after circumstantial evidence indicated that they were involved. The Augustinians then thought to prevent further disturbances by having the viceroy appoint as judge and governor of the town an Indian *principal* of Culhuacán. Troubles continued, however, when the new Indian governor, Don Andrés, seized several *principales* and commoners and jailed them. Other Indians then broke into the jail and allowed the prisoners to escape.

Following this incident, the five or six Indians who were still friendly to the Augustinians told Don Andrés where the town's leaders had hidden more than 4,000 pesos in money and other valuables belonging to the community. Don Andrés collected this wealth and deposited it in the community fund (*caja de comunidad*). This action, however, made the hostile Indian leaders aware that the friars had spies in the town. Thereupon the informants were seized and beaten almost to death, their houses were destroyed, and they were expelled from the town.

When the friars and Don Andrés attempted to prevent the expulsion of the informants, a riot took place in which the friars were pushed about and rudely insulted. The Indians might have done worse things, but fortunately for the Augustinians the *encomendero* Alonso de Bazán happened to be in Teotihuacán. He drew his sword and allowed the friars to beat a retreat to their quarters. Bazán then had the good sense to quit the town with Don Andrés.

Following the report of the Augustinians that Teotihuacán was in a state of revolt, the viceroy and the audiencia agreed that Zorita, "one of the *oidores*, a very Christian man, and well liked by the Indians for his goodness, should go there."[103] Zorita took about ten Spaniards with him, and was also accompanied by several other men led by the *alcalde mayor* of Texcoco. When they were still two leagues from Teotihuacán, Zorita and his group were met by all the town's inhabitants. As a welcoming gift the town's cacique, Don Francisco Verdugo, gave Zorita some roses,

among which were some small leaves suspended which shine like latten-brass. And there were not lacking some who said that in order to bribe him, the Indians had given him roses made of gold and that he would not do justice. The judge became aware of what was said, and sent the gift of roses to the friars so that they might see what they were.[104]

In Teotihuacán, Zorita gathered all the Indians together. His investigation revealed that all the Indians claimed collective responsibility for their insolence and misdeeds—as in the case of the Spanish village of Fuente Ovejuna made famous by Lope de Vega's play of that name: "And so that he might not blame some more than others, and that it might not be said that he had gone for nothing, he had about 60 Indians arrested, and of these he ordered 20 to be placed in *obrajes* (textile sweatshops) to work there for six months and serve as a warning and example to the others." The rest of the Indians having been set free, Zorita returned to Mexico City.

Following Zorita's departure, another peace emissary, the Franciscan friar Juan de Romanones, arrived in Teotihuacán. Admired and respected by the Indians of Teotihuacán, he was sent by his order to aid the Augustinians in their efforts to be accepted as the tutors of the town. This saintly friar preached to the Indians in their own language but failed to persuade them to accept the Augustinians as their guardians. Similar efforts were made by other Franciscans, but the Indians obstinately refused to change their minds.

The conflict was finally settled when the Augustinians left Teotihuacán just before it was completely abandoned by the Indians. In their voluntary exile the Indians made the crown aware of their plight through an account they sent to Spain with the audiencia's *relator*, Hernando de Herrera. After the king ordered that the Indians were not to be forced to receive other priests to instruct them, but only those Franciscan friars they asked to preach, the Indians returned to Teotihuacán.[105]

The Spanish scholar Serrano y Sanz has condemned Zorita for being unjust to the Indians of Teotihuacán in their dispute with the Augustinians. But when one reads Mendieta's account of the affair, it is easy to see why both Benjamin Keen and the Mexican scholar Joaquín Ramírez Cabañas agree that Zorita's sentence was "a graceful way of defending the prestige of authority with the least possible severity."[106]

In addition to his work relating to the Indian question, Zorita had many other duties, one of which was the taking of *probanzas* or depositions by Spaniards in which they related their services on behalf of the crown and their need for *mercedes* before the audiencia. Zorita's signature and those of the other judges can be found on a goodly number of depositions concerning clerics, the religious orders, and the sons of conquerors.[107] An example is the following letter, its subject one of the leading citizens of Mexico City:

Sacred Caesarian Catholic Majesty. At the request of Hernán Pérez de Bocanegra, citizen of this city of Mexico, this royal Audiencia made an inquiry regarding the quality and merits of his person so that it might have recourse to it in supplicating Your Majesty that some grant be given him in conformance with what Your Majesty has ordered. This official inquiry proves his quality, merits and intelligence, and that Hernán Pérez de Bocanegra is a *caballero hijodalgo* and conducts himself as one. He is married, has a wife and married children, and his house is stocked with arms and horses. He holds the *encomienda* of the pueblo of Acámbaro and its subjects for Your Majesty. He is worthy of any grant which Your Majesty may choose to order be given him. Don Luis de Velasco. Doctor Zorita. Doctor Villalobos. Doctor Horozco. Doctor Villanueva.[108]

In 1526, Hernán Pérez de Bocanegra, a native of Córdoba, Spain, arrived in Mexico with Licentiate Luis Ponce de León, appointed by the Council of the Indies to take the Conqueror's *residencia*. Both remained in New Spain. Ponce de León died before taking Cortés's *residencia*, and Hernán Pérez became an *encomendero*. In 1560 the Indians of Acámbaro, in the bishopric of Michoacán, were paying Hernán Pérez a yearly tribute payment of 3,000 pesos in money, wheat, corn, and chickens. The Indians of Apaseo, another *encomienda*, paid him about 1,000 pesos, and 6,000 pesos were realized from his farm holdings around these *encomiendas* in northern Michoacán. This was not the whole of his yearly income, for Hernán Pérez also "owned a vineyard, an inn, and three mills, . . . plus an impressive string of cattle and sheep estancias" in the Acámbaro-Apaseo region.[109]

Hernán Pérez's several sons married well. One son, Bernardino Pacheco Bocanegra, *regidor* in the municipal council, was married to Viceroy Luis de Velasco's niece, the daughter of Francisco Vázquez de Coronado, and received his *encomienda* with his wife. Luis Ponce de León, another son, was married to another niece of the viceroy; he held his *encomienda* through his wife. Still another son, Nuño de Chávez, *corregidor* and heir to his father's *encomienda*, was married to a daughter of Coronado.[110]

All the viceroy's nieces had a great number of relatives in Mexico City through their mother Doña Beatriz, one of five daughters of Alonso de Estrada, the treasurer and governor of the colony in the 1520s.[111] These marriages produced many sons and daughters, and the Bocanegras were related to most of the Creole aristocracy in Mexico City.

Among these aristocratic Creoles related to the Bocanegras were the members of the Ávila family. The conqueror Alonso de Ávila acted as an ambassador for Cortés and auditor for the colony and was then appointed auditor for Yucatán by Francisco de Montejo in 1526. During the time that he was in Yucatán, his brother Gil González de Benavides, was given control of his brother's estate. Gil González was a greedy, cruel, and arrogant man whose avarice stopped at nothing. Given control of his brother's estate, he swindled him out of it, denying that there was a contract between them. Gil González became a leading member of the colonial elite, receiving tribute payments from the *encomiendas* of Cuautitlán, Xaltocan, Zirándaro, Izmiquilpan, and Guaimeo.[112] As for Alonso, he died "almost desperate" in Yucatán, and "it is said that he cursed his brother, and asked God to avenge him, and that neither his brother nor his children should enjoy his estate, and so it came to pass."[113]

Gil González de Benavides's four children did meet tragic ends. One evening his youngest son, a noisy, energetic lad, was playing with other children and fell into a privy filled to overflowing; he drowned in the excrement. An only daughter, María, fell in love with a mestizo youth of humble social rank. When her brothers found out about the affair, the youth was threatened and bought off; the daughter became a nun when she was convinced that her lover, Arrutia, was dead. Years later, María received a letter from her true love, stating that he was alive and well and had returned to Mexico from Spain. Having taken her vows and aware that she could never marry Arrutia, she went crazy and committed suicide. Gil González's two other sons, Alonso de Ávila and Gil González, were killed for their part in the "Cortés-Ávila conspiracy."[114]

Don Martín Cortés, joyously greeted by the Creole aristocrats when he arrived in Mexico City on January 17, 1563, immediately became the new social leader of the colony. Members of both the Bocanegra and Ávila families were constantly seen in his company at the many banquets, balls, masked promenades, and other activities that occupied much of the Creole elite's time.

Frivolity had been common among the city's privileged youths before the arrival of Don Martín, but it seems to have reached extremes after he displaced young Alonso de Ávila as the most important socialite. To meet the costs of conspicuous consumption, many sons of conquerors went into debt. Failing to meet their payments, they were forced to pledge the income of their estates. In this manner the rich merchants of the city became the true lords of these *encomenderos'* estates.[115]

In addition to indulging in costly entertainment, many Creoles gambled and went further into debt. Immorality became, if not more common, at least more notorious. It was rumored, for example, that Martín Cortés was carrying on an affair with Doña Marina Vázquez de Coronado, the wife of Nuño de Chávez Pacheco de Bocanegra. This, gossip had it, was why Don Martín favored the Bocanegras, sons of his father's enemies in the early years of the colony.

Flattered and fawned upon by many important Creoles, Don Martín in turn sought the favor and friendship of Licentiate Jerónimo Valderrama. The visitor general accepted Cortés's offer to stay in his house, and they soon became the best of friends. Meanwhile, the Marqués made an enemy of Don Luis de Velasco by his arrogant attitude and extreme greed.

Cortés was not so forgetful of his wealth that he neglected to take an inventory of it. Soon after he settled in Mexico City, he had one of his agents make a count of his vassals and the total yearly income derived from their payments. This income, according to one estimate, was perhaps 150,000 pesos.[116] News of this fabulous income reached the crown, and "the king, who thought the revenue almost too royal for a subject, . . . directed the solicitor general to notify Cortés that the [crown] had been deceived with regard to the value of his *encomiendas*. Doctor Zorita was consequently deputed by the Audiencia to make the count of the Indians, and the report was against the holder."[117]

Not only did the crown order Cortés's Indians to be counted, but it ordered the viceroy to suspend transmission of *encomiendas* to the third generation. Greatly disturbed by the order, the *encomenderos* held many meetings where they lamented their plight, for most of these grants were already in their third life. The *encomenderos* stated that

before they would consent to this, they would rather lose their lives than allow that to be taken which had been won by their fathers, leaving their sons with nothing. Because they were greatly disturbed, the Devil easily found servants among them to do his work, "By God!", said some, "We're acting like chickens ripe for the plucking. Since the king wishes to take our food and wealth. let's take the kingdom from him. We'll avert this tragedy by revolting and giving the land to the Marqués, for it is his, since his father and our fathers won it by their own efforts."[118]

Rumors of the intended revolt soon reached the viceroy. He also heard that Alonso de Ávila, his brother Gil González, a certain Baltasar de Aguilar, and others had already appointed a *maestre de campo* and other officers. In addition, these flighty youths had given the titles dukes and counts to various leaders, after which they had talked to Martín Cortés about their plans for New Spain.

Though realizing that most of the talk about a revolt was only hot air, the viceroy decided to intervene. He summoned various persons allegedly involved in the conspiracy and warned them in a friendly, gracious manner. The loose talk of the rebellious young Creoles soon ended, and the affair would probably have soon been entirely forgotten had Luis de Velasco continued to govern the colony; unfortunately, he died on July 31, 1564. The void left by the viceroy's death, Bancroft declares, "was painfully felt. The members of the *Audiencia* failed to command respect; they overlooked small offences, and greater ones were engendered thereby."[119]

A number of factors account for the weakness of the government under the audiencia. At the time of the viceroy's death Valderrama was conducting his inspection of the judges, and the court's power "virtually devolved on the *visitador*."[120] Valderrama further weakened the audiencia's authority by suspending some judges. Zorita continued to serve in the audiencia, but during two of the three years the *visita* lasted, his illness prevented him from fully carrying out his duties.[121]

Even before the reduction in its staff and Zorita's illness, the audiencia had more litigants and work than the judges could reasonably handle. In 1558, for example, Velasco requested that more judges and alcaldes be appointed to the court; his letter confirms Mendieta's description of the court in 1562 as "nothing more than the image and picture of hell."[122]

Velasco wrote that only three judges were handling audiencia matters. Although these judges (Zorita, Bravo, and Villalobos) worked as hard as possible in the lawsuits, there was no diminution of work. Many cases had been deferred because they could not be tried and concluded, with great vexations resulting to the parties, the treasury, and the Indians. Velasco noted that this was not the first letter he had written asking that judges and alcaldes be appointed to the court.[123]

The *encomenderos'* first act upon the death of "the Liberator of the Indians" was to have the municipal council ask the crown not to send them any more viceroys. Instead, the crown should appoint Jerónimo Valderrama governor; the cabildo asked that Cortés himself be made captain-general. The crown disregarded this audacious request—a request that reveals the long-range ambitions of Alonso de Ávila, Bernardino de Bocanegra, and other *encomenderos* represented in the cabildo. As Bancroft observed, the *encomenderos* were "anxious to secure the perpetuity of their privilege" and "looked to the possible rule of the Marquis, the chief man among the *encomenderos*, and of Valderrama, his warm friend, as the best means of attaining this object."[124]

As Creole fears and hopes concerning the inheritability of the *encomienda* grew, the *oidores* continued to fall behind in their work. Just before Velasco's death the court reported that the audit of the treasury officials by two judges, scheduled to take place yearly in the months of January and February had not been made owing to pressing daily obligations. For this reason the judges requested that a *contador de cuentas* be appointed to take the audit.[125]

The judges also failed to prosecute public disturbances, and when two of the Bocanegra brothers were arrested for fighting several men with drawn swords in a public street, the court was influenced by Martín Cortés to acquit them of all charges. The Bocanegras' enemies, aware of Cortés's intervention, now included the Marqués among their foes. They began to ignore courtesies previously tendered to Don Martín by all the city's gentlemen, refusing, for example, to take off their hats and escort him through the streets to wherever he was going. This so offended Martín Cortés that only the archbishop's intervention prevented open war between the friends and foes of the Marqués.[126]

As the threat of violence on the city streets continued to grow, on May 6, 1565, the king declared that Cortés must answer charges by the prosecuting attorney of the Council of the Indies that His Majesty had been deceived in the grant of Indians made to the Marqués. Before his death Viceroy Velasco had written the king that Don Martín had more than 60,000 vassals and received tribute payments in the amount of 84,387 pesos, more than double the number of Indians the king had decided to give him. After studying Velasco's letter, the crown's *fiscal* declared that the grant originally made to the Cortés family "was both surreptitious and arreptitious, inasmuch as it had been obtained without stating the correct number of vassals, or the revenue and jurisdiction, and through a representation that it was of little value to the royal patrimony."[127] Cortés received this royal order on September 28, 1565.

Shortly after Cortés was notified that he was being sued, a fleet arrived in Veracruz, "and rumor soon had it that the king's final decision on *encomiendas* had been unfavorable to holders."[128] Once again Alonso de Ávila and his brother Gil proposed rebellion. Disgruntled *encomenderos* flocked to Alonso de Ávila's house; among them were persons who soon gave away the conspiracy. Those who revealed the plot may have done so from feelings of loyalty to the king, or perhaps because they wished to destroy Martín Cortés and his friends.

Plans for the uprising began in September, 1565, and continued with slight interruption until July 16, 1566, when the principal conspirators were arrested. It appears that the rebels planned to kill the royal judges and Licentiate Valderrama. They would then seize the arms in the royal arsenal. While the *oidores* were being killed, other conspirators would dispatch the other royal bureaucrats in the city. Luis Cortés would lead the band that would kill the judges. Licentiate Cristóbal Ayala de Espinosa would lead the attack against other crown officials and kill Luis de Velasco, the son of the deceased viceroy, and Francisco de Velasco, the viceroy's brother.

The bodies of the dead judges and other officials would be exposed in the public square so that all might see them. The royal exchequer's funds would then be given to the soldiers of the city, but merchants and citizens would be done no harm. However, all archival documents would be burned in public view so that the king's name should become a dim memory in Mexico. The conspirators would then make Martín Cortés king, ending tyranny in the land.

Once King Martín Cortés had moved into the palace to dispense justice to his loyal subjects, his brother Luis would leave for Veracruz to take the port and then seize and sink the ships in the harbor, thus preventing news of the uprising from reaching Spain. Meanwhile Martín Cortés, Doña Marina's son, would march north to kill the judges of the Audiencia of Guadalajara and seize the mines of Zacatecas.

After these important places were successfully occupied, an assembly (*cortes*) would be summoned in Mexico City at which all the cities, pueblos, and villas of the kingdom would swear obedience to the new king. The prelates of the church having approved the election of the new sovereign, Dean Alonso Chico de Molina would depart for Rome, well supplied with gifts, to ask the pope to recognize the new Mexican kingdom. Gifts would also be sent to the king of France to persuade him to establish diplomatic relations with Mexico. The new monarchy would establish free trade with all nations for the purpose of attracting trade and profits. Free trade, the retention of the large sums sent each year to the Peninsula, and Mexico's many haciendas, mines, and industries would end the country's dependence on Spain.[129]

Judge Vasco de Puga claimed that until the end of the year 1565 the rebellion was kept so secret that nothing was known about it. Many arms and munitions were stored in Alonso de Ávila's house, where Don Martín, his brothers, and Baltasar de Aguilar gathered each night to set the day for the uprising.[130] A *dueña* of the household, a former employee of Vasco de Puga, overheard the conspirators' talk. Having learned the date of the revolt three days before it was to take place, the woman went to Puga's house early one morning. After telling him everything, the *dueña* warned Puga to take care because the first act of the rebels would be to come to his house to kill him.

On the same day that he learned of the plot, Puga wrote, he informed Licentiate Valderrama and those at the *acuerdo* meeting what was being planned and insistently recommended that Valderrama and the judges investigate the matter. Valderrama, Puga claimed, opposed the idea and forbade the judge to do anything. At twelve o'clock that night Valderrama allegedly met Don Martín Cortés and told him what Puga had said in the administrative session.

Puga claimed that his removal from office eight days after the *acuerdo* meeting came about because Cortés and Valderrama were in agreement that sooner or later Puga would initiate a formal judicial investigation. The matter was then hushed up, "and no arms or munitions were found in Alonso de Ávila's house." Since nothing about the plot was written in the next six months, Puga's news of a planned uprising was the first notice given of the conspiracy.

Following his removal from office Puga left for Spain "to shed light on this matter." At his own expense he brought in the same ship the principal witness concerning the plot, Cristóbal de Oñate. At court Puga gave his version of the conspiracy to His Majesty but was not entirely believed. Cristóbal de Oñate then fled from Puga, leaving Seville for Fuenterrabia, on the French border. Puga wrote:

At this time a dispatch boat came from New Spain with the news of the rebellion. Then, by order of His Majesty, the Lord Bishop of Osma shut himself up with me from one to five in the evening to study the brief I had given His Majesty. At this meeting I explained everything to him; he and Licentiate Ulloa, the Crown's attorney, urgently charged me to find Cristóbal de Oñate. With great effort, in the space of three days and nights, I discovered where he was and sent for him. He was then brought to this court where he stated what he knew and shed light on the whole affair.[131]

Oñate was the nephew of Don Cristóbal de Oñate, conqueror and one of the "silver kings" of Zacatecas. He was hanged for his part in the conspiracy. The Oñates were descendants of Lope Díaz de Haro, the lord of Vizcaya who took Baeza from the Moors in 1227. The conspirator's uncle arrived in Mexico in 1524. He married Doña Catalina de Salazar y de la Cadena, daughter of Gonzalo de Salazar, the first *factor* (business manager) of the exchequer in New Spain. An issue of the marriage was Juan de Oñate, *adelantado* and governor of New Mexico.

The chief conspirators in the plot were Alonso de Ávila and his brother Gil González, Bernardino Pacheco Bocanegra, and the Marqués's brothers, Luis and Martín, knights of the Military Order of Santiago. Associated with the chief plotters were Licentiate Cristóbal Ayala de Espinosa, Dean Alonso Chico de Molina, Diego Rodríguez Orozco, Baltasar and Pedro Quesada, Pedro de Aguilar, Cristóbal de Oñate, and other lesser figures.

A detailed investigation of whether there was an actual conspiracy and how deeply Martín Cortés and his brothers were involved in it still remains to be made. Still, the audiencia judges took it seriously and made numerous arrests. Hernán Pérez de Bocanegra's five sons were put under house arrest, and three were tortured. None confessed, but Bernardino Pacheco de Bocanegra was sentenced to death. Fortunately, Bernardino was related to the principal families of Mexico City, and his mother, his wife, and his relatives, as well as the prelates of the religious orders, begged the judges for his life. After being allowed to file an appeal, he was sentenced "to forfeit his estate and serve twenty years at his cost at the *presidio* of La Goletta in Tunis. Having served this sentence, he would suffer perpetual exile from all the kingdoms and dominions of the king our lord and would suffer death if he violated the terms of this sentence; thus he did not die at that time."[132]

It appears that Martín Cortés was aware of the conspiracy but played an ambivalent role in it. Bancroft's conclusion that the Marqués thought it an impractical plan "devised by hot-headed men"[133] must be qualified. Other students of the affair believe that Cortés "vacillated between ambition and fear" and wanted to "pull the chestnuts from the fire with the cat's paw."[134] After being exiled to Spain, Martín Cortés was finally acquitted of any part in the conspiracy, but he was fined 50,000 ducats and made a forced loan of 100,000 more for war expenses. He never returned to Mexico, and it was only in 1574 that the crown restored his sequestered property.

Alonso de Ávila Alvarado and his brother Gil González were beheaded. In life Alonso had enjoyed an income of 20,000 pesos. He was described as having very fine features, taking great care of his handsome face, very white and elegant in manner, "and so neat and well-dressed that they called him the Lady, for none, of whatever station, took such care to beautify and adorn herself."[135]

That splendid storyteller Juan Suárez tells us that he saw Alonso lose "his life, honor, and estate." He also saw

his head on the gibbet, run through by a large spike driven in from the top of the head, through that dainty skull, brains, and delicate flesh. Without the protection of a plumed hat, or the cap trimmed with pieces of gold that he wore when arrested, that hair which he had so carefully curled and dressed to make it beautiful, and the mustache, once diligently twisted and set, fell limply down his face, exposed to the rain which fell in the public square.[136]

Two other conspirators who had proved a bane to Zorita were arrested by *oidores* Ceynos, Villalobos, and Orozco. These were Diego Rodríguez Orozco and Dean Alonso Chico de Molina. Rodríguez Orozco, *encomendero* of Tutupeque, is an obscure figure.[137] Zorita tells us that this individual had been brought before the audiencia to defend himself against grave charges, and Zorita was one of the judges. His *encomienda* may have been vested in the crown for his part in the conspiracy, for on November 10, 1567, his property was sequestered.[138]

Before his arrest Alonso Chico de Molina had been accused by Archbishop Montúfar of holding heretical beliefs. In 1565, Montúfar noted that all the Mexican bishops had written the crown about the evil lives led by Chico de Molina and Sancho Sánchez de Muñon, the schoolmaster of the cathedral chapter. Imprisoned several times for their improper and disgraceful actions, they were, the archbishop said, two strayed sheep careless of their souls.[139]

Testimony in the trial of the conspirators reveals that Chico de Molina and Fray Luis Cal had talked with Martín Cortés, and both had agreed that Hernando Cortés (and his heir) had more right to the land than did King Philip. It was also said that, once the kingdom was established, the new monarchy's representative, Dean Alonso Chico de Molina, would attempt to have the pope recognize the rebel government and would seek to establish relations with the French king.

These charges were sufficient to have Chico de Molina deported to Spain. Upon his departure Montúfar expressed his satisfaction with the "peace and concord" prevailing in both ecclesiastical and secular affairs now that this pernicious individual was gone. Montúfar was convinced that the dean was implicated in the conspiracy and noted that he was a vindictive, dissolute man capable of bearing false witness. In Madrid, the dean, despite his priestly office and his caballero status, was tortured but did not confess his guilt. Presumed guilty in spite of his silence, Chico de Molina was deprived of his office and remained permanently maimed in one arm from the torture he had suffered.[140]

Zorita's Infirmities and a Lascasian Project

Zorita in this period was frequently absent from audiencia sessions. In 1558 he explained these absences to the crown. In addition to having been partially deaf for four or five years, he also suffered from generally poor health. He believed that his infirmities were the result of his ten years of traveling in lands of contrasting climate and temperature. In the course of his *visitas* in New Granada and Guatemala, Zorita had traveled in the rain, the cold damp of the mountains, and the humid heat of the lowlands. At day's end Zorita many times had been forced to sleep outdoors in desolate places.

Although Zorita claimed that he could still hear and functioned well enough that none found fault with his work, he was especially conscious of his handicap when he talked to his colleagues during public court sessions, for these exchanges involved trading opinions while the judges were sitting on the elevated platform before the vote was taken.

Zorita ascribed his growing deafness and worsened ill-being to bad lodgings and the unhealthy night dews of Mexico City. When he and his wife arrived in the city, they lived in a damp and infectious house that had an irrigation ditch at its base from which emanated a smelly pool discharging evil vapors. Moreover, the evening dews and damps he inhaled on his way home from audiencia consultative sessions gave him "humedades ... en el estómago" and were "very bad and dangerous for the head." Zorita insisted that he wished to continue serving in his office, for his salary was his only means of support, but because his deafness might worsen, the crown should decide whether he should be replaced on the court. He had written the crown about his ailments to relieve his conscience, but he was aware that those who had written to the king had also probably mentioned his deafness and other infirmities, given their nature.[141]

In 1560 the audiencia reported that for more than two years Zorita's deafness had prevented him from effectively performing some duties, especially those dealing with the resolution of cases and during public court days. On these and other occasions, the judges exchanged views before the votes of the individual judges were taken, "and it is awkward to have to speak loudly to him."[142]

Two days before the tribunal wrote the crown about Zorita's illness, Zorita himself wrote to the king recommending that Miguel de Contreras y Ladrón be appointed judge in the Audiencia of Mexico. Zorita's letter suggests that he thought that the crown would soon replace him on the bench and therefore nominated Contreras—an act that demonstrates Zorita's desire to help a man he thought had been wronged.

Contreras had been appointed judge in the Audiencia of New Galicia (Guadalajara) on May 21, 1547. He had arrived in Española in one of the several ships making up the convoy in which Zorita sailed for the Indies in 1548. After presenting his credentials to the Audiencia of Mexico in late 1548 or early 1549, he and his colleague Lorenzo Lebrón de Quiñones journeyed to New Galicia.[143] Zorita noted that Contreras had served as judge in that district for about nine years before being suspended from office after his *residencia* was taken. Because the Royal Council of the Indies had not bothered to review the charges against Contreras, this suspension had now lasted more than three years.

Zorita defended Contreras by noting that reliable persons had told him that Contreras had served well in his office. In the *visitas* Contreras had made of the mines and pueblos held by rich and powerful men, he had upheld the king's provisions for the benefit of the Indians and freed many slaves who had been forced to work in the mines. Because he had offended the powerful, these Spaniards had unjustly accused the judge of immorality and other crimes.

In Spain, Zorita and Contreras had been colleagues in the lawyers' association of Granada. He and Contreras had practiced before the Audiencia of Granada for several years. Later Contreras became a *regidor* in the *Ayuntamiento* of Vélez, Málaga, where he was living when he received his appointment as *oidor*. Contreras, described by Zorita as a good lawyer and a Christian,

now lived in Mexico City and was married to a daughter of
Licentiate Cerrato, "who served Your Majesty so well in these
parts for ten or twelve years that none has surpassed him and few
have equaled him." Cerrato had died a poor and unhappy man,
leaving very little to his children. Moreover, Contreras had so
many children that even if Cerrato had left him and his wife
everything there would have been very little to give to his ten or
twelve children, "most of them daughters and some at the age for
marriage."

Zorita asked the king to order the Council of the Indies to
review the *residencia* charges against Contreras, taking into
account the years of service given to the crown by both Contreras
and Cerrato. Should Contreras be found guilty of some excess or
misdeed, the manner in which the judicial inquiry had been held
should also be taken into account. Given Contreras's great affection for the Indians and his long experience in their affairs and
matters related to judicature, Zorita wrote, it was better for the
crown to be served by Contreras after rebuking him if any guilt
was found than to be served by others of unknown character.
Zorita noted that in Mexico judges who upheld the crown's
interests were greatly resented; he ascribed part of Contreras's
misfortune to his enforcement of unpopular laws in a frontier
district where self-sufficient colonists acted as their own judges.[144]

The crown eventually confirmed Zorita's favorable opinion of
Contreras. In his study of the Audiencia of New Galicia, J. H.
Parry found that Licentiate Pedro Morones, former prosecuting
attorney of the court in Mexico City, who was assigned to investigate the judges of New Galicia, interpreted his commission
as authorizing him to break Contreras and Licentiate Lorenzo
Lebrón de Quiñones. Parry wrote, "The charges against Lebrón
were amply refuted by the detailed clarity of his own reports and
by the testimony of Velasco and the missionaries."[145] Contreras's
guilt or innocence was not as apparent, but it appears that "he too
had been arrested principally because he had offended powerful
interests." In 1562, Contreras was found guilty of one charge,
"that of accepting gifts from litigants." In 1566 he was appointed
senior judge in the Audiencia of New Galicia. In 1572 he was
appointed judge in the Audiencia of Mexico but died before
assuming his duties in that post.[146]

The Council of the Indies did not immediately appoint Contreras to the tribunal in Mexico City but allowed Zorita to resign
his position. On February 10, 1561, Zorita wrote the crown that a

caravel had arrived in the port of New Spain on January 6. It brought the permit authorizing him to return to Spain and a decree granting him one year's salary as moving expenses. How-ever, since his hearing and vigor had improved, and because Viceroy Velasco had asked him not to leave for Spain until the fleet scheduled to arrive in April or May reached port, Zorita was able and eager to continue in his office until then.[147]

Meanwhile, Zorita's friends, among them the provincials of the three orders in Mexico, urged him to remain in New Spain because the Indians needed his protection. After learning that his health and hearing were better, Friars Pedro de la Peña, Francisco de Bustamante, and Fray Agustín de Coruña wrote the crown requesting that the authorization for Zorita's departure be re-voked. They stated that Zorita had worked for the good of the friars, defending them and the Indians of New Spain. Also Zori-ta's excellent counsel was needed in the audiencia, for some newly appointed judges would benefit from his experience.[148] After Viceroy Velasco joined the friars in their request that he remain in Mexico, Zorita heeded his friends' appeal and conceived of a project that showed him to be "a true follower of the teaching of Bartolomé de las Casas."[149]

Zorita, as Keen observes, "knew that the great Dominican had entered among the warlike Indians of the province of Tuzulutlán in Guatemala, and that he had applied his doctrine of conquest by persuasion so successfully that the province was renamed Vera Paz to commemorate its peaceful conquest."[150] In his work on the life of Las Casas, Henry Raup Wagner suggests even closer ideological links between the two men, asserting that Las Casas "carried on an extensive correspondence with the talented Judge Alonso de Zorita."[151]

Wagner's assertion is supported by some circumstantial evi-dence. Las Casas, who praised Zorita's work in Guatemala, may have been directly in touch with Zorita at this time. In 1561, Zorita stated that the bishop of Chiapas had written reprimanding him for seeking permission to leave his post. This indicates that either Las Casas, known as bishop of Chiapas even after he resigned his office in 1550, or Tomás de Casilla, who replaced Las Casas as bishop, wrote to Zorita telling him that he must stay in Mexico, "for it was a question of conscience."[152]

Another bit of evidence that suggests extensive correspondence between Las Casas and Zorita is found in a curious letter of September 1, 1559, sent to Las Casas by Francisco Morales, the royal court's *relator*. This letter, whose contents are very obscure, notes that Zorita may have written Las Casas about Morales's performance of his duties in the Audiencia of Mexico. Morales, who came to Mexico at Zorita's urging, observed that Las Casas had written to Dominican provincial Pedro de la Peña concerning Zorita's work in the audiencia, Zorita's disappointment in not being appointed president of the Audiencia of Guatemala, and the fact that Morales had acted as notary in the *visita* of the pueblos comprising the *encomienda* of Zorita's relative, Gabriel de Aguilera. In this investigation of Aguilera's treatment of and demands on the Indians he held in the Archbishopric of Mexico, Morales had acted as notary. Agustín de Las Casas, the nephew of Bartolomé de Las Casas and the son-in-law of Diego Ramírez, had acted as *visitador*. When Agustín de Las Casas died soon after making this tour of inspection, the *encomenderos* rejoiced, stating that God had heard their prayers.[153]

Thus, although we do not have definite proof that Zorita and Las Casas "carried on an extensive correspondence," it is certain that Zorita added to his firsthand knowledge of Indian affairs by reading manuscripts and published writings of "the very learned and studious Bartolomé de Las Casas."[154] Zorita also learned about the Indians north of Mexico City from lay settlers like Gonzalo de Las Casas, a caballero and person of quality who had written on the peoples of New Spain, especially of the Chichimecas.[155]

Zorita's duties in the audiencia and his interest in the far northern frontier of New Spain led him to make further inquiries. He was aware, for example, that after Alvar Núñez Cabeza de Vaca arrived in Mexico City in 1536, Fray Antonio de Ciudad Rodrigo, the Franciscan provincial, sent three friars on ships commissioned by Don Fernando Cortés to make a voyage of discovery in the South Sea. This expedition of 1538 "arrived in Cíbola, a thickly populated land similar to Spain which extends as far as Florida."[156]

In the same year, Fray Antonio sent Fray Marcos de Niza and the lay brother Onorato to the north by way of the Pacific coast. They formed part of an expedition led by Francisco Vázquez de Coronado in search of new lands. Having passed the lands already discovered and conquered, the friars and Coronado found two roads in the land of Topira north of Culiacán. Coronado elected to explore the road to the right, and the friars chose the road to the left. After a few days, the group led by Coronado reached rugged sierras and was forced to return to San Miguel de Culiacán. Meanwhile, Brother Onorato fell ill, but Fray Marcos in the company of the black slave Estevan and another interpreter followed the road that led to the coast. Fray Marcos came to a land inhabited by a poor people, who treated him well; there he learned of a thickly populated land farther north whose people had houses of two and three stories in enclosed towns on the shore of a great river. The Indians told Fray Marcos that beyond the river were larger pueblos. Zorita noted that this land, rich in turquoise and buffalo, was later discovered by Hernando de Soto. Following Soto's death in that land with half his men, many armed expeditions had been sent in search of that country, "but God kept them hidden, desiring that a barefoot friar should find it."[157]

Zorita also possessed an account, probably written by Fray Gregorio de Beteta, of Fray Luis Cáncer's expedition to Florida in 1549 and his martyrdom in attempting to apply Las Casas's ideal of spiritual conquest in that land.[158] Also, Spanish-Indian conflict continued in New Galicia even after the Mixtón War and the *encomenderos* of that jurisdiction had ignored the New Laws. Aware of the continuous warfare that raged between Spaniards and Chichimecas, Zorita undoubtedly contrasted chronic conflict on the far northern frontier with the apparent success of the Dominicans in pacifying the "Land of War" in Guatemala.

The concern felt by Las Casas and the three orders for the just treatment of New Spain's Indians was apparent as early as 1546. In that year, an ecclesiastical meeting of bishops, friars, and "men of conscience" was held in Mexico City to discuss the instruction and conversion of the Indians, their well-being and civil status. Because Viceroy Mendoza would not permit the bishops to discuss the subject of Indian slavery, Las Casas convoked a second meeting for the friars alone. Although the friars discussed the injustice of past Indian wars and condemned the practice of enslaving Indians captured after they were attacked as rebels, the slave system was in continuous operation in the following years. In fact, Spanish-Indian conflict increased in the next decade, and by 1560 "it seemed that the whole frontier burst into flames."[159]

Three years after the friars' meeting, the Council of the Indies advised Charles V to halt all expeditions of discovery and conquest previously granted; it also recommended that no new expeditions be allowed, giving as a reason the great harm that would be done to the Indians. Should the king decree otherwise, he should order that friars accompany these *entradas*, for their presence would assure the instruction, conversion, and good treatment of the Indians. If new expeditions were allowed, a junta of theologians, jurists, and other experts must be convoked to decide how these expeditions should be conducted. The junta's decisions concerning conquests would have the force of law both in the expeditions authorized by the Council and by the audiencias, "because we do not believe that what has been ordered by the New Laws and other decrees of Your Majesty sufficiently corrects the problem."[160]

This opinion of the council led to the temporary suspension of expeditions of discovery and conquest and to the assemblies of Valladolid, where in 1550–51 Las Casas and Juan Ginés de Sepúlveda clashed in debate over the legality of Spanish conquests. As is well known, the crown reached no definitive decision regarding conquests. It did, however, continue the ban against armed invasions and favored so-called peaceful conquests. "In reality," writes Lino Gómez Canedo, "neither Sepúlveda nor anyone defended the sanguinary methods to which Las Casas referred." Nor did anyone exclude the use of some force or pressure in the evangelization of the Indians. For instance, Bartolomé de Las Casas's idea of a system of fortress-trading posts to be established within the Indian territory of Cumaná (1519–21) "had the same purpose that *presidios* did at a later date: to safeguard the lives and works of the friars and settlers against unjustified attacks by the Indians."[161] Hence what the jurists, theologians, and other experts discussed at Valladolid was the method to be used by the friars in the conversion of the Indians. Should the friars enter Indian territories alone, trusting in the kindness of the natives? Or should the friars enter Indian lands in the company of soldiers or settlers? Or should political conquest precede spiritual conquest? In the last two cases, was the use of force justified?

Answers to these questions varied among individual Franciscans. For example, Sepúlveda claimed that Fray Bernardino de Arévalo, one of the members of the assemblies of 1550–1551, had supported his position. In contrast, Fray Rodrigo de la Cruz wrote the king from Jalisco in 1550 to defend missionary expeditions in which no Spaniards accompanied the friars. But in 1562, Fray Pedro de Ayala, bishop of Guadalajara, informed the crown that missionary expeditions usually failed when they were not preceded by Spanish settlers. On the other hand, Fray Andrés de Olmos proposed the settlement of the coast north of Tampico in

1556, but without conquest, so that the safety of both the Spaniards and the fierce, naked Chichimecas of the coast might not
be endangered. Once these formidable people, nomads without
crops or houses, realized that no harm would be done to them,
they would more easily be subjected.[162]

Since Olmos wrote to Las Casas about his plan before its
approval by the Audiencia of Mexico on November 16, 1556,
Zorita and Las Casas were both aware of this Franciscan project.
Once the Chichimecas in the vicinity of Tampico were converted,
Olmos and his colleagues would depart for Florida from there,
because it was "very near" the province of Pánuco. Olmos's
proposal, similar in some ways to Zorita's project for the Borderlands, was cited by the latter in 1584 as proof of the viability of
spiritual conquest.[163] This idea of peaceful conquest also confirms
the statement by Cervantes de Salazar that in the opinion of many
Spaniards "only one thing [was lacking] to complete the happiness of the province ..., that the Spaniards conquer and put
beneath the dominion of the Emperor the land of Florida, which
one can reach quickly and easily by sea, and the way is not too
difficult by land."[164]

The genesis of Zorita's Las Casas-style offer to pacify the
Indians of the far northern frontier appeared as early as 1558. In a
letter to the crown Zorita stated that in previous communications
he had informed His Majesty that the Orders of Saint Francis and
Saint Dominic intended to send friars to the Indians of Florida
and the Chichimecas "in order to indoctrinate and convert them
to our Holy Catholic Faith." The learned Franciscan Commissary, Francisco de Mena, was even then probably at court and
would give full information on this and other matters. Other
friars from Peru, Chile, and New Spain had left Mexico in a
group bound for the Peninsula, and the Dominican friar Juan de
Torres had also gone to Madrid to give information on the affairs
of Guatemala.[165] Since Mena and Torres undoubtedly saw Las
Casas in Madrid, Zorita was probably indirectly in touch with
Fray Bartolomé at this time. In any case, by 1561 both Zorita and
the Franciscan lay brother Jacinto de San Francisco had written to
the Crown and outlined their plan for the conversion of the
Indians north of Mexico City.

Zorita's offer to peacefully convert the Chichimeca Indians
"had many points resembling the Vera Paz experiment," and
Henry Raup Wagner has noted that "the judge may have received
his plan directly from Fray Bartolomé, or at least encouragement

to try it."[166] Zorita asked to be appointed governor and captain-general of the lands under the jurisdiction of the Audiencia of New Galicia. He would lead an expedition numbering approximately 100 soldiers and 20 Franciscans into the Land of War beyond Culiacán and Chichimeca territory. The region to be entered led to Florida, New Mexico, Copala, lands discovered by Coronado, and other fertile provinces inhabited by large populations ripe for conversion and potentially rich in gold and silver mines. The Indians would be attracted to Christianity and civilization by gifts, affection, good works, and example. Indian messengers at peace with the nomads would be sent to invite the natives to settle in towns and plant crops. A friar would be placed in charge of each Indian town founded, and Spaniards would be forbidden to occupy lands allotted to the Indians. Spaniards allowed by Zorita to enter the land would found settlements a good distance from the Indian towns. No *encomiendas* would be granted by Zorita, and all converted Indians placed in the crown should be exempt from tribute for several years.

The base of operations for this Lascasian project was to be New Galicia. Zorita planned to leave one or more lieutenants in Guadalajara while he personally supervised the pacification and settlement of the Indians. To avoid division of authority between the Audiencia of New Galicia and himself, Zorita asked that this subordinate tribunal be abolished. He defended this part of his plan by pointing out that many citizens of New Galicia had testified that the tribunal was not needed in the region.

Each of the Spaniards who would accompany Zorita and the friars for protection would receive an annual salary of 300 *pesos de tepuzque*, valued at eight *reales*, or 272 *maravedís*. Zorita believed that his plan, once approved, would yield positive results in two years. "In that time His Majesty would risk no more than 50,000 or 60,000 ducats; he could hope to win many thousands of souls for Heaven, many thousands of ducats for the royal treasury, and many great kingdoms and provinces for himself."[167]

Zorita's letter to the crown was sent with a transcript of another letter written by Fray Jacinto de San Francisco. Fray Jacinto's letter was obviously sent to strengthen Zorita's proposal, for this individual had practical experience in the northern Mexican mission field. Fray Jacinto had arrived in the New World in 1515 and had been on at least one of the exploratory expeditions made prior to the epic voyage made with Hernando Cortés in 1519.

As a conqueror, Fray Jacinto had performed many notable services for the crown; they included taking possession of the South Sea for the royal patrimony. Cortés had rewarded him with an *encomienda* comprising various pueblos. His Indians, including many slaves, mined gold until God chose one day to reveal to him that he was bound on the road to hell and eternal punishment, after which he relinquished his *encomienda*, freed his slaves, and donned the habit of the Franciscan order. In 1561, the year of his petition, Fray Jacinto had served God as a lay brother for more than thirty-three years.

Fray Jacinto wrote that from the time of their arrival in New Spain, the Franciscan missionaries had heard of New Mexico, although the truth of this land's existence had not been established. To confirm these reports, and hoping to accomplish as great a conversion of the northern tribes as that achieved by the Franciscans in Mexico, Fray Jacinto and two companions went in search of this land. Several Spaniards sent to protect the three friars accompanied the missionary expedition. Fray Jacinto led the party some 150 leagues north of Mexico City where they met various tribes at war with the Spaniards, "perhaps with good reason." The Indians had treated the friars well, and had requested their children be baptized, "demonstrating their great satisfaction with us." While they were converting these Chichimecas of the north, the viceroy and Franciscan provincial sent word that the friars must return to Mexico City. The friars were told that because Tristán de Luna's expedition in June, 1559, from Mexico to Florida had left few men in the colony, Viceroy Velasco had been unable to send the number of Spaniards necessary for the completion of the mission. Because they were displeased by the departure of the friars and "for other good reasons," the Indians they had visited had since killed certain Spaniards.[168]

Fray Jacinto was eager to return to his chosen mission field, but was fearful that the same pattern of conquest he had witnessed in the past would take place. This type of conquest would result in conversion of the Indians by the friars, the settlement of the former in villages, the arrival of colonists, and the destruction of the Indians from excessive labor, cruelty, and tyranny. The Indians could then rightly state that the friars had deceived them.

In previous conquests, Fray Jacinto pointed out, land belonging to the Indians had been petitioned for by Spaniards; the colonists claimed that because the land was vacant, nobody benefited, and they would make it productive by raising livestock. When officials commissioned to look into the matter agreed with the colonists' claims, the Indians said that the friars, under the pretext of Christianity, gathered them into villages for the purpose of giving the Spaniards their land.

To conserve and protect the Indians of the north, Fray Jacinto proposed that the king should give the Franciscan order the responsibility of pacifying the lands visited by Coronado beyond Zacatecas and San Martín. One hundred Spanish soldiers and an equal number of friendly Chichimecas would initially aid the friars in their work; in time as many as 2,000 friars might be employed in the conversion of the Indians in New Mexico and other lands. The Spanish soldiers who would protect the friars were to be given grants from crown lands or mines to be discovered, and there were to be no *encomiendas*, no enslavement of Indians, no wars, and no killings. The governor and captain-general who would lead the expedition and receive the title of coadjutor and assistant to the Franciscan order should be a zealous Christian chosen by the friars for the crown. Fray Jacinto wrote that it was the opinion of the regular clergy, the Spaniards, and the Indians of Mexico that the man who possessed the qualifications and experience for the plan he envisaged was none other than "Dr. Alonso de Zorita, His Majesty's judge in the Royal Audiencia."[169]

Zorita's petition was probably presented to the Royal Council of the Indies by Las Casas and the Franciscan friar Alonso Maldonado de Buendía in 1562, the same year in which they defended Indian capacity.[170] Las Casas and Maldonado were supported in their effort by the three Mexican provincials who left for Spain in the spring of 1562 "to discuss matters of importance to the service of God, the king, and their supporters." They were prepared to testify concerning Zorita's services and necessity, and hoped that the king might be pleased to grant him the favor "which Our Lord may desire."[171]

Benjamin Keen has noted that the council "evidently found the projects of Fray Jacinto and Zorita fanciful, and Zorita's demands excessive."[172] Zorita's proposal recommended that the cost of churches should be borne by the king and that the Indians should pay no tithes and be free from tribute for ten years; it also asked for 40,000 or 50,000 ducats for the hundred Spaniards he would take with him. In addition, the crown should grant these settlers and their descendants an annual salary in perpetuity and assure

Zorita that for ten years the crown would not take from him the offices he requested, and would grant him an annual salary of 12,000 ducats, as well as all-embracing powers to banish those Spaniards he judged ungovernable.[173] The official reply to Zorita authorized him to try his proposal, but at his own expense, "which," as Wagner notes, "was impossible." Rather than peaceful conquest, the Crown's representatives chose to answer Chichimeca hostility by a policy of "war by fire and blood."

Although Zorita's project was rejected by the crown, it had a certain significance and result. In addition to being "the first of many joint endeavors on behalf of the Indians during the next few years" by Las Casas and the Mexican missionaries,[174] the Zorita-Fray Jacinto plan

may have had some effect in the peaceful settlement of several places beyond Zacatecas in the first half of [the 1560s]. The most important of these settlements, composed of Spaniards, friars, Tarascans, Aztecs, and peaceful Chichimecas, was at Nombre de Dios, strategic for the pacification of the San Martín-Durango region, which had been so close to disaster in the fighting of 1561.[175]

Also, when the policy of *guerra a fuego y sangre* failed to bring peace to the Gran Chichimeca, new policies emerged "which closely resembled the projects of Fray Jacinto and Zorita."[176] Spanish domination of northern Mexico was finally achieved "by a combination of diplomacy, purchase, and religious conversion." Gifts of food and clothing were given the natives, as well as the promise of good land, seed, and agricultural implements to prospective Indians farmers. "Out of the experience of this pacification grew the mission system that was to serve Spain so well in later expansion on the American continent."[177]

Zorita was unaware of the future significance of his plan for spiritual conquest at the time it was rejected. The optimism and renewed vigor he had felt in working with the friars quickly left him when his dream was rebuffed. His idea "of leading a great crusade for the material and spiritual salvation of a world of Indians" gave way to doubts and concerns reflected in the "doleful and querulous tone" of his letters.[178]

Zorita's Retirement

In addition to being deeply troubled by his poverty and the illness he denied, Zorita was also subjected to the *visita* held by

Licentiate Valderrama. As appears from his letters, Zorita continued to serve in his office but was not very effective. In early 1564, Valderrama observed that Zorita's request that he be allowed to retire because he was deaf had been approved, along with a certain grant. This permit to return to Spain had been rescinded when Zorita's hearing had supposedly improved. However, Valderrama noted that in a letter to Doctor Francisco Hernández de Liévana, a member of the Royal Council of the Indies, Maldonado, the audiencia's *fiscal*, "had written more truthfully that Zorita was not physically fit to do his work as a judge."[179]

Valderrama believed that when the friars failed in their effort to have Zorita appointed captain of "the expedition to Copala at Your Majesty's expense," Zorita had changed his mind about retiring. Having decided to continue in his post, Zorita had the friars testify that he was in good health. The friars had consented to do this "because they like him, for good reason in my opinion. But it is certain that he is not in condition to serve, for he cannot hear the proceedings in the trials nor does he understand what his companions vote upon in the administrative sessions." Valderrama noted that when one of the judges voted, Zorita was unable to understand the reason for the vote and was content to know whether his companion had condemned or absolved the defendant. Regretting his shortcomings more than anyone, Zorita would cast his vote so that the sentence would not be decided by it:

If a judge is absent in the review of a case in which he voted so that no sentence resulted, or for any other reason sentence is passed by his vote, he changes his opinion so that it may be remitted. This is very inconvenient, but I absolve my conscience by mentioning it. Should Your Majesty make a decision concerning his post, it is just that he be given the grant previously approved or a larger one. If his *visita* confirms any other things against him, this will have been determined when it is officially transmitted."

Zorita was inspecting Indian villages held in *encomienda* by Martín Cortés when he learned that Valderrama, after asking witnesses testifying before the audiencia if Zorita had a hearing defect, had said that Zorita should be retired with a grant of three or four years' salary. Aware that the crown had been informed that his deafness seriously impaired the administration of justice in cases coming before the court, Zorita defended his capability to the crown in a sorrowful letter which claimed that the witnesses had declared that he did not have a hearing defect, "because if they speak to me in a voice slightly louder than usual, I hear well."

Zorita noted that Valderrama had been discreet in investigating his capacity to serve, but it was entirely possible that what Valderrama had decided might be exaggerated by local citizens who enjoyed spreading rumors and embellishing fact with fancy.

Finally, admitting that he did have a hearing problem which might get worse because he was old and infirm from the many assignments and journeys he had made, Zorita humbly implored the crown to grant him permission to return to Spain. But so that it would not appear that he had been dismissed from office, Zorita requested that he be recalled to Spain to give information relating to the service of God and His Majesty. Should the crown grant this favor, Zorita would be provided with a gracious way of leaving his office.

Zorita pointed out that this favor he requested could have a positive outcome. At that moment the *encomenderos* had gathered in Mexico City with Valderrama's permission to discuss perpetual right to their Indians and the partition of the land. When this matter had been debated in Peru, the crown's commissioners in that viceroyalty had ordered that notice of the question be announced to the Indians so that they might reply to the proposal, "and what service they might give Your Majesty in order to be placed forever in the Royal Crown of Castile." According to Zorita, the opinion and desire of New Spain's Indians to be crown subjects would not be heard unless the crown ordered that they be allowed to discuss the matter and be given the right to choose a person to represent them.[180]

Zorita's wish to represent the Indians was probably discussed with the viceroy, for his letter of February 10, 1564, was shortly followed by Velasco's letter praising Zorita's work and recommending that he be asked to give an account of Mexican affairs to the Council of the Indies once Valderrama's *visita* was completed.[181]

While Zorita waited for permission to return to Spain, Licentiate Jerónimo de Valderrama investigated affairs in the colony. Valderrama, an officious bureaucrat with a bookkeeper's mentality, complained of everyone except his friend Martín Cortés.

To the visitor general, Viceroy Luis de Velasco was inept in matters of government, justice, war and finances. Velasco was also accused of unjustly favoring his relatives and friends, and of having fallen under the pernicious influence of the friars. According to Valderrama, Velasco had allowed the friars to exercise dominion over the Indians in temporal matters, a situation not always compatible with their role as teachers of Christian doctrine. Valderrama stated that if the Indians were oppressed, the fault lay with the regular and secular priests who were not corrected by their provincials and prelates.[182]

Valderrama had an especially low opinion of the Dominicans; to be sure, some, he wrote, were good men,

> but few are qualified or even have a little natural prudence. The dregs of their houses are usually sent from Castile, and on their arrival they find themselves with such absolute authority that they swell up with presumption. This arrogance is enhanced by instruction they suckled from the Bishop of Chiapas. Hence one has great difficulties with them.[183]

Both the viceroy and the judges took advantage of the Indians, but the friars were the worst offenders. The Indians in general were not inclined to work and were addicted to drink, but the most vicious were the Indians raised in the convents. "Since they are lazy and *ladinos* [crafty Spanish-speaking Indians] and favored by the friars, they go about from house to house with flageolets to the great offense of God and harm to the pueblos." Although the friars exempted the Indians from tribute payments, they exploited them in other ways. The viceroy, for example, allowed the Indians to build the friars sumptuous and expensive buildings instead of the humble and modest monasteries required by law; one such building was the convent of Cuiseo, "and that not the largest," where more than 190 Indian servants provided for the friars.[184]

Valderrama's complaints about the friars did not pass unnoticed. On January 2, 1564, Dominican provincial Cristóbal de la Cruz and other dignitaries of the order wrote the crown about these charges. Aware that Valderrama believed the Dominicans hid the most Indians in the tributary counts and exploited them, the friars replied that because walls could not be hidden their buildings should be inspected so that it might be decided whether they were built in accordance with the crown's wishes. The Dominicans had forty-eight houses and monasteries under construction, only three of which were completed. This delay in construction was explained by the fact that the Indians worked voluntarily on the buildings without being bothered by the order. With the exception of a few buildings, most were humble and lacking in novelty or excess. In fact, many of the houses were in such poor shape that the friars risked their health by living in them. Further, the Dominicans pointed out that they did not own the buildings; they belonged to the crown and were used by the Dominicans for the crown's service, propagation, and authority. The friars ended their reply to this charge by noting that all construction had been discontinued until the model and sketch to be followed was received.

The crown was also informed that the Dominicans understood that plans were being made to regulate and modify what they should eat and wear, for "they wish to decree that each minister shall be paid 100 *pesos de oro común* in the manner of day laborers and mercenaries. This sum is spent by a man of middling wealth with a small family on his household each week in this land." Although the Dominicans did not spend this amount on their food and clothing, this salary would prevent them from paying medical bills and other expenses, including the costs of the divine service.

The Dominicans asserted that if the king wished to know how the Dominicans lived and how they performed their office and ministry, His Highness should consult their vicar Don Luis de Velasco. The trustworthy Velasco, in addition to his great skill and experience in governing the kingdom, was also a devout Christian who zealously desired the betterment of the Indians and knew of the great service all the religious had done for the crown in New Spain. There were also many other persons of good intentions who could be trusted to say the same.

Although the order did not know who had made the king believe they were forward, meddling in affairs that did not concern their office and ministry, they were aware that because of these accusations they had lost His Majesty's favor. Because these charges wronged an order that was in the forefront of all who served the king in New Spain, they had decided to write the crown to refute these sinister reports. The Dominicans were especially troubled that Licentiate Valderrama had specifically mentioned these charges, thus singling out the order in the general *visita* and *residencia* that he had proclaimed publicly.

Valderrama's denunciation of the Dominicans to the general public had greatly surprised the friars and had given their rivals and competitors great joy. These opponents now stated that the Dominicans' conduct would be examined and their lapses exposed, "as if we were pagans and publicans deserving of great enmity and punishment." The order did not fear the *visita*, but they were shocked that the king should have believed their detractors. Should impassioned and aspiring persons charge them again with things they had not done and were incapable of doing, the king should suspend judgment until the Dominicans were informed of the charges and allowed to truthfully clear themselves of such deceptions and slanders.

The Dominicans concluded their letter by stating that they feared the frequent and regular counts, computations, and assessments made of the Indians would soon become distasteful to the natives and prove a disservice to the crown:

In exchange for the increase of a bit more money in the royal treasury, the Indians become confused, disturbed, and scandalized, causing them perhaps to believe that we seek them out and care for them not for their bodies and souls but for their wealth. Such treatment makes them sad and they want to die. They perish in great numbers and there is among them much pestilence, so that in a few years there has perished in this land an innumerable amount of people. In this way the loss of the land and the Indians is jeopardized.[185]

In addition to castigating the regular and secular clergy and asking for the removal of the viceroy, Valderrama was severely critical of the judges who numbered six in the years 1560–64: Francisco de Ceynos, Licentiate Luis de Villanueva Zapata, Alonso de Zorita, Pedro de Villalobos, Jerónimo de Orozco, and Licentiate Vasco de Puga. He suspended Villaneuva and Puga, and was sure that the senior judge, Ceynos, was a good man with Indians, whom he liked and helped, though he was too old to handle important, complex litigation: "Before God and my conscience, he is not fit to be a judge, nor is Your Majesty well served by keeping him here."[186]

Although the *oidor* Villalobos was the subject of the worst reports submitted to Valderrama, the visitor general believed that this judge was the ablest magistrate in learning and recitude and that he enjoyed high popular regard.[187] Villalobos was found guilty of various minor charges in 1572 by the Council of the Indies. They included the fault of frequently arriving late for work and quitting early or being absent from audiencia sessions during many days of the year.[188] Villalobos continued to serve in the Mexican tribunal until 1572; he ended his career as the president of the Audiencia of Charcas.

Like Villalobos, Orozco was eventually found guilty of various minor charges. In 1572, the crown appointed him the first governor-president of the reorganized Audiencia of New Galicia. Assuming command of a local force against raiding Indians in 1580, Orozco died defending the province he administered.

As previously noted, Vasco de Puga and Luis de Villanueva Zapata were considered useless and venal judges and suspended by Valderrama. The Council of the Indies eventually confirmed many of Valderrama's serious charges against these two judges in 1571 and 1572. However, the council revoked Valderrama's dismissal of Puga and Villanueva in 1567. Both judges served provisionally in the Mexican audiencia until the council's review of Valderrama charges.

Although Villanueva was condemned to pay 1,500 ducats and suspended from office for ten years, he was readmitted as a judge in 1575. When he died in 1583, Villanueva was serving as senior judge in the audiencia and presided over the government because of the death of the viceroy Lorenzo Suárez de Mendoza, Conde de la Coruña.[189]

In addition to Valderrama's specific charges against the judges, he also claimed that they failed to prosecute criminal cases and that half of the *oidores* were related to citizens by marriage.[190] Some idea of the indignation that Valderrama's accusations produced is suggested by Vasco de Puga's petition to the Council of the Indies in 1575.[191] Puga's condemnation of Valderrama may be considered suspect by those who are aware that Puga claimed that the visitor general's investigation had cost him more than 20,000 ducats in appealing the sentence that ordered his suspension from office for five years and a fine of 4,200 pesos. Still, most of what Puga stated about Valderrama rings true when his venomous letter is compared to Zorita's and the Dominicans' judgment of the visitor general.

Puga wrote the Council of the Indies that when he arrived in New Spain in 1559 he found that all of the judges except himself lacked experience in the many duties required of a judge serving in a royal tribunal. For this reason, he had worked very hard—as was widely known in Mexico and evident from his *visita*—to give the high court order and efficiency. Puga had also become aware that the king was being defrauded in the assessment of tribute payments and counts of Indians. To remedy this situation, he had written a letter to the Council of the Indies in which he offered to save the Indians the 300,000 ducats they were being robbed of annually at the same time that the royal income was increased by

100,000 ducats yearly. After he was commissioned to take the count of the Indians, Puga completed the task in nine months—an assignment he claimed could easily have taken three or more years to complete.[192] Puga's count yielded higher estimates of the Indian population, and he asserted that the "order" that had taken place was being maintained in the 1570s.

In 1563, Puga was recounting and reassessing the provincial towns when he learned that Visitor General Jerónimo Valderrama had arrived in Mexico and accepted Martín Cortés's invitation to stay in the latter's house. Shortly after becoming the Marqués's guest, Valderrama allegedly formed a confederacy with his host and Alonso de Ávila. Puga claimed that in an intimate conversation the three allies agreed that Martín Cortés should be given possession and jurisdiction of his estate. This caused a great deal of work and trouble, for two judges were appointed for this purpose and "they gave him more than what belonged to him, from which resulted litigation in the *Audiencia*." In legal proceedings Cortés was in several instances granted properties that Puga claimed he held unjustly. However, when Puga's arguments lost Cortés other properties, the Marqués and his confederate Valderrama came to hate Puga greatly.

The visitor general's antipathy for Puga increased when the high court's prosecuting attorney, Juan Caballón, died. Valderrama discussed this vacancy in the audiencia with Cortés and they agreed that a certain Licentiate Carvajal, a relative of Alonso de Ávila and Cortés's and Ávila's attorney, should be appointed to the position.

Shortly after Caballón's death, Puga, who was making a tour of inspection, was summoned to the capital to discuss his replacement by Ceynos and the treasury officials. Although ill, Puga quickly returned to Mexico City and convinced the other *oidores* that the royal tribunal "had no need for a prosecuting attorney other than one opposed to the Marqués, for should the reverse occur the interests of His Majesty would be greatly harmed." For this reason, the votes cast for crown prosecutor went to Licentiate Contreras, formerly *oidor alcalde mayor* in New Galicia. Valderrama and Cortés bitterly resented Contreras's appointment and they remained on bad terms with Puga.

A few days after the new *fiscal* was appointed to the audiencia, Puga once again angered Cortés and Valderrama by accusing the high court's chief police officer of an unnatural crime. Because the defendant Gonzalo Cerezo was worth 100,000 ducats and was related to some of Valderrama's relatives, in addition to having been Martín Cortés's lance bearer before becoming the court's perpetual *alguacil mayor*, none of the judges other than Puga had dared accuse him of sodomy.

Once Puga succeeded in having Cerezo suspended from his office, Valderrama and the Marqués sought to have Don Martín Cortés, the son of Doña Marina, appointed to this post. To gain their objective, they had many third parties visit Puga. These flunkies, according to Puga, failed to get him to agree to the appointment, further infuriating Cortés and the visitor general.

In the petition, Puga stated that he had served the crown as a lawyer in Granada prior to his appointment as *oidor*. He had served the crown for twenty years, and had been a judge in the Audiencia of Mexico for sixteen years. After being suspended from office by Valderrama in late 1565, Puga appealed his case personally in Spain and notified the king of the Cortés-Ávila conspiracy. His discovery and disclosure of the plot came six months before its collapse from within.

After being reinstated as *oidor*, Puga was ordered to return to Mexico. He refused to do so unless the charges in his *visita* were reviewed, stating that his trip to Spain had been for this very purpose. After being told that nothing in the *visita* hindered his return to Mexico and that the king would so order, he was reassured by the king and the bishop of Osma that all was well "with many pleasant words."

After returning to Mexico, Puga served well and was appointed general of the Spanish forces when the English ships commanded by John Hawkins arrived at San Juan de Ulúa in September, 1568. Serving at his own cost and without salary, Puga "went as far as Puebla de los Angeles with the flower of the men of New Spain, and had we arrived at the port before the viceroy took charge, the affair would have had a greater success and there would have been less danger than there was."

As is generally known, when Viceroy Martín Enríquez arrived with the Spanish fleet, he found the English ships blocking his entry. After negotiating with Hawkins, Don Martín pledged his word that he would not fire on the fleet if he were allowed to land. Once ashore, the new viceroy of Mexico broke his word and ordered the English ships destroyed. Hawkins and his cousin, Francis Drake, escaped the harbor but later had to abandon 200 men near Pánuco to relieve their overburdened vessels. These men were captured and tried by the Inquisition.

Having shed his armor for the judge's robe, Puga was serving in this capacity when once again he was suspended from office in 1572. He also was "condemned to pay 4,200 pesos, which has been the cause of the total destruction of my life and estate, for I have sold everything I owned to pay my debts and my life is impaired by bad health and the gray hairs my age demands are evidence of this."[192]

To meet expenses, Puga sold his house in Mexico to Lorenzo Porcallo de la Cerda on May 30, 1574, for 18,500 pesos.[193] He was reinstated as *oidor* on August 21, 1575, and died in Mexico.

Zorita was not found as culpable as Villanueva or Puga when the Council of the Indies completed its review of Valderrama's charges against him on February 7, 1572. The council dismissed fifty-three of these charges but did find Zorita guilty of various minor offenses, for example leaving the audiencia before the proper time on days when open court sessions were held and rationalizing his absences by stating that all petitions had been processed. There were also several serious charges of which he was found guilty. One involved a certain Francisco Díaz de Ayala, who had confessed under torture that he had committed an unnatural sex act with Don Juan de Saavedra Cervantes.[194] When the prosecuting attorney requested that the torture be repeated because the confession had been obtained by pressure and the accused had not ratified his confession the day after the ordeal, as was required by law, "Doctor Zorita, the judge handling the case, did not order this done nor did he exercise proper care, with the result that the said Ayala fled the jail and was not punished for this crime."

Zorita's definitive sentence barred him from holding office for three and a half years, and he was ordered to pay 100 ducats. Half of this fine was to go to His Majesty's exchequer to become part of the fines forfeited to the royal treasury for the payment of salaries and expenses of the members of the Council of the Indies. The other half was to be divided equally between the fund that paid transportation costs of friars sailing for the New World and that which paid for the maintenance of the royal halls of the Council of the Indies.

Because Valderrama's complete *visita* of the members of the Audiencia of Mexico is apparently no longer in the Archive of the Indies in Seville, it is difficult to make a valid assessment of the charges the visitor general made against Zorita and the other judges. However, it does appear that Valderrama was an arbi-

trary, insensitive man who found fault with everyone except Martín Cortés and approved the Creole elite's desire to perpetuate the
institution of *encomienda*. Moreover, at least in Zorita's case, it
appears that Valderrama's charges were exaggerated. Zorita naturally claimed that the accusations found in his indictment were
distorted or untrue. But Zorita's assertion that Valderrama was a
biased, hypocritical judge is at least partly supported by the
decision of the Council of the Indies to review Zorita's pleas of
innocence and repeal the remaining period of his suspension and
the fine of 100 ducats.

In a petition to the council dated May 5, 1575, Zorita declared
that he had not acted as a judge in lawsuits brought before the
Audiencia of Mexico during two of the three years that the
Valderrama *visita* lasted. Hence "he could not be charged with an
unjust verdict or partisan judgment, nor was there any complaint
by any of the parties involved in a trial."[195] He also pointed out
that although he was accused and condemned of many charges in
which he had served as judge with Doctors Villalobos and Orozco, these charges were not to be found in the indictments of these
judges.

Several charges against Zorita mentioned legal proceedings in
which he had not served as a judge. In other instances, Zorita was
charged with neglect of duty in matters that took place after he
resigned his office. Many *cargos* listed by Valderrama were shown
to be false by the testimony of notaries and officials of the
exchequer. Had Valderrama carried out his obligation to verify
these charges before listing them, he would have seen that they
were mere fabrications. Zorita was in fact found innocent of these
allegations; he observed that he would have been found innocent
of many others if Valderrama had only acceded to his request that
the visitor general inspect the records of the *libro de acuerdo*.

According to Zorita, other charges of which Valderrama found
him guilty were cut out of whole cloth by the dean of the
cathedral chapter, Alonso Chico de Molina, and the dean's ally
and friend, Diego Rodríguez de Orozco. Both of these individuals had taken part in the Cortés-Ávila conspiracy and were
sent to Madrid as prisoners. They had lived in the same house in
Mexico City and became bitter enemies of Zorita after he acted as
one of the judges hearing accusations brought before the court
against Diego Rodríguez. Appearing as witnesses against Zorita in
the *visita*, Chico de Molina and Diego Rodríguez had lied about
him. Zorita declared that in addition to affirming what suited

their purpose, they prevailed upon others to do the same, "stating this publicly and declaring that they would destroy him, which is the language used in the Indies to terrify judges who do what does not please such people."[196]

From what is known about Chico de Molina and Diego Rodríguez Orozco, neither man can be considered a reliable witness. Diego Rodríguez, for example, claimed to be the son of a conqueror. But the well-informed Francisco Morales wrote King Philip II that Rodríguez's father, "one Maese Tomás," had been a surgeon, a native of Medellín, and an ally of Cortés. This follower of the first Marqués del Valle, "neither a *vecino*, nor settler, nor conqueror, nor having a legitimate wife in Mexico," was nevertheless granted one of the richest and largest *encomiendas* in New Spain, the income of which amounted to some seven or eight thousand pesos in 1563.[197]

Diego Rodríguez, who illegally inherited the *encomienda*, had killed a man in Mexico but was freed by Licentiate Lorenzo de Tejada so that he might marry, as he did, one of Tejada's relatives. In addition to being a murderer, Diego Rodríguez had led a faction against the archbishop of Tlaxcala and had quarreled and litigated with the archbishop, his relatives, and other persons. Further, it was known to the king from reports furnished by both the viceroy and the archbishop that before leaving his wife Rodríguez had treated her like a slave and beaten her cruelly.

From what is known about Jerónimo Valderrama, it appears that he was an ambitious and partisan visitor general who desired to be viceroy of New Spain. Zorita thus appears to have been a victim of unscrupulous and mendacious witnesses and an arrogant, ambitious tax collector who backed the Creole cause and called into question all of Velasco's reform policies. The losers were the Indians and their protectors, including Zorita.

Valderrama's success in weakening the pro-Indian party headed by Luis de Velasco in Mexico stemmed from a number of factors. Not the least of these was the fact that, like many of the faceless men to whom the weak, distrustful, and fearful Philip II turned for counsel, Valderrama was aware that the authoritarian and narrow-minded king was inclined to believe the worst about his officials.

Valderrama arrived in a divided colony. The archbishop had written the king and the Council of the Indies enumerating the faults of the friars and members of the cathedral chapter. The viceroy and the provincials of the Dominican, Franciscan, and Augustinian orders had complained about the archbishop. Various of the judges, royal officials, and *encomenderos* had written bitter letters about Velasco. Velasco complained about the interference of the judges and the crimes of the *encomenderos*. Valderrama, in turn, denigrated the viceroy, the friars, the Indians, the judges, and anyone else who differed with his opinions.

Valderrama's arrival in the divided colony was quickly followed by the death of the viceroy. This made for the weak and ineffective government by the audiencia. As Martín Cortés's partisans fought with his enemies and threatened the peace of the city, Valderrama's use of the *visita general* to remove or inspire fear in the judges rendered them objects of scorn and led to further turmoil and conflict. Power devolved on the despotic visitor general who favored the *encomenderos* and who was nominated by them to be viceroy. Valderrama and the judges, with the exception of Puga, ignored and refused to investigate those individuals who recklessly talked of taking over the kingdom when they learned that the crown had decided that *encomiendas* beyond the third generation should revert to the crown. Having befriended Martín Cortés and the Creole cause, Valderrama returned to Spain in early 1566. His two major accomplishments were the increase of tribute payments by the Indians and reduction of the authority of the judges who remained on the court.

Valderrama's departure for Spain in early 1566 finally allowed the audiencia to impose its authority. Zorita, however, was not among the judges who would investigate the Cortés-Ávila conspiracy to its bitter end. In early 1565, Zorita wrote the king that after Viceroy Velasco had reluctantly given him permission to leave Mexico in June of the previous year he resigned his position. Because several ships had been ready to depart for Spain, Zorita had hastily sold the few things he possessed in his house for much less than they were worth so that he could leave with the *flota*. When he sought to collect what was due him, he was unable to do so because of a lack of coin in the land. For this reason, and because the audiencia officials had yet to be given the indictments so that they could prepare their defenses, although Valderrama had begun his *visita* of the tribunal sixteen months before, Zorita had been forced to remain in Mexico. Were God willing, Zorita was prepared to leave on the next fleet; in the meantime hardship would be his lot because prices in Mexico were great and he was ill, poor, and without office or salary.

Zorita sold his books, his and his wife's clothing, and their household articles and furniture for 8,000 ducats. After finally collecting this sum, "worth less than the value of his personal and household goods when he departed for America," he made ready to leave Mexico for Spain. Burdened by poverty and his infirmities, the aging Zorita's sorrows increased when the lists of charges against the audiencia officials were given to them in late October, 1565.[198] After reading his indictment, Zorita could have applied to himself, and with better reason, Vasco de Puga's observation that the "charges [against him] were as false as they were numerous" and resulted from his defense of the royal interest in New Spain.

CHAPTER 6

Return to Spain and Last Years

SPAIN's economic decline first became apparent during the years Zorita served in the Indies. Under Emperor Charles V human and economic resources were drained to pay for his crusading policy. Castilian interests were neglected or ignored, while this first Hapsburg king financed his wars against German Protestants, France, and the Turks with loans from German bankers. Castilian soldiers fought battles for their warrior-king in his far-flung possessions, and New World bullion was pledged to unite Germany and defend the western Mediterranean against the Ottoman Turks.

Traditional historiography notes that Castilians resented the first years of Charles V's reign. Viewed as an intruder who spoke no Spanish, the young king was surrounded by foreign advisers intent on personal gain. Charles's ambition to become Holy Roman Emperor and his appointment of foreigners to important and lucrative posts showed Castilians that he was more interested in stripping the country's wealth than in ruling after the manner of the Catholic Kings.

More recently Stephen Haliczer has shown that the crown's failure in earlier years to side with the towns against an aristocratic offensive threatening their independence made for the growth of "a powerful urban-based political opposition movement." Political mismanagement and ineptitude produced "a resistance ideology" that manifested itself in the revolt of the *Comuneros* (the rebellion of the Castilian towns in 1520–1521). Many grandees felt slighted by Charles's appointments to important offices and initially failed to support the royal government in its battle with the rebels. But when antiseigneurial revolts and pronouncements threatened to turn the revolt into a social revolution, Castilian magnates pledged their wealth and troops to the royalist cause and more moderate rebels deserted the movement. The defeat of those opposed to an absentee king and heavier tax burdens was assured by the Battle of Villalar on April 23, 1521.[1]

Although the defeat of the *Comuneros* reinforced the power of the upper nobility and allowed Charles to continue his costly policies that sought the religious unity of Christendom and imperial hegemony,[2] dissatisfaction continued. Charles failed to fulfill the aristocracy's political ambitions, and reform proposals by representative of the towns were not satisfied.[3] As late as 1593 the Castilian *cortes* (representative assembly) expressed desires that reflected, in part, the program of the *Comuneros*: it wished to abandon European wars and turn national efforts to developing the New World kingdoms, and it called for a more equitable system of taxation and the retention of American gold and silver. In sum it appears that the *Comuneros* were almost clairvoyant in their fear that Charles's imperial policy and dream of universal empire would create immense problems for Castile.[4]

The Catholic Kings had reaped the benefits of economic expansion, urbanization, and the support of the urban elites, merchants, and the craft guilds. Their Hapsburg successors would preside over a waning economy and society.

Beginning as early as the last half of the fourteenth century, western European experienced a slow and prolonged economic transformation. The development of merchant capitalism and the associated policy of mercantilism was favored by population growth and the increasing power of central governments. It was given impetus by the expansion of European commerce and imperialism into Asia and the New World following the great discoveries. Although the kings of Portugal and Spain financed and directed early explorations, overseas trade could only be undertaken by individuals and groups possessing enough money to wait for a return on their ventures. Those who conquered and settled the New World were largely poor gentlemen and commoners from Spain. Those who benefited most from the settlement and exploitation of America consisted of international merchant-bankers and their creatures. "From the accession of Charles V," the city of Antwerp, in the Netherlands, "was the commercial capital of the Spanish empire, and, in spite of protests that the precious metals were leaving Spain, the market for American silver."[5]

The expansion of the European economy was accompanied by a rise in prices. Theologians at the University of Salamanca and the French political theorist Jean Bodin attributed the steady and continuous inflation to the flood of precious metals arriving from the Indies. Anticipating the quantity theory of money, Martín de Azpilcueta Navarro wrote in 1556 that "money is worth more where and when it is scarce than where and when it is abundant."[6]

Other sixteenth-century figures who commented on the "price

revolution" said that it was due to debasement of coinage, while those who defended the poor blamed wicked landlords, grain merchants, and other monopolists of commodities for the rise in prices and rents.

Adam Smith in the eighteenth century and Earl J. Hamilton in the twentieth gave the quantity theory of money their blessings.[7] More recently other historians have questioned whether the major factor in the rise of prices in the sixteenth century was due to the increased quantity of precious metals.[8] In his discussion of Earl J. Hamilton's study of Spain's price revolution, J. H. Elliott observes that "Spanish prices moved ahead of other European prices" but considers it doubtful that silver from the Indies actually flowed directly into Spanish hands. The king's share of bullion imports, for example, "tended to be mortgaged in advance to his foreign bankers, who might well transfer it abroad at once, without its in any way touching the Spanish economy." C. H. Haring points out that as early as 1608 "the Council of the Indies informed the king that foreign interest in the fleets sent to the Indies amounted to two-thirds of the gold and silver which the royal armadas brought back to Spain."[9]

Another difficulty with the traditional proposed correlation between American treasure and rising prices is that bullion imports of sufficient value "to affect drastically Spanish and European coinage were imported only from about the middle of the sixteenth century onwards and seem to have risen quite sharply until about 1600." However, prices in Spain rose more rapidly in the first half of the sixteenth century. It appears that "there was a 2.8 per cent average annual increase in prices from 1501 to 1562, as compared with a 1.3 per cent average annual increase for 1562–1600." In short, because it appears that American silver arriving in Seville soon left for other parts of Europe, Spain's "high prices and shortage would seem to indicate a credit, rather than a currency, inflation."[10]

In the opinion of B. H. Slicher van Bath, it

was not American gold and silver that transformed the late mediaeval depression into the sixteenth-century boom. Long before the influence of American bullion was felt, prices had begun to rise. It can most probably be attributed, firstly, to the growth of population and, secondly, to the resumption of central European mining, which added to the quantity of money.[11]

Population growth was common to both rich and poor regions in southern Europe. Figures for Spain's population in the sixteenth century differ since "there are no censuses, and few reasonably reliable estimates, of the population of a whole European country before the eighteenth century." Nevertheless, if Braudel is correct, Castile's population may have doubled between 1530 and 1591, from a little over three million inhabitants to almost six million. New lands were brought under the plow, but the cultivation of grains was hindered by at least two factors. Vines and olives brought good profits in the Indies and diverted capital and land to their production, and the crown's favoring of the Mesta, the guild of sheep raisers, closed pastures to other pursuits. Moreover, the crown attempted as early as 1502 to protect consumers by imposing a fixed maximum price for grain. This *tasa del trigo* became permanent in 1539. By this measure peasants' profits were reduced at the same time that grain brokers sold it well above the maximum price. Castile suffered from a food crisis early in the century and was threatened with famine as population growth outran food supplies. By the end of the century the kingdom was relying on imported grain "supplied by the English, Dutch and Hansa merchants."[12]

The discrepancy between profits and wages and the price of goods made for the increase of poverty among peasants and day laborers and "sharply limited the effective market for manufactured goods." In turn, the limited output and the high price of textiles and other manufactures "led to an irresistible demand for the sale of foreign goods in Castile, on the grounds that they were appreciably cheaper." When the crown allowed cheaper foreign textiles to enter the country and prohibited the export of textiles (except to the American colonies) between 1548 and 1552, there was a "sharp depression in the Castilian textile industry." As Elliott observes, these actions by the crown were modified by further legislation in 1555 and 1558. "But ephemeral as was the legislation of 1548–52, its significance was enormous for it marked the point at which the expanding Castilian economy was confronted by its first severe crisis—a crisis which, as the legislation showed, found the country groping in the dark for a way of escape from its dilemmas."[13]

The problems of the commoners, the only group who paid direct taxes, was made more acute by the heavy burden of taxation. Charles V's expenses were enormously higher than those of his grandparents, and his attempt to have Castile pay for his splendid court and imperial ambitions soon aroused public resentment. In the summer of 1520 a Dominican friar, one of the

Juana de Austria, daughter of Charles V of Spain. She is dressed in black satin, with headdress, gorget, shawl, and white wristband (aristocratic feminine attire of the sixteenth century). (Courtesy of Marqués de Lozoya, *Historia de España*)

many clergymen who defended the Comunero cause, preached a sermon at Valladolid praising the rebel towns for "the defense and preservation of their rights." The friar further declared that "Your Majesty had reduced the realm to the poverty in which it stands."[14] Some months later, one of the demands of the revolutionary Junta of Tordesillas declared that the crown should "restrict itself to income from existing forms of taxation and never ask from the Cortes special legislative appropriations [*servicios*]." A complaint was also made of the king's daily food bill, which amounted to 150,000 *maravedís*. This sum was compared with the approximately 15,000 *maravedís* spent for the abundant daily fare of the Catholic Sovereigns, their son Don Juan, and the princesses, who had always had a great number of ladies-in-waiting.[15]

Before Charles's accession, the sales tax (*alcabala*) and the third of the tithes collected from the church accounted for between 80 and 90 percent of the royal income. From 1525 the towns were allowed to compound for the sales tax by paying a fixed sum known as *encabezamiento*. This change in the payment of the sales tax reduced its relative value as prices increased. Charles therefore asked the *cortes* for additional subsidies (*servicios*) amounting to 400,000 ducats a year. Because this tax was paid by commoners, its "general effect was everywhere to place the burden of taxation on the shoulders of those least able to bear it."[16]

During the years he ruled, Charles borrowed 39 million ducats. In 1551 he owed the bankers Fugger, Welser, Schetz, and Spínola 6,800,000 ducats. In return for these loans he had pledged future revenues and granted a huge number of concessions to financiers. The Fuggers and Welsers were given the exploitation of various Spanish mines, the administration of the military orders, and a number of other privileges. By their control of the *encomiendas* belonging to the grand masterships, these bankers, in addition to recovering more than they had lent the crown for these estates, increased the plight of the poor. Their practice of withholding wheat grown on these lands, in anticipation of a higher price, "generally injured the whole kingdom, but especially the *vecinos* within the jurisdiction of the Military Orders."[17]

Both in Germany and Spain, churchmen denounced the greed of the merchant-bankers who drove up prices. That inflation was due, at least in part, to monopolists is supported by a statement made by an employee of the Fuggers; he wrote, "Interest is the euphemistic equivalent of usury; financing is a polite term for robbery."[18]

Another method used to meet expenses was the sale of *juros*, interest bearing bonds secured by crown revenues. Depending on the type of bond sold—a life pension, a perpetual bond, or a redeemable security—the creditor's rate of interest varied from 3 to 7 percent. The crown initially had no problem selling these bonds, but whenever larger sums were needed for Charles's wars, the government exacted forced loans by confiscatng gold and silver remittances from the Indies belonging to private individuals, giving *juros* to victims of deficit financing.

Appropriation of American treasure, writes C. H. Haring,

reached gigantic proportions. Already in 1523, 300,000 ducats were sequestered, all the gold and silver that came on five vessels from the Indies; and in 1535, 800,000 out of the private treasure sent from Peru, most of it, doubtless, remittances from the followers of Pizarro, Six hundred thousand ducats were seized in 1553, and in the winter of 1556–7, just at the outset of Philip II's reign, the unprecedented sum of 1,800,000, bringing disaster to the merchant houses interested in the American trade. In the seventeenth century such forced loans continued to be frequent, amounting in 1629 and again in 1649 to a million ducats.[19]

Zorita became a victim of the crown's financial problems when he arrived in Seville in September, 1566. On his arrival, the Casa de Contratación seized the 8,000 ducats he carried with him. Unable to meet living expenses in Seville after pleading his case with Treasurer Melchor de Herrera and other officials for two months, Zorita finally agreed to a settlement. In return for lending the crown 7,000 ducats, Zorita agreed to accept a *juro* paying 7.14 percent interest. He used the 1,000 ducats returned to him to pay duties, freight charges, and the cost of his stay in Seville and to buy clothes for himself and his wife.[20]

After setting up his household in Granada, Zorita was forced to borrow living expenses and to go to court to petition the king for a pension equal to the salary he had earned as an *oidor*. On April 30, 1567, Zorita was in Madrid and stated that he was "poor, sick, deaf, and impeded in earning a livelihood. He owes 400 ducats which he borrowed which he left for the Indies; he contracted other debts when he returned to these kingdoms."[21]

Zorita's poverty and that of many other subjects reflected the general state of the Castilian economy. In 1552, Philip, Charles's son and heir, wrote the emperor that all of the sums assigned from regular sources of revenue, subsidies from *cortes*, revenues from the military orders, sales of indulgences, and the tax on clerical rents and income were expended until 1555.[22] At the same

time that Philip lamented not having the means to pay the ordinary and obligatory expenses of the Spanish State, Charles V, the
last knight of Europe, fled Innsbruck when Maurice of Saxony
turned against him. The flight to Villach in Carinthia symbolized
the failure of his German policy, brought about "by the defection
not only of Maurice of Saxony, but also of the imperial bankers,
who had finally lost confidence in the Emperor and had failed to
advance the money that was needed to pay his troops."[23]

After abandoning Germany, Charles increasingly relied on
Italian bankers. The Genoese had been active in Spain as early
as 1493, but they were to have, as Braudel observes, "a strangle-
hold" on Philip II's government from an early date.[24]

Succeeding to the throne of Spain in 1556, Philip had a smaller
and more manageable empire than his father. He had also inherited a bankrupt Spain and was forced to suspend interest payments to his creditors in early 1557. To continue paying the
floating debt of some seven million ducats, Philip in 1561 offered
Genoese bankers negotiable state bonds (*juros de resguardo*),
which gave his creditors access to public savings.[25] *Resguardos*
given to a banker as security for a short-term loan were sold to
investors; after the banker's loan was repaid by the crown, he
might buy back these bonds and return them to the exchequer.
The financier also had the right to "give back different bonds
from those he had obtained in deposit, so long as they yielded the
same rate of interest (5 to 7%)and represented the same amount
of capital."[26]

To meet his obligations to the bankers and continue the war
being waged against France—now allied with Pope Paul IV, who
considered Spaniards a "breed of Jews and Moors, dregs of the
earth—the Council of Finance in 1557 recommended that titles of
nobility be sold and the rate of the *encabezamiento* be increased.
Its president, Bishop Juan Suárez de Carvajal, approved the sale
of titles of nobility to *conversos* provided that the person buying
the privilege of *hidalguía* was not opprobrious to the Holy Office
of the Inquisition. The bishop equated the privilege of *hidalguía*
by purchase with the king's custom of granting nobility to a
commoner for having done "signal deeds."[27]

Other means of raising royal revenues included placing a heavy
tax on wool exports; ending free trade between Castile and Portugal by imposing duties of 10 percent on goods crossing the
border; strictly enforcing the royal monopoly on playing cards;
incorporating all salt deposits and the customs revenues of Biscay

into the crown; selling rights of jurisdiction over crown towns and vassals; allowing sons of priests to purchase rights of legitimacy and nobility; and selling municipal offices and other posts in Spain and America.[28]

These and other measures failed to balance expenditures and income, and in the Netherlands Philip's unpaid soldiers turned to looting. The soldiers' violence on people and property was followed by the bitter winter of 1556–57, when hunger killed 20,000 persons in Brussels.[29] In succeeding years Philip would win great victories against the French and the Turks and would assume the hegemony of Europe. But none of his victories proved enduring, and the debt continued to grow. Philip declared bankruptcy for the second time in 1575; the funded debt in this year amounted to 22 million ducats, the floating debt was estimated to total 15 million more. Payments to the bankers were suspended once more in 1596, and again in 1607, 1627, and 1647. Braudel notes that in every instance of state bankruptcy "the brunt of the losses was borne by the taxpayers of Castile, already overburdened with a heavy fiscal load, and by small savers and investors in Spain and Italy."[30]

As is apparent from what follows, Zorita was one of these small losers. His appeals to the king for financial assistance and payment of his annuity went unanswered. War dominated Philip's reign, and the crusade against the Dutch, the French Huguenots, England, the Turks, and the Moriscos of Granada absorbed Philip's attention and weakened the Spanish economy. Spaniards suffered a burden of debts and taxes, and the crown failed to pay interest on annuities held by persons like Zorita.

Born at a time when the nation was receptive to new ideas, Zorita in his last years saw Spain begin to seal herself off against free thought. Economic decline made for a contraction of the spirit; the decrease of the country's merchant and artisan class bolstered the domination of noble ideals held by Old Christians and encouraged the growth of parasitism. It also made for an impoverished peasantry, the multiplication of bandits and vagabonds, and a disdain for commerce and manual labor.[31]

Signs of Spain's decline, fully apparent by 1650, began with the defeat of the Invincible Armada. Then came the crown's declaration of bankruptcy in 1596, followed by crop failure, plague, and inflation. Bankruptcy struck again in 1607, and two years later the truce with the Dutch tacitly recognized the independence of the United Provinces of the Netherlands. When the truce expired, the dream of empire once again beckoned, and the Count-Duke Olivares, a descendant of Lope de Conchillos, plunged Spain into the Thirty Years' War. In 1640, Catalonia and Portugal revolted. In 1643, the Spanish *tercios* commanded by Don Francisco Melo suffered a defeat at Rocroi "such as no Spanish army had experienced for more than a century. Their reputation for invincibility was forever shattered."[32]

Meanwhile, copper coinage had replaced silver and gold in Castile, the Moriscos had been expelled, and the Spanish court "acted as a great magnet, drawing to it from all over the country, the rootless, the dishonest, and the ambitious."[33]

It was in this atmosphere of conflict, despair, and decline that Mateo de Alemán, Miguel de Cervantes, and Francisco de Quevedo wrote their great works. Each in his own way found a world characterized by hypocrisy, folly, and the cleavage between ideals and stark reality.

Mateo de Alemán, the author of a life of Saint Anthony of Padua (1604) and the picaresque novel *Guzmán de Alfarache* (1599), describes man as a ravenous animal dangerous to himself and his neighbors. "All steal, all lie, all cheat; all fail to abide in their honor, and even worse, they approve their misdeeds."

Cervantes's *Don Quixote* is many things to its readers and critics, but this book, written by an elderly, honorable, shabby, and obscure soldier and author constantly in debt, reflects the conflict between the ideal and the real. It thus serves as a social allegory of Spain in the reign of Philip II. Don Quixote remains the loneliest man in literature, an absurd and noble fool who arrives at sanity and reminds us that there are no birds in last year's nest.

Francisco de Quevedo (1580–1645) was a great novelist, satirist, moralist, and poet. He is chiefly known today for his picaresque novel *La vida del buscón* (1606) and his visions of the Last Judgment and hell to be found in *los Sueños*, begun in 1606 and published in 1627. Quevedo could read Hebrew, appreciated the poetry of Fray Luis de León, but attacked all segments of Spanish society, including Jews, women, doctors, bankers, and poets and dramatists who were bores. He characterized the society of his day: "There are many things here that seem to exist and have their being, and yet they are nothing more than a name and an appearance."

Zorita and the War of the Alpujarras

Zorita arrived in Granada with no more than the clothes and personal belongings worn and used by his household. Fortunately for the aged judge, forced into retirement by illness and Valderrama, his wife owned some houses in Granada, and the *juro* he received stated that in return for the 7,000 ducats confiscated by the crown he would receive 500 ducats a year from the revenues paid the king in the Alpujarras.

Granada in the 1560s was still predominantly Moorish, and perhaps 300,000 of the former kingdom's inhabitants were Moriscos, converted Moors or New Christians. Of these, between 30,000 and 45,000 lived in the Albaicín, the Moslem quarter of the city. Each Morisco household in the province paid a special tax called *farda*, the payment of which allowed them the use of their language and dress. In 1563, the *farda* brought the crown 20,000 ducats in revenue.[34]

Since earliest times authors have praised the splendor of Granada: its art and culture; the Alhambra and other wonders; its wealth of natural scenery; its mild, dry climate; its clear, bright sky; and the two rivers of Granada, the Dauro and Genil, which are fed by the snows of the Sierra and flow down to the wheat of the Vega. Granada of the sixteenth century has been depicted as a peaceful town inhabited by refined, sensitive souls who appreciated formalistic and decadent poetry. This inheritance appears to have been preserved, for even today Granada is described as a city where "there are no signs of hurry, rush of work, or ambitious dreams: everybody is content with what he has, and what he has is by no means paltry. The peace of Granada is made for dreams and dreaming."[35]

But the peace of Granada had its dark side. Luxury and opulence contrasted with great poverty, politeness masked cruelty, and prodigality contrasted with greed.[36] Houses in Granada pressed together. Many older houses were in disrepair, their decay ignored by an indifferent class of rich notables who lived in stately villas. Many of the narrow streets were dirty, and persons who found themselves out after dark risked being assaulted and robbed. City ordinances, collected in 1552, show that the city for many years tolerated practices detested by the Inquisition. In 1523, for example, a city ordinance forbade "any man to go about in woman's clothes." This decree, says Caro Baroja, may be placed in the context of what we know about certain medieval

Moslem cities such as Seville or Fez, "where there was a group of men who not only wore women's clothes, but also dedicated themselves to base feminine activities, which greatly shocked travelers and observers." Granada's laws concerning young vagabonds and whores, who were run by a pimp calling himself their "father," also gives us an idea of the similarity of popular sexual behavior in Granada to that of Fez and other cities of Morocco in this period.[37]

Moriscos had other habits that shocked Old Christians. They bathed even in the month of December; males were circumcised after being baptized; they would not eat pork; they enjoyed dances of their ancestral religion (*zambras* and *leilas*); and Morisco men liked fat women. To please their men, the women spent much time sleeping, bathing, and eating; and to make themselves attractive they used henna, painted themselves, tattooed their arms and legs, and wore jewelry after their own fashion, especially medals of religious significance.

Granada's Morisco population was a blend of Syrians, Berbers, native Spaniards, and Jews with an admixture of black, Persian, Hindu, and Turkish blood. Moriscos owned black slaves, considering them an inferior people to be bought and sold; but Morisco men appreciated black women, and some of the leaders who directed the rebellion of the Alpujarras were blackamoors. But as Caro Baroja observes, the distinction between Moriscos and Spaniards was social rather than racial. Social status depended on the lineage and religion of the father. Thus an Old Christian *hidalgo* in Granada was frequently the son and grandson of Moriscos on the female side.[38]

Following the conquest of Granada in 1492, the Moors of Granada had been given generous terms. They were allowed the use of their language, laws, customs, and liberty of person, property, and religion. Moreover, the Moors were not to pay greater tribute than that previously given to their natural rulers. These assurances given to the Moors at first appeared more than empty promises made by the Catholic Kings, for Hernando de Talavera, the queen's confessor appointed archbishop of Granada, admired Moorish charity. This descendant of Jews on his mother's side believed that Moors should adopt Christianity and Spaniards should adopt Moorish generosity.

The Spanish crown had been immediately faced with a dispute over policy concerning the conquered. Religious like Francisco Jiménez de Cisneros opposed Talavera's idea that the Moors could be assimilated and converted by gentleness and instruction. Because Talavera would not allow New Christians to be harmed "in word or deed," this saintly Jeronimite soon ran afoul of Diego Rodríguez Lucero, who became inquisitor of Córdoba in 1499. After denouncing Talavera as a judaizer, Lucero arrested his sister, nieces, and nephew, the dean of the cathedral chapter of Granada. Because the pope held the right to arrest and try bishops, Talavera's inquest was reviewed by Julius II's nuncio, Giovanni Ruffo. Talavera was found innocent on May 21, 1507, but the friar, who was in his seventies, died in Granada of a violent fever on May 14. Before his death he had been shunted aside by Cisneros. In 1502, the Moors, who were offered a choice of conversion or exile, either left for Africa or submitted to baptism.[39]

Because most Moors of the noble class left for North Africa, those who remained were (with the exception of wealthy individuals living in their enclosed villas in the Albaicín quarter) humble, hardworking peasant farmers; small merchants; artisans; and muleteers.

Meanwhile, all the *grandees*, *caballeros*, and *hidalgos* who had served in the conquest of Granada received grants, each according to his status. These *mercedes* consisted of houses, lands, and vassals. Among those who received these grants were at least four of Zorita's relatives: Gonzalo de Córdoba; Don Iñigo López de Mendoza, the second count of Tendilla, related to Zorita's family through his father's marriage with Catalina Suárez de Figueroa; Don Alonso de Aguilar; and the Count of Cabra.

Those Old Christians who did not receive grants included many poor settlers from various parts of Spain. Like other immigrants in different times and places, they had left home to improve their condition. Avid for material gain and with few moral or religious scruples, they soon completed the social and economic subjugation of the Moriscos. Old Christians, including petty officials and priests, exploited these colonized people as ruthlessly as *encomenderos* did their Indian subjects in the New World. The situation of the Moriscos was likened to that of the Indians by Doctor Esteban, the bishop of Orihuela; he wrote in 1595 that Fray Bartolomé de Las Casas's program for the liberation of the Indians in America should be implemented in Spain on behalf of the Moriscos.[40]

Moriscos, said a royal judge of the Audiencia of Granada, were victims of rape, theft, murder, and many other injustices. His report to the crown was confirmed by Francés de Alava, Spain's ambassador to France. In 1569 Alava wrote Philip II's secretary, Gabriel de Zayas, that if troubles existed in Granada the fault lay with the Old Christians. His comments—based upon personal observation and conversations with civil, military, and religious authorities—show that Moriscos were insulted and ruthlessly exploited by Spaniards. Priests participated in the Moriscos' humiliation, and Alava observed that "an entire Morisco village petitioned the archbishop to remove its parish priest." When an investigation of the complaint was made, the villagers again requested that the priest be removed—or else be married off, "for all our children are born with eyes as blue as his."[41]

Zorita does not tell us what he thought of the Moriscos, but in 1584 he wrote that, although the secular clergy had been in charge of the religious instruction of the Moriscos of Granada for more than 70 years, the Moriscos had received little benefit from these priests. This result had been anticipated by the regular clergy and might have been averted if the crown had assigned friars instead. Zorita concluded that the work of the secular clergy in Granada had mainly consisted in saying mass and in punishing those Moriscos who did not attend church services; seldom if ever had they given them instruction.[42]

Spanish exploitation of the Moriscos was rationalized by the Old Christians' fear, hatred, and envy of these people. Generally speaking, commoners and hidalgos alike passionately detested them. Those least hostile were the great nobles of Granada, virtual sovereigns over the Moriscos, who gave them "a third of the crops together with the 'ordinary services' and many arbitrary gifts and loans."[43] At least in part, nobles like Don Iñigo López de Mendoza, fourth Count of Tendilla and third Marqués of Mondéjar, protected the Moriscos from the church and the Audiencia of Granada because they recognized the truth of the proverb "the more Moors the more profit" ("quien tiene moro, tiene oro," or "a más moros, más ganancia").[44]

Like Sancho Panza, commoners might say that, though poor, they were Old Christians and owed nothing to anybody. This statement, however, contradicted reality, for commoners seduced by chivalric ideals deferred to nobles; seeking to rise, they looked upward. Nobles looked down on commoners and often treated them with little respect. Deference to the nobility in Granada was mingled with hatred, for commoners resented the protection of the Moriscos by the magnates. Commoners also felt threatened by Moriscos, for with the exception of religion and custom, Old and New Christians were legal and social equals. Moriscos, however, appear to have been a thriftier people, and this trait aroused working-class resentment. As Sancho also noted, "Where envy rules, virtue cannot live, nor can liberality exist where there is want."[45]

Hidalgos were inordinately proud of their purity of blood (*limpieza de sangre*) but often lacked wealth and office. Hence they also resented the alleged wealth of the Moriscos. Poor hidalgos were often so conscious of their lineage that they preferred to go hungry rather than betray the aristocratic ideals they aped. As one can observe in the portrait of the hungry hidalgo and his *apariencia* in the picaresque novel *Lazarillo de Tormes*, poor nobles reflected one aspect of the Baroque: form without content, tragicomic and ridiculous figures without purpose. Lazarillo's description of the poor master he served includes the line: "Oh Lord, how many of these must you have scattered throughout the world, suffering for that dismal concept they call honor what they would not suffer for You."[46]

Prejudice against Moors was common among most Spaniards, and Cervantes can be included in this group. This great figure of Spanish literature, who was old, poverty-stricken, and battle-scarred from fighting the Moors, wrote in his *Coloquio de los perros* (1613) the following lines:

Oh friend Cipion, how many things I could tell you about this Moorish rabble, did I not fear this would take at least two weeks! And if I were to go into details, I should need two months! But since I must say something, I shall generally relate what I particularly noted about these good people. Among so many, seldom does one find anybody who fully believes in the sacred Christian law, for their sole purpose is to hoard and guard what they earn. To do this, they work and do not eat. If a *real* worth its face value comes into their possession, they condemn it to life imprisonment and eternal darkness; so that, always earning and never spending, they have accumulated most of the money in Spain. Moriscos are Spain's money-box, clothes moth, its magpies, and weasel; everything is gathered up, everything is hidden, and everything is swallowed up. Consider that they are many and that each day they earn little or much, and take into account that a slow fever kills as certainly as a burning one.[47]

Cervantes also claimed that the Moriscos lacked continence and disdained higher education. Their only science was to rob Christians, and they all married and multiplied. "I have heard that

Don Miguel de Cervantes Saavedra, author of *Don Quixote*, as he appeared in 1600. (Courtesy of Bradley Smith, *Spain: A History in Art*)

twelve sons of Joseph entered Egypt. When Moses rescued them from captivity, they numbered 600,000 not counting women and children. From this can be inferred how ours will multiply, since we have incomparably greater numbers."[48]

Hatred and envy was fed by fear. Old Christians considered Moriscos to be a fifth column in contact with the Turks and Moors. This charge was given some basis by Moslem pirates who plundered coastal towns and enslaved Spanish citizens. Within Granada itself, nobles frequently sheltered Moriscos who had been involved in feuds or were contrabandists. These delinquents would usually settle down to a peaceful life after receiving asylum. When the crown suppressed the right of asylum by lords, also limiting the right of sanctuary in churches to three days, the exiles fled to the mountains and became bandits (monfíes).

Morisco brigands were organized into bands led by "captains." Leaving their mountain fastnesses, the monfíes pillaged, robbed, and murdered "in order to live." Two of these bandits, the brothers Lope and Gonzalo Xeñiz, formerly of Bérchul in the Alpujarras, were responsible for a great number of crimes. Just prior to the revolt of 1568, these bandits had killed a merchant and several other Christians returning from a fair.[49]

An uneasy concord between Moriscos and Christians in Granada was maintained during the reign of Charles V. Although Charles issued various decrees imposing restrictions on the Moriscos, he allowed these prohibitions to be eluded, disregarded, or suspended. An example is the Edict of Granada, issued in 1526; if it had been enforced, all traces of Islam would have ended. Charles, however, suspended the edict when the Moriscos paid him 80,000 ducats.

Things might have continued in this fashion had it not been for the end of the war between France and Spain in 1559. The Peace of Cateau-Cambrésis left Philip free to impose religious unity in Spain. It also allowed him to resume Castile's traditional crusade against Moslems within and beyond its borders.

Following the discovery of Protestant cells in Spain, heterodoxy from 1558 on "was treated as a threat to the state and religious establishment."[50] After eradicating the "Lutheran" menace, Philip II allowed the president of the Council of Castile and future inquisitor general, Diego de Espinosa, and the president of the Audiencia of Granada, Pedro Deza, to persuade him that the Islamic customs and language of the Moriscos had prevented the conversion of these people. Deza, a bitter enemy of the captain-general of Granada, Don Iñigo de Mendoza, was convinced that an end should be put to Don Iñigo's protection of the Moriscos from the audiencia, the church, and the Inquisition.

On January 1, 1567, Philip issued a pragmatic suppressing Arabic language, dress, and customs. This royal decree, a reenactment of the ordinance of 1526, had numerous regulations. Moriscos must learn Spanish within three years; all books written in Arabic must be delivered to Deza within thirty days, and those returned after being inspected could be used by the Moriscos for only three years; all public baths were to be closed; Morisco women must discard the veil, and Moorish dress was prohibited after a year; the regulation against Moriscos bearing arms was to be strictly enforced; Moorish names were not to be used, and the use of henna by women was forbidden; Moriscos might not possess Moorish slaves, and permission to keep black slaves must be obtained from Deza; the doors of the Moriscos' houses must be kept open on Christian holy days so that Islamic ceremonies might end.

The Moriscos bargained with the crown at the same time that they asked for help from North Africa and Turkey. When they saw that the crown would not rescind the decree, they covertly organized their revolt at the hospital they maintained in Granada and at meetings held by their Confraternity of the Resurrection. They appointed as their king Don Hernando de Valor, a *regidor* of the cabildo who claimed descent from the Ommayad founder of the independent emirate of Córdoba; the name he assumed, Aben Humeya (Ibn Umayyah), refers to his ancestors who ruled al-Andalus between 756 and 1031.[51]

On December 23, 1568, the residents of Cádiar, a settlement in the district of Ugíjar, in the Alpujarras, killed while they were sleeping and unarmed a Captain Herrera and the forty horsemen he had billeted in the village. The Moriscos then fled to the high sierra to await the Moslem troops they believed would join them for the forthcoming war against the Spaniards.[52]

The leaders of the rebellion chose the Alpujarras as the place to fight their war with good reason. The region had access to the sea, and Moslem troops from North Africa and Turkey would have little difficulty entering the region; it also had an abrupt, rocky terrain and difficult passes, and its rude and fierce settlers were convinced that they were fighting a holy war (*jihad*).

The mountainous region of the Alpujarras, in the provinces of Granada and Almería, consists of a long valley bordered by the slopes of the Sierra Nevada and the coastal range. Although much of the region is barren, rugged land, it also has broad, open plains and rivers that flow to the sea. On the level, well-watered tracts of land in the valley the Moriscos cultivated a variety of crops.[53]

Following the murder of Captain Herrera and his men, the Moriscos of Cádiar joined a poorly armed group of 6,000 men determined to take Granada. Fortunately for Zorita and other citizens of the capital, heavy snow fell and blocked the passes and footpaths in the Alpujarras. Despite the heavy snowfall, the black captain Fárax Aben Fárax, a resolute leader of the rebels and a rival of Aben Humeya, led a band of 150 *monfíes* into the Albaicín on the night of December 24–25. When the Moriscos of the Albaicín ignored his call to arms by failing to open their doors to the bandits, the attack failed. If the Moriscos of Granada had attempted to take the city, they would have met little resistance from the fearful Spaniards. The Count of Tendilla, who had chosen to guard the Alhambra, had only forty soldiers and fifty horses, while the *corregidor* Juan Rodríguez de Villafuerte had been unable to muster more than twenty-three men to guard the remaining part of the Spanish quarter.[54]

Although Granada remained in the possession of the Spaniards, more than 180 Morisco settlements rose up in the Alpujarras in the next week. The rebels tortured and killed those who would not renounce the Catholic faith; systematically destroyed and profaned churches, sacred vessels, images, and ornaments; and parodied and mocked the rites of the Christians. During the rebellion the Moriscos, according to one report, killed forty-nine priests and three friars in the Alpujarras and the Lecrín Valley. Another account claims that the Moriscos killed 86 priests and friars, 111 Christian adults, more than 50 children, and a number of women, including 4 *moriscas* who refused to abjure the faith.[55]

The torture and killing of priests, the looting and burning of churches and Christian homes, the decapitation and burning of images after tearing out their eyes, the whipping of the image of Christ at Berja, and the indecent manner in which the Virgin's image at Bayarcal was desecrated gave evidence of the Moriscos' hatred of the Christians' God and his saints. These actions also indicate that the Moriscos felt they were fighting a holy war against the enemies of Islam.[56] Spaniards captured by the Moriscos who were not killed were sold as slaves in North Africa for arms and munitions.

Spaniards, for their part, became fanatical in defense of Chris-

tianity. Even the Count of Tendilla, who had protected the
Moriscos, ordered a general massacre at Guajaras in retaliation for
a previous defeat. In other instances the aim of the Spaniards was
simply plunder. Many military movements were really slave raids
in which Morisco males were slaughtered; the women and children were then taken to Granada and sold. In their search for
slaves and treasure, Spanish soldiers "stole cats, caldrons, turn-
spits, kneading troughs, reels, cow bells, and other worthless
things, all simply because they would not give up the right to
plunder."[57]

During the war the Count of Tendilla was replaced by Don
John of Austria, the king's half brother. To aid the new supreme
commander, seasoned troops were brought in from Italy. Meanwhile, Deza had the greater number of the Moriscos living in the
Albaicín moved to other parts of Spain, and Philip ordered the
proclamation of a war of extermination (*guerra a fuego y sangre*).

The war was marked by bungling, rapacity, dissension, and
fearful brutality on the part of the Spanish forces, but their
superior numbers and the failure of the North Africans to send
more than a few hundred volunteers to aid the Moriscos made the
defeat of the rebels a foregone conclusion. Aben Aboó, who
succeeded Aben Humeya as king, held out until early 1571, but
most had surrendered by the autumn of 1570.

Those Moriscos who were expelled during the war went to live
in towns of the ancient kingdoms of Seville, Córdoba, and Jaén.
Those left in Granada when the war ended were sent to Estrema-
dura and Galicia. Others were deported to Chinchilla, Albacete,
villages in La Mancha, the province of Toledo, Castilla la Vieja,
and León. Twelve thousand peasant families replaced the Moriscos in the deserted villages of Granada.

Among those Moriscos remaining in Granada was Aben Aboó.
By Deza's order, Gonzalo Xeñiz was offered a pardon if he
would kill his king. After dispatching Aben Aboó, Gonzalo
brought his body to the capital; the pardoned bandit and his
followers were marched through the streets with Aben Aboó's
body mounted on a horse and dressed as though he were still
alive. Zorita may have been in the crowd that saw Gonzalo kiss
the hands of Deza and the Count of Arcos. After paying his
respects to the count and the president of the audiencia, he
handed them the rebel leader's weapons, "saying that, like a good
shepherd, if he could not bring the sheep to his master he at least
brought the pelt."[58]

If Zorita did not witness this scene, he had occasion to look upon the Morisco leader's face many times thereafter; Aben Aboó's "corpse was drawn and quartered and the head, in an iron cage over the arch of the Puerta del Rastro, for years looked out on the Alpujarras."[59]

The War of the Alpujarras brought new woes for Zorita. In his petition to the crown of May 5, 1575, he noted that because of the rebellion he had not been paid his annuity for two years. Moreover, he was presently owed seven years' payments on the annuity, a sum amounting to 3,500 ducats.[60] Zorita noted that he had returned to Spain with funds less than the value of his household goods given him by his parents when he departed for the Indies. To pay moving expenses from Mexico to Spain, he had even sold his large collection of books, leaving him and his wife with no more than the clothes and personal belongings they brought to Granada. Having become a *vecino* of Granada, Zorita, who lived in the parish district of the cathedral church, found himself unable to support his household; he therefore filed a petition for assistance from his parents in the Audiencia of Granada.

Zorita's appearance in court must have been humiliating; some twenty years before he had served as legal advocate for indigent persons before the audiencia. Zorita, no longer a royal judge, without funds, and awaiting the outcome of his *visita*, must have felt a pang of bitterness entering the audiencia chambers, staffed by a president, sixteen *oidores* who judged civil cases, four *alcaldes de corte* who judged criminal cases, three *alcaldes de hijosdalgo* in charge of cases concerning the nobility, and two attorneys for the crown. He may also have noticed the dissension among the judges; these members of the royal tribunal, said Diego Hurtado de Mendoza, fought each other like cats and dogs, and the envy and discord they felt for each other was comparable to that found in a convent of friars.[61]

In addition to the aid he received from his parents, Zorita also borrowed from his younger brother. Juan Pérez, although burdened with debts in Peru, had allowed Zorita to sell his share of the inheritance left by their father in 1570. But Juan Pérez de Zorita secured this loan (*censo*) by encumbering the property Zorita held in Granada through his wife. Zorita still owed this and other debts to his brother in 1575. Moreover, because the crown had failed to pay Zorita's annuity, a fourth of the houses he and his wife owned in Granada had not been repaired and were no longer habitable.

Pressed for money to pay his debts, Zorita may have thought

of his more prosperous relatives. An instance he may have re-
membered was the power of attorney that his brother-in-law
Alonso de Aguilera, *vecino* of Córdoba, gave Alonso Sánchez de
Ahumada and Cristóbal de la Becerra on December 5, 1554.
Aguilera had authorized these two citizens of Seville to collect
from the merchant Alonso de Medina ten gold bars minted in
Chile worth 4,802 *pesos de oro* that Zorita had sent him in five
different ships from Santo Domingo.[62]

Zorita's problems in these years were increased by litigation
between himself and Juan Pérez with their brothers and sisters.
This lawsuit was finally resolved on October 25, 1572, when
Zorita filed a document with Diego de la Fuente, the secretary of
the Royal Audiencia. The brief stated that Zorita, with power of
attorney given him by Juan Pérez in 1570, had a lawsuit pending
with other brothers and sisters over the inheritance left them by
their deceased parents. All the heirs excepting Doña Inés and
Doña Ana, nuns represented by the convent of Santa Inés, had
now agreed to settle their differences out of court. They now
proposed to give the convent in Córdoba 600 ducats if it agreed
to renounce all other claims to the inheritance sought on behalf of
the two sisters.[63]

Zorita and Other Losers at Court

While the War of the Alpujarras was being fought, the position of
Spain in the Mediterranean was rapidly deteriorating. Moslem
raids on the coasts of Italy and Spain continued, and the Turks
now demanded the island of Cyprus from Venice. When the
Venetians asked for aid from the Catholic powers of Europe,
Pope Pius V called for an alliance against the Turks and persuaded Philip II to come to the aid of Christendom. In April,
1570, the pope, Spain, and Venice formed the Holy League
against the infidel.

On October 7, 1571, the great Christian fleet led by Don John
of Australia virtually destroyed the Turkish fleet in the Bay of
Lepanto, the narrowest part of the Gulf of Corinth. The Catholic
force sank, burned, or captured some 200 ships, killed or took
prisoner some 33,000 Turks, and freed about 15,000 Christian
galley slaves. In the battle Miguel de Cervantes lost the use of his
left hand for the greater glory of the right." He later described
Lepanto as "the noblest occasion that past or present ages have
seen or future ones may hope to see."

Cervantes and other soldiers returned to Spain only to suffer hunger and want. Like Zorita, who preceded Cervantes to Madrid, the soldier and other thousands in their need all sought *mercedes* or regular employment. As they waited for audiences at court, the judge and the soldier walked the streets, forming part of an unemployed population seeking posts, pensions, back pay, and relief from their creditors. Zorita and Cervantes differed from other casualties of history, however, in their love of learning and sympathy for the problems of the oppressed as revealed in their writings. What Cervantes said of himself is applicable to Zorita, who had sold his large collection of books: "I am an avid reader of anything, even though it be but scraps of paper in the streets."[64]

Various kinds of people described in the literature of the Golden Age might have been seen in this city of many colors. When Charles began his reign, Madrid had about 5,000 inhabitants. When Philip succeeded him they numbered some 45,000. After 1561 it became the capital of Spain; by the end of the century its population had grown to 107,000.[65]

The roads leading to Madrid, a new city where many went to seek their fortune, were filled with a "steady procession of poor travelers, civil servants without posts, captains without companies, humble folk in search of work, trudging behind a donkey with empty saddle bags, all faint with hunger and hoping that someone, in the capital, would settle their fate." Like other cities of Europe, great wealth contrasted with abject poverty and idealism contrasted with realism. Great piety was evident, as well as blind and obstinate passion resulting in public disturbances and quarrels.[66]

The poor and humble in search of work mingled with vagrants and soldiers. A hardened veteran might be seen on his way to a brothel; another might be seen in the company of some lost, submissive girl. Other soldiers were young recruits who would eventually see duty in the Netherlands, the North African presidios, Portugal, or Italy. Although Spain was in decline, the *tercios* were still considered to be invincible. After taking Portugal for Philip II in 1580, the soldiers commanded by the duke of Alba said that they had won the country in fifty-eight days in the way "the kingdom of Heaven is won, that is, by fasting on bread and water."[67]

Unemployed hidalgos wandered the streets, and during the reign of Philip II this term came to mean a member of the lower nobility who lacked jurisdictional rights of *señorío*. Frequently without house and land, many hidalgos, impoverished by the price revolution, boasted of their lineage but lived in arrogant misery, giving rise to the type found in the picaresque novel *Lazarillo de Tormes* (1554) and its successors.

Priests abounded, and the first anti-hero of the picaresque novels, Lazarillo, tells us that not a few priests and friars robbed the poor and stole from their orders to provide for their mistresses. One of Lazarillo's masters is a priest who gives him an onion for his ration every fourth day; another is an archbishop whose mistress he marries. Most Spaniards identified with the religiosity of the Counter-Reformation, but proverbs of the time suggest a popular view that many clerics led irregular lives. Examples are *Gorriones y frailes son malas aves* ("Sparrows and friars are birds of ill omen") and *Putas y frailes andan a pares* ("Whores and friars go in pairs").[68] Beggars competed with priests, and one of Lazarillo's masters, a cruel, blind, cunning beggar offered up prayers for pennies. Almost all his customers were "inn-keepers, barmaids, candy sellers, whores, and other common women."

Madrid, like other cities of Spain, had an underworld; the favorite haunt of beggars, pickpockets, cutthroats, and other dregs of society was the Puerta del Sol. From Cervantes we gain some idea of the underworld in Spanish cities. An example is the innkeeper who dubs Don Quixote knight. In his travels he had lived in the disreputable localities of Seville, Granada, Córdoba, and other cities. Before retiring with his illgotten gains, his quick fingers and nimble feet had seen much exercise; "he had done many wrongs, bedded many widows, seduced many virgins, and cheated various prostitutes." His many crimes had made him well known in almost all the royal tribunals and courts of Spain.[69]

In Philip's day, Madrid had a few great families; still fond of their country estates where all important ceremonies and festivities were held, their houses in the city were only temporary residences. They were often "violent and uncouth, although there were brilliant exceptions." After Philip's death the aristocracy flocked to Madrid, taking a "certain perverse pleasure in descending to low society, mingling with the sophisticated crowd of the big city."[70] Aristocrats there and in other parts of Spain appear to have suffered frequently from syphilis. In 1560 Cipriano de Valera stated, "No longer is one held for a gentlement who has not had two or three *mudas*." In 1605, Gaspar Lucas Hidalgo

Philip II (1556–98). Known as Philip the Prudent, this sedentary king was his own secretary and ruled over a bureaucratic Spanish empire centered in Madrid. (Courtesy of Marqués de Lozoya, *Historia de España*)

affirmed that "*bubas*, without exception, were ordinarily the property and the exclusive privilege of noble women and lords."[71]

Philip's court had few outstanding personalities representing the great aristocracy; his confidants were lesser figures, such as the priest Gonzalo Pérez, a man of obscure origins. Because Philip was reluctant to delegate responsibility, departmental heads tended their own areas and were given limited access to other affairs of state; isolated officials thus created their own sources of information. "Secrecy, and resultant suspicion and intrigues, permeated the entire administration, and one of the most frequent words used in official correspondence was the verb '*disimular*' which means 'to hide one's real intentions.'"[72] The king's suspicion and lack of confidence in his bureaucrats led to delay, mediocrity, and conservativism in all branches of government. Just before his death in 1586, Philip's minister, Cardinal Granvelle, wrote that the final ruin of Spain was imminent: "All business is left in the air; the administration is dominated by corrupt and dishonest officials who are not to be trusted, and the same is happening in judicial and financial affairs and in the running of the army and the fleet."[73]

Factions contended at court, and the more than 4,000 members of the royal household found life "expensive, demanding and often tedious." Courtiers relieved their boredom by gambling and courting ladies-in-waiting or might be diverted by dwarfs, jesters, and buffoons. At times a serious crime could be the subject of conversation, as happened in 1572, when Don Gonzalo Chacón, the count of Montalbán's brother, raped a lady-in-waiting to the king's sister, or in 1583, when four servants of the count of Melgar murdered the royal councillor Don Alonso Gutiérrez.[74] Until his death in 1568, Don Carlos, the king's deranged son, "kept even that most gossip-loving of cities, Madrid, fully supplied with stories of his eccentricity."[75]

Zorita's petitions to the crown are few but revealing. In 1575 he observed that he and his brother Juan Pérez were without an estate and in debt after serving the king faithfully and well for so many years. In the course of their duties both he and Juan Pérez had spent what they had inherited from their parents, and Zorita and his wife were ill and without means. Moreover, Juan Pérez, before departing for the Indies, had rendered the emperor great services in North Africa. Between 1540 and 1544 he had seen combat at Alborán, in the capture of Tlemcen and Mostaganem, in the king's galleys, and was present at the death of Caramani and the imprisonment of Ali Hamet, "all at his own cost and with the help of his parents." As was apparent from Juan Pérez's *probanza* given to the council by Juan de la Peña Vallejo and from the judicial proceedings before former governor and president of the Audiencia of Lima, Lope García de Castro, the crown had yet to give Zorita's brother the *merced* he merited.

Zorita also noted that he had served the crown on his return to Spain. He did not mention whether these duties had to do with the Morisco uprising, but did say that the costs incurred and the hard work involved should be considered in his request for repeal of his suspension and the fine of 100 ducats he had been sentenced to pay. He requested that should the fine be forgiven the crown lien on 200 *pesos de tepuzque* still owed Zorita for household goods he had sold in Mexico be discharged; if this sum had already been collected, it should be returned to his creditor in New Spain. Zorita further observed that if he were to be found innocent of the false charges in the *visita* taken by Valderrama, the dishonor and affliction he had suffered for the last eleven years would finally be removed.

In compensation for his losses and many years of service, Zorita asked to be given special licenses for ships to carry goods to various ports in the Indies; these *registros* would allow him to dispatch goods to the New World without having to wait for the annual *flota*. He also asked for the office of notary to the royal official handling the property of intestates for Mexico City and its district and the post of secretary to the *alcalde mayor's* court having jurisdictional authority of Tlaxcala, Tepeaca, and Huejotzingo. The council denied Zorita these notorial offices, but it did recommend a review of the matter of his suspension and fine.[76]

The crown may have paid Zorita all or part of his annuity and repealed his suspension and fine, for petitions after this date no longer refer to these matters. Instead, on June 25, 1576, Zorita asked for the return of the two books that he had submitted to the council for examination before publication. In its resolution to this petition the council ordered these books to be found and returned to Zorita. The extract of the petition does not give the title of Zorita's books, but the "Suma de los tributos" and the "Recopilación de las leyes de Indias" are mentioned in later petitions. What is not clear is why the council still had not given Zorita permission to publish these books two years after their submission.[77]

In early 1578 the council finally gave Zorita permission to

publish his "Suma de los tributos" for a period of twenty years,
but it stipulated that the Spanish text must be translated into
Latin. It appears that the council did not want the work published in Spanish because of its somber assessment of Spanish
tribute policy. After receiving the decision Zorita asked to be
allowed to print the work in the original Spanish, as was customary, citing Latin quotations from authorities on the saints and
other matters within the body of the work in the margin of the
text. He gave as his reasons his advanced age, the difficult work
and time involved in translating the book, and the fact that,
except for members of royal tribunals, few persons in the New
World knew Latin.[78]

The earlier decision of the council prevailed; its resolution that
Zorita publish the work in Latin was confirmed by the comment
"Lo proveído" at the end of the extract to Zorita's petition. Two
other references mention the "Suma de los tributos"; both reiter-
ate the council's original decision that the book, if published,
must be translated into Latin.[79] In a citation in the "Recopilación de
las cosas notables de la Nueva España", Zorita wrote that this
work on pre- and post-Conquest tribute was written "at not little
cost and work" in Spanish and in Latin.[80]

On March 3, 1578, the council mentioned Zorita's "Relación
de las leyes de Indias." In response to Zorita's demand that this
compilation of the Laws of the Indies be returned, the council
noted that the book had been reviewed by Doctor Gómez de
Santillán but failed to say whether the book had been approved
for publication.[81]

Zorita's Last Years and Death

Zorita's appeals to the king for financial assistance were ignored.
But if his annuity was finally paid, this sum and the rents he and
his wife received from some of the houses she owned in Granada
allowed him to pay his creditors and live out his last years in
honorable poverty. Despite his financial problems and illness,
Zorita's last years were busy and fruitful. He remained interested
in Indian affairs and may have served the king in the revolt of the
Moriscos of the Alpujarras.

Zorita in these years continued writing his books and summaries and corresponded with pro-Indian friends of the regular
clergy in Mexico. Fray Gerónimo de Mendieta for example,
wrote that his order had commissioned him to write a history;

would Zorita send him a manuscript by Fray Toribio de Motolinía on the Indians of New Spain? Zorita promptly sent him the work with a religious of the Franciscan order. Although Zorita had known Mendieta for only a short time in Mexico, he was aware that this missionary was a scholar of great ability who was fluent in Náhuatl and Otomí. Mendieta, who had arrived in Mexico in 1554, completed his *Historia* in 1596. The venerable and scholarly Fray Domingo de la Anunciación also wrote to inform Zorita that he and Fray Vicente de Las Casas were writing a history of the Dominican order in Mexico.

Other friends told Zorita of Mexican affairs. One of these was Gonzalo de Las Casas, a native of Trujillo, Spain, where he had excellent houses and a good *mayorazgo*. Described by Zorita as a caballero of quality and virtue, Las Casas had in *encomienda* a flourishing town in the Mixteca and also owned some fine houses in Mexico City. He had lived in Mexico for many years and had written on the peoples of New Spain, especially of the Chichimecas. Las Casas had lent Zorita these writings when he went to Granada on business.[82]

Despite their differences over the matter of their inheritance, Zorita's brothers and sisters admired, respected, and undoubtedly felt a deep affection for him. Members of Zorita's family lived in Córdoba, and the property they owned in Cañete and Montoro was an item of discussion in the early 1570s.

After the death of Zorita's father in 1570, Zorita spent three years reconciling differences concerning the estate. His brothers and sisters finally agreed to withdraw the lawsuit pending before the Audiencia of Granada and had Zorita represent them in their dispute with the abbess of Santa Inés, who acted as advocate for their sisters Doña Ana and Doña Inés, who had taken vows and lived at the convent. Zorita's request for dismissal of the suit noted that his sister Lucía de Zorita and her husband, Don Alonso de Aguilera, were *vecinos* of the parish of San Pedro in Córdoba; Miguel Díaz de Zorita, *vecino* and *jurado* of Córdoba, lived in Cañete; his sister Elvira de Zorita Villavicencio also lived in Córdoba with her second husband, Licentiate Alonso de Mesa.[83]

Although the date of Zorita's death is unknown, we can assume it was the year that he completed his "Relación de las cosas notables de la Nueva España." When death came for Zorita in 1585, he was working on a philosophical and devotional work entitled "Discursos de la vida humana."

With his death Spain lost one of the noblest and most attractive figures of the sixteenth century. In his life and works Zorita represents that exalted Spanish humanism expressed by Cervantes, who has Don Quixote counsel Sancho to be "clement, for while the attributes of God are all equal, that of mercy shines brighter and is greater in our opinion than justice."[84]

Having received all the sacraments, this clear-sighted man of great integrity probably died peacefully in bed. In matters of justice he always sought to uncover the truth, but in questions of equity he recognized the higher law of charity. "With one foot in the stirrup" and on the point of riding forth on his last journey, this modest, unpretentious, honorable man departed the world knowing that he had employed his knowledge and talents to protect and represent the oppressed Indians of the New World. His efforts were a part of that larger crusade led by Fray Bartolomé de Las Casas.

CHAPTER 7

Alonso de Zorita: Anthropologist and Historian

ZORITA as historian belongs to the second generation of Spanish writers interested in the New World and its inhabitants. He and his contemporaries had at their disposal the accounts of conquerors, first settlers, missionaries, court historians, and other cultivated Europeans. Zorita utilized a wide variety of works, including the letters of Cortés, accounts and letters of other conquerors, and works like Francisco López de Gómara's *Historia de las Indias*. For his ethnographic writing Zorita drew primarily on nineteen years of experience and observation in the royal tribunals of Santo Domingo, Guatemala, and Mexico; his period of service in New Granada as *juez de residencia*; and the invaluable treatises of scholarly friars like Motolinía. Indian elders and lords also supplied Zorita with accounts of pre-Conquest society.

Like many other educated men of his day, Zorita had a deep interest in the civilizations of Greece and Rome. The findings of humanists reached an ever-growing number of university students and members of court circles and inspired them to take up the new learning.[1] Zorita's taste for Latin classical literature is shown in frequent references to writers like Horace, Cicero, Quintilian, Priscian, Plutarch, Pliny, Lucan, Tacitus, Virgil, and Livy.

Zorita had also read the devotional literature of his day and the writings of the church fathers. Nowhere in his work is there a sense of polarity between the "pagan" and the "Christian" past or between the sacred and profane works he cites. Zorita, an orthodox Roman Catholic who cited contemporaries like Sir Thomas More and Erasmus, warned his readers that in his relation of these authors' accounts of historical events he had quoted nothing offensive to pious ears and had thus conformed to the criteria of censorship used by the Inquisition in grading books on its indices.[2] It appears from Zorita's warning to his readers that he knew that the Index of Prohibited Books issued by the Inquisition in 1559 listed sixteen of Erasmus's works; since his history of New Spain was completed in 1585, Zorita was also aware that the indices of 1583 and 1584 listed Thomas More's *Utopia*, a forbidden work requiring expurgation.[3]

Zorita's mentality was essentially that of a Spanish humanist and pro-Indian reformer who, in the manner of Las Casas and other mendicant chroniclers, compared the native peoples of the New World with the advanced peoples of antiquity, to the advantage of the former. It is also evident that Zorita, in his administration of justice and in his writings, was guided by the scholastic teaching that positive law must conform to the natural law, which reflected divine reason. Like the Stoics and Saint Augustine, he believed that all men descended from Adam and therefore should enjoy full equality before the law.

Zorita's works demonstrate that he was a competent thinker of considerable learning; his writings show that he appreciated the eloquence of writers like Quintilian, Saint Jerome, and other Latin and church authors. And Zorita, like a number of his contemporaries, was given to long, rambling, discursive sentences. Much of his work appears to have been written hastily; his style generally lacks subtlety, polish, and the well-turned phrase. Yet if Zorita was unable to rise to the heights of rhetorical brilliance achieved by a writer like Gómara, his ardent defense of the Indians against the charge that they were "barbarians" included a relativist line of argument that anticipated Michel de Montaigne's celebrated comment, "Everyone calls barbarian what is not his own usage."[4] Further, Zorita's inquiries into native history, land tenure, and inheritance laws may be considered true "exercises in applied anthropology, capable of yielding a vast amount of information about native customs and society," an example of what Europe saw or failed to see in an age confronted with a strange new world.[5]

Zorita's Works

In retirement Zorita completed several works, the most important being his *Brief and Summary Relation of the Lords of New Spain*. Between 1567 and 1585 Zorita also completed three compendiums.

The "Suma de los tributos," now lost, dealt with pre- and post-Conquest tribute payments and was first written in Spanish. The Royal Council of the Indies granted Zorita permission to publish the work in 1578, provided it were translated into Latin. The council may have desired to restrict this work to a small reading public because Zorita wrote that the modest exactions of the Aztec lords and priests had been replaced by excessive tribute and labor demands under Spanish rule. Zorita translated the "Suma" into Latin, but apparently it was never published. Serrano y Sanz is probably correct in his opinion that the contents of this compendium were incorporated into Zorita's later works.[6]

Zorita wrote another "Suma" on the lords and lordships of pre-Conquest Mexico; this work discussed the benefits derived by the lords from their dominions and whether their rule was advantageous to their subjects. This summary was also probably incorporated into his later works.[7]

A third "Suma" written by Zorita asked whether the Indians should pay tithes and examined "the disadvantages there are in this."[8] Zorita's opinion in this matter included in his *Brief Relation* differs slightly from his earlier recommendation.

In 1558, Zorita wrote the crown that the prelates of New Spain had told the judges that "under penalty of hell and eternal damnation" they were obliged to send an opinion to the king that the Indians should pay tithes. He noted that the friars, of the opposite opinion, threatened the judges with the same penalty. "Both propositions," said Zorita, "are defended by learned and very virtuous Christians."[9]

In this letter Zorita wrote that, because the Indians were so heavily burdened, their miserable state would only be worsened if they were obliged to pay tithes. The Indians paid tribute and other impositions to their *encomenderos*, caciques, and lords, as well as to many other persons whose only aim was to rob and molest them. They constructed and furnished ornaments for monasteries and churches in their towns and supported the friars. They also sustained the clerics in addition to paying their salaries. Further, the Indians were constantly occupied in public works (repairing of roads and bridges, fountains and buildings and maintaining irrigation ditches) and the herding of livestock.[10]

Should the crown nevertheless decide that the Indians must pay additional tax, Zorita recommended that this imposition be in the form of a general assessment based on the nature of the products yielded by the lands. Each tributary would then be told what he must pay, and those who grew cacao and cotton—crops yielding higher profits—should be apportioned a higher assessment. The total of tribute payments should be divided into ten parts: seven-tenths for the *encomenderos*, two-tenths for community expenses and its *señores* and caciques, and one-tenth for the tithes.[11] In his

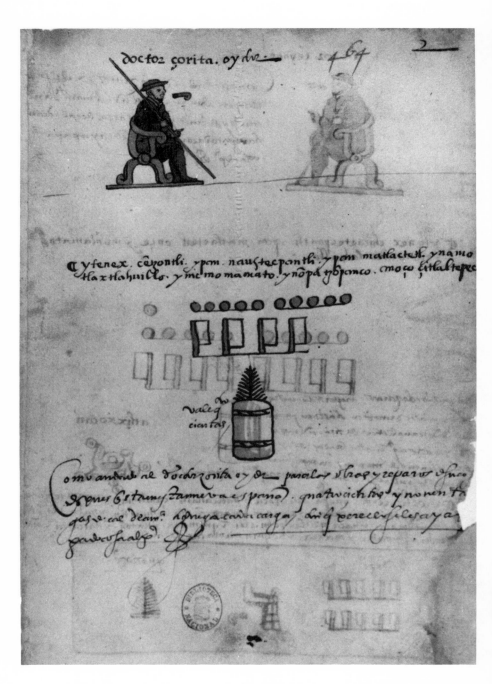

Stylized sketch of Alonso de Zorita showing work ordered on his house in New Spain. (Courtesy of *Pintura del gobernador, alcaldes y regidores de México: Códice Osuna*)

Illustration from *Pintura del gobernador, alcaldes y regidores de Mexico: Códice Osuna* (Madrid: Servicio de Publicaciones del Ministerio de Educación y Ciencia, 1973).

Doctor Zorita, oidor

(figure)

La cal del (doctor Zorita, oidor). Cuatrocientas noventa (cargas) que no se han pagado por lo que se fué a cargar alla en Tzompanco o Citlatepec. (See Luis Chávez Orozco, ed., *Códice Osuna*, Ediciones del Instituto Indigenista Interamericano, México, D. F., 1947, page 265).

Vale cuatro cientos   (figures)

Como han dado al doctor Zorita oidor para las obras y reparos de su casa después que entro en esta Nueva España cuatrocientas y noventa cargas de cal de a media fanega cada carga, sin que por el se les haya pagado cosa alguna. (rúbrica).

Brief Relation, Zorita slightly modified his position concerning tribute payments by recommending that one-tenth of the general assessment should be the portion applied to tithes but that the remaining nine-tenths of the tribute should be divided equally between the *encomenderos* and the natural lords.[12]

In his seventy-third year Zorita was working on a manuscript entitled "Discursos de la vida humana," a long work that he found very difficult. Whether this philosophical and devotional work survives or was completed is unknown. Serrano y Sanz, no admirer of Zorita's a style or erudition, stated that this treatise was probably "one of those products of the mind condemned from birth to eternal solitude," useful only to its creator.[13]

The full title of the work completed in 1574 is "Leyes y ordenanzas reales de las Indias del mar Océano por las cuales primeramente se han de librar todos los pleitos civiles y criminales de aquellas partes y lo que por ellas no estuviere determinado se ha de librar por las leyes y ordenanzas de los reinos de Castilla." This manuscript of 373 folio pages, known as "Recopilación de las leyes de Indias," is in the Biblioteca del Real Palacio in Madrid, listed as MS 1813. Zorita made this compilation of the laws of the Indies during the time he served as an *oidor* in the New World and dedicated the work to Philip II. Serrano y Sanz, who discovered the manuscript, stated in 1909 that no mention of it was to be found in historical studies of New World legislation. He intended to publish it but never carried out the project.

The manuscript's dedication to Philip II states that after he returned to Spain Zorita learned that the king had ordered all the *cédulas* and decrees for the government of the overseas colonies to be arranged in the order of their issuance and published with royal letters pertaining to government and justice in the Indies, so that judges, lawyers, and litigants might have access to these laws. Zorita assembled these materials in the form of books and titles but summarized the substance of what had been decreed "as was decided in the Cortes of Segovia regarding the compilation of the laws of these kingdoms, noting only where and when and by whom it was decided."[14] Although the contents of this work have a certain value, an examination reveals that most of the laws duplicate those to be found in the compilations made by Vasco de Puga in 1563 and by Diego de Encinas in 1596.[15] Moreover, because Zorita placed the decrees and ordinances he compiled by subject but did not include the decisions of the crown in specific instances, particulars regarding persons are missing and the historical value of the work is lessened. Zorita's collection was based on decrees addressed to the viceroys and judges of the royal courts of New Spain and Guatemala.

"Relación de las cosas notables de las Nueva España y de la conquista y pacificatión della y de la doctrina y conversión de los naturales," a work of 633 folio pages, is preserved in the Biblioteca del Real Palacio, where it is listed as MS 59. Serrano y Sanz published part one of this major work in 1909 under the title *Historia de la Nueva España por el doctor Alonso de Zorita (siglo XVI)*. Before its publication by Serrano y Sanz as volume 10 of the series entitled *Colección de libros y documentos referentes a la historia de América*, part of the manuscript was printed by the Idamor Moreno Press. The only copy of this edition—consisting of seven chapters numbering 129 pages—is preserved in the Biblioteca Nacional, Madrid, listed as R23075; the title page has the number 46083. Published under the title *Historia de la Nueva España*, the edition ends with chapter 7, which treats of the fruits of Spain that grew in Mexico and were sold among the Indians; page 1 of the book has the words "No llegó a tirarse."

Part one of the "Relación" treats in part of the geography and ancient history of New Spain. Part two (folios 166 to 260) is almost an exact duplicate of the *Brief and Summary Relation of the Lords of New Spain*. Part three treats of the conquest of Mexico and also has four chapters dealing with events in Guatemala and Nicaragua. Zorita mentions, for example, the destruction of Santiago de Guatemala on September 10, 1541. Part four, which begins on folio 455, treats of the conversion and instruction of the Indians of New Spain.

Serrano y Sanz observed that in this work Zorita recapitulated everything to be found in his other writings concerning Mexico. He also claimed that the work had little originality, for the author copied most of its contents from other works without the least misgiving. Although Serrano y Sanz believed that both Zorita and Bartolomé de Las Casas lacked the training to write of the rich inheritance still apparent among the Indians shortly after their conquest, he published part one of the "Relación" "in its entirety because from beginning to end it is inspired by many sources which have been lost, such as the writings by Juan Cano, Gonzalo de Las Casas, Don Pablo Nazareo, Fray Andrés de Olmos, and other authors expressly quoted by Zorita."[16]

Serrano y Sanz's severe judgment of Zorita's "Relación" and

other works is largely motivated by his dislike for this loyal disciple of Las Casas. He claims that Zorita—either from inner conviction or because it was fashionable—was as zealous as Las Casas in defending the freedom of the Indians and their good treatment but that both complacently accepted black slavery.[17] Serrano is correct in stating that Zorita's major work is largely derivative and suffers from pedantry and the inclusion of irrelevant material, but he fails to mention that these offenses were customary faults of sixteenth-century historiography. Further, Zorita carefully cited his sources, unlike several pioneer historians of Mexico and colonial America. For instance, Juan de Torquemada referred to his Indian sources "in very general terms"; Gómara "tells us virtually nothing about his sources"; and Antonio de Herrera y Tordesillas not only "carried to an extreme the abusive privilege claimed by contemporary historians of pillaging the works of others without indicating the source" but deliberately hid sources, forged them, or twisted their original meanings.[18]

As honest in his writings as in his life, Zorita, in his valuable bibliographical introduction to the "Relación," indicates whether he only knew of a work or had used it as a source. A reading of the history also indicates that he made critical use of his sources. Thus he followed Fray Francisco de las Navas's *relación* in his discussion of the four classes of Aztec tribute payers but disagreed with Gómara and other writers concerning the pre-Conquest tribute system. His catalogue of some forty-four published and manuscript sources is the first descriptive account of works on the subject of the Indies; Zorita is thus the first bibliographer of the New World.[19]

Important sources cited by Zorita include Fray Toribio de Motolinía; Fray Andrés de Olmos; Fray Bartolomé de Las Casas; Fray Francisco de las Navas; the Indian principal Don Pablo Nazareo, married to a daughter of a brother of Montezuma; and Juan Cano, a Spaniard who married a daughter of Montezuma.

Zorita called Motolinía the best author he had read on the subject of the Indies. He took Motolinía's book to Spain when he left Mexico. Some years later, Fray Gerónimo de Mendieta wrote Zorita requesting the loan of this manuscript so that he might incorporate its findings into his *Historia eclesiástica indiana*. Robert Ricard collated Zorita's and Mendieta's citations from Motolinía and concluded that the work used by these writers was neither Motolinía's *Historia de los indios de la Nueva España*, nor the *Memoriales* but a much larger work that has been lost.[20]

Ricard's conclusion is supported by Georges Baudot. He finds that Motolinía's *History of the Indians of New Spain* is an abbreviated forerunner of the friar's lost definitive work entitled "Relación de las cosas, idolatrías, ritos y ceremonias de la Nueva España," written between 1556 and 1560. According to Baudot, this lost manuscript included other writings attributed to Motolinía.[21]

Zorita also used a summary of a book on Indian antiquities by Fray Andrés de Olmos. This friar, who arrived in Mexico in 1528 with Bishop Juan de Zumárraga, mastered Náhuatl, Totonac, Tepehuan, and Huastec and wrote many books and treatises. In 1533 the president of the Audiencia of Mexico, Don Sebastián Ramírez de Fuenleal, and the head of the Custody of the Holy Gospel, Fray Martín de Valencia, commissioned Olmos to write a book on Indian antiquities to serve as a guide in Franciscan efforts to refute native religious beliefs. This work, completed in 1539 and based on information obtained from Olmos's interviews with the most ancient Indians and from pictographic annals, was sent to Spain. The original and several copies were apparently lost, but it is possible that Olmos's great work survives as the partly unpublished "Códice del Museo de America."[22] In any case, no versions of this history remained in Mexico.

Some years later it appears that the Council of the Indies and Fray Bartolomé de Las Casas requested a copy of Olmos's work on Mexican antiquities. Unable to comply, Olmos reviewed his notebooks and memory and wrote a summary of what was contained in his original work. Part of this summary was used by Zorita and Las Casas in their writings.[23]

Zorita also mentions that he used several *memoriales* by Fray Francisco de las Navas. When Zorita arrived in Mexico, Navas was acting as the local superior of the Convent of Saint Francis in Tepeaca. Navas's writings were one source for Zorita's comments on the rules of succession among the Indians.[24]

"Relación de las cosas notables de la Nueva España"

Because much of what Zorita wrote in his major work, "Relación de las cosas notables," is pedantic and irrelevant, few readers today would find it interesting literary fare. Granted the defects of Zorita's style, his frequent digressions, and inclusion of irrelevant materials, the book nonetheless makes a valuable contribution to our understanding of Aztec society.

Zorita's vision of the Aztec state is a blend of medieval and

Renaissance-humanist thought. On the one hand, he is rigidly orthodox in matters of theology and relies on biblical-patristic traditions to condemn Indian religious practices. On the other hand, the Renaissance-humanist elements of his thought are demonstrated by his relativism, his attempt to understand Indian civilizations by comparing them to Old World societies representing approximately the same state of development, and the fact that his descriptions of Indian government and life were based on personal observations, contemporary authors, and informants.

Zorita's attitude toward Aztec culture, as found in this book, is similar to views held by middle-of-the-road realists like Motolinía, Sahagún, and Fray Diego Durán. Unlike the *Brief and Summary Relation*, which minimizes or rationalizes the dark side of Aztec civilization, Zorita's major work condemns Aztec religion and views the Conquest as divinely ordained because it prepared the way for the evangelization of the Indians; this view is held by Indian haters like Sepúlveda and Gómara. Yet Zorita, like Las Casas, condemned Spanish crimes against the Indians, ardently defended native crown subjects, and praised Aztec character and cultural achievements. Zorita in the "Relacíon" thus adheres to the views of a moderate like Motolinía and agrees with him that Mexico was a transplanted hell before the Indians' conversion.

Although Zorita condemned Aztec religion and defended the Conquest because it was a preliminary to the conversion of the Indians, he rejected the idea of Indian inferiority. Like Bartolomé de Las Casas, Zorita discussed the customs of New Spain's Indians within the framework of universal history. Zorita saw the uniformity of mankind in its seeming variety and recognized that the wandering generations of Adam had over time arrived at different states of development. Peoples differed in cultural attainment and ranged from the most primitive to those possessing all the trappings of civilization and true religion.

According to Zorita, early man in the Old World lived like the Chichimecas and ate raw meat, as did the nomads, Troglodytes, Scythians, and Huns. Zorita also observed that cannibalism was practiced in the Old World and noted that Saint Jerome mentions that the British Scots ate human flesh and held women in common. Moreover, "Erasmus in his commentaries states that even today there are some among the Saxons who still eat raw meat, especially that of the pig."[25]

In his comparison of Aztec civilization to such approximate counterparts as the Greek, Roman, and Hebrew cultures, Zorita

was influenced by a popular historical theory of the Renaissance
—the Platonic doctrine of historical regression, which taught that
time is the enemy of man. This idea held that history is retro-
gressive and that man inevitably falls from a Golden Age of simplicity, happiness, and long life that is finally replaced by an
Iron Age characterized by deviation from the natural law.[26]

The idea of the Golden Age was fused with its Christian
parallel, the Garden of Eden, where man's first parents lived
before the Fall; the Platonic doctrine of degeneration was combined with the Christian idea that with Adam's disobedience
"man, corrupt by choice and condemned by justice, has produced
a progeny that is both corrupt and condemned."[27]

Zorita, like other legalistic and scholastic Spaniards who described the Indians in the sixteenth century, believed in the continuing degeneration of humankind. However, humanists like
Peter Martyr, Las Casas, and Zorita were aware of cultural differences and evolution and the distances separating civilized nations
from peoples still living in primitive simplicity. They also were
convinced that Europeans had experienced greater retrogression
than had other societies. The contrast between a Europe in decline and a society still apparently living in the Golden Age of
innocence was made by Peter Martyr shortly after Columbus's
discovery. He wrote that the Indians living in the state of nature
"go naked, they know neither weights nor measures, nor that
source of all misfortune, money; living in a golden age, without
laws, without lying judges, without books, satisfied with their
life, and in no wise solicitous for the future."[28]

Zorita, it is clear, accepted primitivist doctrine and its incor-
poration of the Indian into the Noble Savage tradition. However,
humanists like Zorita were products of European societies who
cherished the achievements and values of Western civilization.
Zorita was also a zealous Catholic, aware of scholastic-theological
thought which, in addition to promoting the idea of a universal
state and a universal church, taught that "the Christian era introduced the last period of history, the old age of humanity, which
would endure only so long as to enable the Deity to gather in the
predestined number of saved souls."[29] Further, Zorita was an
admirer and supporter of the mendicant orders and a friend of
friars like Mendieta, a member of the pro-Indian party in the
Franciscan order who praised Zorita's work on behalf of the
Indians in Mexico. Zorita was aware that Mendieta believed that
his fellow missionaries had been "given the unique opportunity

of creating, on the eve of the end of the world, a terrestrial paradise where a whole race of men would be consecrated to evangelical poverty."[30]

Primitivist traditions and Christian apocalyptic eschatology are apparent in Zorita's comparison of Indian practices and customs with those of barbaric peoples of earlier times and of the Greeks and Romans. Primitivism and millennialism are not incongruent, for they are in essence "opposite sides of the same coin of human aspiration for a way of life dramatically opposite in complexity and organization from the present."[31] At the same time, Zorita could look backward to an Indian Golden Age in which people lived happily under the rule of native lords, and look forward to a Christian utopia that would redeem the confused and tragic life of the Indians in the reign of Philip II.

Zorita's "Relación" sought to prove that Indians had been unjustly defamed by those who claimed they lacked intelligence and gratitude. Indians, said Zorita, were a generous and creative people who reasoned well and spoke eloquently. In agreement with Las Casas, Zorita declared that God had created the simple Indians without evil and duplicity. Indians, extremely obedient to their natural lords and to Christians, were the most patient and peaceful people in the world. More delicate than princes, these humble people had little stamina and died quickly from exhaustion and illness. Because Indians lived in abject poverty, they lacked pride, ambition, and greed. After comparing their food and clothing to those of the ascetic early fathers of the Church who separated themselves from the world in the Egyptian desert, Zorita stated that because of their clear, deliberate, and lively minds, the Indians would be the most blessed people in the world once they had knowledge of the true God.[32]

Although Zorita's major work is largely concerned with the character of Aztec civilization, the "Relación" is also important for information on the Spanish borderlands. Part four, which treats of the conversion and instruction of the Indians of New Spain, has two chapters dealing with the early history of Florida and New Mexico.

Zorita's interesting account of Fray Luis Cáncer de Barbastro's 1549 expedition to Florida adds significant details to those found in published traditional sources by Woodbury Lowery, Andrés G. Barcía, Fray Agustín Dávila Padilla, and Father V. F. O'Daniel.[33] Zorita's account also differs in certain respects from the accounts of the Cáncer expedition, and from that completed by Fray Gregorio de Beteta for the viceroy's information. Some of these differences have to do with the name of a friar from the Basque provinces (called Fray Diego de Salamanca by Zorita and Fray Diego de Tolosa and Fray Diego de Peñalosa by Lowry), the time elapsed between the departure from Havana and the sighting of the Florida coast, the number of female interpreters, the landing and the number of Indians met on the coast, and Fray Luis Cáncer's initial impression of Juan Muñoz, the Spanish captive who had come to Florida with Hernando de Soto and served the Indians for more than ten years before his escape.

Zorita's discussion of Fray Marcos de Niza and Onorato's expedition to the north in 1538 confirms that the Indians beyond San Miguel de Culiacán had extensive contacts and traded with the sedentary Indians of New Mexico in pre-Conquest times. Zorita observed that the poor Indians visited by Fray Marcos had obtained much turquoise and other articles from the Pueblo Indians. They also told Fray Marcos they went at times of labor in a thickly populated land inhabited by people who had houses of two and three stories. These people were gathered in many enclosed towns on the shore of a great river. This information, although derivative, is one more example of why the Southwest may be considered the far-northern frontier of Mexico before the colonization of New Mexico by Don Juan de Oñate in 1598.[34]

Zorita's "Relación" is an insightful and informative recapitulation of what other authors have written. Zorita's work also contains numerous descriptions of post-Conquest Indian society based on personal observations and demonstrates that the comparative framework of his own cultural tradition led him to be concerned with Greek deductions and Christian doctrine about the nature and destiny of man, the superiority of Christianity over pagan religion, and the just treatment of the conquered Indians.

Brief and Summary Relation of the Lords of New Spain

Zorita's pedantic style and numerous classical citations make the "Relación de las cosas notables" tedious reading and obscure its wealth of valuable data. Much more interesting is the *Brief and Summary Relation of the Lords of New Spain*, although this work tends to idealize the reality of Aztec political organization.

The *Brief Relation's* importance was recognized long before its publication in the nineteenth century. Part two of Zorita's "Rela-

ción de las cosas notables" is, for example, almost an exact duplicate of the *Brief Relation*, and the entire work is a manuscript
copy of the sixteenth century. Another manuscript of the *Brief
Relation* is preserved in the Biblioteca de la Real Academia de la
Historia in Madrid. This copy, of 135 folio pages, forms volume
26 of the Muñoz Collection, and is numbered A/68 at the end of
the book. A note says: "This copy was made by me, Lorenzo
Boturini, Señor de Hono, from the original which is in the
Colegio de San Pedro y San Pablo de la Compañía de Jesús. The
original has 144 useful folio pages, and has become the property
of His Majesty." A sentence follows the note: "From the Boturini copy Don Diego Panes, Lt. Col. of Artillery, made another,
from which has been copied the present work. Madrid, March 9,
1791. J. B. Muñoz." Another manuscript copy of the *Brief Relation* preserved in the Biblioteca del Real Palacio appears to be a
copy of the Muñoz text made in the last decade of the eighteenth
century; it has 236 folio pages and is listed as MS 1481.[35]

Fray Agustín de Vetancourt first mentioned Zorita's *Brief Relation* in his *Teatro Mexicano* (1698), where he wrote that Zorita
was the author of a manuscript owned by Carlos de Sigüenza y
Góngora but failed to give the title of the work. The first explicit
citation of the *Brief Relation* is by Lorenzo Boturnini Benaduci,
an eighteenth-century scholar-adventurer. Giving the work's correct title, he stated that the manuscript in his possession was a
copy of the original manuscript but failed give the location of the
original.

Francisco Javier Clavijero (1731–87) mentioned Zorita in his
bibliographical introduction to his *Historia Antigua de México*
and stated that Zorita's original manuscript was preserved in the
Jesuit Colegio de San Pedro y San Pablo, in Mexico City.[36] This
manuscript later became the property of the Mexican scholar José
F. Ramírez; García Icazbalceta made a copy from it in 1867.
According to Joaquín Ramírez Cabañas, this copy is probably the
manuscript of Zorita's work owned by the Biblioteca Nacional de
México.[37]

In his introduction to the 1891 edition García Icazbalceta noted
that Ramírez had two other copies of the *Brief Relation*, one of
which was in Boturini's hand. The Boturini copy had been examined by García Icazbalceta, and a note at the end of the
manuscript stated that Boturini had copied the work in November, 1738, from the original, preserved in the Colegio de San
Pedro y San Pablo. Boturini had also written that the original

manuscript had a comment stating that it had come into the possession of one Licentiate Pensado in 1683.

It appears that the presumed original manuscript of the *Brief Relation* owned by Pensado fell into the hands of Sigüenza y Góngora and eventually found its way into the library of the Jesuits in Mexico City. The location of the manuscript owned by Ramírez was not known to García Icazbalceta.

The first edition of the *Brief Relation* was published in French by Henri Ternaux-Compans in 1840. This unreliable edition was translated from the Muñoz manuscript, another unreliable edition, published in 1864 and found in volume 2 of the *Colección de documentos inéditos* ... (Madrid, 42 vols., 1864–84). The first acceptable edition of the *Brief Relation* was prepared by García Icazbalceta in 1891; it was republished in 1941.[38]

Joaquín Ramírez Cabañas utilized García Icazbalceta's text for his edition, published in 1942. Although he omitted some of García Icazbalceta's notes, his intelligent summary of Zorita's life and the importance of the work points out that after four centuries Zorita had still not found an impartial writer to argue his case so that he might be rendered the complete justice due him.[39]

Zorita finally found such a defender in 1963. In addition to making the *Brief Relation* available to a wider reading public, Benjamin Keen's introduction to his brilliant English version confirms that Zorita as a judge and author was one of the most admirable characters in the pro-Indian reform party in the Spanish colonies.

Zorita's Idyllic Image of Aztec Society

Zorita's *Brief Relation* compares an idealized Indian past with a dismal present, contrasting a Golden Age of virtue and voluntary communal labor with an Iron Age of misery and forced labor. The tone of the work, a vigorous defense of Indian character and achievement, is immediately set by an account of the Aztec rules of succession.

The customs of the Indians varied in different provinces, wrote Zorita, but in Tenochtitlán and other cities the oldest son of the ruler's principal wife usually succeeded to the supreme lordship. However, ability to govern and the qualities of courage and fortitude, rather than close relationship to the supreme lord, determined which of the ruler's descendants would be chosen as successor.

The rulers' fortitude led Zorita to observe that the more noble the Indian, the more humility he displayed. But he added that admirable qualities were general throughout Indian society. Indians who followed traditional ways were long-suffering, obedient, teachable, humble, and repentant when rebuked for having misbehaved. In contrast, those Indians who had been made slaves or who dealt with Spaniards had lost their natural simplicity and goodness.[40]

Zorita concluded that in matters of succession and election of rulers all the Indians did "conformed to Natural Law, and in some degree to the Divine Law, and even to Civil and Canon Law, although they were ignorant of this."[41] Supreme and lesser lords benefited their subjects, said Zorita, and order and justice marked the Aztec state. There were few lawsuits, truth prevailed, and all were equal under the law.

Zorita approved of the swift, exact, and severe nature of Aztec justice. Magistrates appointed by the supreme lords functioned in the manner of a royal audiencia. Appeals from lesser judges were heard by twelve superior judges who ruled on cases in consultation with the supreme ruler. Aztec judges had great skill in gathering evidence and passing sentence, and they and all the other ministers of justice showed great rectitude in their rulings.[42]

Aztec judges, said Zorita, punished the offense of sodomy by death, for they held it a grave transgression and an act seen only among beasts. "Intercourse with animals was unknown among them." Zorita also contrasted Indian drunkenness after the Conquest with Indian sobriety under their natural lords. No one could drink wine (pulque) when the Indians were pagans without express permission of lords or judges, and its use was allowed only to sick persons or those more than fifty years of age. Public officials found guilty of this offense were removed from office and barred from holding posts in the future; men and women found guilty of drunkenness had their hair cropped in the marketplace, after which the offenders' houses were razed.

Like Motolinía, Zorita believed that Indians sometimes chose evil over good because they were blinded by idolatry. An example is the following passage:

Both male and female transvestites were condemned to death, and Fray Toribio says that in two other provinces far from Mexico sodomy was tolerated because the Devil led them to believe that their gods had this custom and that therefore it was licit. However, the Indians regarded it as evil and considered the person who committed this act infamous.[43]

Zorita also noted that some Indians were so addicted to drinking both native and Castilian wine that in their drunken state they often killed each other and committed great iniquities and sins. Other Indians living in remote places and not yet Christians imbibed until they could drink no more; they then had wine poured into their system through the anal passage.

The laws punishing liars, perjurers, adulterers, and drunkards to be found in the *Brief Relation* are also described in part two of Zorita's larger "Relación." In the latter work Zorita gives other examples of the nature of Aztec justice. He noted that the pregnant woman who aborted her infant was killed, as was the woman who aided her in this crime; whoever did violence to a virgin was put to death; anyone who injured or killed with poison was given the death penalty, and this punishment applied to the person who supplied the potion.

Persons found guilty of committing adultery were put to death, but if the evidence was circumstantial, the accused were tortured before sentence was passed. If a husband killed his unfaithful wife, he was executed because he had broken the law requiring him to take her before the judges for sentencing.

Zorita cited Fray Andrés de Olmos as his source when he observed that Aztec judges warned those being tried to tell the truth, reminding the accused that their god knew what was hidden in their hearts. If the accused was found guilty but still claimed to be innocent, he was enclosed in a wooden cage until he confessed or died. Whoever committed a crime against the state or was found guilty of grand theft was put to death, and his relatives were also subject to this penalty.[44]

Zorita anticipated Montaigne's cultural relativism when he criticized Cortés for calling the Aztecs barbarians. Stating that Cortés had also declared that Aztec mode of life was much the same as in Spain, with as much harmony and order, Zorita carefully analyzed the use of the term. He noted that men frequently call peoples of different speech, customs, and religion "barbarians," for what is not one's usage is called foreign or barbarous. He concludes that the Aztecs, a people of great ability and intelligence, were the equals of the ancients in their achievements.[45]

Zorita's account of the Aztec peasantry depicts them as living in a New World earthly paradise. The men did light communal work in their towns with much merriment, and without being hurried. Work ended early and they returned to their small, cozy houses to enjoy the company of their families, a warm fire, and the food prepared by their wives.[46]

Zorita's idyllic picture of ancient Mexico may be questioned for a number of reasons, Even if his account of Aztec civilization is essentially correct, we still know very little about other Indian societies of central Mexico in pre- and post-Conquest times.[47] Moreover, Spanish accounts of the Aztecs and other Indian groups were written from a variety of motives and many were set down long after the Conquest. Writings on the history and culture of ancient Mexico by Indians also pose problems.

Native accounts (as recorded by Sahagún, Durán, Juan de Tovar, Ixtlilxóchitl, Muñoz Camargo, and Chimalpahin) have considerable value but may be questioned. Individuals like Ixtlil-xóchitl wrote many decades after the Conquest, and information compiled by Sahagún and Durán was recorded many years after the destruction of Tenochtitlán. Moreover, divergencies exist in the Indian histories, and authorities differ in their interpretations of Indian codices; in the absence of other documentation their differences remain unresolved. Further, after the Aztecs gained control of much of Middle America, they burned those accounts that slighted them and created a "new history" and cosmogony. Finally, native reports are ambivalent and reflect the ambiguous social and political status of Indian and mestizo historians under Spanish rule.[48]

Zorita's rosy picture of enlightened Aztec aristocrats exercising a mild rule over blissful commoners is obviously unreal; it also differs markedly from other Spanish accounts that describe Indian lords' oppression of the peasantry, the unfavorable status of Indian women, marked inequities of wealth, human sacrifice, ritual cannibalism, and "bestial drunkenness" in the 1520s.[49]

Zorita's sources for pre-Conquest Indian society included oral and written accounts supplied by Indian elders and lords. But it appears that "Zorita's compassion for the suffering of the natives caused him to overlook the possibility of exaggeration in the picture they themselves drew of their former felicity."[50] Zorita's informants, like other conquered peoples, felt a great nostalgia for the past. Like all unhappy peoples, they looked backward in time "to find a Garden of Eden, a Golden Age, a pastoral Arcadia. Fields distant in time (and sometimes in space) are greener. 'By the waters of Babylon we sat down and wept when we thought of thee, o Zion.'"[51]

Zorita's image of the Indians as noble, generous, and creative people is part of the Noble Savage convention, also found in Peter Martyr's *Decades,* the seventeenth-century Jesuit *Relations,* and the writings of Rousseau. Zorita fails to discuss the dark side of Aztec civilization, which included war as a predominant cultural trait, human sacrifice in great numbers, and the neglect of subjects in times of famine.[52] These omissions leave Zorita open to criticism. Still, if population growth is indicative of a flourishing culture, it is apparent that Indians lived better under their native lords than they did under the Spaniards. It also appears that their tribute burdens were lighter.

The Somber Present in the Brief Relation

Zorita's account of the condition of the Indians under Spanish rule contrasts greatly with his picture of pre-Conquest society. The evils he depicted, however, were based on personal experiences and observations of the sad state of the Indians in New Granada, Guatemala, and Mexico. Moreover, Zorita's negative assessment of Indian conditions in the years 1548–66 conforms with views held by the majority of his contemporaries and most modern scholars.

Zorita stressed the poverty of the Indians, their constant hunger and endless labor, and the decrease of the population. Even in Zorita's time, some Indians had lost so much land to Spaniards that they had no space in which to plant.[53] Zorita also maintained that the peace and concord that had existed in ancient Mexico had been replaced by a topsy-turvy state of affairs in which whirl was king.

Encomenderos and the audiencia had ruined and humiliated many Indian lords by replacing them with Indian commoners. Tribute collectors had done the same, and these representatives of *encomenderos* exploited the Indians in every way imaginable. No harmony remained, wrote Zorita, for Indian commoners under Spanish rule had lost all fear and shame; the evil consequences were "false swearing, hatreds, enmities, ruin of towns and provinces, and great wickedness on the part of those who urge them on in order to rob them, all leading to confusion so great that a solution now appears hopeless."[54]

All men were against the Indians, the land had lost its splendor, chaos was the norm, and acculturated Indian officials were cunning, shameless creatures who lacked all sense of decency. Misery was intensified because of Spanish crimes, and the native popula-

tion had declined by two-thirds. Labor and tribute systems had
devastated Indians everywhere, and would destroy them completely if remedial action was not provided.[55]

Zorita's account supports the view of Bartolomé de Las Casas
and a significant number of his contemporaries who stressed the
great evils of the Conquest and its aftermath. These advocates of
reform urged the Spanish monarch to protect his Indian subjects
against the unjust demands and cruel treatment of their new
lords. The *Brief Relation* also forms part of that impressive body
of evidence amassed in recent years which supports the claim that
the Black Legend's substantive content, "stripped of its rhetoric
and emotional coloration, and with due regard for its failure to
notice less dramatic forms of Spanish exploitation of the Indians
(land usurpation, peonage, and the like) . . . is no legend at all."[56]
The Spanish Conquest was followed by new patterns of life and
labor that transformed the Indians into a victimized minority
group. Indian lands in Mexico and elsewhere were expropriated,
social systems were destroyed, custom and religion were forbidden, and Indians reacted to their subordinate status in various
ways—drunkenness, apathy, disregard of kindship obligations,
intragroup violence, criminal behavior, and emulation of the
worst traits of their conquerors.[57]

A reading of the *Brief Relation* and other sixteenth-century
documents also confirms that in contrast to Spanish laws for the
protection of the Indians, which were seldom enforced, exploita-
tive laws were vigorously implemented, "wherefore there is no
end to the destruction of the Indians."[58] As Eric Wolf and other
modern scholars have noted, between the time of Cortés's arrival
and the middle of the seventeenth century, perhaps 85 percent of
Middle America's Indian population had been eradicated; "only a
seventh remained to turn the wheels of paradise. Like the baroque
altars soon to rise in the colony, the splendor and wealth of the
new possession but covered a grinning skull."[59] While epidemic
disease and famine may have accounted for many deaths, their
results are directly related to mistreatment of Indians and the
disruption of their societies.

Zorita's Account of Aztec Society

Granted that Zorita exaggerated the role of the Aztec nobility in
defending and benefiting their subjects, it is clear that Aztec
society, at least at the upper levels, consisted of supreme lords

and officials who sought to make order and justice prevail in their dominions. As Zorita noted, if population increase is a mark of good government, the natural lords governed well.[60] In addition to conveying this impression of Aztec life, Zorita tells us a great deal about the types of Indian nobility, land tenure, and the social and political organization of the Aztec state.

Zorita carefully differentiated between the various orders of the aristocracy. Supreme lords, or *tlatoques*, had command over provinces and towns. These chief speakers had civil and criminal jurisdiction and the government and command of all their territory and people. In addition to having patrimonial lands and serfs, supreme lords enjoyed certain lands called *tlatocamilli*. Because these "lands of the lordship" were not privately owned but passed with the lordship, the lord might not dispose of this type of land; but he might rent it if he pleased. If the income from these lands did not suffice to meet the king's traditional obligation of hospitality to all who came to this house, he spent income received from his privately owned estate for this purpose.

Below the supreme rulers were *tectecutzin* or *teules*, who served as governors and ministers of justice for life, and at court they might act as courtiers, guards, messengers, and majordomos. Those sons of *teules* who did not succeed their fathers kept their status as nobles. Houses of these lords were called *teccalli*. Their subjects, the *teccallec*, paid them the tribute ordinarily paid to the supreme lord. Because the supreme ruler rewarded these lords with greater or lesser dignities and *encomiendas*, some had command and dominion of more people than others.

In his study of noble lineages in ancient Mexico, Pedro Carrasco observes that the term *teccalli*, translated literally means "seignorial house". He also notes that various documents of the sixteenth century equate the term with the Spanish concept of *mayorazgo*, or an entailed estate. He therefore concludes that the *teccalli* was essentially an entity subordinate to a lord which comprised the lands of the chief house with its dependents. The lord exercised authority over the lands and peasants he controlled, and participated in the political organization of the lordship in its entirety. Members of the *teccalli*, or at least the dominant sector, considered themselves to be descendants of the seignorial house and acted as a corporate lineage in the economic and political system.[61]

Lords of the third kind were called *chinancallec*, or *calpullec* in the singular. These lords governed *calpultin*, kinship groups of ancient lineage gathered into wards or barrios. This type of lord was compared by Zorita to the *pariente mayor*, or senior kinsman, in Biscay or the Montaña. Ward members farmed a parcel of land for their chief elder's maintenance, and gave him household service.

Lords of the fourth kind were called *pipiltzin* (*pipiltin*). This order of nobility had various ranks, for Zorita stated that the term in Spanish meant nobles or caballeros. Members of this rank of nobility included all the sons, grandsons, and great-grandsons of the supreme rulers and sons of *tectecutzin*. These lords, like the rest of the nobility, paid no tribute because they were caballeros, hidalgos, and warriors.

Zorita reveals that the Aztec nobility paid no tribute, did not work the land, and received various benefits denied commoners. Subjects of lords worked their fields and rendered personal service. Zorita also states that some lords had "direct dominion" of their estates, a type of landholding that "was of immemorial antiquity and had the consent of the supreme rulers." By ancient custom lords holding privately owned estates might bequeath to each son such serfs (*mayeques*) and land as he preferred, because these were not entailed estates.[62]

Scholars have differed over the nature of the social organization of ancient Mexico, and whether the great nobles had patrimonial estates. As Pedro Carrasco observes, modern students of Aztec society have associated the concept of patrimonial estates with its logical corollary, the idea of social classes "based upon the private ownership of the material means of production." He claims that this is the theoretical focus found in more or less explicit form in the works of Lewis H. Morgan and Adolph F. Bandelier, who denied there were social classes, and in those studies by Manuel Moreno, Alfonso Caso, Paul Kirchhoff, and Friedrich Katz which affirm the existence of social classes in the Aztec state. According to Carrasco, modern scholars from Moreno (1931) to Katz (1966) all adhere to the concept "that social classes are based upon the private ownership of the means of production and that the state is the organism that has the function of assuring the dominion of the proprietary class."[63]

Carrasco, like other scholars, cites Zorita in distinguishing several ranks within the Aztec ruling group. But he agrees with those anthropologists who argue that in primitive economies what we call economy is a by-product of other social institutions. He thus concludes that in Aztec society there was no distinction between public and private life. Hence land and other economic resources controlled and regulated by the government "could be acquired and held only together with the political office for which they provided the economic basis."[64] By making no distinction between the economically powerful and the governing personnel of the Aztec state, Carrasco makes the state the only proprietor and the ruling group a class of managers rather than owners of private landed property.

In addition to denying that privately owned estates existed in pre-Conquest Mexico, both Carrasco and Mexican scholar Alfredo López Austin attribute a static character to Aztec society.[65] They thus make it appear that this society practiced an "Asiatic mode of production." This phrase was originally coined by Karl Marx to account for a type of stationary society marked, in part, by the absence or slight importance of private property in land, the central control of public works, and the decentralized nature of production in local communities subordinated to the supreme proprietor—the state. Depending upon one's view, the concept was later developed or distorted by Karl Wittfogel in various works on Oriental despotism, equated with what he called "hydraulic societies."[66]

The revisionist idea that no patrimonial estates existed in Aztec Mexico rests on theory rather than fact. Zorita's statement that permanent fiefs existed is supported by other reliable sources.[67] Available sources support the claim that the spoils of conquest transformed the Aztec tribe—originally composed of several kinship groups called *calpultin*—into a state in which various types of property, including patrimonial estates, were found. In short, one can agree with Pedro Carrasco that the Aztec economy was politically organized, and that production by artisans and the market mechanism were secondary activities in an economy marked by reciprocity and redistribution, yet argue that patrimonial estates and other forms of private property were important aspects of this economy.

Zorita lists as commoners those who were merchants, artisans, free peasant farmers, serfs, and slaves. His remarks confirm that in a society marked by division of labor, wealth and privilege differed according to the individual's position in the social structure.

Zorita's description of merchants as a privileged group is supported by other sources. Sahagún's Indian informants described this intermediate group between the nobility and the commoners as mean, stingy, and selfish. Some merchants, said Oviedo, had privately owned estates; like lords and their relatives, merchants might sell and gamble with their lands as they pleased, sowing and harvesting them but paying no tribute.[68]

Artisans included specialists in the art of gold and silver work, feather-workers, and skilled stonecutters and masons. Zorita also noted that in the 1550s there was a numerous class of carpenters, engravers, weavers, painters, blacksmiths, locksmiths, bridlemakers, cutlers, beadworkers, and lathe turners. Others made stockings, shoes, doublets, gloves, and any number of things.[69]

Unlike free peasant farmers, serfs (*mayeques* or *tlamaitec*) were bound to the land of their lords. Passed on to heirs of their masters, serfs paid a part of their harvest as rent or worked a piece of land for the lord. Rent and service varied according to the number of serfs and their agreement with the lord.

It appears that one became a *mayeque* by birth, for Zorita noted that the ancestors of the serfs were included among the first conquerors of the land but received no part of it. The same thing happened when the Spaniards took Mexico; some conquerors were given land and Indians but others obtained neither.[70]

Zorita clearly distinguished between serfs and tenants. Serfs were permanently attached to the land, but tenants rented land from its owner for a certain period. Like other free commoners, tenants only gave personal service to the supreme ruler; they also did communal labor on the tribute fields farmed for the chief speaker. Zorita also distinguished between serfs and those tribute payers called *teccallec*; the latter were not automatically inherited by a lord, and they held lands in their wards.[71]

Very little is known about the economic and social roles of serfs in Aztec society. Because some slaves did the same work as serfs—and serfs may not have differed greatly in status from free peasant farmers—it is not clear whether *mayeques* formed a distinct servile and oppressed class. Motolinía either refers to serfs or slaves when he states that "slaves live virtually free on their masters' landed properties and inheritances, cultivating a certain part of it for their masters and a part of it for themselves. They also have their houses and their wives and children. Hence slavery here is not such as to induce the slaves to flee and desert their masters." He probably refers to slaves, for Zorita notes that in each town's tribute fields "the rulers kept slaves who guarded and worked the fields with the aid of the townspeoples."[72]

If recent estimates are correct that serfs constituted perhaps 33 percent of the Aztec population, whereas slaves made up about 5 percent it is obvious that Aztec society more closely resembled the estate system of medieval Europe than that of ancient Rome or classical Greece.[73]

Zorita says very little about slaves in the *Brief Relation* but notes in the larger "Relación de las cosas notables" that slavery among the Aztecs differed markedly from European slavery. The children of Aztec slaves were born free, and slaves gave limited rather than ordinary service to their masters. Moreover, a slave who had served for some years or wished to marry might gain his freedom if a brother or relative agreed to take his place.[74]

Slaves largely consisted of prisoners of war not sacrificed or freemen sentenced to slavery for various crimes. But some people became slaves by choice. Players addicted to the ball game or to *patolli*, a kind of dice game, lost everything and sold themselves. Some women sold themselves in order to live and dress well. The average price of a slave was 20 *mantas*, or one load of cloth. "Because some mantles are larger and better than others, one load is worth more than another. Because the same is true of slaves, a higher price was paid for those who were fitter than others." Those who sold themselves were allowed their liberty until they had spent their price, which was hardly ever more than a year; when this was gone they became slaves.[75]

Zorita's *Brief Relation* also includes the most complete description of the *calpulli*, the basic unit of Aztec social organization and landholding. Zorita's account of this kinship group shows that the *calpulli* was an administrative unit which had educational, military, and religious functions.

Although scholars agree that the *calpulli* was an administrative unit and a landholding group, and Zorita suggests that it was a kin group, its nature and significance is still disputed. Those who stress bonds of kinship as pre-dominant in these clans, lineages, or barrios, equated by Zorita to the "tribes" of Israel, risk making the *calpulli* more egalitarian than it was. Those who stress territorial bonds as its predominant characteristic tend to make the *calpulli* a mere political division of the centralized Aztec state.

In his study of the *calpulli*, Arturo Monzón notes that this unit of social organization had the characteristics of a clan, a territory, and a guild. Although it appears that craft specialization may have been practiced by some *calpultin*, Zorita clearly states that all classes, including merchants and artisans, were found in each *calpulli*. On the other hand, Zorita also states that merchants were members of recognized lineages and could not follow this occupation except by inheritance or by royal permission.[76]

The word *calpulli*, as Hugo G. Nutini and Pedro Carrasco observe, may be applied to different things and one should take care in assigning a precise meaning to this term.[77] Hence Zorita may have meant either that merchants and artisans were to be found in each of the four great sections (barrios) of Tenochtitlán or that these classes were to be found in the several subdivisions of these four "quarters." In either case, Zorita's description indicates that there was not a close degree of relationship between *calpulli* and particular occupations. Further, Zorita's statement that the tribute of the rich merchants was the most valuable of all payments given to the supreme ruler clearly shows that social and economic inequality existed in the *calpulli*. Finally, Zorita's statement that some members of the *calpulli* cultivated poor land or had to request land of their elder suggests that not all peasant farmers belonging to this social unit enjoyed the same opportunity.[78]

Monzón's extensive citations and interpretations of Zorita and other historical sources largely support his conclusion that the *calpulli* was essentially a strongly stratified ambilateral clan with a tendency toward endogamy in marriage. Although members shared kinship, degrees of relationship to the ancestral elder varied. Those most closely related to the real or mythical ancestral heads and the lords of Mexico on the maternal side constituted a privileged minority and formed the apex of the pyramidal clan; the base of the pyramid represented those most distantly related to distinguished ancestors. Monzón also suggests that because only six barrios had schools of higher learning (*calmecac*) reserved for children of the nobility, these *calpultin* were "nobler" than the others.

Monzón's idea that the Aztec *calpulli* was endogamous is supported by Zorita's statement that the members of one *calpulli* would not allow people of another ward to work their lands, for this would result in the mixing of the two groups and destroy lineage divisions.[79] On the other hand, other sources indicate that the only impediment to marriage among the Aztecs was that between parents and children or between siblings.[80]

The Aztec *calpulli* may have been egalitarian at the time of the tribe's arrival in the Valley of Mexico. This was not the case on the eve of the Conquest. In his *Relación*, Zorita noted that some poor couples would agree to sell one of their sons into slavery.

After this son had served his master for several years, it was not uncommon for his parents to release him from bondage by exchanging him for another son. Not only was the master delighted to do this, but he would give the parents three or four blankets or loads of corn for the new slave.[81]

Another method of making slaves was called "the old servitude." In time of famine one or two families would sell a son, and all members of these families would pledge to replace him with another slave if he died. The families were released from this permanent obligation only if the slave died in his master's house or if the master took property acquired by the slave.[82]

Zorita states that many people sold themselves into slavery in 1505, a year of great famine. Aware of the evils brought about by the custom of "the old servitude," Nezahualpilli, lord of Texcoco, abolished debt slavery and freed those households obligated to perform service in perpetuity. It appears that the rulers of Tenochtitlán and other towns abolished slavery for debt when they received this news.[83]

While Zorita's account of slavery among the Aztecs shows that reform took place, it also indicates that shortly before the Conquest communal and internal solidarity in the *calpulli* had declined. The *calpulli*, as Friedrich Katz notes, does not appear to have had any responsibility for those unable to fend for themselves. Members of starving or needy families sold into slavery prior to the end of debt servitude in 1505 appear to have been bought by rich commoners, for nobles chiefly relied on the labor of conquered peoples or serfs.[84]

Although the *calpulli* had largely become an administrative unit under Montezuma II, it still retained its communal lands and this provided its members some collective security. Tribute demands may have been heavy, but may be considered modest in comparison to the crushing burdens imposed by the Spaniards after the Conquest. Hence Zorita's idealized portrait of the Indian aristocracy's beneficial rule, despite its obvious exaggerations, has a factual basis.

In his defense of the lords of Mexico and the tribute system, Zorita refuted the charges of writers like Gómara who claimed that the ruler of Mexico was a cruel tyrant who made nobles and commoners pay tribute in excessive amounts. After pointing out that Indian nobles paid no tribute, Zorita denied that commoners (*villanos y pecheros*) paid a third of their yearly produce to the state, and even had their food assessed by collectors. Nor was it true that if they failed to pay their taxes, they might be enslaved and their children sacrificed. Zorita stated that these and other errors to be found in the works of Gómara and other writers were not intentional, for they had been deceived by accounts of interested parties who portrayed Indians as barbarians lacking reason.[85]

The order that prevailed in tribute collection continued, said Zorita, for a short time after the Conquest. In the next two decades things changed drastically, in great part due to the "arbitrary actions of the *encomenderos*, who stripped the lords of their authority if they would not do the Spaniards' will in regard to tribute and personal service. In the lord's place they would set up some *macehual* who would do all that was demanded of him." Stewards and tribute collectors of *encomenderos* followed the examples of their mastes.[86] The change that had taken place was evident as early as 1538, when Cortés wrote the Royal Council of the Indies that some members of the calpultin had left them because tribute was excessive or for other reasons.[87]

Zorita's writings reveal a sixteenth-century Christian humanist and a pro-Indian reformer. Like Las Casas he was interested in Indian cultures both for their own sake and to make cross-cultural comparisons. Zorita also admired the Indians' character and many of their customs. Although aware of the many cultural styles to be found among the various Indian societies, Zorita recognized what some anthropologists and historians of our day have contended were "certain persistent characteristics that distinguish Indian life from European life." Cultural traits mentioned by Zorita that are discussed as basic features of the uncorrupted Indian's personality by Wilcomb Washburn, Harold Driver, and Alvin M. Josephy, Jr.,[88] are: (1) Indian religiosity; (2) the Indian's close relationship and identification with nature; (3) a generalized love of children and a gentle, affectionate, and indulgent treatment of infants and minors; (4) a complex judicial system whose central concept was retributive justice; (5) the uncorrupted Indian's faithfulness to his pledged word; (6) a varied but persistent pattern of generosity; (7) and an impassivity and reserve interpreted by some in terms of dignity, and by others in terms of dullness.[89]

Given Zorita's intimate knowledge of the Indians, and the fact that the characteristics he portrays are found in the writings of so many explorers, settlers, missionaries, and travelers who visited Indians at different times and on different frontiers, it appears that the so-called myth of the Noble Savage has some factual basis. Were Zorita and Montaigne mistaken in their portrait of the Indian and his ways? Or did their contemporaries give a false picture of Indian life when they described the Indian as an ignorant and ignoble savage?

Zorita describes the social order of the Aztecs as an estate system on the eve of the Conquest. In this hierarchic society, marked by gradations of rank within the nobility and the commoners, prestige and power—or their absence—were still mainly based on hereditary relationships to the land. Vertical social mobility was possible, but social status was largely determined by birth.

Nobles held both entailed and patrimonial estates, while free peasant farmers held communal lands. Merchants were a rising class; nobles considered them a group of ambitious rivals, and poorer commoners resented their greedy ways. Landless peasants worked the land on the nobles' patrimonal estates; these serfs paid no tribute to the ruler but served in time of war. Anyone might become a slave.

Scholars ranging from William H. Prescott to Friedrich Katz have praised Zorita's ethno-historical sense and cite him as a primary source.[90] More recently, anthropologist H. R. Harvey challenged some of Zorita's statements relating to land tenure, but recognizes the *Brief Relation* as "the most comprehensive source on land tenure" in pre-Conquest Mexico.[91] Ethnographers like Robert M. Carmack have paid tribute to Zorita's "special competence" in his account of the Guatemalan Indians' method of government and tribute system.[92]

As an author Zorita has a number of faults. He lacks a polished style and a major theme, and his frequent digressions and citations of legal and scholastic authorities reflect contemporary Spanish practice. Dualism also marks his *Relación*, where he is harshly critical of native religion.[93] He also is a pedant and moralist in his failure to recognize that laws against sexual misconduct and drunkenness do not necessarily ensure high morality. Further, Zorita obviously exaggerated when he described ancient Mexico as a Lost Eden in his *Brief Relation*.

Granted the above defects, Zorita's works contain a vast amount of valuable information on ancient and colonial Mexico. Moreover, his idealized view of the Indian past found in the *Brief Relation* was subsequently modified in his larger *Relación*. Yet both works ardently defend Indian capacity and correctly point out the remarkable achievements of the Aztecs in education, jurisprudence, child rearing, government, and other aspects of culture. Another positive feature is a relativist line of argument in his comparisons across cultures. Finally, Zorita's works, like those of Las Casas and a significant number of other Spaniards, confirm that part of the Black Legend that deals with the cruelities of the Spanish Conquest and its aftermath.

As a royal judge and writer, Zorita was a worthy representative of that group of pro-Indian reformers who saw the contradiction between the many laws issued in favor of the Indians and their lack of enforcement. Zorita defended Indian rights, condemned Spanish cruelties and the countless crimes he had personally seen, and sought reform of policy that largely ignored the evils of a labor system that was destroying the conquered.

In conclusion, what Arnold J. Toynbee said about the religious temper of the Middle Ages may be applied to that small group of Indian defenders to which Zorita belonged:

In the eyes of the medieval Western Christian, when he looked abroad upon the World, the Heathen, wandering unkempt in the wilderness, were neither incurably unclean nor irretrievably lost. Potentially, they were Christians like himself; and he looked forward to a time when all the lost sheep would be gathered into the fold. Indeed, he looked forward to this with assurance as the foreordained consummation of terrestrial history, the fulfillment of God's purpose in the World.[94]

Glossary of Spanish and Nahuatl Terms

THIS glossary contains basic definitions applicable to the terms used in this book. Most of the terms defined in the text are omitted from this list.

abogado de pobres Counsel appointed by the crown for those individuals who could not afford to pay for one.

acuerdo Consultative session of the audiencia in which it acted as a council of state. Decisions were called *autos acordados* and recorded in the *libro de acuerdo*.

adelantado Title given to some of the New World governors in the sixteenth century. In medieval Castile the *adelantado* was a royal deputy who exercised civil and judicial functions over a large district. During the period of the long crusade against the Moslems, military and civil governors of frontier provinces were called *adelantados de frontera*. The *adelantado de frontera* had extensive military, executive, and judicial powers because of his exposed position. About thirty-five *adelantados* served in the New World. Christopher Columbus conferred the title on his brother Bartholomew, but it appears that the first crown appointment of *adelantado* went to Juan Ponce de León in 1512. Juan de Oñate, the conqueror and settler of New Mexico, received the last appointment. The *adelantado* in the New World can be compared to the colonial proprietor of the English colonies. The office of *adelantado* ended when a royal governor assumed control of a frontier province.

alcabala Sales tax.

alcaide Fortress commander.

alcalde ordinario Magistrate of a municipality who also had administrative duties.

alcalde mayor District administrator. Subdivisions of local jurisdictions were governed by officials called *alcaldes mayores, corregidores,* and *gobernadores*. The district administered by a *gobernador* was usually a larger territory than that of the *corregimiento* or the *alcaldía mayor*.

alguacil Police chief or constable.

armada Fleet or squadron. As early as 1522 a fleet known as the Armada de la carrera de Indias was organized. The Armada de barlovento guarded the Caribbean region.

audiencia Highest royal court of appeals within a jurisdiction. In the New World the audiencia had limited legislative and executive powers. In addition to its judicial responsibilities, the audiencia served as a council of state to the viceroy and assumed his powers when he was absent or unable to rule. Audiencias far from the seat of the viceroyalty were presided over by a senior judge, who might hold the offices of governor and captain-general. The first royal court was established in Santo Domingo in 1511.

avería An export-import tax used to support the cost of the military armada escorting merchant ships to and from the Indies.

bachiller Individual holding the first degree in the sciences and liberal arts.

barrio (1) *Calpulli* or territorial division of a pre-Conquest Indian town. (2) Ward or quarter of a colonial town or city.

bubas Syphilitic pustules.

caballería Land given to a cavalryman amounting to perhaps 100 acres. Varying in size, *caballerías* were supposed to be five times as large as the land alloted to a foot soldier; the grant included land for farming, grazing, and a house.

caballero Member of the lesser nobility; knight.

cabildo Municipal council.

cacique Local ruler or chieftain.

caja de comunidad Community fund used to defray municipal expenses.

calpisqui, pl. *calpixque* Indian tribute collector or steward; overseer.

calpullec Head or elder (senior kinsman) of a *calpulli*.

calpulli Territorial and political kinship unit. The Aztec *calpulli* has been described as a patrilineal clan tending toward exogamy which did not recognize private property in land. It has also been defined as an ambilateral clan with a tendency toward endogamy in marriage. The latter definition is probably correct. The *calpulli* (ward or barrio) was the basic social unit of organization and landholding in pre-Conquest Mexico. The land held by a member of the *calpulli* might be transmitted to heirs. It appears that the size of landholdings in the *calpulli* varied widely; because plots were of unequal size and independent of the size of the family of the possessor, economic and social inequality existed within the *calpulli*.

cargos Indictment (list of charges) contained in the report prepared by the *juez de residencia* upon completion of the judicial review of an official's conduct during his term of office.

Casa de Contratación House of Trade responsible for the regulation and development of commerce. Situated in Seville, this agency enforced the laws relating to the New World trade, collected duties, attempted to control emigration, maintained a nautical school, and generally controlled traffic and commerce.

castellano In the Indies the *castellano's* equivalent was the *peso de oro de minas* worth 450 *maravedís*. The *castellano* weighed one-fiftieth mark; the mark was equivalent to 7.40 troy ounces.

caudillo (1) "Strong man" or chief. (2) Cruel and petty regional tyrant.

cédula A decree.

censo   (1) Annuity. (2) Annual rent. (3) Lease. (4) Mortgage.

ciudadandos honrados   Members of the urban patriciate and the lesser nobility.

colegio   Secondary school; a preparatory school leading to the bachelor's degree. (2) Self-governing constituent body of a university offering living quarters and instruction but not granting degrees. (3) Organized body of persons engaged in a common pursuit or having common interests or duties; a guild or association.

colegio mayor   University college offering specialized studies. A bachelor's degree was necessary for admission.

comendador mayor   Knight commander of a military order in Spain.

confirmador de privilegios   Attester of royal concessions.

contador   Comptroller. Collection of revenues by exchequer officials was organized in each Spanish colony; these officials consisted of a treasurer, a comptroller, a business manager (*factor*), and an inspector (*veedor*).

converso   A Jewish convert to Christianity; *moriscos*, Moslem converts to Christianity, were also called *conversos*.

corregidor   A district governor equivalent to an *alcalde mayor*.

corregidores de pueblos de indios   Indian towns that paid tribute to the crown, grouped into *corregimientos*. *Corregidores de indios* exercised judicial and political authority over the Indians; they were sometimes assisted in their duties by *tenientes*. *Corregidores* were often petty tyrants.

cortes   Consultative assembly of a Spanish kingdom. The states-general (*cortes*) of Castile were organized into three estates: the clergy, the nobility, and the towns.

cuenta   Count of Indians paying tribute. (2) Statement of accounts.

custodio   Head of a Franciscan custody, or mission district, responsible to his minister provincial.

descargos   Defense pleas of a *residenciado*.

Ducat (ducado de Castilla)   Standard gold coin of Castile after 1497; its value was fixed at 375 *maravedís*.

encomendero   Holder of an *encomienda*.

encomienda   Originally a formal grant of Indian crown vassals (it did not include Indian lands) to a favored Spanish conqueror or colonist. The Indians were initially required to perform labor services and give tribute to their *encomendero*. The colonist in turn was obliged to protect and Christianize his charges and rendered military service in defense of the colony. In granting *encomiendas*, the crown intended both to reward deserving colonists and to incorporate the Indians into Christian civilization by placing them under the tutelage of responsible Spaniards. *Encomienda*, so excellent in intent, proved a hideous slavery and contributed to the virtual extinction of the natives of the Antilles. When this labor system was brought to the mainland, it also served as a factor in the demographic catastrophe witnessed there.

escribano de cámara   Office of notary attached to an audiencia; the clerk of the royal tribunal.

escribano de juez de bienes de difuntos   Notary or scribe assisting the judge who settled the property of intestates, or of persons who died without heirs in the colonies or on the voyage to or from the Indies.

escribanía del juzgado del alcalde mayor   Office of a notary serving in a provincial governor's court of justice.

estancia   (1) Rural estate. (2) Cattle ranch. (3) Landed property.

entrada   Expedition into Indian territory.

factor   (1) Business agent. (2) Officer of the exchequer who disposed of tribute in kind received from the Indians; he also made purchases and completed commercial transactions in which crown monies were involved. (3) Executive head of the Casa de Contratación.

fanega   Grain measure of about 1.6 bushels.

fiscal   (1) Crown attorney. (2) Indian sacristan.

fuero   Charter of rights and privileges granted to a town or province; it defined the relationship between vassal and overlord.

gentileshombres   Gentlemen and members of the lesser nobility.

hacienda   (1) Large rural estate. (2) Plantation. (3) In colonial New Mexico a small farm.

hidalgo   Member of the lesser nobility.

hijosdalgo   See *hidalgo.*

información   (1) Legal brief. (2) Judicial inquiry and process. (3) Investigation.

juez de residencia   Specially designated commissioner in charge of a judicial review of an official's conduct. The *residencia* was taken at the end of the official's term of office.

jurado   (1) Municipal official. (2) Juryman.

justicia   In Aragon a high official whose primary duty was to defend the ancient privileges of the kingdom against any infringement by officials of the king or the nobility.

justicia mayor   Chief justice; the deputy of the governor who presided in the municipal council.

ladino   (1) *Negro ladino*, a Spanish-speaking black from the Iberian Peninsula who had been baptized and had some knowledge of Spanish ways. Non-Christian black slaves from Guinea used as laborers in commercial agriculture were called *bozales*. (2) Acculturated. (3) Sagacious, cunning, crafty, treacherous.

letrado   (1) Legist trained in the civil law. (2) Lawyer, advocate, counselor.

libro de acuerdo   Secret ledger of the audiencia in which the votes of the judges were recorded by the president or senior judge of the court.

licenciado   (1) Licentiate. (2) Graduate of a university.

macehual, macegual   Indian commoner.

maestre de campo   Officer of superior rank commanding a certain number of troops.

manta Blanket or mantle, an essential article of Indian dress in pre-Conquest Mesoamerica. The tribute *manta* was a cotton cloth about one yard wide and four yards long.

maravedí Spanish copper coin worth perhaps $.007 in pre-1934 U.S. gold dollars. According to Benjamin Keen, board and room at an inn in the late fifteen century "seems to have cost a minimum of 9 maravedís a day."

Mark or *marco* Basic unit of monetary weight. The gold mark was worth fifty *castellanos,* each of eight *tomines* (twelve grains). The silver mark was equivalent to eight ounces (*onzas*); each ounce was divided into eighths (*ochavos*); the *ochavo* contained seventy-five grains.

maroon See *negros cimarrones.*

mayeque Indian serf permanently attached to the land.

mayorazgo Entailed estate or the right of succession to such an estate.

merced Royal favor or grant.

mestizo In the first half of the sixteenth century, a person of Indian and Spanish background, accepted as a Spaniard if born in wedlock who might inherit his father's *encomienda.* Later, mestizos came to form a separate group in the caste system.

militares Members of the lesser nobility; nobility of the sword.

morisco Moorish convert to Christianity; the name of these New Christians.

nao Square-rigged ship or vessel.

negros cimarrones Black slaves who fled their captivity and became runaways; maroons.

oidor Judge of an audiencia.

patache Ship employed to attend other ships or a warship that provides logistic support.

pechero Taxpayer; commoner.

peso Unit of currency. A *peso de a ocho reales* was worth 272 *maravedís.* The *peso de oro común* or the *peso corriente* was an uncoined gold unit worth perhaps 300 *maravedís.* Until 1592 a *peso ensayado* and a *peso de oro* were each worth 450 *maravedís.* The *peso de minas* was worth 450 *maravedís;* the peso *de oro de tipuzque* (also spelled *tepuzque*) was an uncoined unit of gold and copper valued at 272 *maravedís.*

pesquisa secreta First or secret part of a judicial inquiry, or *residencia.*

pillalli Patrimonial estates of the Indian nobility in Mexico.

pipiltzin Aztec nobles or lords equivalent to Spanish caballeros or native *principales.*

principal Member of the Indian aristocracy.

probanza Legal deposition; proof of services.

procurador Agent. In the sixteenth century towns in the New World were authorized to elect *procuradores,* or agents, to represent their interests before the Royal Council of the Indies. In the seventeenth century New World municipalities commissioned resident *procuradores* in Spain to look after their interests.

propios   Public lands.

provisor   Ecclesiastical judge; bishop's vicar-general.

pueblo   Indian village or town.

real   Silver coin worth thirty-four *maravedís*.

receptor   Receiver of evidence for the audiencia.

Recusation (*recusación*)   Right to challenge a judge considered suspect because his impartiality was in doubt; it consisted of a written objection presented in an administrative session of the court.

regidor   Municipal councilor.

registrador   Master or clerk of records.

relator   Official of the royal tribunal who summarized evidence for the judges; court reporter or legal secretary.

repartimiento   (1) Allotment of Indians or an *encomienda*. After the New Laws of 1542–1543 abolished forced labor, the *repartimiento* became an institution for the use of Indians in labor gangs to work in mines, factories, farms and ranches, and public works for a prescribed period of time. Thus compulsory paid labor regulated by laws replaced forced personal services.

requerimiento   (1) Legal summons or demand. The notorious *Requerimiento* was a document drawn up by Juan López de Palacios Rubios to be used by conquistadors before making war on the bewildered Indians. The proclamation called upon the natives to acknowledge the supremacy of the pope and the sovereignty of the Castilian crown over their lands. Should the bewildered Indians refuse to heed the summons, they might be warred upon and enslaved.

residencia   Judicial review or hearing held at the end of an official's term of office.

rico-hombre   "Rich man" or magnate; grandee.

señor natural   Legitimate, hereditary lord whose superior birth and qualities entitled him to dominion in accord with divine, natural, and human law and reason.

sisa   Excise tax.

tamemes   Indian porters.

tasación   Statement of the legal tribute an *encomendero* could demand from his *encomienda*.

tectecutzin (*tectecuhzin*)   Indian nobles just below the supreme ruler; they were compared by Zorita to *comendadores* of Spain; they performed various services and had lands and peasants.

teniente de gobernador   Provincial governor's deputy.

tercio   Regiment of infantry.

teules   See *tectecutzin*.

tierras frías   Temperate highland region.

tierras calientes   Hot coastal lowlands

tlamaitec   *Mayeque*, or serf.

tlatoque, singular *tlatoani*   Supreme lords.

vara de justicia   Symbol of jurisdictional authority.

vecino   Recognized citizen and voter of a Spanish municipality who was the head of a household and usually a property holder. Residents of a town who were not citizens were called *habitantes* or *moradores*.

veedor   Inspector.

villa   Municipality or town just below a city in importance.

visitador   Official delegated to hold an official inquiry, or *visita*.

visita   (1) Official inquiry. The *visita* was similar to the *residencia*, but various authorities have noted that a general *visita* applied to a whole body of magistrates rather than to an investigation of the conduct of an individual officeholder. The general *visita* might take place at any time and might include an examination of the royal tribunal's officials, the officials of the exchequer, enforcement procedures relating to particular laws, the general political and economic conditions of the colony, and other matters. A *visitador general* did not pass sentence but was granted wide powers and could suspend from office any magistrate he deemed incompetent. A general *visita* usually lasted for a minimum of two years. (2) Provincial tours of inspection made by judges of the audiencia made every three years. (3) Community under the jurisdiction of a monastery town (*cabecera*).

zabra   Armed vessel.

Notes

Preface

1. Benjamin Keen in Alonso de Zorita, *Life and Labor in Ancient Mexico: The Brief and Summary Relation of the Lords of New Spain*, trans. Benjamin Keen, p. 56; cited hereafter as Zorita, *Life and Labor in Ancient Mexico*.
2. Ibid., p. 18; William H. Prescott, *Mexico and the Life of the Conqueror Fernando Cortés*, 1:58 *n*; Manuel Orozco y Berra, *Historia antigua y de la conquista de México*, p. 276; François Chevalier, *Land and Society in Colonial Mexico: The Great Hacienda*, trans. Alvin Eustis, Lesley Byrd Simpson, pp. 16–22; Friedrich Katz, *Situación social y económica de los aztecas durante los siglos XV y XVI*, p. 4; J. H. Elliott, *The Old World and the New, 1492–1650*, p. 33; George Kubler, *Mexican Architecture of the Sixteenth Century*, 1:48.
3. See Louis Wirth in Karl Mannheim, *Ideology and Utopia: An Introduction to the Sociology of Knowledge*, trans. Louis Wirth and Edward Shils, pp. x–xxx.
4. Aubrey F. G. Bell, *Cervantes*, p. 158.
5. Ibid., p. 213.

Chapter 1

1. Karl Kautsky, *Thomas More and His Utopia, with a Historical Introduction*, trans. H. J. Stenning, p. 63.
2. Carl J. Friedrich, *The Age of the Baroque, 1610–1660*, p. 96.
3. Fernand Braudel, *The Mediterranean and the Mediterranean World in the Age of Philip II*, trans. Siân Reynolds, 2:716.
4. J. Huizinga, *The Waning of the Middle Ages* pp. 56–57.
5. Ibid.
6. J. H. Elliott, *Imperial Spain, 1469–1716*, p. 32.
7. Braudel, *The Mediterranean World*, 2:727.
8. Huizinga, *The Waning of the Middle Ages*, p. 58; Charles E. Chapman, *A History of Spain*, p. 412.
9. J. Vicens Vives, ed., *Historia de España y América*, 3:395–96; Miguel de Cervantes Saavedra. "El celoso estremeño," in *Obras completas*, ed. A Valbuena Prat, p. 902. See also Francisco de Quevedo, *El buscón*, p. 235; Alexander A. Parker, *Literature and the Delinquent: The Picaresque Novel in Spain and Europe, 1599–1753*, pp. 56–73.
10. Eric Wolf, *Sons of the Shaking Earth*, pp. 152–75; Mariano Picón-Salas, *A Cultural History of Spanish America from Conquest to Independence*, pp. 27–41.
11. The concept in its practical aspects was, of course, "employed as a means of assuring the subjection of the masses of the people through control of their already established *señores*—" Robert S. Chamberlain, "The Concept of the *Señor Natural* as Revealed by Castilian Law and Aministrative Documents," *Hispanic American Historical Review* 19 (May, 1939): 130–37.

12. Vicens Vives, *Historia de España y América*, 2:435.

13. The institution of *mayorazgo*, which began in the reign of Alfonso X (1252–84), was confirmed and extended by the Cortes of Toro in 1505 under Ferdinard and Isabella and is only one example of the perpetuation of the existing social order by the Catholic Kings.

14. Vicens Vives, *Historia de España y América*, 2:444.

15. Miguel de Cervantes Saavedra, *Don Quijote de la Mancha*, p. 580. This line is quoted and commented on by Tomás Thayer Ojeda and Carlos J. Larrain, *Valdivia y sus compañeros*, pp. 79–80.

16. J. Vicens Vives, "The Economy of Ferdinand and Isabella's Reign," in Roger Highfield, ed., *Spain in the Fifteenth Century, 1369–1516: Essays and Extracts by Historians of Spain*, pp. 251–53.

17. Huizinga, *The Waning of the Middle Ages*, p. 57. See also Alfonso García Valdecasas, *El hidalgo y el honor*, pp. 11–15.

18. Rafael Altamira y Crevea, *Historia de España y de la civilización española*, 3:532.

19. Braudel, *The Mediterranean World*, 1:243.

20. Elliott, *Imperial Spain*, p. 291.

21. H. G. Koenigsberger and G. L. Mosse, *Europe in the Sixteenth Century*, p. 36.

22. Marqués de Lozoya, *Historia de España*, 1:5.

23. Braudel, *The Mediterranean World*, 2:705, 725–26, 729.

24. Cervantes, *Don Quijote*, p. 200–201.

25. Joaquín García Icazbalceta, ed. *Nueva colección de documentos para la historia de México*, 3:xi–xxxix.

26. Joaquín García Icazbalceta, ed., *Colección de documentos para la historia de México*, 2:vii, 333.

27. Manuel Serrano y Sanz, "Vida y escritos del Doctor Alonso de Zorita," in Alonso de Zorita, "Historia de la Nueva España," ed. *Colección de libros y documentos referentes a la historia de América*, 10:vii.

28. *Libro de peticiones al consejo de Indias, Madrid, Monday, January 27, 1578*, Entry 28, Archivo General de Indias, Indiferente General, Leg. 1086. Cited hereafter as AGI, with appropriate information.

29. Jerónimo de Zurita in his memorial claims the same coat of arms as that of Alonso de Zorita's family, and it is probable that the Zuritas of Aragon also had their origin in Jerez de la Frontera and Zorita de los Canes in Guadalajara, Spain. "Memorial de Jerónimo de Zurita a Felipe III sobre su limpieza de sangre," Real Academia de la Historia, Colección de Don Luis de Salazar y Castro, vol. A–110, fols. 337–41; JFA de Ustarroz and DJ Dormer, *Progreso de la historia en Aragón y vida de sus cronistas*, p. 8.

30. J. Corominas, *Diccionario crítico etimológico de la lengua castellana*, 4:883.

31. For a more detailed genealogical study of Zorita's forebears, see Ralph H. Vigil, "Alonso de Zorita, Early and Last Years," *Americas* 32 (April, 1976): 501–13.

32. Harold Livermore, *A History of Spain*, p. 275.

33. Luis García de Valdeavellano, *Curso de historia de las instituciones españolas de los orígenes al final de la edad media*, p. 545.

34. Jean Hippolyte Mariéjol, *The Spain of Ferdinand and Isabella*, trans. and ed. Benjamin Keen, p. 45.

35. Ibid., p. 38.

36. Elliott, *Imperial Spain*, p. 110.

37. Norman F. Cantor, *Medieval History: The Life and Death of a Civilization*, p. 155.

38. Friedrich Heer, *The Medieval World*, p. 315, Stephen H. Haliczer, "The Castilian Urban Patriciate and the Jewish Expulsions of 1480–92," *American Historical Review* 78 (February, 1973): 35–58. Julio Caro Baroja observes that the majority of Castilian *conversos* became sincere Roman Catholics, "and even more, Catholics of a group so select that from it came saints such as St. Teresa and St. Juan de Dios; mystics like the blessed Juan de Ávila or Father Diego de Estella; religious administrators like Diego Laínez or Polanco in the Company of Jesus; jurists like Father Vitoria; philosophers, like Luis Vives, or humanists and poets, like Fray Luis de León." See his *Inquisición, brujería, y criptojudaísmo*, p. 44.

39. Elliot, *Imperial Spain*, p. 217; Henry Kamen, *The Spanish Inquisition*, p. 123.

40. Kamen, *The Spanish Inquisition*, p. 63.

41. On March 23, 1554, the elder Zurita and his wife sold their grange of Peralejo on the boundary of the villa of Montoro to the Holy Office for a redeemable *censo* of 75,000 *maravedís*, Archivo de Protocolos, Córdoba, Oficio 1, Protocolo 27, fols. 255v.–257. For other sales and purchases of land by Zorita's father and mother, see Vigil, "Alonso de Zorita: Early and Last Years," *Americas*, pp. 504–505.

42. Elliott, *Imperial Spain*, p. 217.

43. Zorita, *Historia de la Nueva España*, p. 28.

44. Vicens Vives, *Historia de España y América*, 2:16, 46–47.

45. Nina Epton, *Andalusia* p. 254.

46. J. Morales Rojas, *Córdoba*, p. 43.

47. Braudel, *The Mediterranean World*, 1:82.

48. Vicens Vives, *Historia de España y América*, 3:171; José de la Torre y del Cerro, "La industria de la seda en Córdoba," in *Obras*, 1:177–81.

49. *Colección de documentos inéditos para la historia de España*, 8:521–28.

50. Mariéjol, *Ferdinand and Isabella*, pp. 287–88.

51. Henry Charles Lea, *A History of the Inquisition of Spain*, 1:128–29.

52. Washington Irving, *The Conquest of Granada*, pp. 339–46.

53. Kamen, *The Spanish Inquisition*, p. 28.

54. Antonio Rodríguez Villa, ed., *Crónicas del Gran Capitán*, pp. 548–49.

55. W. H. Prescott, *History of the Reign of Ferdinand and Isabella*, 3:305; Mary Purcell, *The Great Captain, Gonzalo Fernández de Córdoba*, pp. 216–17.

56. Richard L. Kagan, *Students and Society in Early Modern Spain*, p. 6.

57. Angel Valbuena Prat, *La vida española en la edad de oro según sus fuentes literarias*, pp. 167–86.

58. Kagan, *Students and Society*, p. 8.

59. Ibid., p. 23.

60. Ludwig Pfandl, *Cultura y constumbres del pueblo español de los siglos XVI y XVII*, pp. 177–78.

61. Kagan, *Students and Society*, p. 32.

62. Zorita, *Historia de la Nueva España*, p. 6. Zorita stated on October 20, 1585, that he was seventy-three years old. This means that he was born in either 1511 or 1512.

63. José de la Torre y del Cerro, "Los fundadores de las Córdobas de América," in *Obras*, pp. 345–56.

64. Américo Castro, "The Spanish Sense of Nobility," in H. B. Johnson, Jr., ed., *From Reconquest to Empire*, pp. 185–208.

65. *Probanza of the Services of Juan Pérez de Zorita, La Plata, October 16, 1583*, AGI, Patronato 127, Ramo 12. This *probanza* can be found in Roberto Levillier, ed., *Gobernación del Tucumán: Probanzas de méritos y servicios de los conquistadores*, pp. 527–54. Cited hereinafter as *Probanza—Juan Pérez de Zorita*.

66. *Probanza—Juan Pérez de Zorita*; R. Trevor Davies, *The Golden Century of Spain, 1501–1621*, p. 102.

67. *Probanza—Juan Pérez de Zorita*.

68. Hernández Girón, who rebelled on November 13, 1553, represented those Spaniards who resented the reduction of *encomienda* tributes and the crown decree forbidding forced personal service or labor by Indians. "Later, as the rebellion proceeded, Francisco Hernández had more than 300 Ethiopian [black] soldiers, and in order to do them honor and raise their courage and ardor, he gave them an independent command." Garcilaso de la Vega, *Royal Commentaries of the Incas and General History of Peru*, 2:1356.

69. For the location of these settlements, see map in Roberto Levillier, *Nueva crónica de la conquista del Tucumán, 1542–1563*, vol. 1, lámina 36.

70. *Probanza—Juan Pérez de Zorita*.

71. Ibid.

72. Tomás Thayer Ojeda, *Formación de la sociedad chilena y censo de la problación de Chile en los años de 1540 a 1565*, 3:82–84.

73. Luis de Roa y Ursúa, *El reyno de Chile, 1535–1810*, p. 222.

74. *Probanza—Juan Pérez de Zorita*.

75. Hipólito Sancho, "Diego Fernández de Zurita, Alcaide de Arcos, Embajador en Granada," *Revista de historia y de genealogía española*, 1:18–19; Gonzalo Argote de Molina, *Nobleza de Andalucía*, p. 423; Juan Luis Espejo, *Nobiliario de la antigua capitanía general de Chile*, 1:282–83.

76. "I, Francisco de Zurita, legitimate son of my lord Miguel Díaz de Zurita, who servel as *jurado* of the city of Córdoba and is presently a *vecino* of the villa of Cañete, grant with full knowledge that dowry and wealth which I received by my marriage with you, Doña Ana de Góngora, my wife, daughter of the illustrious Lord Captain García de Góngora, who is in glory, *vecina* of the said city of Córdoba, to wit: 468, 360 *maravedís* in standard currency given me with yourself in the said marriage by the illustrious lord Francisco de Góngora, prebendary of the holy church of Córdoba and vicar-general of His Majesty in the chapel of the kings of that city and your uncle and the brother of the said Lord Captain, your father." Signature: Francisco de Zorita, Córdoba, September 24, 1576. APC, Córdoba, Oficio 30, Protocolo 39, fols. 1593–1595.

77. Letter of Pedro de Valdivia to the crown, October 15, 1550, in *Crónicas del reino de Chile*, p. 65.

78. The careers of Zorita's brothers and sisters are outlined in José de la Torre y del Cerro, *Obras*, pp. 349–51.

79. Guillermo Lohman Villena, *Los americanos en las órdenes nobiliarias, 1529–1900*, 2:91, 187.

80. J. M. Batista i Roca notes that Ferdinand and Isabella transformed the medieval administration of Spain "into that of a Renaissance state, expanded and

adopted to become the instrument of government of a world-wide monarchy."
G. R. Potter, ed., *The New Cambridge Modern History*, Vol. 1: The Renaissance, 1493–1520, p. 328.

81. Elliott, *Imperial Spain*, p. 75.

82. Quoted by José A. Maravall, "La formación de la conciencia estamental de los letrados," *Revista de estudios políticos*, pp. 53–81.

83. However, even the Inquisitor was first a "man of laws" before he was a theologian. See Julio Caro Baroja, *El Señor Inquisidor y otras vidas por oficio*, p. 19.

84. R. B. Merriman, *The Rise of the Spanish Empire in the Old World and in the New*, 3:353.

85. Quoted by Otis H. Green, *Spain and the Western Tradition*, 3:101.

86. Elliott, *Imperial Spain*, p. 76.

87. Mariéjol, *Ferdinand and Isabella*, p. 176.

88. E. N. van Kleffens, *Hispanic Law until the End of the Middle Ages*, p. 18.

89. J. T. Vance, *The Background of Hispanic-American Law: Legal Sources and Judicial Literature of Spain*, p. 87.

90. Cantor, *Medieval History*, pp. 140, 340.

91. Kleffens, *Hispanic Law*, p. 221.

92. Mariéjol, *Ferdinand and Isabella*, p. 130.

93. García de Valdeavellano, *Historia de las instituciones españolas*, pp. 458–59.

94. Ibid., p. 460; Elliott, *Imperial Spain*, p. 88; Mariéjol, *Ferdinand and Isabella*, pp. 147–48.

95. Cantor, *Medieval History*, p. 341.

96. Manuel Serrano y Sanz, ed., "Discurso de la vida del ilustrísimo y reverendísimo señor Don Martín de Ayala," in *Autobiografías y memorias*, pp. 211–38.

97. Ibid., "La vida y cosas notables del señor obispo de Zamora, Don Diego de Simancas," pp. 151–210.

98. Baroja, *El Señor Inquisidor*, p. 19.

99. Zorita, *Historia de la Nueva España*, pp. 17. A search of the *incomplete* list of *Pruebas de cursos y bachilleramientos* before 1546 failed to reveal Zorita's name. I was aided in this search by the Reverend Florencio Marcos, the gracious and kindly *bibliotecario* of the Archivo de la Universidad de Salamanca.

100. Helene Wieruszowski, *The Medieval University*, p. 93; Vicente de la Fuente, *Historia de las universidades, colegios y demás establecimientos de enseñanza en España*, 2:39–40.

101. Vicens Vives, *Historia de España y América*, 3:15. Salamanca's population increased during the sixteenth century and included 24, 765 persons in 1594. The university itself matriculated between 5,000 and 7,000 students a year in the last half of the sixteenth century. Kagan, *Students and Society*, p. 197.

102. Aubrey F. G. Bell, *Luis de León, 1527–1591: A Study of the Spanish Renaissance*, p. 66.

103. Miguel de Cervantes Saavedra, "La tía fingida," in *Novelas ejemplares*, pp. 158–68.

104. Francisco de Quevedo, *The Scavenger*, trans. Hugh A. Harter, pp. 45–49. See also Valbuena Prat, *La vida española*, pp. 43–45.

105. Caro Lynn, *A College Professor of the Renaissance: Lucio Marineo Sículo*

Among the Spanish Humanists, p. 23.

106. Myron P. Gilmore, *Humanists and Jurists: Six Studies in the Renaissance,* p. 14.

107. Saint Augustine, *The City of God,* p. 365.

108. Zorita, *Historia de la Nueva España,* p. 13.

109. Henry Raup Wagner and Helen Rand Parish, *The Life and Writings of Bartolomé de las Casas,* p. 106, n. 37; p. 227, n. 3.

110. Justus M. Van der Kroef, "Francisco de Vitoria and the Nature of Colonial Policy," *Catholic Historical Review* 35 (April, 1949–January, 1950): 129–62.

111. Wagner and Parish, *Bartolomé de las Casas,* p. 106.

112. Reginaldo de Agostino Iannarone, "Genesis del pensamiento colonial en Francisco de Vitoria," in Francisco de Vitoria, *Relectio de Indis o libertad de los Indios,* ed. L. Pereña and J. M. Pérez Prendes, p. xxxiv.

113. Van der Kroef, *Francisco de Vitoria,* pp. 151–52.

114. Ibid., p. 159. For a less kindly view of Vitoria's *Relecciones,* see Father Manuel M. Martínez, "Las Casas on the Conquest of America," in Juan Friede and Benjamin Keen, eds. *Bartolomé de Las Casas in History: Toward as Understanding of the Man and His Work,* pp. 309–49.

115. Stephen Gilman, *The Spain of Fernando de Rojas: The Intellectual and Social Landscape of La Celestina,* p. 301. An idea of the books of law possessed by a humanist lawyer of the sixteenth century is gained from the inventory of Fernando de Rojas's forty-four titles listed by Gilman in this study.

116. Lynn, *A College Professor of the Renaissance,* p. 214; Kagan, *Students and Society,* pp. 161–62.

117. Cervantes, *Don Quijote de la Mancha,* p. 1021.

118. Juan Huarte de San Juan, "Examen de ingenios," in *Obras escogidas de filósofos,* 65:403–520.

119. Letter of Miguel Díez de Armendáriz to *Adelantado* Sebastián de Benalcázar, Santa Fe de Bogotá, April 27, 1547, in Pedro de Aguado, *Historia de Venezuela,* ed. Jerónimo Bécker, 2:90.

120. Bell, *Luis de León,* p. 69; H. Rashdall, *The Universities of Europe in the Middle Ages,* ed. F. M. Powicke and A. B. Emden, 2:89.

121. Kagan, *Students and Society,* p. 89; Elliott, *Imperial Spain,* p. 312.

122. Fuente, *Historia de las universidades,* 2:39–40.

123. Bell, *Luis de León,* p. 74.

124. Enrique Esperabé-Arteaga, *Historia pragmática e interna de la Universidad de Salamanca,* 1:170; Gilman, *The Spain of Fernando de Rojas,* p. 288; Bell, *Luis de León,* 73–75

125. See the illustrations from *Pintura del gobernador, alcaldes y regidores de México: Códice Osuna,* app. 1.

126. Antonio Domínguez Ortiz, *La sociedad española en el siglo XVII,* 1:170.

127. Cervantes, *Don Quijote de la Mancha,* p. 645.

128. Zorita, *Historia de la Nueva España,* p. 242.

129. Alonso de Zorita, "Relación de las cosas notables de la Nueva España y de la conquista y pacificación della y de la doctrina y conversión de los naturales," fol: 455.

130. Bell, *Luis de León,* p. 48; Marcel Bataillon, *Erasmo y España: Estudios sobre la historia espiritual del siglo XVI,* p. 218.

131. Americo Castro, *Semblanzas y estudios españoles*, p. 146. See also Bataillon, *Erasmo y España*, pp. 718, 723. Sixteen of Erasmus's works were included in Fernando de Valdés's Index of 1559. Gaspar de Quiroga's list of 1583 includes the *Adages*, except the editions expurgated by Paulo Manucio.

132. Esperabé-Arteaga, *Historia pragmática*, 1:171.

133. Lewis Hanke, *The Spanish Struggle for Justice in the Conquest of America*, p. 29.

134. Serrano y Sanz, ed., *Autobiografías y memorias*, p. 152.

135. Zorita, *Historia de la Nueva España*, pp. 3–4; Hipólito R. Sancho, *Diego Fernández de Zurita*, 1:35. One of Hernando de Vega's ancestors was Lorenzo Suárez de Figueroa, grand master of the Military Order of Santiago. Diego Fernández de Zurita, one of Zorita's forebears, married Mencia Suárez de Moscoso in 1428. She was the daughter of Ruy Barba de Moscoso, "the brother of Lorenzo Suárez de Figueroa, lord of Zafra and grand master of Santiago."

136. Elliott, *Imperial Spain*, p. 312. See also Kagan, *Students and Society*, pp. 88–105. Kagan writes that in a report to Philip II, Hernando de Vega in 1585 recommended appointment of *colegiales* in the Indies for the good of the royal service and "because they are commonly well-born, virtuous, and *letrados*; they would govern well and even for the places in this council [of the Indies] they would be most appropriate."

137. For the duties and privileges of lawyers and *abogados de pobres* in Spain, see Antonio Xavier Pérez y López, *Teatro de la legislación universal de España y las Indias*, 1:24–71.

138. Ernesto Schäfer, *El Consejo Real y Supremo de las Indias*, 2:120–21; Kagan, *Students and Society*, pp. 84–85. Schäfer observes that in 1550 the salary of an *oidor*, or royal judge, in the Audiencia of Mexico was 650,000 *maravedís*, or 1,733 ducats. In 1571, the salary of an *abogado de pobres* was 90,000 *maravedís*, approximately 13.8 percent of a judge's yearly income.

139. Antonio Ubieto, et al., *Introducción a la historia de España*, p. 259.

140. Louis Bertrand and Sir Charles Petrie, *The History of Spain*, p. 140.

141. Ibid., p. 142.

142. *Petition of Zorita to the Royal Council of the Indies, Madrid, May 5, 1575*, AGI, Indif. Gen., Leg. 1385.

143. *Letter of Zorita to the Crown, Mexico, July 20, 1561*, AGI, Audiencia de México, Leg. 68. For women in the Golden Age, see Pfandl, *Cultura y costumbres*, pp. 125–31.

144. Peter Laslett, *The World We Have Lost: England Before the Industrial Age*, p. 2.

145. "Cartas del Licenciado Jerónimo Valderrama y otros documentos sobre su visita al gobierno de Nueva España," in France V. Scholes and Eleanor B. Adams, eds., *Documentos para la historia del México colonial*, 7:226–27, 245.

146. *Colección de documentos inéditos para la historia de España*, 10:182.

147. See R. H. Vigil, "Alonso de Zorita, Early and Last Years," pp. 503–504, and the works cited in the footnotes there.

148. See Julio Caro Baroja, *Los judíos en la España moderna y contemporánea*, 3:289; and Ramón Cárande, *Carlos V y sus banqueros*, 3:54, 63.

149. Caro Baroja, *Los judíos en la España moderna*, 3:294–95.

150. Ibid., 2:213, 271, 301; 3:287–99. This brilliant and exhaustively documented study demonstrates that the designation Old Christian was ascribed

rather than actual and validates Cervantes's statement in *El retablo de las maravillas* that the two most common "infirmities" in the Spain of the Golden Age were illegitimacy and some Jewish ancestry.

Chapter 2

1. *Appointment of Alonso de Zorita as Judge in the Audiencia of Santo Domingo, Madrid, May 21, 1547*, AGI, Audiencia de Santo Domingo, Leg. 868, fol. 364v.

2. *License given to Alonso de Zorita Allowing Passage of Four Negro Household Slaves to the Indies Free of Charge, Monzón, August 2, 1547*, AGI, Audiencia de Santo Domingo, Leg. 868, fols. 37–370v.

3. C. H. Haring, *Trade and Navigation Between Spain and the Indies in the time of the Hapsburgs*, pp. 71, 201–207. The orders for the sailing of vessels in semiannual, protected fleets were not consistently observed in the 1540s, "but from 1550 onward the system of periodical convoys between Spain and America was well established, although *registros* or special licenses for individual sailings to minor ports were occasionally granted." C. H. Haring, *The Spanish Empire in America*, p. 325.

4. *Power of Attorney Given by Licentiate Alonso de Zorita to Juan Pérez de Zorita and Licentiate Turiel, Córdoba, March 11, 1548*, APC, Oficio 23, Protocolo 10.

5. Francisco López de Gómara, *Annals of the Emperor Charles V*, ed. Roger Bigelow Merriman, pp. 113, 138–39.

6. Ibid., pp. 136–37; Carande, *Carlos V y sus banqueros*, 2:56.

7. José de la Torre y del Cerro, "Gonzalo Jiménez de Quesada," in *Obras*, pp. 335–41. A Captain Joan de Zorita, perhaps a relative of Alonso de Zorita, had sailed for Darién in 1514 and served in Panama under Governor Pedrarias Dávila. See Gonzalo Fernández de Oviedo, *Historia general y natural de las Indias*, 3:349–50.

8. Vicens Vives, *Historia de España y América*, 3:228.

9. Pfandl, *Cultura española*, pp. 204–206; Cervantes, *Don Quijote*, p. 49.

10. Elliot, *Imperial Spain*, p. 205.

11. Antonio Domínguez Ortiz, *La sociedad española en el siglo XVII*, 1:140.

12. Mateo Alemán, *The Rogue, or the Life of Guzmán de Alfarache*, trans. James Mabbe, pt. 1, chap. 2, p. 28.

13. Ruth Pike, *Aristocrats and Traders: Sevillian Society in the Sixteenth Century*, p. 17; Cervantes, "El coloquio de los perros," in *Novelas ejemplares*, 2:231.

14. Alemán, *The Rogue*, pt. 2, chap. 6, p. 309.

15. Julio Caro Baroja, *Los judíos en la España moderna*, 3:294.

16. Pike, *Aristocrats and Traders*, pp. 44, 213–14; C. H. Haring, *Trade and Navigation*, pp. 264–65.

17. *Testament of Departure by Alonso de Zorita Before Pedro Sánchez, Crown Notary, Sanlúcar de Barrameda, April 28, 1548*, AGI, Audiencia de México, Leg. 100.

18. For the translation of this license, see Ralph H. Vigil, "Negro Slaves and Rebels in the Spanish Possessions, 1503–1558." *Historian* 33 (August, 1971): 637–55.

19. Samuel Eliot Morison, *Admiral of the Ocean Sea: A Life of Christopher Columbus*, pp. 514, 536. The *seguidilla* that follows may have been written by Lope de Vega: "Río de Sevilla/cuan bien pareces/con galeras blancas/y ramos verdes!" A newer form of this poem is found in an eighteenth-century song of Seville admired by Federico García Lorca: "Qué bien pareces!/Ay río de Sevilla,/qué bien pareces!/lleno de velas blancas/y ramos verdes" (How fine you look!/Oh river of Seville,/how fine you look!/full of white sails/and green branches").

20. Benjamin Keen, trans. and ed., *Readings in Latin-American Civilization, 1492 to the Present*, pp. 103–105. See also Keen, *Life and Labor in Ancient Mexico*, p. 22.

21. *Letter of Alonso de Grajeda to the Crown, Santo Domingo, June 23, 1548*, AGI, Audiencia de Santo Domingo, Leg. 49. Zorita's voyage of forty-four days was a bit longer than the average, which was "made in thirty-five or forty days." Gonzalo Fernández de Oviedo, *Natural History of the West Indies*, trans. and ed. Sterling A. Stoudemire, p. 7.

22. *Letter of the Audiencia of Santo Domingo to the Crown, Santo Domingo*, May 13, 1549, AGI, Audiencia de Santo Domingo, Leg. 49.; Oviedo, *Historia general*, 1:140. Licentiate Hurtado de Mendoza arrived in Española in late April of 1549.

23. The best short description of the duties of a royal judge in the Indies is found in C. H. Haring, *The Spanish Empire in America*, pp. 119–37.

24. Pike, *Aristocrats and Traders*, pp. vii, 52–72, 80–81.

25. Oviedo, *Natural History of the West Indies*, p. 12; Samuel Eliot Morison, *The European Discovery of America: The Southern Voyages, A. D. 1492–1616*, pp. 268–69; Otto Schoenrich, *The Legacy of Christopher Columbus*, 1:251–307; *Residencia of Licentiates Alonso López de Cerrato, Alonso López de Grajeda, and Alonso de Zorita, President and Judges of the Audiencia of Santo Domingo, Santo Domingo, 1553*, Legs. 75–80, AGI, Justicia, Leg. 77. Cited hereafter as *Residencia—Cerrato, Grajeda, and Zorita* with appropriate information.

26. Oviedo, *Natural History*, p. 11; Oviedo, *Historia general*, 1:77.

27. J. M. Incháustegi Cabral, ed., *Reales cédulas y correspondencia de gobernadores de Santo Domingo, de la regencia del cardenal Cisneros en adelante*, 2:581–88.

28. Schäfer, *El Consejo Real y Supremo de las Indias*, 2:122.

29. C. H. Haring, *The Spanish Empire in America*, p. 136.

30. *Letter of the Cabildo of Santo Domingo to the Crown, Santo Domingo, June 20, 1555*, AGI, Audiencia de Santo Domingo, Leg. 73.

31. Oviedo, *Historia general*, 1:77.

32. C. H. Haring, *The Spanish Empire in America*, p. 14; *Letter of the Audiencia of Santo Domingo to the Royal Council of the Indies, Santo Domingo, September 25, 1551*, AGI, Audiencia de Santo Domingo, Leg. 74. See also Troy S. Floyd, *The Columbus Dynasty in the Caribbean, 1492–1526*, pp. 274–75.

33. G. A. Mejía Ricart, *Historia de Santo Domingo*, 5:207; Oviedo, *Historia general*, 1:79–80.

34. Oviedo, *Historia general*, 1:78. *Cassia fistula*, or drumstick tree, is "an East Indian leguminous tree brought by the Spaniards to the New World. The juice of the seed of the pods was widely used in medicine as a mild laxative." Oviedo, *Natural History*, p. 9. Fourteen sugar mills were in operation by 1518,

and by the 1530s and throughout the 1560s there were approximately thirty-four, most which were water-powered. José Antonio Saco, *Historia de la esclavitud de la raza africana en el Nuevo Mundo y en especial en los países américo-hispanos,* 1:203; Mervyn Ratekin, "The Early Sugar Industry in Española," *Hispanic American Historical Review* 34 (February, 1954): 1–19.

35. *Letter of the Audiencia of Santo Domingo to the Royal Council of the Indies, Santo Domingo, July 27, 1549,* AGI, Audiencia de Santo Domingo, Leg. 49.; Girolamo Benzoni, *History of the New World,* p. 78; Oviedo, *Historia general,* 1:66–67; Bartolomé de Las Casas, *Doctrina,* p. 5; Bartolomé de Las Casas, *Historia de las Indias,* 3:346; Sherburne F. Cook and Woodrow Borah, *Essays in Population History: Mexico and the Caribbean,* 1:376–410; E. G. Bourne, *Spain in America, 1450–1580,* pp. 213–14; Carl O. Sauer, *The Early Spanish Main,* pp. 65–69. See also David Henige, "On the Contact Population of Hispaniola: History as Higher Mathematics," *Hispanic American Historical Review* 58 (May, 1978): 217–37.

36. Benzoni, *History of the New World,* pp. 77–78.

37. *Letter of the Audiencia of Santo Domingo to the Crown, Santo Domingo, April 24, 1545,* AGI, Audiencia de Santo Domingo, Leg. 49.

38. *Letter of the Audiencia of Santo Domingo to the Royal Council of the Indies, July 27, 1549.*

39. *Residencia—Cerrato, Grajeda, and Zorita,* Justicia, Leg. 75, fols. 523v–524, 554. For the best edition and commentary on the New Laws, see Antonio Muro Orejón, ed., *Las Leyes Nuevas de 1542–1543: Ordenanzas para la gobernación de las Indias y buen tratamiento y conservación de los indios.* Articles 21 and 23 abolishing Indian slavery can be found on p. 12; the commentary on these articles can be found on p. 40.

40. *Residencia—Cerrato, Grajeda, and Zorita,* Justicia, Leg. 75, fol. 623.

41. Ibid., Leg. 75, fols. 635v–636; *Letter of Zorita to the Crown, Mexico, July 20, 1561,* AGI, Audiencia de México, Leg. 68; Keen, *Life and Labor in Ancient Mexico,* p. 24.

42. Oviedo, *Historia general,* 1:125.

43. Magnus Mörner, *Race Mixture in the History of Latin America,* p. 38; *Residencia—Cerrato, Grajeda, and Zorita,* Justicia, Leg. 75, fols, 668v–670.

44. *Letter of the Audiencia of Santo Domingo to the Crown, Santo Domingo, October 20, 1538,* AGI, Audiencia de Santo Domingo, Leg. 49.

45. *Letter of Alonso de Cerrato to the Crown, Santo Domingo, July 27, 1546,* AGI, Audiencia de Santo Domingo, Leg. 49.

46. *Letter of Alonso de Cerrato to the Crown, Santo Domingo, June 15, 1546,* AGI, Audiencia de Santo Domingo, Leg. 49.

47. Vigil, "Negro Slaves and Rebels," pp. 649–51.

48. Saco, *Historia de la esclavitud,* 1:301; Ángel Rosenblat, *La población indígena y el mestizaje en América,* 1:87; Juan López de Velasco, *Geografía y descripción universal de las Indias,* pp. 49–55. In the 1570s Velasco observed that Santo Domingo had 500 *vecinos* but had formerly had 1,000.

49. Saco, *Historia de la esclavitud,* 1:221.

50. Ruth Pike, *Enterprise and Adventure: The Genoese in Seville and the Opening of the New World,* pp. 131–32.

51. Enrique Otte, "Una carta inédita de Gonzalo Fernández de Oviedo," *Revista de Indias* 65 (July–September, 1956): 435–58.

52. Manuel Giménez Fernández, *Bartolomé de las Casas,* 2:1122–124.

53. *Residencia—Cerrato, Grajeda, and Zorita*, Justicia, Leg. 77.

54. *Colección de documentos inéditos relativos al descubrimiento, conquista y colonización de las posesiones españolas en América y Oceanía*, 1:521. Cited hereafter as DII.

55. Otte, "Una carta inédita," p. 457.

56. Julio Caro Baroja, *los judíos en la España moderna*, 2:330–31.

57. *Letter of Licentiate Grajeda to the Crown, Santo Domingo, June 16, 1553*, AGI, Audiencia de Santo Domingo, Leg. 75; *Residencia—Cerrato, Grajeda, and Zorita*, Justicia, Leg. 77. This Alonso Rodríguez may have been related to an Alonso Rodríguez of Medina del Campo "who had been burnt at the stake in Spain for heresy." In 1528 it was alleged that the heretic Alonso Rodríguez was the grandfather of Blas de Villasante, the treasurer of the island of Puerto Rico. Pike, *Enterprise and Adventure*, p. 140.

58. Giménez Fernández, *Bartolomé de las Casas*, 1:320–21.

59. *Residencia—Cerrato, Grajeda, and Zorita*, Justicia, Leg. 75, fol. 652.

60. *Royal cédula authorizing Ochoa de Luyando to sell licenses for the passage of 1,000 Negro slaves to Española, Valladolid, March 22, 1550*, AGI, Indif. Gen. 424, tomo 22, fols. 107–108v.

61. Saco, *Historia de la esclavitud*, 3:28–29.

62. Ibid., p. 39.

63. López de Velasco, *Geografía y descripción universal*, p. 53.

64. Ángel Rosenblat, "Base del español de América: Nivel social y cultural de los conquistadores y pobladores," *Revista de Indias*, 125–26 (July–December, 1971): 13–75.

65. James Lockhart, *Spanish Peru, 1532–1560: A Colonial Society*, p. 99.

66. Salvador de Madariaga, *Spain: A Modern History*, pp. 20–21; Rosenblat, "Base del español de América," p. 60; Kamen, *The Spanish Inquisition*, p. 18.

67. Braudel, *The Mediterranean World*, 2:681.

68. R. H. Tawney, *Religion and the Rise of Capitalism: A Historical Study*, p. 27.

69. Saco, *Historia de la esclavitud*, 2:18.

70. Norman F. Martin, *Los vagabundos en la Nueva España, siglo XVI*, p. 15.

71. Rosenblat, *Base del español de América*, p. 57. "In 1557 Philip II, to meet his pressing financial necessities, ordered one thousand *hidalguías* sold to persons of all classes without question of defect of lineage, and later sovereigns followed the same practice." C. H. Haring, *The Spanish Empire in America*, p. 213.

72. Lockhart, *Spanish Peru, 1532–1560*, p. 78.

73. *Residencia—Cerrato, Grajeda, and Zorita*, Justicia, Leg. 75, fol. 645.

74. Ibid., Leg. 75, fol. 642v.

75. Ibid., Leg. 75, fols. 652–653v.

76. Tawney, *Religion and the Rise of Capitalism*, p. 37; Lockhart, *Spanish Peru, 1532–1560*, p. 78.

77. Tawney, *Religion and the Rise of Capitalism*, p. 80.

78. Pike, *Aristocrats and Traders*, p. 25.

79. Cervantes, *Don Quijote*, p. 396; for the translation, see Miguel de Cervantes Saavedra, *The Ingenious Gentleman Don Quixote de la Mancha*, trans. Samuel Putnam, p. 345 [italics added].

80. France V. Scholes, "The Spanish Conqueror as a Business Man," offprint from *New Mexico Quarterly* 28 (Spring, 1958): 1–29; José Durand, *La transformación social del conquistador*, 2:64–72; François Chevalier, *Land and Society in Colonial Mexico*, p. 307; Caro Baroja, *Los judíos en la España moderna*, 2:345–347.

81. *Residencia—Cerrato, Grajeda, and Zorita, Justicia*, Leg. 75, fols. 546–547v.

82. *Probanza of Licentiate Alonso de Zorita, Santiago de Guatemala, August 16, 1554*, Archivo General de Centro América, A. 1.29, Leg. 4678, Expediente 40245, Guatemala, 1600. I wish to express thanks to William L. Sherman for giving me a copy of this document.

83. Caro Baroja, *Los judíos en la España moderna*, 2:323–24.

84. Bartolomé Bennassar, *The Spanish Character: Attitudes and Mentalities from the Sixteenth to the Nineteenth Centuries*, trans. Benjamin Keen, pp. xi, 121; Vicens Vives, *Historia de España y América*, 1:385–86.

85. Vives, *Historia de España y América*, 1:397; Norman F. Cantor, *Medieval History: The Life and Death of a Civilization*, p. 490.

86. Quoted by Caro Baroja, *Los judíos en la España moderna*, 2:324–25. See also Carlos G. Noreña, *Studies in Spanish Renaissance Thought*, pp. 220–21.

87. Bennassar, *The Spanish Character*, p. 121; Kamen, *The Spanish Inquisition*, p. 122.

88. *Información sobre servicios de Alonso de Zorita, México, 1562*, AGI, Justicia, Leg. 1029, no. 7, Ramo 1. Cited hereinafter as *Información—Alonso de Zorita*. This *probanza* may also be found in Zorita, *Historia de la Nueva España*, pp. 438–92, and in AGI, *Audiencia de México*, Leg. 100. The translation is by Keen, *Life and Labor in Ancient Mexico*, p. 19.

89. *Información of President Alonso de Maldonado and the judges of the Audiencia of Santo Domingo concerning the Cathedral Chapter of Santo Domingo, Santo Domingo, 1556*, AGI, Audiencia de Santo Domingo, Leg. 11, fols. 21–21v.

90. Ibid., fol. 24.

91. Otte, "Una carta inédita," p. 454.

92. *Información of the Audiencia of Santo Domingo concerning the Cathedral Chapter of Santo Domingo, Santo Domingo, January 20, 1549*, AGI, Audiencia de Santo Domingo, Leg. 10.

93. Ibid. See also Claudio Miralles de Imperial y Gómez, "Del linaje y armas del primer cronista de Indias," *Revista de Indias* 71 (January–March, 1958): 73–126.

94. Archbishop Alonso de Fuenmayor may have died in office in 1554. See Schäfer, *El Consejo Real y Supremo de las Indias*, 2:599. This is only a supposition, for the testimony of Don Pedro de Rivera, the dean of the Cathedral, indicates that the archbishop may have died in 1553. Rivera declared that "cuando vinó a ésta ciudad a la iglesia catedral della por dean que puede haber tres años poco más o menos halló que era fallecido el arzobispo don Alonso de Fuenmayor poco había." *Información concerning the Cathedral Chapter, Santo Domingo, 1556*, fol. 3v.

95. C. H. Haring, *The Spanish Empire in America*, p. 208.

96. Bennassar, *The Spanish Character*, pp. 97–98, 242–44; Vicens Vives, *Historia de España y América*, 3:86.

97. López de Velasco, *Descripción universal de las Indias*, pp. 19–20.

98. *Sentences Confirmed by the Royal Council of the Indies in the Residencia of Alonso de Fuenmayor, Juan de Vadillo, and Iñigo López de Cervantes de Loaisa, Valladolid, April 27, 1548,* AGI, Escribanía de Cámara, Leg. 1184; *Letter of Fuenmayor to the Royal Council of the Indies, Santo Domingo, January 16, 1542,* AGI, Audiencia de Santo Domingo, Leg. 49.

99. *Letter of Alonso de Cerrato to the Crown, Santo Domingo, November 16, 1546,* AGI, Audiencia de Santo Domingo, Leg. 49. Cerrato noted that the decree forbidding the passage of all persons and arms to Peru was acted upon in Española but was laxly enforced by the officials of the port of Seville.

100. After their suspension, Fuenmayor and Vadillo left Española for Spain to plead their *residencia* charges. Fuenmayor arrived in Seville in July, 1544, according to the *List of Passengers who arrived from Santo Domingo, Seville, July, 1544,* AGI, Indif. Gen., Leg. 2048.

101. *Sentences Confirmed by the Royal Council of the Indies in the Residencia of Alonso de Fuenmayor, Juan de Vadillo, and Iñigo López de Cervantes de Loaisa, Valladolid, April 27, 1548.*

102. Oviedo, *Historia general,* 1:140.

103. *Letter of the Royal Officials to the Crown, Santo Domingo, April 23, 1544,* AGI, Audiencia de Santo Domingo, Leg. 74.

104. *Letter of Francisco Bravo to the Crown, Santo Domingo, March 24, 1550,* AGI, Audiencia de Santo Domingo, Leg. 78.

105. "He is charged with insulting those who appeared before him in court by calling them knaves, thieves, traitors, and other evil words so insulting that citizens came to feel they would be dishonored if they appeared before him to ask for justice." *Residencia—Cerrato, Grajeda, and Zorita,* Justicia, Leg. 75, fol. 526v. See also G. A. Mejía Ricart, *Historia de Santo Domingo,* 5:202; William L. Sherman, "Indian Slavery and the Cerrato Reforms," *Hispanic American Historical Review* 51 (February, 1971): 25–50.

106. *Residencia—Cerrato, Grajeda, and Zorita,* Justicia, Leg. 75, fol. 554v.

107. *Letter of Cerrato to the Crown, Santo Domingo, Oct. 8, 1547,* AGI, Audiencia de Santo Domingo, Leg. 49.

108. Oviedo, *Historia general,* 1:140–41.

109. Otte, "Una carta inédita," pp. 457–58.

110. Oviedo, *Historia general,* 1:lxiii. The Aragonese *converso* Lope de Conchillos y Quintana was the great-grandfather of the Count-Duke Olivares (1578–1645), the favorite of Philip IV. Conchillos, in addition to receiving an annual salary of 100,000 *maravedís* as Ferdinand the Catholic's principal secretary, was the beneficiary of the absentee *encomienda* system initiated by Ferdinand; he also received other posts, rights, advantages, and sinecures, all of which furnished him about 4 million *maravedís* annually in 1516. In 1508, Ferdinand appointed Miguel de Pasamonte, a creature of Conchillos and his dispatcher of the royal mail, to the post of treasurer general of the Indies; Pasamonte held perhaps 700 Indians in the islands.

111. Enrique Otte, "Gonzalo Fernández de Oviedo an Kaiser Karl über die zustände in Santo Domingo," in *Spanische Forschungen der Görresgesellschaft,* 1st ser., (Münster, 1956), 2:165–70.

112. *Residencia—Cerrato, Grajeda, and Zorita,* Justicia, Leg. 77.

113. *Letters of Alonso Maldonado to the Crown, Santo Domingo, July 23, 1553, and April 16, 1554,* AGI, Audiencia de Santo Domingo, Leg. 71. Grajeda was subsequently appointed *oidor* in the Audiencia of Santa Fe in New Granada

and served in that tribunal from 1557 to 1560. He returned to the Audiencia of Santo Domingo in 1560 and was still serving as a judge in 1565.

114. *Letter of the Cabildo of Santo Domingo to the Crown, Santo Domingo, June 20, 1555,* AGI, Audiencia de Santo Domingo, Leg. 73.

115. *Letter of Francisco Bravo to the Crown, Santo Domingo, March 24, 1550.*

116. *Residencia—Cerrato, Grajeda, and Zorita,* Justicia, Leg. 78.

117. A. P. Newton, *The European Nations in the West Indies, 1493–1688,* pp. 50–52; P. A. Means, *The Spanish Main, Focus of Envy, 1492–1700,* p. 56.

118. Mejía Ricart, *Historia de Santo Domingo,* 5:84.

119. *Letter of the Audiencia of Santo Domingo to the Crown, Santo Domingo, April 24, 1545,* AGI, Audiencia de Santo Domingo, Leg. 49.

120. *Letter of the Audiencia of Santo Domingo to the Crown, Santo Domingo, Oct. 16, 1548,* AGI, Audiencia de Santo Domingo, Leg. 49.

121. *Letter of the Audiencia of Santo Domingo to the Crown, Santo Domingo, January 23, 1549,* AGI, Audiencia de Santo Domingo, Leg. 49.

122. *Letter of the Audiencia of Santo Domingo to the Crown, Santo Domingo, May 13, 1549,* AGI, Audiencia de Santo Domingo, Leg. 49.

123. *Letter of the Audiencia of Santo Domingo to the Crown, Santo Domingo, April 11, 1552,* AGI, Audiencia de Santo Domingo, Leg. 49. The *Audiencia* estimated that the proposed fort at La Yaguana would cost four or five thousand *pesos* and would consist of a *casa fuerte* with a tower surrounded by high adobe walls with embrasures, where a dozen pieces of ordinance would be placed.

124. *Letter of the Royal Officials to the Crown, Santo Domingo, August 15, 1552,* AGI, Audiencia de Santo Domingo, Leg. 71; *Letter of Alonso Maldonado to the Crown, Santo Domingo, February 13, 1553,* AGI, Audiencia de Santo Domingo, Leg. 49.

125. *Letter of Alonso Maldonado to the Crown, Santo Domingo, February 13, 1553;* Otte, "Una carta inédita," p. 446.

126. *Letter of Alonso Maldonado to the Crown, Santo Domingo, February 13, 1553.*

127. *Petition of Zorita to the Royal Council of the Indies, Madrid, May 5, 1575,* AGI, Indif. Gen., Leg. 1385. See also Keen, *Life and Labor in Ancient Mexico,* p. 24; *Información—Alonso de Zorita;* Zorita, *Historia de la Nueva España,* p. 450.

128. *Letter of the Royal Officials to the Crown, Santo Domingo, December 6, 1552,* AGI, Audiencia de Santo Domingo, Leg. 71.

129. C. H. Haring, *The Spanish Empire in America,* p. 321.

130. *Letter of the Audiencia of Santo Domingo to the Crown, Santo Domingo, July 27, 1546,* AGI, Audiencia de Santo Domingo, Leg. 49.

131. *Letter of the Audiencia of Santo Domingo to the Crown, Santo Domingo,* AGI, Audiencia de Santo Domingo, Leg. 49, March 9, 1550.

132. *Residencia—Cerrato, Grajeda, and Zorita,* Justicia, Leg. 75, fols. 664v., 668v.–670, and Leg. 77. The most serious accusation against Zorita was submitted by Miguel Díez de Armendáriz who claimed that Zorita had fraudulently acquired 190 emeralds belonging to the crown in Santa Marta. This charge was dismissed by the Council of the Indies in Valladolid on April 29, 1557, after being investigated by Licentiate Agreda, the crown's prosecuting attorney.

133. *De oficio al Licenciado Zorita para que vaya a servir en el Audiencia de*

los Confines, Monzón, July 11, 1552, AGI, Audiencia de Guatemala, Leg. 386; *Letter of the Cabildo of Santo Domingo to the Crown, Santo Domingo, February 17, 1553*, AGI, Audiencia de Santo Domingo, Leg. 73.

Chapter 3

1. Lesley Byrd Simpson, *The Encomienda in New Spain: The Beginnings of Spanish Mexico*, p. 132.

2. Juan Friede, ed., *Documentos inéditos para la historia de Colombia*, 6:325–29; 7:183–84. Cited hereafter as DIC.

3. Marcos Jiménez de la Espada, ed., *Cartas de Indias*, p. 751.

4. DIC, 7:185–86.

5. Alberto y Arturo García Carraffa, *Enciclopedia heráldica y genealógica hispano-americana*, 11:74; Elliott, *Imperial Spain*, p. 29; Livermore, *A History of Spain*, p. 150; Vicens Vives, *Historia de España y América*, 2:263.

6. *Lawsuit of Miguel Díez de Armendáriz with the heirs of Pedro de Ursúa for the sum of 2,000 pesos, Madrid, October 10, 1573*, AGI, Justicia, Leg. 1122, fol. 2.; DIC, 9:50; Aguado, *Historia de Venezuela*, 2:90. One of the witnesses in the lawsuit also calls Miguel Díez's parents Juan Díez and María de Beonza. After living with Martín Díez, María de Abenza married Pedro de Garmendi, also called Garmendia; by this marriage Miguel Díez's mother had Pedro de Garmendi. This half brother of Miguel Díez had two children, Pedro and Juana de Garmendi.

7. Antonio Ballesteros y Beretta, *Historia de España y de la civilización española*, 3:732.

8. *Residencia of Licentiate Miguel Díez de Armendáriz taken by Licentiate Alonso de Zorita, Cartagena, June 1, 1551*, AGI, Justicia, Leg. 550, fols. 65, 80.; *Probanza of Miguel Díez's Descargos Before Licentiate Pedro Gómez de Montalvo, Alcalde Ordinario of Cartagena, Cartagena*, January 22, 1555. AGI, Justicia, Leg. 555, fol. 25.; Miguel Díez presented this *probanza* in Valladolid on November 6, 1556. He attempted to absolve himself of the charge that he had put on mourning clothes when news of the Peace of Crespy was received in Cartagena by declaring that he was sorrowing for Doña Graciana Díez de Armendáriz, his aunt. He claimed that this was widely known "because when various individuals asked why he was in mourning he showed them the letters telling him that she was dead."

9. *Letter of Zorita to the Crown, Cartagena, October 31, 1551*, AGI, Audiencia de Santa Fe, Leg. 187.; Zorita, *Historia de la Nueva España*, p. 380.

10. Caro Baroja, *El Señor Inquisidor*, p. 146.

11. Ibid., p. 124.

12. Ibid., p. 128.

13. Pedro de Aguado, *Historia de Santa Marta y Nuevo Reino de Granada*, 1:490; Clements Robert Markham, *The Conquest of New Granada*, p. 174.

14. DIC, 8:83.

15. Caro Baroja, *El Señor Inquisidor*, p. 126.

16. Rodney Gallop, *A Book of the Basques*, p. 34.

17. Julio Caro Baroja, *The World of the Witches*, trans. O. N. V. Glendinning, pp. 158–59; Keen, *Life and Labor in Ancient Mexico*, p. 25.

18. Caro Baroja, *El Señor Inquisidor*, p. 127; *Petition of Miguel Díez to the*

Crown's Fiscal Claiming That 3,000 Ducats Yearly Should Be Paid to Him from May 10, 1551, to September 4, 1556, AGI, Justicia, Leg. 1118. In this petition Miguel Díez noted that he had left Spain for New Granada on July 10, 1544, in the *flota* commanded by Juan López de Archuleta.

19. DIC, 8:295–96; Germán Arciniegas, *The Knight of El Dorado: The Tale of Don Gonzalo Jiménez de Quesada and His Conquest of New Granada, Now Called Colombia,* trans. Mildred Adams, p. 216.

20. Hayward Keniston, *Francisco de los Cobos, Secretary of the Emperor Charles V,* p. 286; DIC, 7:432; DIC, 5:69–71.

21. Aguado, *Historia de Venezuela,* pp. 90–91; DIC, 8:108–109.

22. For details on the legal process of recusation, the right to challenge a judge considered suspect because his impartiality was in doubt, See José María Mariluz Urquijo, *Ensayo sobre los juicios de residencia indianos,* pp. 66–69.

23. DIC, 8:119.

24. *Residencia of Alonso López de Ayala by Alonso de Zorita, Cartagena, 1551,* AGI, Justicia, Leg. 562.; *Residencia of Juan Ortiz de Zárate by Licentiate Zorita, Santa Marta, 1551,* AGI, Justicia, Leg. 557.

25. Juan Friede, *Vida y luchas de Don Juan del Valle, primer obispo de Popayán y protector de indios,* p. 104.

26. DIC, 8:153–55; Oviedo, *Historia general,* 26. 5:28–30. See also Emilio Robledo, *Vida del Mariscal Jorge Robledo.*

27. Antonio de Herrera y Tordesillas, *Historia general de los hechos de los castellanos en las Islas e Tierra Firme del Mar Océano,* vol. 4, dec. 7, lib. 3, chap. 5.

28. DIC, 8:207.

29. Robledo, *Vida del Mariscal Jorge Robledo,* p. 218; DIC, 8:318: "And he strangled a *comendador* named Hernán Rodríguez de Sosa, whose wife and child came in the company of the said Robledo; in the same fashion he strangled a certain Ledesma and hanged one Juan Márquez and one Cristóbal Díaz."

30. DIC, 8:177, 319.

31. *Residencia of Licentiate Miguel Díez,* Justicia, Leg. 551; *the Crown's fiscal versus the heirs of Miguel Díez de Armendáriz Regarding the Payment of 1,000 Pesos He Was Fined in His Residencia, Madrid, 1574,* AGI, Justicia, Leg. 1122.

32. *Residencia of Miguel Díez,* Justicia, Leg. 550, fol. 140.

33. *The Crown's Fiscal Versus the Heirs of Miguel Díez, Madrid, 1574,* Justicia, Leg. 1122.

34. *Residencia of Miguel Díez,* Justicia, Leg. 550, fol. 37v.

35. *Probanza of Miguel Díez's descargos,* Justicia, Leg. 555, fols. 350–350v.

36. *Residencia of Miguel Díez,* Justicia, Leg. 550, fol. 54v.

37. *Rollo of the residencia taken of Miguel Díez de Armendáriz by Judges Zorita, Montaño, and Briceño, Valladolid, May 9, 1558,* AGI, Justicia, Leg. 561; DIC, 8:306–307.

38. Bernard Moses, *The Spanish Dependencies in South America,* 1:155.

39. DIC, 8:314–15.

40. Juan de Castellanos, *Obras,* 4:498.

41. Ibid., 4:495–96.

42. DIC, 9:50–51.

43. Ibid., 8:347–48.

44. Ibid., 8:349–51; 9:30–34, 340–57; Castellanos, *Obras,* 9:499.

45. DIC, 10:14–15. The Audiencia of Santo Domingo authorized Zorita as *juez de residencia* and governor of New Granada to draw a salary amounting to that which he received as *oidor* and the salary paid the governor of New Granada. See *Letter of Zorita to the Crown, Santo Domingo, October 12, 1549,* AGI, Audiencia de Santo Domingo, Leg. 49.

46. Juan Friede, "Creación de la Real Audiencia," *Boletín Histórico Antiguo* 37 (Bogotá, 1950):75–80; Herrera y Tordesillas, *Historia general,* vol. 4, dec. 8, lib. 4, chap. 11; Lucas Fernández Piedrahita, *Historia general de las conquistas del Nuevo Reino de Granada,* 4:62–63.

47. Keen, *Life and Labor in Ancient Mexico,* pp. 25–28.

48. *Letter of Zorita to the Crown, Santo Domingo, October 12, 1549.*

49. *Letter of Zorita to the Crown, Santo Domingo, December 12, 1549,* AGI, Audiencia de Santo Domingo, Leg. 49.

50. *Royal cédula Authorizing Zorita 2,100 Ducats Yearly in Addition to His Salary as Oidor for the Period of His Stay in New Granada as Juez de Residencia, Valladolid, September 6, 1550,* AGI, Audiencia de Santa Fé, Leg. 533, fol. 136.; DIC, 10:87–91; *Información—Alonso de Zorita.*

51. *Royal decree Appointing Alonso de Zorita Juez de Residencia of New Granada, Valladolid, June 9, 1549,* AGI, Audiencia de Santa Fe, Leg. 533, bk. 1, fols. 61–62.; *Petition of Zorita to the Royal Council of the Indies, Madrid, May 5, 1575,* AGI, Indif. Gen., Leg. 1385.

52. *Letter of the Audiencia of Santa Fe, Mompox, February 12, 1550,* AGI, Audiencia de Santa Fe, Leg. 60.

53. *Letter of Zorita to the Crown, Santa Marta, February 27, 1550,* AGI, Audiencia de Santo Domingo, Leg. 49.; Aguado, *Historia de Santa Marta,* 1:510–11.

54. *Información—Alonso de Zorita.* When Mercado died, the office of *contador* of the province of Santa Marta was left vacant, and Miguel Díez appointed Andrés López de Galarza, the brother of Licentiate Juan de Galarza, comptroller of the treasury of Santa Marta and the New Kingdom until His Majesty should decree otherwise. See *Probanza of Miguel Díez's descargos,* Justicia, Leg. 555, fol. 27. Andrés López de Galarza was paid an annual salary of 400,000 *maravedís* and also received a very good *repartimiento* of Indians in Pamplona in spite of being a royal bureaucrat. Also, when Miguel Díez heard that Licentiate Galarza had arrived in Cartagena, he sent the judge a piece of fine gold worth 1,000 pesos. *Residencia of Miguel Díez,* Justicia, Leg. 550, fols. 47–49.

55. For a short description of *residencia* procedures, see John J. Finan, ed., *A List of Spanish Residencias in the Archives of the Indies, 1516–1775: Administrative Judicial Reviews of Colonial Officials in the American Indies, Philippines and Canary Islands,* comp. José María de la Peña y de la Cámara, pp. v–viii.

56. *Información—Alonso de Zorita;* Keen, *Life and Labor in Ancient Mexico,* p. 29.

57. DIC, 10:350.

58. *Letter of Zorita to the Crown, Cartagena, April 28, 1551,* AGI, Audiencia de Santo Domingo, Leg. 49; Zorita, *Historia de la Nueva España,* pp. 338–59.

59. DIC, 10:323.

60. *Letter of Zorita to the Crown, April 28, 1551.*

61. *Información Compiled in Cartagena at the Request of Licentiate Zorita, Juez de Residencia of the New Kingdom, Concerning Various Incivilities Com-*

mitted Against Him, Cartagena, April 4, 1551, AGI, Escribanía de Cámara, Leg. 1184.

62. *Sentence of Luis de Manjarres, Lieutenant Governor of Santa Marta, Toledo, March 29, 1560*, AGI, Escribanía de Cámara, Leg. 1184.

63. DIC, 9:341.

64. Ibid., p. 337; Ernesto Restrepo Tirado, *Historia de la provincia de Santa Marta*, 1:214. Zorita's sentence was reduced by the Council of the Indies. On March 29, 1560, the council decreed that Manjarres should be exiled from the Indies for six months and fined the amount he received in income from his *encomienda* of the Marsh and Dorosino for two years. On June 1, 1560, the council ordered Manjarres' Indians in Bonda to be returned to him if they had been taken from him; they should be restored with the income they would have given in a two-year period. Half of the income received during the two years the *encomienda* was confiscated was to go to the king's exchequer, and the other half should be given to the Indians of Bonda.

65. *Letter of Zorita to the Crown, Cartagena, October 31, 1551*, AGI, Audiencia de Santa Fé, leg. 187.

66. DIC, 9:341.

67. *Residencia of Licentiate Miguel Díez Taken by Zorita*, Justicia, Leg. 550, fols. 56v., 36v and 243v.

68. Keen, *Life and Labor in Ancient Mexico*, p. 210; Alonso de Zorita, *Breve y sumaria relación de los señores de la Nueva España*, p. 145.

69. Zorita, *Breve y sumaria relación de los señores de la Nueva España*, p. 208; Keen, *Life and Labor in Ancient Mexico*, p. 270.

70. *Residencia of Alonso López de Ayala, Cartagena, 1551*, Leg. 562.

71. *Opinion of Zorita Concerning the Religious Instruction of the Indians, Granada, March 10, 1584*, AGI, Patronato, Leg. 231, no. 1, Ramo 7.; Zorita, *Historia de la Nueva España*, pp. 493–527; Keen, *Life and Labor in Ancient Mexico*, p. 31.

72. Keen, *Life and Labor in Ancient Mexico*, p. 31.

73. *Información—Alonso de Zorita; Letter of Zorita to the Crown, Santo Domingo, September 23, 1552*, AGI, Audiencia de Santo Domingo, Leg. 49; Keen, *Life and Labor in Ancient Mexico*, p. 33.

74. Keen, *Life and Labor in Ancient Mexico*, p. 33.

75. *Letter of Miguel Díez to the Crown, Santo Domingo, September 29, 1551*, AGI, Audiencia de Santo Domingo, Leg. 78.

76. *Letter of the Royal Council of the Indies to the Crown, Valladolid, August 3, 1551*, AGI, Indif. Gen., Leg. 737, Ramo 2. Of the original appointments to the Audiencia of Santa Fé, only four were acted upon. Gutierre de Mercado, as has been noted, died at Mompox, and another judge, Francisco Briceño, went to Popayán to hold the *residencia* of Sebastián de Benalcázar.

77. *Royal Decree of the Crown Ordering Miguel Díez to Return to New Granada, Monzón, July 8, 1552*, AGI, Audiencia de Santa Fé, Leg. 533, fols. 218–19.; *Letter of Miguel Díez to the Crown, Santo Domingo, February 23, 1553.*, AGI, Audiencia de Santo Domingo, Leg. 49.

78. *Letter of Doctor Juan Maldonado to the Crown, Cartagena, July 26, 1554*, AGI, Audiencia de Santo Domingo, Leg. 49.

79. Juan Friede, *Vida y lucheas de Don Juan del Valle*, p. 162.

80. Ibid., p. 161; Schäfer, *El Consejo Real y Supremo de las Indias*, 2:129–30.

81. Juan Rodríguez Freile, *The Conquest of New Granada*, trans. William C. Atkinson, p. 63; José Manuel Groot, *Historia eclesiástica y civil de Nueva Granada*, 1:247; *Letter of Zorita to the Crown, Mexico, July 20, 1561*, AGI, Audiencia de México, Leg. 68.; Keen, *Life and Labor in Ancient Mexico*, p. 30.

82. *Letter of Zorita to the Crown, October 13, 1551*.

83. *Residencia of Licentiates Góngora and Galarza, Santa Fe de Bogotá, July 21, 1553*, AGI, Justicia, Leg. 566, fol. 4.

84. *Letter of Zorita to the Crown, April 28, 1551*.

85. *Residencia of Licentiates Góngora and Galarza, July 21, 1553*, Justicia, Leg. 566.

86. *Letter of Zorita to the Crown, October 13, 1551*.

87. Archivo Nacional de Colombia, ed., *Libro de acuerdo del audiencia del Nuevo Reyno, 1551–1556*, 1:93; Gerardo Reichel-Dolmatoff, *Datos históricos-culturales sobre las tribus de la antigua gobernación de Santa Marta*, p. 25.

88. *Libro de acuerdo del audiencia del Nuevo Reyno*, 1:140.

89. Caro Baroja, *El Señor Inquisidor*, p. 116. See also Emiliano Jos, *La expedición de Ursúa al Dorado, la rebelión de Lope de Aguirre y el itinerario de los "marañones"*, pp. 15, 223–34; Fray Pedro Simón, *Historia de la expedición de Pedro de Ursúa al Marañon y de las aventuras de Lope de Aguirre*, pp. 41–43.

90. *Probanza of Miguel Díez's Descargos*, Justicia, Leg. 555, fols. 9, 15v.

91. Jiménez de la Espada, *Cartas de Indias*, p. 752; *Lawsuit of Miguel Díez with the Heirs of Pedro de Ursúa, Madrid, October 10, 1573*, Justicia, Leg. 1122.

92. *Lawsuit of Miguel Díez with the Heirs of Pedro de Ursúa, Madrid, October 10, 1573*.

93. *Ibid.* The lawsuit noted that Pedro de Ursúa had a brother named Tristán de Ursúa who married Doña Juana de Mearin; both were dead at the time of the lawsuit's completion in 1573.

94. Moses, *The Spanish Dependencies*, 1:277; Markham, *The Conquest of New Granada*, p. 174. See also Ernesto Restrepo Tirado's assertion that Miguel Díez was the best governor New Granada had seen up to his time and that he was the only true lay protector of the Indians in New Granada. *Historia de la provincia de Santa Marta*, 1:223.

95. *The Crown's Fiscal Versus the Heirs of Miguel Díez, Madrid 1574*, Justicia, Leg. 1122.

96. Ibid. Zorita's findings in this charge was included in his final sentence, but he did fine Miguel Díez 30 *marcos de oro* for each appeal that Miguel Díez denied the condemned men. The council fined Miguel Díez 30 gold ducats.

97. Ibid.; *Rollo of the Residencia Taken of Miguel Díez de Armendáriz, Valladolid, May 9, 1558*, Justicia, Leg. 561; *Hernando García Versus Licentiate Miguel Díez de Armendáriz, Valladolid, August 21, 1553*, AGI, Justicia, Leg. 556. *Pedro Rodríguez de Salamanca Versus Miguel Díez de Armendáriz, Santa Fé, January 8, 1552*, AGI, Justicia, Leg. 554.

98. Keen, *Life and Labor in Ancient Mexico*, p. 25.

99. *The Crown's Fiscal Versus the Heirs of Miguel Díez, Madrid, 1574*, Justicia, Leg. 1122.

100. Juan Rodríguez Freile, *The Conquest of New Granada*, p. 64. Benalcázar appealed his sentence to the crown and prepared to leave for Spain from Cartagena. On April 28, 1551, Pedro de Heredia wrote the crown charging Judges Góngora and Galarza with interference in the *residencia* of Miguel Díez

held by Zorita. He also noted that, while he was writing the letter, "*Adelantado* Benalcázar died; he arrived here four or five days ago on his way to those kingdoms with his *residencia*." *Letter of Pedro de Heredia to the Crown, Cartagena, April 28, 1551,* AGI, Audiencia de Santa Fe, Leg. 37.

101. Fray Pedro Simón, *Noticias historiales de las conquistas de Tierra Firme en las Indias Occidentales,* 6:200–209. Heredia determined to seek the protection of the Council of the Indies and departed for Spain; he drowned within sight of Spain in late January, 1555, along with Góngora and Galarza.

102. C. H. Haring, *The Spanish Empire in America,* p. 40.

103. *Last Will and Testament of Doctor Lope Díez Aux de Armendáriz, Former President, Governor, and Captain General of the Kingdom of New Granada, Cartagena, August 20, 1585,* Archivo Histórico de Protocolos, Madrid, Protocolo 3299, fols. 277–79.; Schäfer, *El Consejo Real y Supremo de las Indias,* 2:80 (n. 51), 130 (n. 207), 498, 504, 440; Andrés Cavo, *Los tres siglos de Méjico durante el gobierno español,* pp. 189–92.

Chapter 4

1. William L. Sherman, *Forced Native Labor in Sixteenth-Century Central America,* pp. 130, 404, n. 11; Jiménez de la Espada, *Cartas de Indias,* 3:776.

2. Hubert Howe Bancroft, *History of Central America,* 2:305.

3. Sherman, *Forced Native Labor,* p. 139.

4. Ibid., pp. 132, 140; Bancroft, *History of Central America,* 2:308.

5. Sherman, *Forced Native Labor,* p. 146; Jiménez de la Espada, *Cartas de Indias,* 2:448; Sherman, "Indian Slavery and the Cerrato Reforms," pp. 25–50.

6. López de Velasco, *Descripción universal de las Indias,* p. 156; Sherman, *Forced Native Labor,* pp. 151–52; Ernesto Chinchilla Aguilar, *Blasones y heredades,* p. 242. Gracias a Dios was settled to exploit the rich silver and gold mines of the surrounding area. Situated on top of a hill to defend it from Indians, the land under its jurisdiction was described as "broken country with lofty mountain ridges." No gold or silver were being mined in 1620 for lack of workers, and its 60 *vecinos* were principally occupied in raising mules, wheat, and other products for export to neighboring provinces. Antonio Vázques de Espinosa, *Compendio y descripción de las Indias Occidentales,* p. 165.

7. López de Velasco, *Descripción universal de las Indias,* p. 146.

8. Ibid.

9. Dorothy H. Popenoe, *The Story of Antigua Guatemala,* pp. 36–38.

10. Domingo Juarros, *Compendio de la historia de la ciudad de Guatemala,* 1:112, 260; Severo Martínez Peláez, *La patria del criollo,* p. 77; Salvador Rodríguez Becerra, *Encomienda y conquista, los inicios de la colonización en Guatemala,* pp. 168–70.

11. Herbert Cerwin, *Bernal Díaz: Historian of the Conquest,* p. 123.

12. Ibid., p. 70.

13. Ibid., pp. 9–10.

14. Ernesto Chinchilla Aguilar, *El ayuntamiento colonial de la ciudad de Guatemala,* p. 173.

15. Martínez Peláez, *La patria de criollo,* p. 306.

16. Ibid., p. 308.

17. López de Velasco, *Descripción universal de las Indias,* p. 146.

18. Alonso de Zorita, "Relación de las cosas notables de la Nueva España y

de la conquista y pacificación della y de la doctrina y conversión de los naturales," MS no. 59, chap. 34, fols. 438–40; Fray Toribio de Motolinía, *Memoriales*, pp. 210–16.

19. Motolinía, *Memoriales*, p. 214.

20. Zorita, "Relación de las cosas notables de la Nueva España, Chapter 35, fols. 441–43.

21. *Appointment of Zorita as Oidor in the Audiencia de los Confines, Monzón, July 11, 1552.*

22. *Appointment of Licentiate Juan de Galarza as Oidor in the Audiencia de los Confines, Monzón, July 11, 1552*, AGI, Audiencia de Guatemala, Leg. 386, fol. 45v.

23. Jiménez de la Espada, *Cartas de Indias*, 2:448.

24. Sherman, *Forced Native Labor*, pp. 145–47.

25. On May 15, 1553, Zorita wrote the crown stating that he intended to begin his journey to Guatemala in June. *Letter of Zorita to the Crown, Santo Domingo, May 15, 1553*, AGI, Audiencia de Santo Domingo, Leg. 49.

26. Keen, *Life and Labor in Ancient Mexico*, p. 36.

27. *Letter of the Audiencia of Guatemala to the Crown, Santiago de Guatemala, September 20, 1553*, AGI, Audiencia de México, Leg. 100.

28. Keen, *Life and Labor in Ancient Mexico* p. 36.

29. Sherman, "Indian Slavery and the Cerrato Reforms," p. 48.

30. Murdo J. MacLeod, *Spanish Central America: A Socioeconomic History, 1520–1720*, pp. 55–56.

31. Ibid.

32. Ibid., pp. 110–14.

33. Ibid., p. 114.

34. Sherman, *Forced Native Labor*, p. 153.

35. Bancroft, *History of Central America*, 2:234.

36. Sherman, *Forced Native Labor*, pp. 159–61.

37. MacLeod, *Spanish Central America*, p. 108.

38. Marcel Bataillon, "Las Casas y el licenciado Cerrato," in *Estudios sobre Bartolomé de Las Casas*, pp. 281–90; Bernal Díaz del Castillo, "Letter to the Crown, February 22, 1552," in *Historia de la conquista de la Nueva España*, pp. 589–92; Sherman, *Forced Native Labor*, pp. 167–72.

39. Sherman, *Forced Native Labor*, p. 172.

40. *Letter of Zorita to the Crown, Mexico, March 20, 1560*, AGI, Audiencia de México, Leg. 68.

41. *Letter of Fray Tomás de la Torre to the Crown, Santo Domingo de Cobán, Verapaz, May 22, 1553*, AGI, Audiencia de Guatemala, Leg. 8.

42. Christopher Lutz, "Santiago de Guatemala, 1541–1773: The Socio-Demographic History of a Spanish American Colonial City" (Ph. D. diss., University of Wisconsin, 1976), p. 66; Francisco Antonio de Fuentes y Guzmán, *Obras históricas*, p. 205; Juarros, *Compendio de la historia de la ciudad de Guatemala*, 1:111–12; 2:213.

43. Cerwin, *Bernal Díaz*, pp. 125–31; Sherman, *Forced Native Labor*, p. 412, n. 5.

44. Ibid.

45. Bataillon, "Las Casas y el licenciado Cerrato," p. 286; Sherman, *Forced Native Labor*, pp. 71, 158, 161; Rodríguez Becerra, *Encomienda y conquista*, pp. 168–70.

46. Sherman, *Forced Native Labor*, p. 414, n. 5.

47. Bancroft, *History of Central America*, 2:180.
48. *Letter of Fray Tomás de la Torre, Santo Domingo de Cobán, Verapaz, May 22, 1553*; MacLeod, *Spanish Central America*, p. 53.
49. Bancroft, *History of Central America*, 2:274–88.
50. Zorita, *Historia de la Nueva España*, p. 514.
51. Antonio de Herrera, *Historia general*, vol. 4, dec. 8, lib. 10, chap. 20.
52. *Letter of the Audiencia of Guatemala to the Crown, Santiago de Guatemala, September 6, 1554*, AGI, Audiencia de Guatemala, Leg. 9.
53. Ibid.; *Letter of the Royal Officials to the Crown, Santiago de León, provincia de Guatemala, April 27, 1556*, AGI, Audiencia de Guatemala, Leg. 9.
54. *Información—Alonso de Zorita*; Zorita, *Historia de la Nueva España*, pp. 465–66.
55. Zorita, *Historia de la Nueva España*, p. 514.
56. J. H. Parry, *The Audiencia of New Galicia in the Sixteenth Century: A Study in Spanish Colonial Government*, p. 40; Francisco del Paso y Troncoso, ed., *Epistolario de la Nueva España*, 9:244–46.
57. Paso y Troncoso, ed., *Epistolario*, 9:245–46.
58. Ibid.
59. Ibid.
60. Sherman, *Forced Native Labor*, p. 163.
61. Ibid., p. 163.
62. Jiménez de la Espada, *Cartas de Indias*, 2:415.
63. Manuel Giménez Fernández, "Fray Bartolomé de Las Casas: A Biographical Sketch," in Friede and Keen, *Bartolomé de Las Casas in History*, pp. 67–125.
64. Bancroft, *History of Central America*, 2:327.
65. Sherman, *Forced Native Labor*, p. 164.
66. Zorita, *Historia de la Nueva España*, pp. 509–10.
67. *Letter of Fray Tomás de la Torre, Santo Domingo de Cobán, May 22, 1553*.
68. Zorita, *Historia de la Nueva España*, p. 510.
69. Federico Argüello Solórzano and Carlos Molina Argüello, eds., *Monumenta Centroamericae Histórica: Colección de documentos y materiales para el estudio de la historia y de la vida de los pueblos de la América*, 1:530.
70. *Royal Decree of the Prince to the Audiencia of Guatemala, Madrid, April 17, 1553*, AGI, Audiencia de Guatemala, Leg. 9.
71. *Royal Decree of the Prince to the Audiencia of Guatemala, Toro, January 18, 1552*, AGI, Audiencia de Guatemala, Leg. 386, fol. 22; Bancroft, *History of Central America*, 2:234. See also William L. Sherman, "Tlaxcalans in Post-Conquest Guatemala," offprint from *Tlalocan* 6 (1970):124–39.
72. *Royal Decree of the Prince to the Audiencia of Guatemala, Madrid, April 17, 1553*.
73. *Letter of the Audiencia to the Crown, Santiago de Guatemala, September 6, 1554*, AGI, Audiencia de Guatemala, Leg. 9.
74. Sherman, *Forced Native Labor*, pp. 182, 225–26.
75. *Letter of Cerrato to the Crown, Santiago de Guatemala, August 27, 1554*, AGI, Audiencia de Guatemala, Leg. 9.
76. *Información of the Cabildo of Santa Marta Against Licentiate Alonso de Zorita, Santa Marta, September 12, 1551*, AGI, Justicia, Leg. 1123. This complaint was sent to Secretary Juan de Samano of the Council of the Indies by

Licentiate Martín Ruiz de Agreda, the crown's *fiscal*, on December 9, 1552; *Residencia—Cerrato, Grajeda, and Zorita*, Justicia, Leg. 75, fols. 345v–347v.

77. *Letter of Zorita to the Crown, Cartagena, October 13, 1551*, AGI, Audiencia de Santa Fe, Leg. 187; *Residencia—Cerrato, Grajeda, and Zorita*, Justicia, Leg. 75, fols. 657–58, 662v–64, 855–58v.

78. *Letter of Cerrato to the Crown, Santiago, August 27, 1554.*

79. *Residencia—Cerrato, Grajeda, and Zorita, Justicia, Leg. 77.* Juan Bautista Muñoz adds the following remarks to a copy of Zorita's letter of October 13, 1551, to be found in the Biblioteca de la Real Academia de la Historia, Madrid. Muñoz does not mention where he obtained the additional material contained in the brackets of the letter. "I realize that I have been charged with taking certain emeralds from the king's strong-box in Santa Marta [*Responde completament a este cargo*]; that I attempted to sell an Indian woman for 100 pesos [*Satisface*]; that I took the funds deposited in the royal exchequer of those who died without heirs or intestate [*Satisface*]." Muñoz concludes: "He mentions other accusations made by persons in Santa Marta and the New Kingdom, but it seems clear that given the absence of other evidence, none has any substance, which proves how little these charges would affect Zorita." See *Colección de Muñoz*, vol. 68 or 85, fols. 68–68v.

80. Sherman, *Forced Native Labor*, p. 226.

81. *Letter of Cerrato to the Crown, Santiago, August 27, 1554.*

82. Sherman, *Forced Native Labor*, p. 185.

83. Bancroft, *History of Central America*, 2:358–59.

84. *Letter of Diego de Robledo to the Crown, Santiago de Guatemala, April 10, 1556*, AGI, Audiencia de Guatemala, Leg. 9; Schäfer, *El Consejo Real y Supremo de las Indias*, 2:472.

85. *Visita of Licentiate Zorita to the pueblo of Totonicapa (1554)*, in Rodríguez Becerra, *Encomienda y Conquista*, pp. 162–67.

86. Ibid.; *Commission to Licentiate Zorita to Make a Visita of the Pueblos Under the Jurisdiction of the Audiencia, Santiago de Guatemala, March 5, 1554*, AGI, Audiencia de México, Leg. 100.

87. See Zorita's letter of December 6, 1553, in Antonio de Remesal, O. P., *Historia general de las Indias Occidentales y particular de la gobernación de Chiapa y Guatemala*, 2:260; *Letter of Zorita and Pedro Ramírez to the Crown, Santiago de Guatemala, November 5, 1555*, AGI, Audiencia de Guatemala, Leg. 9.

88. Keen, *Life and Labor in Ancient Mexico*, p. 272.

89. Ibid.

90. Zorita, "Relación de las cosas notables de la Nueva España," fol. 539.

91. Ibid.

92. Bancroft, *History of Central America*, 2:360.

93. *Letter of Provincial Domingo de Coro and Friars Alonso de Norena, Domingo de Azcona, Tomás de Cárdenas, and Jerónimo de San Vicente, Santiago de Guatemala, May 14, 1556*, AGI, Audiencia de Guatemala, Leg. 168; *Letter of the Audiencia to the Crown, Santiago de Guatemala, April 21, 1556*, AGI, Audiencia de Guatemala, Leg. 9.

94. Bancroft, *History of Central America*, 2:358–59.

95. *Letter of Vicar Tomás de Cárdenas and Fray Juan de Torres to the Crown. Santo Domingo de Sacapula, December 6, 1555*, AGI, Audiencia de Guatemala, Leg. 168.

96. Ibid.

97. Keen, *Life and Labor in Ancient Mexico*, p. 35.

98. Ibid.; *Información—Alonso de Zorita*.

99. *Letter of Fray Juan de Torres, Guatemala, November 17, 1555*, AGI, Audiencia de Guatemala, Leg. 168.

100. Ibid.

101. Ibid., Bancroft, *History of Central America*, 2:359.

102. *Letter of Zorita to the Crown, Mexico, July, 20, 1561*, AGI, Audiencia de México, Leg. 68.

103. *Letter of Fray Juan de Torres, Guatemala, November 17, 1555*.

104. *Letter of Fray Tomás de la Torre, Guatemala, November 8, 1555*, AGI, Audiencia de Guatemala, Leg. 168.

105. Bancroft, *History of Central America*, 2:375–76.

106. *Letter of the Franciscans in Guatemala to the Crown, Santiago de Guatemala, January 1, 1556*, AGI, Audiencia de Guatemala, Leg. 168.

107. Ibid.

108. Ibid.

109. *Letter of Diego de Robledo to the Crown, Santiago, April 10, 1556*.

110. *Letter of Friars Cárdenas and Torres to the Crown, Santo Domingo de Sacapula, December 6, 1555*.

111. *Letter of Diego de Robledo to the Crown, Santiago de Guatemala, November 7, 1555*, AGI, Audiencia de Guatemala, Leg. 965.

112. *Letter of Pedro Ramírez de Quiñones to the Crown, Santiago de Guatemala*, May 20, 1556, AGI, Audiencia de Guatemala, Leg. 9.

113. Ibid.

114. Giménez Fernández, "Fray Bartolomé de Las Casas," in *Bartolomé de Las Casas in History*, p. 102.

115. *Letter of Diego de Robledo to the Crown, Santiago de Guatemala, April 10, 1556*.

116. Ibid.; On April 21, 1556, the audiencia reported that Licentiate Juan Márquez, *fiscal* of the royal tribunal, had died "ready to set out as *alcalde mayor* and *juez de residencia* of the province of Nicaragua." *Letter of the Audiencia of Guatemala to the Crown, Santiago, April 21, 1556*.

117. Paso y Troncoso, *Epistolario de la Nueva España*, 9:244.

118. Ibid.; Bataillon, *Estudios sobre Bartolomé de Las Casas*, p. 284.

119. *Letter of Zorita to the Crown, Mexico, January 10, 1558*, AGI, Audiencia de México, Leg. 68; Zorita, *Historia de la Nueva España*, pp. 400–405. Robledo received 400 gold pesos a year from these Indians. See MacLeod, *Spanish Central America*, p. 115.

120. *Letter of Zorita to the Crown, Mexico, January 10, 1558*.

121. Some historians call him Núñez de Landecho, but Bernal Díaz calls him Juan Martínez de Landecho. See also *Colección de documentos inéditos relativos al descubrimiento, conquista y organización de las antiguas posesiones de Ultramar*, 2:17, 165, 167.

122. Remesal, *Historia general*, 2:342; Bernal Díaz del Castillo, *Historia de la conquista de la Nueva España*, pp. 561–62.

123. Remesal, *Historia general*, 2:342.

124. Bancroft, *History of Central America*, 2:367.

125. Bernal Díaz del Castillo, *Historia de la conquista de la Nueva España*, p. 561.

126. Sherman, *Forced Native Labor*, p. 308.

127. *Letter of Antonio Mejía to the Crown, Guatemala, July 30, 1557*, AGI, Audiencia de Guatemala, Leg. 9.

128. *Letter of Fray Tomás de la Torre, Santo Domingo de Cobán, Verapaz, May 22, 1553.*

129. Bataillon, *Estudios sobre Bartolomé de las Casas*, p. 286.

130. Sherman, *Forced Native Labor*, p. 139.

131. *Letter of Antonio de Mejía to the Crown, Guatemala, July 30, 1557*.

132. Ibid.

133. Ibid.

134. Bancroft, *History of Central America*, 2:367.

135. *Letter of Antonio de Mejía to the Crown, Guatemala, July 30, 1557*.

136. DII, 7:162–67.

137. Ibid.; Sherman, *Forced Native Labor*, p. 205.

138. DII, 7:163.

139. Ibid., pp. 165–66.

140. *Letter of the Exchequer Officials to the Crown, Santiago de León, Guatemala, April 27, 1556*. The treasury officials were Francisco de Castellanos and Francisco de Ovalle. On April 20, 1556, Zorita wrote to the crown recommending that Ovalle, *factor* and *veedor* of the exchequer in Guatemala, be given a similar position in Mexico City. *Letter of Zorita to the Crown, Guatemala, April 20, 1556*, AGI, Audiencia de Guatemala, Leg. 9. Because Zorita's letter in behalf of Ovalle and the treasury officials' letter criticizing the audiencia would have been read at the same time by the officials of the Royal Council of the Indies, it is reasonable to assume that the treasury officials were complaining of the inefficient work of judges other than Zorita.

141. Keen, *Life and Labor in Ancient Mexico*, p. 36.

142. Sherman, *Forced Native Labor*, p. 185.

143. *Letter of the Audiencia of Mexico to the Crown, Mexico, July 9, 1556*, AGI, Audiencia de México, Leg. 100.

144. Keen, *Life and Labor in Ancient Mexico*, pp. 33–36.

145. Ibid., pp. 101–102.

Chapter 5

1. Zorita, *Historia de la Nueva España*, pp. 174, 215.

2. López de Velasco, *Descripción universal de las Indias*, pp. 98–99; Toribio de Motolinía, *Motolinía's History of the Indians of New Spain*, trans. Francis Borgia Steck, O.F.M., p. 260.

3. Zorita, *Historia de la Nueva España*, p. 175; Francisco Cervantes de Salazar, *México en 1554*, p. 56.

4. Zorita, *Historia de la Nueva España*, p. 180.

5. Ibid., p. 279.

6. Cervantes de Salazar, *México en 1554*, p. 24. The author also notes that copper coinage (*vellón*) was not to be found in Mexico. It thus appears that when "Cervantes was writing this dialogue the 200,000 pesos in copper coins, which Viceroy Antonio de Mendoza had ordered minted in 1542, had disappeared." See Francisco Cervantes de Salazar, *Life in the Imperial and Loyal City of Mexico in New Spain and the Royal and Pontifical University of Mexico*

as Described in the Dialogues for the Study of the Latin Language Prepared by Francisco Cervantes de Salazar for Use in His Classes and Printed in 1554 by Juan Pablos, trans. Minnie Lee Barrett Shepard, p. 28, n. 47.

7. Zorita, *Historia de la Nueva España*, p. 176.

8. Ibid., pp. 178–79.

9. Cervantes de Salazar, *México en 1554*, p. 66.

10. Ibid., p. 69.

11. Arthur Scott Aiton's article on the mint, written in 1931, did not determine the exact location of the mint. See Arthur Scott Aiton, "The First American Mint," *Hispanic American Historical Review* 11 (May, 1931): 198–215.

12. Zorita, *Historia de la Nueva España*, p. 178.

13. Cervantes de Salazar, *México en 1554*, p. 11; Pedro Henríquez Ureña, "Escritores españoles en la Universidad de México," *Revisita de Filología* 22 (Madrid, 1935):61–65; Francisco Esteve Barba, *Cultura virreinal*, p. 282.

14. Joaquín García Icazbalceta, *Obras*, 1:345–46; Julio Jiménez Rueda, *Historia de la cultura en México*, p. 273.

15. Henríquez Ureña, "Escritores españoles en la Universidad de México," p. 64. The author quotes from the *Crónica de la Real y Pontificia Universidad de México*, a seventeenth-century work by Cristóbal Bernardo de la Plaza y Jaén, published in two volumes by the modern Universidad Nacional de México in 1931.

16. Ibid., p. 65. The privileges and immunities of the university were the same as those of the University of Salamanca. Cervantes de Salazar, *México en 1554*, p. 22.

17. Zorita, *Historia de la Nueva España*, p. 175; Steck, *Motolinía's History of the Indians of New Spain*, p. 260.

18. Zorita, *Historia de la Nueva España*, p. 189.

19. Ibid., p. 190.

20. Frank Tannenbaum, *Slave and Citizen: The Negro in the Americas*, p. 53.

21. Zorita, *Historia de la Nueva España*, p. 191.

22. Zorita, "Relación de las cosas notables de la Nueva España," fol. 455.

23. Angel Rosenblat, *La población indígena y el mestizaje en América*, 2:137–38. It should be noted that Rosenblat's comment regarding *gente de razón* is not absolutely correct. Nicolás León states that this term referred not to color or race but to "intelligence." All non-Indians, whether colored or white, were *gente de razón*. All Indians, in addition to being people of color, were *gente sin razón*. In other words, Indians were considered to be "minors," restricted in their liberty of movement, forbidden to buy wine, and incapable of concluding contracts. See Nicolás León, *Las castas del México colonial, o Nueva España*, p. 8.

24. Zorita, "Relación de las cosas notables de la Nueva España," fol. 300; Zorita, *Historia de la Nueva España*, p. 185. Zorita's estimate of the income of Xilotepec is not in agreement with Chevalier's statement that around 1560 "Jilotepec brought in 17,000 pesos, divided equally between Francisco de Velasco, the second viceroy's brother and Doña Beatriz de Andrade's heir, and Luis de Quesada, Juan Jaramillo's successor." Chevalier, *Land and Society in Colonial Mexico: The Great Hacienda*, p. 118.

25. Baltasar de Obregón, *Historia de los descubrimientos antiguos y mo-*

dernos de la Nueva España, pp. 42, 51. For further information on the Jaramillo family, see Francisco A. de Icaza, *Diccionario autobiográfico de conquistadores y pobladores de Nueva España*, 1:4; Francisco López de Gómara, *Cortés: The Life of the Conqueror by His Secretary*, trans. and ed. Lesley Byrd Simpson, p. 346; F. W. Hodge and T. H. Lewis, eds., *Spanish Explorers in the Southern United States, 1528–1543*, p. 279.

26. Zorita, *Historia de la Nueva España*, pp. 191–92.

27. Joaquín García Icazbalceta et al., *Investigación histórica y documental sobre la aparición de la Virgen de Guadalupe*, pp. 91–92.

28. Ibid., pp. 92–93.

29. José Ugarte, S.J., *Cuestiones históricas guadalupanas*, pp. 69, 73, 74.

30. Jacques Lafaye, *Quetzalcóatl and Guadalupe: The Formation of Mexican Consciousness, 1531–1813*, trans. Benjamin Keen, p. 216.

31. Ibid., pp. 238–42, xi.

32. John Leddy Phelan, *The Millennial Kingdom of the Franciscans in the New World*, p. 51.

33. Zorita, *Historia de la Nueva España*, pp. 15–16.

34. Zorita, "Relación de las cosas notables," fols. 267–75.

35. Ibid., fol. 272.

36. Lafaye, *Quetzalcóatl and Guadalupe*, p. 150; Hernán Cortés, *Hernán Cortés: Letters from Mexico*, tr. A. R. Pagden, p. 86.

37. Lafaye, *Quetzalcóatl and Guadalupe*, p. 195.

38. Manuel Orozco y Berra, *Noticia histórica de la conjuración del Marqués del Valle, 1565–1568*, 347–62.

39. Lafaye, *Quetzalcóatl and Guadalupe*, p. 144.

40. Ibid., p. 152.

41. Ibid., p. 193.

42. Peggy K. Liss, *Mexico Under Spain, 1521–1556: Society and the Origins of Nationality*, p. 109.

43. Keen, *Life and Labor in Ancient Mexico*, p. 133.

44. Mariano Cuevas, *Historia de la iglesia en México*, 2:37; Gonzalo Aguirre Beltrán, *La población negra de México*, p. 174.

45. Lafaye, *Quetzalcóatl and Guadalupe*, p. xvi.

46. Quoted by Fernando Benítez, *The Century After Cortés*, trans. Joan MacLean, p. 242.

47. Orozco y Berra, *Noticia histórica*, document no. 1 following the first 72 pages, pp. 6–8.

48. Ibid., pp. 42–44, 74, 101.

49. Quoted by Cuevas, *Historia de la iglesia en México*, 2:30. Mendieta's estimate of the number of daughters fathered by Spaniards is found on p. 24.

50. Francisco del Paso y Troncoso, ed., *Epistolario de la Nueva España*, 15:134.

51. Ibid., 14:156. Téllez contrasted the judges' actions with that of Don Antonio de Mendoza, who owed 100,000 ducats after serving as viceroy for fifteen years, and Don Luis de Velasco "who in two or three years owes more than 20,000 *pesos*."

52. María Justina Sarabia Viejo, *Don Luis de Velasco, virrey de Nueva España, 1550–1564*, p. 43.

53. Ibid., p. 45.

54. Ernesto Schäfer, *El Consejo Real y Supremo de las Indias*, 2:119.

55 *Información*—*Alonso de Zorita*; *Letter of the Audiencia of Mexico to the Crown*, Mexico, March 22, 1560, AGI, Audiencia de México, Leg. 68.

56. Paso y Troncoso, *Epistolario*, 15:99–101, 14:155–58; J. Ignacio Rubio Mañé, *Don Luis de Velasco, el virrey popular*, p. 89.

57. The audiencia's practice of suspending Velasco's orders until his decisions were finally settled created great difficulties for those Indian communities whose lands had been usurped. Chevalier notes that Velasco was usually successful in removing *estancias* endangering villages in the vicinity of Mexico City and Puebla. Chevalier, *Land and Society in Colonial Mexico*, pp. 99–100.

58. Sarabia Viejo, *Don Luis de Velasco*, p. 55.

59. Ibid.

60. Quoted in Vicente Riva Palacio, ed., *México a través de los siglos*, 2:373.

61. Ibid.

62. Joaquín García Icazbalceta, ed., *Nueva colección de documentos para la historia de México; Cartas de religiosos de Nueva España, 1539–1594*, p. 19. The two other individuals mentioned as suitable judges were the *contador* Montealegre and Doctor Sedeño, former *fiscal*.

63. Woodrow Borah, "The Spanish and Indian Law: New Spain," in George A. Collier, *et al.*, eds., *The Inca and Aztec States, 1400–1800*, pp. 265–88. A "new unified judicial jurisdiction for Indian cases, civil and criminal, in which the Indians were defendants" was finally established between 1591 and 1593.

64. Lesley Byrd Simpson, *The Encomienda in New Spain*, p. 144.

65. Charles Gibson, *The Aztecs Under Spanish Rule: A History of the Indians of the Valley of Mexico, 1519–1810*, pp. 62, 92, 198.

66. Riva Palacio, *México a través de los siglos*, 2:362; Keen, *Life and Labor in Ancient Mexico*, p. 40; Gibson, *The Aztecs Under Spanish Rule*, p. 63.

67. Benjamin Keen, *The Aztec Image in Western Thought*, pp. 72–73; G. Micheal Riley, *Fernando Cortés and the Marquesado in Morelos, 1522–1547: A Case Study in the Socioeconomic Development of Sixteenth-Century Mexico*, p. 20; Bernardo García Martínez, *El Marquesado del Valle: Tres siglos de régimen señorial en Nueva España*, pp. 39–40. García Martínez points out the difference between an *encomienda* holding and a *señorío* but states that nevertheless Cortés's dominions appeared in the setting of the *encomienda* system as one more *encomienda*.

68. This "true fief in perpetuity," the "envy, admiration, and goal of all encomenderos" was formed into an entailed estate in 1535. Simpson, *The Encomienda in New Spain*, p. 164.

69. Riley, *Fernando Cortés and the Marquesado in Morelos*, p. 34. Bancroft states that the *cédula* confirming the grant was issued at Toledo on March 16, 1562. See his *History of Mexico*, 2:580.

70. Keen, *Life and Labor in Ancient Mexico*, p. 40; Simpson, *The Encomienda in New Spain*, p. 167.

71. DII, 4:461.

72. Paso y Troncoso, *Epistolario de la Nueva España*, 10:42–44.

73. Keen, *Life and Labor in Ancient Mexico*, p. 41; García Martínez, *El Marquesado del Valle*, p. 167.

74. Benjamin Keen, "The White Legend Revisited: A Reply to Professor Hanke's 'Modest Proposal,'" *Hispanic American Historical Review* 51 (May 1971): 336–55.

75. The *calpulli*, or group of houses, was the basic unit of Aztec social

organization and was usually translated by the Spanish chroniclers as barrio or quarter. Both a territorial and a kinship organization, the *calpulli* had lost much of its autonomy to the strong Aztec central government described by the Spaniards at the time they arrived in Mexico. Jacques Soustelle, *Daily Life of the Aztecs on the Eve of the Spanish Conquest*, p. 7; Benjamin Keen, *The Aztec Image in Western Thought*, pp. 20–21.

76. "Sobre el modo de tributar los indios de Nueva España a Su Majestad, 1561–1564," in France V. Scholes and Eleanor B. Adams, eds., *Documentos para la historia del México colonial*, 5:29–31, 49–53; hereafter cited as Scholes and Adams with appropriate information.

77. Keen, *Life and Labor in Ancient Mexico*, pp. 42–43.

78. Scholes and Adams, 5:76. See also Walter V. Scholes, *The Diego Ramírez Visita*, 20 (4):58–62.

79. Scholes and Adams, 5:116–17.

80. *Colección de documentos inéditos para la historia de Ibero-Americana*, 1:365–66; Gibson, *The Aztecs Under Spanish Rule*, p. 200; Francisco González de Cossío, ed., *El libro de las tasaciones de pueblos de la Nueva España, Siglo XVI*.

81. Simpson, *The Encomienda in New Spain*, p. 151.

82. José Miranda, *El tributo indígena en la Nueva España durante el siglo XVI*, pp. 9–12.

83. Walter V. Scholes, *The Diego Ramírez Visita*, p. 14.

84. José Miranda, *España y Nueva España en la época de Felipe II*, p. 72.

85. Miranda, *El tributo indígena*, pp. 15, 138; Simpson, *The Encomienda in New Spain*, pp. 152–53.

86. Simpson, *The Encomienda in New Spain*, pp. 150–51.

87. Ibid., p. 151.

88. Ibid., pp. 151–52; Miranda, *El tributo indígena*, pp. 229–32.

89. Gibson, *The Aztecs Under Spanish Rule*, p. 202. See also Silvio A. Zavala, *La encomienda indiana*, p. 164.

90. Miranda, *El tributo indígena*, pp. 17–22.

91. Keen, *Life and Labor in Ancient Mexico*, pp. 12–13. See also Miranda, *El tributo indígena*, pp. 133–37; Haring, *The Spanish Empire in America*, p. 283.

92. Scholes, *The Diego Ramírez Visita*, p. 84.

93. Keen, *Life and Labor in Ancient Mexico*, p. 278.

94. Ibid., p. 227.

95. Ibid., pp. 231, 241.

96. Ibid.

97. Paso y Troncoso, *Epistolario de la Nueva España*, 9:146–56.

98. Ibid., p. 153.

99. Ibid., p. 151; *Letter of Francisco Morales to the Crown, Mexico, October 1, 1563*, AGI, Audiencia de México, Leg. 168. See also Paso y Troncoso, *Epistolario de la Nueva España*, 9:234–48.

100. Ibid., 9:243.

101. Ibid.

102. Lino Cómez Canedo, *Evangelización y conquista: Experiencia Franciscana en Hispanoamérica*, p. 48.

103. Gerónimo de Mendieta, *Historia eclesiástica indiana*, 2:205.

104. Ibid.; Keen, *Life and Labor in Ancient Mexico*, p. 44.

105. Mendieta, *Historia eclesiástica*, 2:207–208.

106. Serrano y Sanz in his introduction to Zorita, *Historia de la Nueva España*, p. lxvi; Joaquín Ramírez Cabañas, in his preface to Zorita, *Breve y sumaria relación de los señores de la Nueva España*, p. xv; Keen, *Life and Labor in Ancient Mexico*, p. 44.

107. Depositions signed by the president, Zorita, and other members of the Mexican tribunal can be found in audiencia files entitled *Informaciones de oficio y parte del distrito de dicha audiencia, México, 1552–1559, 1560–1561, 1562–1563*, AGI, Audiencia de México, Legs. 205, 206, 207. Information can be found regarding the services and needs of the following individuals: Hortuño de Ibarra, Diego de Fuentes, Gaspar López, Juan Troyano, Diego Ramírez, Alonso Balades [Valdés?], Francisco de Morales, Antonio de los Ríos, the Dominican Order, Baltasar Díez de Angulo, Martín López, Andrés García, Diego Díaz Cantero, Diego Juárez, Juan de Oliver, Antonio de Herrera, Gaspar Ochoa de Lejalde, Álvaro de Vega, Sancho Ortiz de Agurto, Doctor Sedeño, Bartolomé de Saldaña, Francisco Rodríguez Santos, Pedro Garcés, Juan Ugarte de la Cruz, García de Guilar (*sic*), Juan Baptista María, Juan de Cueva, *Licenciado* Caballero, Juan Gutiérrez. This does not exhaust the list of individuals asking for *mercedes*.

108. *Letter of the Audiencia of Mexico to the Crown, Mexico, 1560*, AGI, Audiencia de México, Leg. 97.

109. Bernal Díaz del Castillo, *Historia verdadera*, p. 468; Paso y Troncoso, *Epistolario*, 9:3; Chevalier, *Land and Society in Colonial Mexico*, p. 120.

110. "Cartas del licenciado Jerónimo Valderrama y otros documentos sobre su visita al gobierno de Nueva España, 1563–1565," in Scholes and Adams, 7:230. The other two sons of Hernán Pérez were Hernando de Córdoba and Francisco Pacheco.

111. Doña Beatriz was the viceroy's sister-in-law. She was married to Don Francisco de Velasco, the viceroy's brother, and held "half the province of Xilotepeque." Ibid., 7:207, 211.

112. Artemio de Valle-Arizpe, *La casa de los Ávila*, p. 31. Gil González inherited from his brother the *encomienda* of Cuautitlán, Xaltocan, and Zumpango. J. Ignacio Rubio Mañé, *Introducción al estudio de los virreyes de Nueva España, 1535–1746*, 2:12.

113. Juan Suárez de Peralta, *Tratado del descubrimiento de las Indias: Noticias históricas de Nueva España*, p. 132.

114. The mother of these unfortunate children was Doña Leonor de Alvarado, niece of the conqueror Pedro de Alvarado. See Rubio Mañé, *Introducción*, 2:12.

115. Suárez de Peralta, *Tratado del descubrimiento de las Indias*, p. 113.

116. Suárez de Peralta declared that Cortés's annual income from *encomienda* vassals was more than 150,000 *pesos de a ocho reales* but that if one estimated the sum in *ducados de Castilla* "one would not lie." Suárez de Peralta, *Tratado del descubrimiento de las Indias*, p. 114.

117. Ibid.; Hubert Howe Bancroft, *History of Mexico*, 2:585.

118. Suárez de Peralta, *Tratado del descubrimiento de las Indias*, p. 114.

119. Bancroft, *History of Mexico*, 2:605.

120. Ibid., p. 603.

121. *Petition of Zorita to the Royal Council of the Indies, Madrid, May 5, 1575*, AGI, Indif. Gen., Leg. 1385.

122. Quoted by Keen, *Life and Labor in Ancient Mexico*, p. 37; Joaquín García Icazbalceta, *Nueva colección de documentos para la historia de México*, p. 18; *Letter of Luis de Velasco to the Crown*, AGI, Audiencia de México, Leg. 19.

123. Ibid.

124. Bancroft, *History of Mexico*, 2:602–603 (italics and capitals added).

125. *Letter of the Audiencia of Mexico to the Crown, Mexico, February 20, 1564*, AGI, Audiencia de México, Leg. 19.

126. Bancroft, *History of Mexico*, 2:606; Suárez de Peralta, *Tratado del descubrimiento de las Indias*, p. 118.

127. Bancroft, *History of Mexico*, 2:607.

128. Ibid.

129. Luis González Obregón, *Rebeliones indígenas y precursores de la independencia mexicana en los siglos XVI, XVII, y XVIII*, pp. 154–56.

130. *Petition of Licenciado Vasco de Puga to the President of the Council of the Indies, Madrid, May 28, 1575*, AGI, Indif. Gen., Leg. 1385. Vasco de Puga is chiefly known as compiler of his *Cedulario*, a valuable collection of laws and royal decrees in force within the jurisdiction of the Audiencia of Mexico. The collection is not complete and there are errors in names and dates, but it remains an important source for Mexican history in the sixteenth century. The first edition appeared in 1563. See Vasco de Puga, *Provisiones, cédulas, instrucciones para el gobierno de la Nueva España*.

131. J. Lloyd Mecham, *Francisco de Ibarra and Nueva Vizcaya*, pp. 22–23; for Cristóbal de Oñate's confession, see Orozco y Berra, *Noticia histórica*, document no. 5, pp. 279–328.

132. Suárez de Peralta, *Tratado del descubrimiento de las Indias*, p. 148.

133. Bancroft, *History of Mexico*, 2:609.

134. Fernando Benítez, *The Century After Cortés*, p. 199; Luis González Obregón, *Rebeliones indígenas*, p. 151.

135. Suárez de Peralta, *Tratado del descubrimiento de las Indias*, p. 127.

136. Ibid., p. 129.

137. Scholes and Adams 7:390. See also Francisco A. de Icaza, *Diccionario autobiográfico de conquistadores y pobladores de Nueva España*, 2:4–5.

138. Orozco y Berra, *Noticia histórica*, p. 59. In 1560, Diego Rodríguez Orozco collected 4,500 pesos from the *encomienda* of Tututepec. Chevalier, *Land and Society in Colonial Mexico*, p. 118.

139. Paso y Troncoso, *Epistolario de la Nueva España*, 9:107–109, 10:87–88. Chico de Molina and the Cabildo of the Cathedral defended themselves to the crown by accusing the archbishop of many faults, including those of extreme greed, tyranny, and arrogance. They claimed, among other things, that Montúfar failed to visit and confirm Indians living in poor villages, that he practiced simony and nepotism, and that he used the funds of the hermitage of Our Lady of Guadalupe, amounting to more than 10,000 pesos, for his own use. Other funds belonging to the archbishopric were used by Montúfar to work some very rich mines he had bought. Ibid., 9:109–18.

140. Ibid., 10:220–24; Luis González Obregón, *Rebeliones indígenas*, p. 188.

141. *Letter of Zorita to the Crown, Mexico, January 25, 1558*, AGI, Audiencia de México, Leg. 68; Zorita, *Historia de la Nueva España*, pp. lxvii–lxxi; Keen, *Life and Labor in Ancient Mexico*, p. 45; *Información—Alonso de Zorita*.

142. *Letter of the Audiencia of Mexico to the Crown, Mexico, March 22, 1560*.

143. Ernesto Schäfer, *El Consejo Real y Supremo de las Indias*, 2:493; J. H. Parry, *The Audiencia of New Galicia in the Sixteenth Century*, p. 41.

144. *Letter of Zorita to the Crown, Mexico, March 20, 1560*; Serrano y Sanz in Zorita, *Historia de la Nueva España*, pp. lxxi–lxxiv.

145. Parry, *The Audiencia of New Galicia*, p. 77.

146. Ibid., p. 79.

147. *Letter of Zorita to the Crown, Mexico, February 10, 1561*, AGI, Audiencia de México, Leg. 68.

148. Joaquín García Icazbalceta, ed., *Nueva colección de documentos para la historia de México: Códice Franciscano, siglo XVI*, pp. 229–30; hereafter cited as *Códice Franciscano*.

149. Wagner and Parish, *Bartolomé de las Casas*, p. 229.

150. Keen, *Life and Labor in Ancient Mexico*, p. 46.

151. Wagner and Parish, *Bartolomé de las Casas*, p. 228.

152. *Letter of Zorita to the Crown, Mexico, July 20, 1571*, AGI, Audiencia de México, Leg. 68; Zorita, *Historia de la Nueva España*, p. 422; Keen, *Life and Labor in Ancient Mexico*, p. 46. See also Ralph H. Vigil, "Bartolomé de Las Casas, Judge Alonso de Zorita, and the Franciscans: A Collaborative Effort for the Spiritual Conquest of the Borderlands," *The Americas* 38 (July, 1981): 45–57.

153. *Colección de documentos inéditos para la historia de Ibero-Americana*, 1:229–34. Gabriel de Aguilera held the *encomienda* of Guaçalingo in the Archbishopric of Mexico. The tribute paid by the Indians in cloth and corn was worth 1,500 pesos. See Paso y Troncoso, *Epistolario de la Nueva España*, 9:16. Complaints by Indians against Aguilera for imposing excessive tribute payments and killing thirteen Indians may be found in ibid., 14:101–108.

154. Zorita, *Historia de la Nueva España*, p. 10.

155. Ibid., p. 21.

156. Zorita, "Relación de la las cosas notables de la Nueva España," fol. 496.

157. Ibid., fols. 496–97; Steck, *Motolinía's History of the Indians of New Spain*, pp. 255–56.

158. Zorita, "Relación de las cosas notables de la Nueva España," fols. 521–38.

159. Wagner and Parish, *Bartolomé de las Casas*, pp. 161–65; Philip Wayne Powell, *Soldiers, Indians, and Silver: The Northward Advance of New Spain, 1550–1600*, pp. 71, 109.

160. Gómez Canedo, *Evangelización y conquista*, p. 79.

161. Ibid., pp. 79–80.

162. Ibid., p. 80.

163. Ibid., pp. 80, 250–54.

164. Cervantes de Salazar, *México en 1554*, pp. 145–46.

165. *Letter of Zorita to the Crown, Mexico, January 10, 1558*, AGI, Audiencia de México, Leg. 68; Zorita, *Historia de la Nueva España*, pp. 400–405.

166. Wagner and Parish, *Bartolomé de las Casas*, p. 229.

167. *Letter of Zorita to the Crown, Mexico, July 20, 1561*, AGI, Audiencia de México, Leg. 68; Zorita, *Historia de la Nueva España*, pp. 417–31; Keen, *Life and Labor in Ancient Mexico*, p. 49.

168. Joaquín García Icazbalceta, *Códice Franciscano*, pp. 217–28.

169. Ibid., p. 227.

170. Wagner and Parish, *Bartolomé de las Casas*, p. 230. Wagner's supposition is given as fact by Ángel Losada, who states that Zorita's project was

presented by these two individuals. He notes that a manuscript version of the petition can be found in the Biblioteca Nacional de Paris among the papers for Veracruz. Ángel Losada, *Fray Bartolomé de las Casas a la luz de la moderna crítica histórica*, pp. 363–64.

171. *Letter of Zorita to the Crown, Mexico, April 12, 1562*, AGI, Audiencia de México, Leg. 68.

172. Keen, *Life and Labor in Ancient Mexico*, p. 49.

173. García Icazbalceta, *Colección de documentos para la historia de México*, 2:333–42. This petition, called a rough draft of Zorita's project by Serrano y Sanz, is the same as the *Memorial del Licenciado Zorita, oidor de la Audiencia de Méjico, sobre la población de Florida y Nuevo Méjico* to be found in the Archivo Histórico Nacional, Madrid. It is listed as *Cartas de Indias, Sección de Diversos, no. 170*, and was taken to Spain with Fray Jacinto's letter by Fray Alonso Maldonado.

174. Wagner and Parish, *Bartolomé de las Casas*, p. 231.

175. Powell, *Soldiers, Indians, and Silver*, p. 94.

176. Keen, *Life and Labor in Ancient Mexico*, p. 50.

177. Powell, *Soldiers, Indians, and Silver*, p. 204.

178. Keen, *Life and Labor in Ancient Mexico*, p. 50.

179. Scholes and Adams, 7:51–52.

180. *Letter of Zorita to the Crown, Mexico, February 10, 1564*, AGI, Audiencia de México, Leg. 18; Serrano y Sanz, in Zorita, *Historia de la Nueva España*, pp. lxxxiv–lxxxviii. The letter of the *encomenderos* requesting that Indian villages be assigned permanently to Spaniards in Mexico may be found in Paso y Troncoso, *Epistolario de la Nueva España*, 10:4–12.

181. *Letter of Luis de Velasco to the Crown, Mexico, February 26, 1564*, AGI, Audiencia de México, Leg. 19; Scholes and Adams, 7:343–44.

182. Scholes and Adams, 7:44–45.

183. Ibid., 7:46.

184. Ibid., 7:59, 69.

185. *Letter of the Dominican Order to the Crown, Mexico, January 2, 1564*, AGI, Audiencia de México, Leg. 280.

186. Scholes and Adams, 7:51.

187. Ibid., 7:52.

188. Ibid., 7:370.

189. Although Schäfer states that Villanueva served as judge in the Audiencia of Guatemala from 1579 to 1582 and as *fiscal* in the Audiencia of Lima in the 1590s, Rubio Mañé observes that Villanueva's son was actually *fiscal* in the *Audiencia* of Lima. Ernesto Schäfer, *El Consejo Real y Supremo de las Indias*, 2:452, 468, 490; Rubio Mañé, *Introducción al estudio de los virreyes de Nueva España*, p. 8.

190. Scholes and Adams, 7:48.

191. *Petition of Licentiate Vasco de Puga to the President of the Council of the Indies, Madrid, May 28, 1575*. Although the reverse of this petition is dated May 28, 1575, its contents indicate that Puga wrote it on board ship in the middle of the winter prior to his arrival in Spain.

192. Ibid. In 1560, Puga wrote the crown that it was being defrauded of 80,000 ducats a year. In 1561 he revised his figure to 200,000 ducats, stating that he had learned more about the land and its people. "Sobre el modo de tributar los indios," in Scholes and Adams, 5:11–12.

193. García Icazbalceta, *Obras*, 4:54.

194. Scholes and Adams, 7:372–77. It is curious that this individual should have the first name of Miguel de Cervantes Saavedra's grandfather and youngest brother. See Aubrey F. G. Bell, *Cervantes*, p. 63.

195. *Petition of Zorita to the Royal Council of the Indies, Madrid, May 5, 1575.*

196. Ibid.

197. *Colección de documentos inéditos para la historia de Ibero-Americana,* 1:364–65.

198. Scholes and Adams, 7:185.

Chapter 6

1. Stephen Haliczer, *The Comuneros of Castile: The Forging of a Revolution, 1475–1521.*

2. Ibid., p. 207.

3. Ibid., pp. 211–30.

4. Marqués de Lozoya, *Historia de España*, 15:294. The *cortes* was the equivalent of the French estates general and the English parliament; see Mariéjol, *Ferdinand and Isabella*, pp. 132–45.

5. Tawney, *Religion and the Rise of Capitalism*, p. 68.

6. Quoted by H. G. Koenigsberger and G. L. Mosse, *Europe in the Sixteenth Century*, p. 26.

7. Earl J. Hamilton, *American Treasure and the Price Revolution in Spain, 1501–1650.*

8. Braudel, *The Mediterranean World*, 1:517–42; Carlo M. Cipolla, "The So-called 'Price Revolution': Reflections on 'the Italian Situation,'" in Peter Burke, ed., *Economy and Society in Early Modern Europe: Essays from Annales*, pp. 43–46; Alexandre R. E. Chabert, "More About the Sixteenth-Century Price Revolution," in ibid., pp. 47–53. Chabert points out that Cipolla's interpretation of prices in Italy does not invalidate the quantitative theory as he defines it.

9. Elliott, *Imperial Spain*, pp. 188–96; Haring, *The Spanish Empire in America*, p. 315.

10. Koenigsberger and Mosse, *Europe in the Sixteenth Century*, p. 28.

11. B. H. Slicher van Bath, *The Agrarian History of Western Europe, A.D. 500–1850*, p. 195.

12. Braudel, *The Mediterranean World*, 1:405; Elliott, *Imperial Spain*, pp. 186, 116; Koenigsberger and Mosse, *Europe in the Sixteenth Century*, p. 41; Slicher van Bath, *The Agrarian History of Western Europe*, p. 195.

13. Elliott, *Imperial Spain*, pp. 188–93.

14. Henry Latimer Seaver, *The Great Revolt in Castile: A Study of the Cumunero Movement of 1520–1521*, p. 303.

15. Ibid., p. 167; Marqués de Lozoya, *Historia de España*, 15:297.

16. Elliott, *Imperial Spain*, pp. 199–201.

17. Carande, *Carlos V y sus banqueros*, 2:392.

18. Ibid., 1:259.

19. C. H. Haring, *The Spanish Empire in America*, p. 297.

20. *Información—Alonso de Zorita.*

21. Ibid.

22. Carande, *Carlos V y sus banqueros*, 3:396.

23. Elliott, *Imperial Spain*, pp. 206–207.

24. Braudel, *The Mediterranean World*, 1:343.
25. Ibid., 1:501–502.
26. Jaime Vicens Vives, *An Economic History of Spain*, trans. Frances M. López-Morillas, p. 383.
27. Carande, *Carlos V y sus banqueros*, 3:423.
28. Merriman, *The Rise of the Spanish Empire in the Old World and in the New*, 4:440–41; Jean H. Mariéjol, *Philip II: The First Modern King*, trans. Warre B. Wells, p. 341; C. H. Haring, *The Spanish Empire in America*, pp. 165–66, 289.
29. Mariéjol, *Philip II*, p. 39.
30. Braudel, *The Mediterranean World*, 1:511.
31. Kamen, *The Spanish Inquisition*, p. 122.
32. R. Trevor Davies, *Spain in Decline, 1621–1700*, pp. 65–67.
33. Elliott, *Imperial Spain*, p. 311.
34. Julio Caro Baroja, *Los moriscos del reino de Granada*, pp. 56–57; Henry Charles Lea, *The Moriscos of Spain: Their Conversion and Expulsion*, p. 217.
35. Enrique Sordo, *Granada*, p. 16.
36. Caro Baroja, *Los moriscos*, p. 60.
37. Ibid., pp. 60, 157–58.
38. Ibid., p. 65.
39. Kamen, *The Spanish Inquisition*, p. 60; Mariéjol, *Ferdinand and Isabella*, pp. 50–51.
40. Caro Baroja, *Los moriscos*, p. 8.
41. Braudel, *The Mediterranean World*, 2:787.
42. Zorita, *Historia de la Nueva España*, p. 497.
43. Lea, *The Moriscos*, p. 186.
44. Caro Baroja, *Los moriscos*, p. 23.
45. Cervantes, *Don Quijote*, p. 479.
46. Quoted by Caro Baroja, *Los moriscos*, p. 22.
47. Cervantes, "Coloquio de los perros," in *Novelas ejemplares*, p. 273.
48. Ibid., pp. 273–74.
49. Caro Baroja, *Los moriscos*, pp. 163–64.
50. Kamen, *The Spanish Inquisition*, p. 86; Lea, *The Moriscos*, pp. 226–28.
51. Anwar G. Chejne, *Islam and the West, The Moriscos: A Cultural and Social History*, p. 23.
52. Diego Hurtado de Mendoza, *Guerra de Granada*; ed. Bernardo Blanco-González, pp. 123–24.
53. Ibid., pp. 125–26; Gerald Brenan, *South from Granada*, pp. 12–18.
54. Caro Baroja, *Los Moriscos*, p. 174.
55. Ibid., p. 176.
56. Ibid., p. 177.
57. Merriman, *The Rise of the Spanish Empire in the Old World and the New*, 4:91.
58. Lea, *The Moriscos*, p. 262.
59. Ibid.
60. *Petition of Zorita to the Royal Council of the Indies, Madrid May 5, 1575.*
61. Caro Baroja, *Los moriscos*, pp. 148–49.
62. *Power of Attorney Given by Alonso de Aguilera to Alonso Sánchez de Ahumada and Cristóbal de la Becerra, Córdoba, December 5, 1554*, APC, Oficio 21, Protocolo 38, fols. 2048–2049.
63. *Copy of a Legal Document Filed Before the Audiencia of Granada on*

Behalf of Zorita and Juan Pérez de Zorita, Granada, Oct. 25, 1572, APC, Oficio 37, Protocolo 40, fols. 1249–1250.

64. Cervantes, *Don Quijote*, p. 93; the translation is Putnam's.

65. Vicens Vives, *Historia de España y America*, 3:22.

66. Braudel, *The Mediterranean World*, 2:740; Pfandl, *Cultura española*, p. 174.

67. Merriman, *The Rise of the Spanish Empire*, 4:476.

68. José Bergua, ed., *Refranero español precedida del libro de los proverbios morales de Alonso de Barros*, pp. 146, 434.

69. Cervantes, *Don Quijote*, p. 49.

70. Braudel, *The Mediterranean World*, 2:712.

71. Quoted by Pfandl, *Cultura española*, p. 173.

72. John Lynch, *Spain Under the Hapsburgs*, 1:180.

73. Elliott, *Imperial Spain*, pp. 272–73.

74. Geoffrey Parker, *Philip II*, pp. 169–74.

75. Sir Charles Petrie, *Philip II of Spain*, p. 158.

76. *Petition of Zorita to the Royal Council of the Indies, Madrid, May 5, 1575.*

77. *Extract of a petition of Zorita to the Royal Council of the Indies, Madrid, Monday, June 25, 1576*, AGI, Indif. Gen., Leg. 1085, fol. 185, punto 1.

78. *Extract of a petition of Zorita to the Royal Council of the Indies, Monday, January 27, 1578, Entry 28*, AGI, Indif. Gen., Leg. 1086.

79. *Extract of a petition of Zorita to the Royal Council of the Indies, Madrid, Wednesday, January 29, 1578*, AGI, Indif, Gen., Leg. 1086, fol. 29v; *Extract of a petition of Zorita to the Royal Council of the Indies, Madrid, Tuesday, February 4, 1578*, AGI, Indif. Gen., Leg. 1086, fol. 40, punto 5.

80. "Relación de las cosas notables," fol. 273.

81. *Extract of a petition of Zorita to the Royal Council of the Indies, Madrid, Monday, March 3, 1578*, AGI, Indif. Gen., Leg. 1086, fol. 68v., punto 6.

82. Zorita perhaps refers to a work by Las Casas that included his *Noticia de los Chichimecas y justicia de la guerra que se les ha hecho por los españoles*. Las Casas's ability as a writer is confirmed by Harold E. Driver, who notes that the "simple style" of his report describing the Chichimecas of what is today Querétaro and Guanajuato "is almost poetic at times." Harold E. Driver, ed., *The Americas on the Eve of Discovery*, pp. 19–23.

83. *Copy of a Legal Document Filed by Doctor Alonso de Zorita on Behalf of Himself and Various Relatives Withdrawing the Lawsuit Pending Before the Audiencia of Granada, Córdoba, October 9, 1573*, APC, Oficio 4, tomo 12.

84. Cervantes, *Don Quijote*, p. 842.

Chapter 7

1. Myron P. Gilmore, *The World of Humanism, 1453–1517*, p. 183.

2. Zorita, *Historia de la Nueva España*, p. 28. Zorita probably defended the Inquisition for the same reason as Las Casas: "Loyal to his mission and aware of the rocks among which he must navigate, Las Casas protected himself and stressed his support for the Inquisition in order to avoid difficulties." Ángel Losada, "The Controversy Between Sepúlveda and Las Casas in the Junta of Valladolid," in Friede and Keen, eds., *Bartolomé de Las Casas: Toward an Understanding of the Man and His Works*, pp. 279–306.

3. Kamen, *The Spanish Inquisition*, p. 100.

4. Elliott, *The Old World and the New, 1492–1650*, pp. 46–47.

5. Ibid., pp. 33, 6.

6. Serrano y Sanz, in Zorita, *Historia de la Nueva España*, p. xcvii.

7. Ibid., p. 25.

8. Ibid.

9. Georges Baudot, "L'institution de la dîme pour les indiens du Mexique: remarques et documents," *Mélanges*, pp. 167–221.

10. Ibid.

11. Ibid., p. 203.

12. Keen, *Life and Labor in Ancient Mexico*, p. 253.

13. Serrano y Sanz, in Zorita, *Historia de la Nueva España*, pp. cvii–cviii.

14. "Recopilación," MS 1813. For the contents of this work, see Serrano y Sanz, in Zorita, *Historia de la Nueva España*, pp. ci–cvii.

15. Vasco de Puga, *Provisiones, cédulas, instrucciones para el gobierno de la Nueva España*; Diego de Encinas, *Cedulario Indiano*.

16. Serrano y Sanz, in Zorita, *Historia de la Nueva España*, pp. cviii–cix.

17. Ibid., pp. xiii–xiv. Serrano y Sanz undoubtedly knew that Las Casas eventually opposed Negro slavery, as is apparent in his *Historia de las Indias*, 3:177.

18. Howard F. Cline, "A Note on Torquemada's Native Sources and Historiographical Methods," *Americas* 25 (April, 1969):372–86; López de Gómara, *Cortés: The Life of the Conqueror*, pp. xx; Miguel Maticorena Estrada, "Sobre las 'Decadas' de Antonio de Herrera: La Florida," *Anuario de estudios americanos* 23 (1958):29–62.

19. Francisco Esteve Barba, *Cultura virreinal*, p. 884.

20. Robert Ricard, "Remarques bibliographiques sur les ouvrages de Fr. Toribio Motolinía," *Journal de la Société des Americanistes* 25 (1933):139–51. See also Steck's comment in *Motolinía's History of the Indians of New Spain*, p. 53.

21. Georges Baudot, *Utopie et histoire au Mexique: Les premiers chroniqueurs de la civilisation mexicaine, 1520–1569*, pp. 327–86. Baudot's reconstruction of the contents of Motolinía's lost definitive work on the things of New Spain may be found on pp. 373–82.

22. Howard F. Cline, "Torquemada and His Franciscan Predecessors: Further Notes on Sources and Usages in the Monarquía Indians," in *HMAI Working Papers:80*, pp. 1–67. See also Mendieta, *Historia eclesiástica indiana*, 2:81–82; Baudot, *Utopie et histoire au Mexique*, pp. 159–240.

23. Baudot, *Utopie et histoire au Mexique*, pp. 169, 221. A copy of this work was sent to Las Casas by Olmos in 1547.

24. Navas, like Olmos, was a great linguist and after 1540 served as a missionary to the Popolocas; one of his works on the calendar and the festivals of the month celebrated by the Indians is preserved in the Archivo Histórico del Museo Nacional de Antropología de México. Johanna Broda, "Algunas notas sobre crítica de fuentes del México antiguo," *Revista de Indias* 25 (January–December, 1975): 123–65.

25. Zorita, *Historia de la Nueva España*, pp. 86–88.

26. J. B. Bury, *The Idea of Progress: An Inquiry into Its Origin and Growth*, pp. 9–15.

27. Saint Augustine, *The City of God*, pp. 278–79.

28. Francis Augustus MacNutt, trans., *De Orbe Novo: The Eight Decades of*

Peter Martyr D'Anghera, 1:79, 103–104.
    29. Bury, *The Idea of Progress,* p. 21.
    30. John Leddy Phelan, *The Millennial Kingdom of the Franciscans,* p. 58. Like Motolinía's account, Zorita's relation of the life of Fray Martín de Valencia has the passage: "The man of God persevered in his holy desires and the Lord deigned to visit and console him. One night during the season of Advent he was with the friars when the chorus was chanting the fourth hour or sext. When the chanting started, he began to sense a new manner of devotion and experienced a great consolation in his soul. He reflected on the conversion of the infidels and while meditating on this he found in many of the psalms he recited devout understanding concerning this aspiration, particularly in the psalm which begins *Eripe me de inimicis* [Psalm 58(59):2] which twice reiterates the verse, 'Each evening they return, they snarl like dogs and prowl about the city.' This servant of God spoke to himself and said 'Oh, when will this be? When will this prophecy be fulfilled? When will this evening be? By chance, is this the time and will I be found worthy to witness this conversion?' *We are already in the afternoon and end of our days, and in the world's final age*'" (italics added). "Relación de las cosas notables," fol. 482; Steck, *Motolinía's History,* pp. 231–32.
    31. Robert F. Berkhofer, Jr., *The White Man's Indian: Images of the American Indian from Columbus to the Present,* p. 72.
    32. Zorita, *Historia de la Nueva España,* pp. 281–82.
    33. "Relación de las cosas notables," fols. 521–38. For published sources of this expedition see Woodbury Lowery, *The Spanish Settlements Within the Present Limits of the United States, 1513–1561,* p. 418; Andrés G. Barcía, *Chronological History of the Continent of Florida,* trans. Anthony Kerrigan; Fray Agustín Dávila Padilla, *Historia de la fundación y discurso de la provincia de Santiago de México de la Orden de Predicadores;* V. F. O'Daniel, *Dominicans in Early Florida;* Buckingham Smith, ed., *Colección de varios documentos para la historia de Florida y Tierras Adyacentes,* pp. 190–202. The last few paragraphs of the Buckingham Smith document agree in particulars with Zorita's account, and these paragraphs and the several explanatory notes were obviously written by Fray Gregorio. It appears that the source used by Zorita was a report written by Fray Gregorio at a later date; it served to correct Fray Luis Cáncer's incomplete and very general summary of the expedition written before his death and completed by Beteta. Zorita did not acknowledge Fray Gregorio as the author of this account of the Cáncer expedition because he probably realized that the friar did not wish to emphasize his heroic actions and good sense throughout the disastrous enterprise. Beteta's account clearly shows that Cáncer was an incredibly naïve man whose imprudence and failure to heed advice led to his death at the hands of the Indians.
    34. "Relación de las cosas notables." fols. 496–97.
    35. Marcos Jiménez de la Espada gave this information to García Icazbalceta; my examination of the manuscript indicates that the manuscript is an eighteenth-century copy. See Joaquín García Icazbalceta, ed., *Nueva colección de documentos para la historia de Nueva España: Pomar.—Zurita.—Relaciones Antiguas,* p. xv; cited hereafter as *Relaciones de Texcoco y de Nueva España.*
    36. Francisco Javier Clavijero, *Historia antigua de México,* p. xxvii. Clavijero also stated that Boturini's collection of Mexican antiquities was sequestered by the Mexican government and was preserved in the archive of the viceroy.

37. Ramírez Cabañas, *Breve y sumaria relación*, p. xxii. Another copy of the *Brief Relation* is preserved in the New York Public Library. Keen, *Life and Labor in Ancient Mexico*, p. 55.

38. DII, 2:1–126; *Relaciones de Texcoco y de Nueva España*, p. 15.

39. Ramírez Cabañas in Zorita, *Breve y sumaria relación*, p. vii.

40. Keen, *Life and Labor in Ancient Mexico*, pp. 94–95.

41. Ibid., p. 104.

42. Ibid., p. 128.

43. "Relación de las cosas notables," fol. 203v. For comparison, see Motolinía, *Memoriales*, p. 264.

44. "Relación de las cosas notables," fols. 202–203v.

45. Keen, *Life and Labor in Ancient Mexico*, pp. 169–73.

46. Ibid., p. 203.

47. Ronald Spores, *The Mixtec Kings and Their People*, p. 3.

48. For an example of two interpretations of *Lámina* 13 of the *Lienzo de Tlaxcala*, the famous pictorial account of the Conquest, and how differences may be resolved by documentation, see Ralph H. Vigil, "A Reappraisal of the Expedition of Pánfilo de Narváez to Mexico in 1520," *Revista de Historia de América* 77–78 (January–December, 1974): 101–25. See also Miguel León-Portilla, *Los antiguos mexicanos a través de sus crónicas y cantares*, pp. 90–97; Keen, *The Aztec Image in Western Thought*, pp. 127–30.

49. Oviedo, *Historia general*, 4:248–51. For Indian drunkenness, see Steck, *Motolinía's History*, pp. 95–96.

50. García Icazbalceta, *Relaciones de Texcoco y de la Nueva España*, p. xviii; Keen, *Life and Labor in Ancient Mexico*, p. 69.

51. Ronald Hilton, "Is Intellectual History Irrelevant? The Case of the Aztecs," *Journal of the History of Ideas* 33 (April–June, 1972): 337–44.

52. Friedrich Katz, *Situación social y económica de los aztecas durante los siglos XV y XVI*, pp. 183, 189; Friedrich Katz, *The Ancient American Civilizations*, trans. K. M. Lois Simpson, p. 195.

53. Keen, *Life and Labor in Ancient Mexico*, p. 109.

54. Ibid., p. 118.

55. Ibid., pp. 175, 202, 205, 216.

56. Benjamin Keen, "The Black Legend Revisited: Assumptions and Realities," *Hispanic American Historical Review* 49 (November, 1969): 703–19; see also Lewis Hanke, "A Modest Proposal for a Moratorium on Grand Generalizations: Some Thoughts on the Black Legend," *Hispanic American Historical Review* 51 (February, 1971):112–27; Benjamin Keen, "The White Legend Revisited: A Reply to Professor Hanke's 'Modest Proposal'" in ibid, (May, 1971):336–55. The Black Legend of Spanish cruelty and injustice in the Old World and the New has as its theme Spain as dispoiler. It had thrived wherever anti-Hispanism has served a purpose. The counterpoint to the Black Legend is the White Legend, which emphasizes Spain's civilizing mission and the humanitarian aspects of Spain's colonial policy.

57. See, for example, Keen, *Life and Labor in Ancient Mexico*, pp. 120, 123, 126, 133, 204, 225, 231, 239–40.

58. Ibid., p. 216. As late as 1585 the Franciscans compared the *repartimiento's* implementation to that of men who "would walk out to gather herds of sheep and would go and allot and entrust them into the hands of wolves, so that these could take them to their dens." Richard Stafford Poole, "The Franciscan Attack

on the Repartimiento System (1585)," in John Francis Bannon, ed., *Indian Labor in the Spanish Indies: Was There Another Solution?* pp. 66–75.

59. Wolf, *Sons of the Shaking Earth*, p. 195.

60. Keen, *Life and Labor in Ancient Mexico*, p. 218.

61. Pedro Carrasco, "Los linajes nobles del México antiguo," in Pedro Carrasco, Johanna Broda, et al., *Estratificación social en la Mesoamérica prehispánica*, pp. 19–36. See also Pedro Carrasco, "Royal Marriages in Ancient Mexico," in H. R. Harvey and Hanns J. Prem, ed., *Explorations in Ethnohistory: Indians of Central Mexico in the Sixteenth Century*, pp. 41–81.

62. Keen, *Life and Labor in Ancient Mexico*, p. 183.

63. See Carrasco's introduction to *Estratificación social en la Mesoamérica prehispánica*, p. 8. Carrasco cites the following works: Lewis H. Morgan, *Ancient Society, or Researches in the Lines of Human Progress from Savagery Through Barbarism to Civilization* (1877), ed. Leslie A. White; Adolph F. Bandelier, "On the Distribution and Tenure of Land, and Customs in Respect to Inheritance among the Ancient Mexicans," *Reports of the Peabody Museum* 11 (Cambridge, Mass., 1878): 385–448; Adolph F. Bandelier, "On the Social Organization and Mode of Government of the Ancient Mexicans," *Reports of the Peabody Museum* 12 (Cambridge, Mass., 1879): 557–669; Manuel Moreno, *La organización política y social de los aztecas*; several studies by Alfonso Caso, the gist of which may be found in his "Land Tenure Among the Ancient Mexicans," *American Anthropologist* 65 (August, 1963): 863–78; Paul Kirchhoff, "Land Tenure in Ancient Mexico: A Preliminary Sketch," *Revista de estudios antropológicos* 14 (1954–55): 351–61; Katz, *Situación social y económica de los aztecas*.

64. Pedro Carrasco, "Social Organization of Ancient Mexico," in Robert Wauchope, ed., *Handbook of Middle American Indians*, 10:349–75; Pedro Carrasco, "The Political Economy of the Aztec and Inca States," in George Collier, et al., *The Inca and Aztec States, 1400–1800*, pp. 23–39; Carrasco, *Estratificación social en la Mesoamérica prehispánica*, p. 8.

65. Alfredo López Austin, "Organización política en el altiplano central de México durante el posclásico," *Historia Mexicana* 23 (April–June, 1974): 515–50; for Carrasco's opinion that "the economy of ancient Mexico can be described as a variant of what has been called the Asiatic mode of production," see Pedro Carrasco, "La economía del México prehispánico," in Pedro Carrasco and Johanna Broda, eds., *Economía política e ideología en el México prehispánico*, pp. 15–76.

66. See, for example, reviews by Arnold Toynbee and I. A. Levada in Anne M. Bailey and Josep R. Llobera, eds., *The Asiatic Mode of Production, Science and Politics*, pp. 164–67, 182–94.

67. See Fernando de Alba Ixtlilxóchitl, *Obras históricas*, p. 2:91; Diego Durán, *Historia de las Indias de Nueva España*, 1:96, 101, 114; Juan de Torquemada, *Monarquía Indiana*, 2:545–46. See also Gibson, *The Aztecs Under Spanish Rule*, p. 263; Soustelle, *Daily Life of the Aztecs*, pp. 81–93.

68. Bernardino de Sahagún, *General History of the Things of New Spain, Florentine Codex*, trans. and ed. A. O. J. Anderson and C. E. Dibble, vol. 8, (book 7), p. 23; Oviedo, *Historia general* 4:249.

69. Zorita, *Historia de la Nueva España*, pp. 293–99.

70. For a different view, see Frederic Hicks, "Mayeque y calpuleque en el sistema de clases del México antiguo," in Carrasco, *Estratificación social en la Mesoamérica prehispánica*, pp. 67–77.

71. Keen, *Life and Labor in Ancient Mexico*, p. 187.

72. Steck, *Motolinía's History*, p. 196; Keen, *Life and Labor in Ancient Mexico*, p. 187.

73. Katz, *The Ancient American Civilizations*, p. 225.

74. "Relación de las cosas notables," fol. 216.

75. Ibid., fol. 217. Zorita believed that the laws and customs of Texcoco and Mexico (Tenochtitlán) were generally followed in making slaves but noted that in provinces inhabited by groups speaking other languages "they had other laws and customs for making slaves." Ibid., fol. 216. For a discussion of the confusion and contradictions to be found on this subject in colonial and modern sources, see Yolotl González Torres, "La esclavitud entre los mexica," in Carrasco, *Estratificación social en la Mesoamérica prehispánica*, pp. 78–87. For a discussion of prehispanic slavery in Central America, see Sherman, *Forced Native Labor*, pp. 15–19.

76. Arturo Monzón, *El calpulli en la organización social de los Tenocha*; Keen, *Life and Labor in Ancient Mexico*, pp. 181–83.

77. Hugo G. Nutini, "Clan Organization in a Nahuatl-speaking Village of the State of Tlaxcala, Mexico," *American Anthropologist* 63 (February, 1961): 62–78; Carrasco, "Social Organization of Ancient Mexico," p. 364.

78. Keen, *Life and Labor in Ancient Mexico*, pp. 187, 107–108. See also H. R. Harvey, "Aspects of Land Tenure in Ancient Mexico," in H. R. Harvey and Hanns J. Prem, *Explorations in Ethnohistory*, pp. 83–102, for the range in size of landholdings of Aztec commoners in the sixteenth century.

79. Keen, *Life and Labor in Ancient Mexico*, p. 107.

80. Fray Diego Durán stated that one might marry within or outside his own ward, and Zorita in his major work wrote that "masters frequently married their female slaves, and women did the same with their male slaves." Also, Carrasco's study of ward membership and marriage in sixteenth-century Chiauhtla, north of Texcoco, indicates that "endogamy was not absolute," and "in mixed marriages patrilocal residence and patrilocal affiliation predominated." "Relación de las cosas notables," fol. 220; Carrasco, "Social Organization of Ancient Mexico," p. 367.

81. "Relación de las cosas notables," fol. 219.

82. Ibid. Zorita also noted that "Fray Andrés de Olmos says in his *relación* that if the slave fled and was not found, his relatives were taken as slaves, and the Bishop of Chiapas says in his treatise that they would take the nearest relation, so that servitude never ended for many subjects." Ibid., fol. 220.

83. Ibid., fol. 219.

84. Katz, *The Ancient American Civilizations*, p. 229.

85. *Relación de las cosas notables*, fols. 252–53.

86. Keen, *Life and Labor in Ancient Mexico*, p. 114.

87. Monzón, *El calpulli*, p. 39.

88. Wilcomb E. Washburn, *The Indian in America*, pp. 11–24; Harold Driver, *Indians of North America*, pp. 431–55; Alvin M. Josephy, Jr., *The Indian Heritage of America*, pp. 22–29.

89. Keen, *Life and Labor in Ancient Mexico*, pp. 96–97, 163, 124–26, 135–40.

90. See, for example, Lucio Mendieta Núñez, *El derecho precolonial*.

91. Quoted by Harvey, "Aspects of Land Tenure in Ancient Mexico," in *Explorations in Ethnohistory*, p. 84.

92. Robert M. Carmack, *Quichean Civilization*, p. 108.

93. Before receiving the knowledge of God and his Holy Gospel, says Zorita, the Indians "were in the condition of beasts made servants of the Devil." "Relación de las cosas notables," fol. 456. Zorita also compares the labors of the friars in Mexico to those of Hercules in cleaning the Augean stable, a comparison earlier made in a different context by Erasmus in his *Adages*. See Margaret Mann Phillips, *The "Adages" of Erasmus: A Study with Translations*, pp. 191, 209. The Mexican stable that the friars cleansed was "full of infernal filth." Zorita was of the opinion that the Indians before their conversion were unworthy of the figure of man—created in God's image and likeness—because they lacked knowledge of their Creator.

94. Arnold J. Toynbee, *A Study of History*, 1:224.

Bibliography

Unpublished Material

Archivo General de Indias, Seville
  Audiencia de Guatemala: Legajos 8, 9, 45, 168, 386, 965.
  Audiencia de México: Legajos 18, 19, 68, 97, 100, 168, 205–207, 280.
  Audiencia de Santa Fe (Bogotá): Legajos 16, 37, 60, 187, 533.
  Audiencia de Santo Domingo: Legajos 10, 11, 49, 71, 73–75, 78, 868.
  Escribanía de Cámara: Legajo 1184.
  Indiferente General: Legajos 424, 737, 1085, 1086, 1385, 2048.
  Justicia: Legajos 75–80, 550, 552, 554–57, 561, 562, 566, 1029, 1118, 1122, 1123.
  Patronato Real: Legajos 127, 231.
Archivo Histórico de Protocolos, Córdoba
  Oficio 1, tomo 27; Oficio 4, tomo 12; Oficio 7, tomo 1; Oficio 12, tomo 6; Oficio 21, tomos 26, 38, 47, 49; Oficio 23, tomo 10; Oficio 30, tomo 39; Oficio 37, tomo 40.
Archivo Histórico de Protocolos, Madrid
  Protocolo 3299, fols. 277–79.
Archivo General de Centro América, Guatemala
  Legajo 4678.
Biblioteca Nacional, Madrid
  Zorita, Alonso de. "Historia de Nueva España." MS R23075. This is an incomplete edition of the "Relación de las cosas notables," printed by the Idamor Moreno Press, in 1908.
Biblioteca de la Real Academia de la Historia, Madrid
  Colección de Juan Bautista Muñoz. Vol. 26, or (A/68), vol. 68, or (A/112/85).
  Colección de Don Luis de Salazar y Castro. Vol. A-110.
Biblioteca del Real Palacio, Madrid
  Zorita, Alonso de. "Leyes y ordenanzas reales de las Indias del mar Océano por las cuales primeramente se han de librar todos los pleitos civiles y criminales de aquellas partes y lo que por ellas no estuviere determinado se ha de librar por las leyes y ordenanzas de los reinos de Castilla. "MS 1813 (1574).
  Zorita, Alonso de. "Relación de las cosas notables de la Nueva España y de la conquista y pacificación della y de la doctrina y conversión de los naturales." MS 59 (1585).
Other
  Cline, Howard F. "Torquemada and His Franciscan Predecessors:

345

Further Notes on Sources and Usages in the Monarquía Indiana.
"In HMAI Working Papers: 80, pp. 1–67. Library of Congress
Reference Department, Hispanic Foundation, March 20, 1969.
Lutz, Christopher H. "Santiago de Guatemala, 1541–1773: The
Socio-Demographic History of a Spanish American Colonial City."
Ph.D. dissertation, University of Wisconsin, 1976.
Pescador del Hoyo, M. del Carmen. "Archivo Histórico Nacional.
Documentos de Indias: Siglos XV–XIX: Catálogo de la serie ex-
istente en la Sección de Diversos." Madrid, 1954.

Published Works

Aguado, Pedro de. *Historia de Santa Marta y Nuevo Reino de Granada.*
2 vols. Madrid: Publicaciones de la Real Academia de la Historia,
1916–17.
———. *Historia de Venezuela.* Edited by Jerónimo Bécker 2 vols.
Madrid: Imprenta y Editorial Maestre, 1950.
Aguirre Beltrán, Gonzalo. *La población negra de México.* 2nd ed.
Mexico City: Fondo de Cultura Económica, 1972.
Aiton, Arthur Scott. "The First American Mint." *Hispanic American
Historical Review* 11 (May, 1931): 198–215.
Alba Ixtlilxóchitl, Fernando de. *Obras históricas.* 2 vols. Mexico City:
UNAM, Instituto de Investigaciones Históricas, 1977.
Alemán, Mateo. *The Rogue, or the Life of Guzmán de Alfarache.*
Translated by James Mabbe. Oxford: William Turner, 1630.
Altamira y Crevea, Rafael. *Historia de España y de la civilización
española.* 4 vols. Barcelona: Sucesores de Juan Gili, 1928.
Archivo Nacional de Colombia, ed. *Libro de acuerdo del audiencia del
Nuevo Reyno, 1551–1556.* 2 vols. Bogotá: Editorial Antena, 1947–
48.
Arciniegas, Germán. *The Knight of El Dorado: The Tale of Don Gonza-
lo Jiménez de Quesada and His Conquest of New Granada, Now
Called Colombia.* Translated by Mildred Adams. New York:
Greenwood Press, 1968.
Argote de Molina, Gonzalo. *Nobleza de Andalucía.* Jaen: López Viz-
caíno, 1866.
Argüello Solórzano, Federico, and Carlos Molina Argüello, eds.
*Monumenta Centroamericae Histórica: Colección de documentos y
materiales para el estudio de la historia y de la vida de los pueblos
de la America Central.* Managua: Instituto Centroamericano de
Historia, 1965.
Augustine, Saint. *The City of God.* Translated by Gerald G. Walsh, S.J.,
et al. Foreword by Etienne Gilson. Garden City, N.Y.: Image
Books, 1958.

Bailey, Anne M., and Josep R. Llobera, eds. *The Asiatic Mode of Production, Science and Politics.* London, Boston, and Henley: Routledge & Kegan Paul, 1981.

Ballesteros y Berretta, Antonio. *Historia de España y de la civilización española.* 12 vols. Barcelona: Casa Editorial P. Salvat, 1922.

Bancroft, Hubert Howe. *History of Central America.* 3 vols. San Francisco: History Publishing Co., 1882–86.

_____. *History of Mexico.* 6 vols. San Francisco: History Publishing Co., 1883–88.

Bandelier, Adolph F. "On the Distribution and Tenure of Land, and Customs in Respect to Inheritance Among the Ancient Mexicans." *Reports of the Peabody Museum* 11:385–448. Cambridge, Mass., 1878.

_____. "On the Social Organization and Mode of Government of the Ancient Mexicans." *Reports of the Peabody Museum* 12. Cambridge, Mass., 1879.

Bannon, John Francis, ed. *Indian Labor in the Spanish Indies: Was There Another Solution?* Boston: D.C. Heath, 1966.

Barcía, Andrés G. *Chronological History of the Continent of Florida.* Translated by Anthony Kerrigan. Gainesville: University of Florida Press, 1951.

Bataillon, Marcel. *Erasmo y España: Estudios sobre la historia espiritual del siglo XVI.* Mexico City: Fondo de Cultura Económica, 1966.

_____. *Estudios sobre Bartolomé de las Casas.* Barcelona: Ediciones Península, 1976.

Baudot, Georges. "L'institution de la dîme pour les indiens du Mexique: remarques et documents." In *Mélanges,* pp. 167–221. Madrid: Casa de Velázques, 1965.

_____. *Utopie et histoire au Mexique: Les premiers chroniqueurs de la civilisation mexicaine, 1520–1569.* Toulouse: Editions Edouard Privat, 1976.

Bell, Aubrey F. G. *Luis de León, 1527–1591: A Study of the Spanish Renaissance.* Oxford: At the Clarendon Press, 1925.

_____. *Cervantes.* New York: Collier Books, 1961.

Benitez, Fernando. *The Century After Cortés.* Translated by Joan Maclean. Chicago: University of Chicago Press, 1965.

Bennassar, Bartolomé. *The Spanish Character: Attitudes and Mentalities from the Sixteenth to the Nineteenth Centuries.* Translated and with a Preface by Benjamin Keen. Berkeley: University of California Press, 1979.

Benzoni, Girolamo. *History of the New World.* London: Hakluyt Society, 1857.

Bergua, José, ed. *Refranero español precedida del libro de los proverbios morales de Alonso de Barros.* Madrid: Ediciones Ibéricas, n.d.

Berkhofer, Robert F., Jr. *The White Man's Indian: Images of the Ameri-*

can Indian from Columbus to the Present. New York: Vintage Books, 1979.

Bertrand, Louis, and Sir Charles Petrie. *The History of Spain.* New York: Collier Books, 1971.

Bourne, Edward Gaylord. *Spain in America, 1450–1580.* Edited by Benjamin Keen. New York: Barnes & Noble, 1962.

Braudel, Fernand. *The Mediterranean and the Mediterranean World in the Age of Philip II.* Translated by Siân Reynolds. New York: Harper and Row, 1972–73.

Bravo Ugarte, José. *Cuestiones históricas guadalupanas.* Mexico City: Editorial Jus, S.A., 1966.

Brenan, Gerald. *South from Granada.* New York: Grove Press, n.d.

Broda, Johanna. "Algunas notas sobre crítica de fuentes del México antiguo." *Revista de Indias* 25 (January–December, 1975): 123–65.

Burke, Peter, ed. *Economy and Society in Early Modern Europe: Essays from Annales.* London: Routledge & Kegan Paul, 1972.

Bury, J. B. *The Idea of Progress: An Inquiry into Its Origin and Growth.* New York: Dover Publication, 1955.

Cantor, Norman F. *Medieval History: The Life and Death of a Civilization.* New York: Macmillan, 1969.

Carande, Ramón. *Carlos V y sus banqueros.* 3 vols. Madrid: Sociedad de Estudios y Publicaciones, 1943–67.

Carmack, Robert M. *Quichean Civilization.* Berkeley and Los Angeles: University of California Press, 1973.

Caro Baroja, Julio. *Los moriscos del reino de Granada.* Madrid: Instituto de Estudios Políticos, 1957.

――――. *Los judíos en la España moderna y contemporánea.* 3 vols. Madrid: Ediciones Arion, 1962.

――――. *El Señor Inquisidor y otras vidas por oficio.* Madrid: Alianza Editorial, 1968.

――――. *The World of the Witches.* Translated by O. N. V. Glendinning. Chicago: University of Chicago Press, 1973.

――――. *Inquisición, brujería, y criptojudaísmo.* Madrid: Ariel, S.A., 1972.

Carrasco, Pedro, Johanna Broda, et al. *Estratificación social en la Mesoamérica prehispánica.* Mexico City: Instituto Nacional de Antropología e Historia, 1976.

Carrasco, Pedro and Johanna Broda, eds. *Economía política e ideología en el México prehispánico.* Mexico City: Editorial Nueva Imagen, S.A., 1978.

Caso, Alfonso, "Land Tenure Among the Ancient Mexicans," *American Anthropologist* 65 (August, 1963): 863–78.

Castellanos, Juan de. *Obras.* 4 vols. Bogotá: Editorial ABC, 1955.

Castro, Américo. *Semblanzas y estudios españoles.* Princeton, N.J.: Ediciones Insula, 1956.

Cavo, Andrés. *Los tres siglos de Méjico durante el gobierno español.* Jalapa: Tipografía Veracruzana de A. Ruiz, 1870.

Cervantes Saavedra, Miguel de. *Don Quijote de la Mancha.* Barcelona: Editorial Juventud, 1958.

_____. *The Ingenious Gentleman Don Quixote de la Mancha.* Translated by Samuel Putnam. New York: Modern Library, 1949.

_____. *Novelas ejemplares.* Buenos Aires: Editorial Sopena Argentina S.R.L., 1939.

_____. *Obras completas.* Edited by A. Valbuena Prat. Madrid: Aguilar, S.A. de Ediciones, 1965.

Cervantes de Salazar, Francisco. *México en 1554.* México: Ediciones de la Universidad Nacional Autónoma, 1952.

_____. *Life in the Imperial and Loyal City of Mexico in New Spain and the Royal and Pontifical University of Mexico as Described in the Dialogues for the Study of the Latin Language Prepared by Francisco Cervantes de Salazar for Use in His Classes and Printed in 1554 by Juan Pablos.* Translated by Minnie Lee Barrett Shepard, Introduction and Notes by Carlos E. Castañeda. Westport, Conn. Greenwood Press, 1970.

Cerwin, Herbert. *Bernal Díaz: Historian of the Conquest.* Norman: University of Oklahoma Press, 1963.

Chamberlain, Robert S. "The Concept of the *Señor Natural* as Revealed by Castilian Law and Administrative Documents." *Hispanic American Historical Review* 19 (May, 1939): 130–37.

Chapman, Charles E. *A History of Spain.* New York: Macmillan, 1965.

Chejne, Anwar G. *Islam and the West, the Moriscos: A Cultural and Social History.* Albany: State University of New York Press, 1983.

Chevalier, François. *Land and Society in Colonial Mexico: The Great Hacienda.* Translated by Alvin Eustis, Edited with a Foreword by Lesley Byrd Simpson. Berkeley and Los Angeles: University of California Press, 1970.

Chinchilla Aguilar, Ernesto. *El ayuntamiento colonial de la ciudad de Guatemala. Guatemala City: Editorial Universitaria, 1961.*

_____. *Blasones y heredades.* Guatemala City: Ministerio de Educación, 1975.

Clavijero, Francisco Javier. *Historia antigua de México.* Mexico City: Editorial Porrúa, 1968.

Cline, Howard F. "A Note on Torquemada's Native Sources and Historiographical Methods" Reprint from *Americas* 25 (April, 1969): 372–86.

Colección de documentos inéditos para la historia de España. 112 vols. Madrid: Imprenta de la Viuda de Calero, 1842–95.

Colección de documentos inéditos para la historia de Ibero-Americana. 14 vols. Madrid: Editorial Ibero-Africano-Americana, 1927–32.

Colección de documentos inéditos relativos al descubrimiento, conquista y colonización de las posesiones españolas en América y Oceanía. 42 vols. Madrid: Imprenta de Manuel B. de Quiros, 1864–84.

Colección de documentos inéditos relativos al descubrimiento, conquista y organización de las antiguas posesiones de Ultramar. 21 vols. Madrid: Sucesores de Rivadeneyra, 1885–1928.

Collier, George A. et al., eds. *The Inca and Aztec States, 1400–1800.* New York: Academic Press, 1982.

Cook, Sherburne F., and Woodrow Borah. *Essays in Population History: Mexico and the Caribbean.* 3 vols. Berkeley, Los Angeles, London: University of California Press, 1971.

Corominas, J. *Diccionario crítico etimológico de la lengua castellana.* 4 vols. Madrid: Gredos, 1954.

Cortés, Hernán. *Hernán Cortés: Letters from Mexico.* Edited and translated by A. R. Pagden. New York: Grossman, 1971.

Crónicas del reino de Chile. Madrid: Biblioteca de Autores Españoles, 1960.

Cuevas, Mariano. *Historia de la iglesia en México* 5 vols. Mexico City: Editorial Patria, S.A., 1946.

Davies, R. Trevor. *The Golden Century of Spain, 1501–1621.* London: Macmillan, 1937.

_____. *Spain in Decline, 1621–1700.* London: Macmillan, 1970.

Dávila Padilla, Fray Agustín. *Historia de la fundación y discurso de la provincia de Santiago de México de la orden de predicadores.* Mexico City: Editorial Academia Literaria, 1955.

Díaz del Castillo, Bernal. *Historia de la conquista de la Nueva España.* Introduction and notes by Joaquín Ramírez Cabañas. Mexico City: Editorial Porrúa, 1966.

Domínguez Ortiz, Antonio. *La sociedad española en el siglo XVII.* 2 vols. Madrid: Consejo Superior de Investigaciones Científicas, 1963.

Driver, Harold. *Indians of North America.* Chicago and London: University of Chicago Press, 1975.

Driver, Harold, ed. *The Americas on the Eve of Discovery.* Englewood Cliffs, N.J.: Prentice-Hall, 1964.

Durán, Diego. *Historia de las Indias de Nueva España.* 2 vols. and Atlas. Mexico City: Editora Nacional, 1967.

Durand, José. *La transformación social del conquistador* 2 vols. Mexico City: Porrúa y Obregón, S.A., 1953.

Elliott, J. H. *Imperial Spain, 1469–1716.* New York: New American Library, 1966.

_____. *The Old World and the New, 1492–1650.* Cambridge: At the University Press, 1972.

Encinas, Diego de. *Cedulario Indiano.* 4 vols. Madrid: Ediciones Cultural Hispánica, 1945–46.

Epton, Nina. *Andalusia.* London: Weidenfeld and Nicholson, 1968.

Espejo, Juan Luis. *Nobiliario de la antigua capitanía general de Chile*. 2 vols. Santiago de Chile: Imprenta Universitaria, 1917–21.

Esperabé-Arteaga, Enrique. *Historia pragmática e interna de la Universidad de Salamanca*. 2 vols. Salamanca: Imp. y Lib. de Francisco Núñez Izquierdo, 1914.

Esteve Barba, Francisco. *Cultura virreinal*. Barcelona: Salvat Editores, S.A., 1965.

Fernández de Oviedo, Gonzalo. *Natural History of the West Indies*. Translated and edited by Sterling A. Stoudemire. Chapel Hill: University of North Carolina Press, 1959.

———. *Historia general y natural de las Indias, Islas y Tierra Firme del Mar Océano*. 5 vols. Madrid: Biblioteca de Autores Españoles, 1959.

Fernández Piedrahita, Lucas. *Historia general de las conquistas del Nuevo Reino de Granada*. 4 vols. Bogotá: Editorial ABC, 1942.

Finan, John J., ed. *A List of Spanish Residencias in the Archives of the Indies, 1516–1775: Administrative Judicial Reviews of Colonial Officials in the American Indies, Philippines and Canary Islands*. Compiled for the Hispanic Foundation in the Library of Congress by José María de la Peña y de la Cámara. Washington, D.C.: Library of Congress, 1955.

Floyd, Troy S. *The Columbus Dynasty in the Caribbean, 1492–1526*. Albuquerque: University of New Mexico Press, 1973.

Friede, Juan. *Vida y luchas de Don Juan del Valle, primer obispo de Popayán y protector de indios*. Popayán: Edición conmemorativa del IV Centenario de la muerte del primer Obispo de Popayán, auspiciada por el Arzobispado de ésta ciudad, 1961.

———. "Creación de la Real Audiencia," *Boletín Histórico Antiguo* 37 (Bogotá, 1950): 75–80.

Friede, Juan, ed. *Documentos inéditos para la historia de Colombia*. 10 vols. Bogotá: Academia Colombiana de Historia, 1955–60.

Friede, Juan, and Benjamin Keen, eds. *Bartolomé de Las Casas in History: Toward an Understanding of the Man and His Works*. DeKalb: Northern Illinois University Press, 1971.

Friedrich, Carl J. *The Age of the Baroque, 1610–1660*. New York: Harper & Row, 1962.

Freile, Juan Rodríguez. *The Conquest of New Granada*. Translated by William C. Atkinson. London: Folio Society, 1961.

Fuente, Vicente de la. *Historia de las universidades, colegios y demás establecimientos de enseñanza en España*. 4 vols. Madrid: Imprenta de la viuda è hija de Fuentenebro, 1884–89.

Fuentes y Guzmán, Antonio de. *Obras históricas*. Madrid: Biblioteca de Autores Españoles, 1969.

Gallop, Rodney, *A Book of the Basques*. Reno: University of Nevada Press, 1970.

García Carraffa, A. and A. *Enciclopedia heráldica y genealógica hispa-*

noamericana. 59 vols. Madrid: Antonio Marzo, 1920–36.

García Granados, Rafael. *Diccionario biográfico de historia antigua de Méjico.* 3 vols. Mexico City: Instituto de Historia, 1953.

Garcia Icazbalceta, Joaquín. *Obras.* 10 vols. New York: Burt Franklin, 1968.

———, ed. *Nueva colección de documentos para la historia de Mexico.* Mexico City: Andrade y Morales, 1886–91.

———, ed. *Colección de documents para la historia de México.* 2 vols. Mexico City: J. M. Andrade, 1858–66.

———, ed. *Nueva colección de documentos para la historia de México: Cartas de religiosos de Nueva España, 1539–1594.* 5 vols. Mexico City: Editorial Salvador Chávez Hayhoe, 1941.

———, ed. *Nueva colección de documentos para la historia de Nueva España: Códice Franciscano, siglo XVI.* Mexico City: Editorial Salvador Chávez Hayhoe, 1941.

———, ed. *Nueva colección de documentos para la historia de México: Pomar.—Zurita.—Relaciones Antiguas.* Mexico City: Editorial Salvador Chávez Hayhoe, 1941.

———, et al. *Investigación histórica y documental sobre la aparición de la Virgen de Guadalupe.* Mexico City: Ediciones Fuente Cultural, 1952.

García Martínez, Bernardo. *El Marquesado del Valle: Tres siglos de régimen señorial en Nueva España.* Mexico City: El Colegio de Mèxico, 1969.

García de Valdeavellano, Luis. *Curso de historia de las instituciones españoles de los orígines al final de la edad media.* Madrid: Revista de Occidente, 1968.

García Valdecasas, Alfonso. *El hidalgo y el honor.* Madrid: Revista de Occidente, 1958.

Garcilaso de la Vega. *Royal Commentaries of the Incas and General History of Peru.* 2 vols. Austin: University of Texas Press, 1966.

Gibson, Charles. *The Aztecs Under Spanish Rule: A History of the Indians of the Valley of Mexico, 1519–1810.* Stanford, Calif.: Stanford University Press, 1964.

Gilman, Stephen. *The Spain of Fernando de Rojas: The Intellectual and Social Landscape of La Celestina.* Princeton, N.J.: Princeton University Press, 1972.

Gilmore, Myron P. *The World of Humanism, 1453–1517.* New York: Harper & Row, 1962.

———. *Humanists and Jurists: Six Studies in the Renaissance.* Cambridge, Mass.: Harvard University Press, 1963.

Giménez Fernández, Manuel. *Bartolomé de Las Casas.* 2 vols. Seville: La Escuela de Estudios Hispano-Americanos, 1953–1960.

Gómez Canedo, Lino. *Evangelización y conquista: Experiencia Franciscana en Hispanoamérica.* Mexico City: Editorial Porrúa, 1971.

González de Cossío, Francisco, ed. *El libro de las tasaciones de pueblos de la Nueva España, Siglo XVI.* México: Archivo General de la Nación, 1952.

González Obregón, Luis. *Rebeliones indígenas y precursores de la independencia mexicana en los siglos XVI, XVII, y XVIII.* Mexico City: Ediciones Fuentes Cultural, 1952.

Green, Otis H. *Spain and the Western Tradition: The Castilian Mind in Literature from El Cid to Calderón.* 4 vols. Madison, Milwaukee, and London: University of Wisconsin Press, 1968.

Groot, José Manuel. *Historia eclesiástica y civil de Nueva Granada.* 5 vols. Bogotá: Biblioteca de Autores Colombianos, 1957.

Haliczer, Stephen H. "The Castilian Urban Patriciate and the Jewish Expulsions of 1480–92." *American Historical Review* 78 (February, 1973): 35–58.

———. *The Comuneros of Castile: The Forging of a Revolution, 1475–1521.* Madison: University of Wisconsin Press, 1981.

Hamilton, Earl J. *American Treasure and the Price Revolution in Spain, 1501–1650.* Cambridge, Mass: Harvard University Press, 1934.

Hanke, Lewis. *The Spanish Struggle for Justice in the Conquest of America.* Boston, Toronto: Little, Brown, 1965.

———. "A Modest Proposal for a Moratorium on Grand Generalizations: Some Thoughts on the Black Legend." *Hispanic American Historical Review* 51 (February, 1971): 112–27.

Haring, C. H. *Trade and Navigation Between Spain and the Indies in the Time of the Hapsburgs.* Cambridge, Mass.: Harvard University Press, 1918.

———. *The Spanish Empire in America.* New York: Oxford University Press, 1952.

Harvey, H. R. and Hanns J. Prem, eds. *Explorations in Ethnohistory: Indians of Central Mexico in the Sixteenth Century.* Albuquerque: University of New Mexico Press, 1984.

Heer, Friedrich. *The Medieval World.* New York: New American Library, 1962.

Henige, David. "On the Contact Population of Hispaniola: History as Higher Mathematics." *Hispanic American Historical Review* 58 (May, 1978): 217–37.

Henríquez Ureña, Pedro. "Escritores españoles en la Universidad de México." *Revista de filología de Madrid* 22 (Madrid, 1935): 61–65.

Herrera y Tordesillas, Antonio de. *Historia general de los hechos de los castellanos en las Islas e Tierra Firme del Mar Océano.* 4 vols. Madrid: Imprenta Real, 1601–15.

Hodge, Frederick W., and T. H. Lewis, eds. *Spanish Explorers in the Southern United States, 1528–1543.* New York: Barnes & Noble, 1953.

Highfield, Roger, ed. *Spain in the Fifteenth Century, 1369–1516: Essays and Extracts by Historians of Spain*. Translated by Frances M. López-Morillas. New York, Evanston, San Francisco, London: Harper & Row, 1972.

Hilton, Ronald. "Is Intellectual History Irrelevant? The Case of the Aztecs." *Journal of the History of Ideas* 33 (April–June, 1972): 337–44.

Huarte de San Juan, Juan. "Examen de ingenios," in *Obras escogidas de filósofos*. Madrid: Biblioteca de Autores Españoles, 1953.

Huizinga, J. *The Waning of the Middle Ages*. Garden City: Doubleday & Co., 1924.

Hurtado de Mendoza, Diego. *Guerra de Granada*. Edited by Bernardo Blanco-González. Madrid: Editorial Castalia, 1970.

Icaza, Francisco A. de. *Diccionario autobiográfico de conquistadores y pobladores de Nueva España*. 2 vols. Mexico City: Edmundo Aveña Levy, 1969.

Incháustegui Cabral, J. M., ed. *Reales cédulas y correspondencia de gobernadores de Santo Domingo, de la regencia del cardenal Cisneros en adelante*. 5 vols. Madrid: Colección histórico-documental trujilloniana, 1958.

Irving, Washington. *The Conquest of Granada*. New York: E.P. Dutton, 1910.

Jiménez de la Espada, Marcos, ed. *Cartas de Indias*. Madrid: Ministerio de Fomento, 1877.

Jiménez Rueda, Julio. *Historia de la cultura en México*. Mexico City: Editorial Cultura, 1951.

Johnson, H. B., Jr., ed. *From Reconquest to Empire*. New York: Alfred A. Knopf, 1970.

Jos, Emiliano. *La expedición de Ursúa al Dorado, la rebelión de Lope de Aguirre y el itinerario de los "marañones."* Huesca: Imprenta V. Campo, 1927.

Josephy, Alvin M., Jr. *The Indian Heritage of America*. New York: Bantam Books, 1976.

Juarros, Domingo. *Compendio de la historia de la ciudad de Guatemala*. 2 vols. Guatemala: Tipografía Nacional, 1936.

Kagan, Richard L. *Students and Society in Early Modern Spain*. Baltimore & London: Johns Hopkins University Press, 1974.

Kamen, Henry. *The Spanish Inquisition*. New York: New American Library, 1971.

Katz, Friedrich. *Situación social y económica de los aztecas durante los siglos XV and XVI*. Mexico City: Universidad Nacional Autónoma de México, 1966.

––––––. *The Ancient American Civilizations*. Translated by K. M. Lois Simpson. New York: Praeger Publishers, 1972.

Kautsky, Karl. *Thomas More and His Utopia, with a Historical Introduction*. Translated by H. J. Stenning. New York: International Publishers, 1927.

Keen, Benjamin. "The Black Legend Revisited: Assumptions and Realities." *Hispanic American Historical Review* 49 (November, 1969): 703–19.

———. "The White Legend Revisited: A Reply to Professor Hanke's 'Modest Proposal.'" *Hispanic American Historical Review* 51 (May, 1971): 336–55.

———. *The Aztec Image in Western Thoguht.* New Brunswick, N.J.: Rutgers University Press, 1971.

Keen, Benjamin, ed. *Readings in Latin-American Civilization, 1492 to the Present.* Boston: Houghton Mifflin, 1967.

Keniston, Hayward. *Francisco de los Cobos, Secretary of the Emperor Charles V.* Pittsburgh, Pa.: University of Pittsburgh Press, 1958.

Kirchhoff, Paul. "Land Tenure in Ancient Mexico: A Preliminary Sketch." *Revista de Estudios Antropológicos* 14 (1954–55): 351–61.

Kleffens, E. N. van. *Hispanic Law Until the End of the Middle Ages.* Edinburgh: University Press, 1968.

Koenigsberger, H. G., and G. L. Mosse. *Europe in the Sixteenth Century.* New York: Holt, Rinehart and Winston, 1968.

Kubler, George. *Mexican Architecture of the Sixteenth Century.* 2 vols. New Haven, Conn.: Yale University Press, 1948.

Lafaye, Jacques. *Quetzalcóatl and Guadalupe: The Formation of Mexican Consciousness, 1531–1813.* Translated by Benjamin Keen, Foreword by Octavio Paz. Chicago and London: University of Chicago Press, 1976.

Las Casas, Bartolomé de. *Doctrina.* Mexico City: Ediciones de la Universidad Nacional Autónoma, 1941.

———. *Historia de las Indias.* 3 vols. Edited by Agustín Millares Carlo with a Preliminary Study by Lewis Hanke. Mexico City: Fondo de Cultura Económica, 1965.

Laslett, Peter. *The World We Have Lost: England Before the Industrial Age.* New York: Charles Scribner's Sons, 1965.

Lea, Henry Charles. *A History of the Inquisition of Spain.* 3 vols. New York: Macmillan, 1908.

———. *The Moriscos of Spain: Their Conversion and Expulsion.* New York: Greenwood Press, 1968.

León, Nicolás. *Las castas de México colonial, o Nueva España.* Mexico City: Talleres gráficos del Museo Nacional de Arqueología, Historia y Etnografía, 1924.

León-Portilla, Miguel. *Los antiguos mexicanos a través de sus crónicas y cantares.* Mexico City: Fondo de Cultura Económica, 1961.

Levillier, Roberto. *Nueva crónica de la conquista del Tucumán, 1542–1563.* Buenos Aires: Sucesores de Rivadeneyra, 1926.

Levillier, Roberto, ed. *Gobernación del Tucumán: Probanzas de méritos y servicios de los conquistadores.* Madrid: Sucesores de Rivadeneyra, 1919.

Liss, Peggy K. *Mexico Under Spain: 1521–1556: Society and the Origins of Nationality.* Chicago and London: University of Chicago Press, 1975.

Livermore, Harold. *A History of Spain.* London: George Allen & Unwin, 1958.

Lockhart, James. *Spanish Peru, 1532–1560: A Colonial Society.* Madison: University of Wisconsin Press, 1968.

Lohmann Villena, Guillermo. *Los americanos en las órdenes nobiliarias, 1529–1900.* 2 vols. Madrid: Consejo Superior de Investigaciones Científicas, 1947.

López Austin, Alfredo. "Organización política en el altiplano central de México durante el posclásico." *Historia Mexicana* 23 (April–June, 1974): 515–50.

López de Gómara, Francisco. *Annals of the Emperor Charles V.* Edited by Roger Bigelow Merriman. Oxford: At the Clarendon Press, 1912.

————. *Cortés: The Life of the Conqueror by His Secretary.* Translated and edited by Lesley Byrd Simpson. Berkeley and Los Angeles: University of California Press, 1964.

López de Velasco, Juan. *Geografía y descripción universal de las Indias.* Madrid: Biblioteca de Autores Españoles. 1971.

Losada, Angel. *Fray Bartolomé de Las Casas a la luz de la moderna crítica histórica.* Madrid: Editorial Tecnos, 1970.

Lowery, Woodbury. *The Spanish Settlements within the Present Limits of the United States, 1513–1561.* New York and London: G.P. Putnam's Sons, 1911.

Lozoya, Marqués de. *Historia de España.* 137 vols. to date. Barcelona: Salvat Editores, 1967.

Lynch, John. *Spain Under the Hapsburgs.* 2 vols. New York: Oxford University Press, 1965.

Lynn, Caro. *A College Professor of the Renaissance: Lucio Marineo Sículo among the Spanish Humanists.* Chicago: University of Chicago Press, 1937.

MacLeod, Murdo J. *Spanish Central America: A Socioeconomic History, 1520–1720.* Berkeley: University of California Press, 1973.

MacNutt, Francis Augustus. *De Orbe Novo: The Eight Decades of Peter Martyr D'Anghera.* 2 vols. Translated from the Latin with Notes and Introduction. New York and London: G.P. Putnam's Sons, 1912.

Madariaga, Salvador de. *Spain: A Modern History.* New York: Frederick A. Praeger, 1960.

Mannheim, Karl. *Ideology and Utopia: An Introduction to the Sociology of Knowledge.* Translated by Louis Wirth and Edward Shils, Introduction by L. Wirth. New York: Harcourt, Brace & World, 1936.

Maravall, José A. "La formación de la conciencia estamental de los letrados." *Revista de estudios políticos,* (Madrid, July–August, 1953): 53–81.

Mariéjol, Jean H. *Philip II: The First Modern King.* Translated by Warre B. Wells. New York: Harper & Brothers, 1933.

_____. *The Spain of Ferdinand and Isabella.* Translated and edited by Benjamin Keen. New Brunswick, N.J.: Rutgers University Press, 1961.

Mariluz Urquijo, José María. *Ensayo sobre los juicios de residencia indianos.* Seville: Escuela de Estudios Hispano-Americanos, 1952.

Markham, Clements Robert. *The Conquest of New Granada.* London: Smith, Elder, 1912.

Martin, Norman F. *Los vagabundos en la Nueva España, siglo XVI.* Mexico City: Editorial Jus, 1957.

Martínez Peláez, Severo. *La patria del criollo.* Guatemala City: Editorial Universitaria, 1971.

Maticorena Estrada, Miguel. "Sobre las 'Decadas' de Antonio de Herrera: La Florida." Reprint from *Anuario de estudios Americanos* 23 (1958): 29–62.

Means, P. A. *The Spanish Main, Focus of Envy, 1492–1700.* New York: Gordian Press, 1935.

Mecham, J. Lloyd. *Francisco de Ibarra and Nueva Vizcaya.* Durham, N. C.: Duke University Press, 1927.

Mejía Ricart, G. A. *Historia de Santo Domingo.* 8 vols. to date. Ciudad Trujillo: Pol. Hnos., 1948–1954.

Mendieta, Gerónimo de. *Historia eclesiástica indiana.* 4 vols. Mexico City: Editorial Salvador Chávez Hayhoe, 1945.

Mendieta Núñez, Lucio. *El derecho precolonial.* Mexico City: Porrúa Hermanos, 1937.

Merriman, R. B. *The Rise of the Spanish Empire in the Old World and in the New.* 4 vols. New York: Macmillan, 1918–34.

Miralles de Imperial y Gómez, Claudio. "Del linaje y armas del primer cronista de Indias." *Revista de Indias,* no. 71 (January–March, 1958): 73–126.

Miranda, José. *El tributo indígena en la Nueva España durante el siglo XVI.* Mexico City: El Colegio de México, 1952.

_____. *España y Nueva España en la época de Felipe II.* Mexico City: Universidad Nacional Autónoma de México, 1962.

Monzón, Arturo. *El calpulli en la organización social de los Tenocha.* Mexico City: Universidad Nacional Autónoma de México, 1949.

Morales Rojas, J. *Córdoba.* Barcelona: Editorial Planeta, 1966.

Moreno, Manuel. *La organización política y social de los aztecas.* Mexico City: Instituto Nacional de Antropología e Historia. 1962.

Morgan, Lewis H. *Ancient Society, or Researches in the Lines of Human Progress from Savagery through Barbarism to Civilization (1877).* Edited by Leslie A. White. Cambridge, Mass.: Harvard University Press, 1964.

Morison, Samuel E. *Admiral of the Ocean Sea: A Life of Christopher Columbus.* Boston: Little, Brown, 1942.

————. *The European Discovery of America: The Southern Voyages. A. D. 1492–1616.* New York: Oxford University Press, 1974.

Mörner, Magnus. *Race Mixture in the History of Latin America.* Boston: Little, Brown, 1967.

Moses, Bernard. *The Spanish Dependencies in South America.* 2 vols. New York: Cooper Square, 1965.

Motolinía, Fray Toribio de [Benavente]. *Memoriales.* Mexico City: Edmundo Aviña, 1967.

————. *Motolinía's History of the Indians of New Spain.* Translated by Francis Borgia Steck. Washington. D.C.: Academy of American Franciscan History, 1951.

Muro Orejón, Antonio, ed. *Las leyes nuevas de 1542–1543: Ordenanzas para la gobernación de las Indias y buen tratamiento y conservación de los indios.* Seville: Escuela de Estudios Hispano-Americanos, 1961.

Newton, A. P. *The European Nations in the West Indies, 1493–1688.* London: A. & C. Black, 1933.

Noreña, Carlos G. *Studies in Spanish Renaissance Thought.* The Hague: Martinus Nijhoff, 1975.

Nutini, Hugo G., "Clan Organization in a Nahuatl-Speaking Village of the State of Tlaxcala, Mexico." *American Anthropologist* 63 (February, 1961): 62–78.

Obregón, Baltasar de. *Historia de los descubrimientos antiguos y modernos de la Nueva España.* Mexico City: Secretaría de Education Pública, 1924.

O'Daniel, V. F. *Dominicans in Early Florida.* New York: United States Catholic Historical Society, 1930.

Orozco y Berra, Manuel. *Noticia histórica de la conjuración del Marqués del Valle, 1565–1568.* Mexico City: R. Rafael, 1853.

————. *Historia antigua y de la conquista de México.* 4 vols. Mexico City: Tipografía de Gonzalo A. Esteva, 1880.

Otte, Enrique. "Gonzalo Fernández de Oviedo an Kaiser Karl über die zustände in Santo Domingo. In *Spanische Forschungen der Görresgesellschaft.* 1st ser. Münster, 1956. 2: 165–70.

————. "Una carta inédita de Gonzalo Fernández de Oviedo." *Revista de Indias* 65 (1956): 435–58.

Parker, Alexander A. *Literature and the Delinquent: The Picaresque Novel in Spain and Europe, 1599–1753.* Edinburgh: University Press, 1967.

Parker, Geoffrey. *Philip II.* Boston-Toronto: Little, Brown, 1978.

Parry, J. H. *The Audiencia of New Galicia in the Sixteenth Century.* Cambridge: Cambridge University Press, 1948.

Paso y Troncoso, Francisco del, ed. *Epistolario de la Nueva España.* 16 vols. Mexico City: Antigua Librería Robredo, de José Porrúa e Hijos, 1939–42.

Pérez y López, Antonio Xavier. *Teatro de la legislación universal de España y las Indias*. 28 vols. Madrid: Imprenta de M. González, 1791–98.

Petrie, Sir Charles. *Philip II of Spain*. London: Eyre & Spottiswoode, 1963.

Pfandl, Ludwig. *Cultura y costumbres del pueblo español de los siglos XVI y XVII*. Barcelona: Casa Editorial Araluce, 1929.

Phelan, John Leddy. *The Millennial Kingdom of the Franciscans in the New World*. Berkeley and Los Angeles: University of California Press, 1970.

Phillips, Margaret Mann. *The "Adages" of Erasmus: A Study with Translations*. Cambridge: University Press, 1964.

Picón-Salas, Mariano. *A Cultural History of Spanish America from Conquest to Independence*. Translated by Irving A. Leonard. Berkeley and Los Angeles: University of California Press, 1968.

Pike, Ruth. *Enterprise and Adventure: The Genoese in Seville and the Opening of the New World*. Ithaca; N.Y.: Cornell University Press, 1966.

_____. *Aristocrats and Traders: Sevillian Society in the Sixteenth Century*. Ithaca, N.Y., and London: Cornell University Press, 1972.

Pintura del gobernador, alcaldes y regidores de México: Códice Osuna. Madrid: Servicio de Publicaciones del Ministerio de Educación y Ciencia, 1973.

Popenoe, Dorothy H. *The Story of Antigua Guatemala*. Dalton, Mass.: Studley Press, 1973.

Potter, G. R., ed. *The New Cambridge Modern History*. vol. 1: *The Renaissance, 1493–1520*. Cambridge: Cambridge University Press, 1957.

Powell, Philip Wayne. *Soldiers, Indians and Silver: The Northward Advance of New Spain, 1550–1600*. Berkeley and Los Angeles: University of California Press, 1952.

Prescott, William H. *Mexico and the Life of the Conqueror Fernando Cortés*. 2 vols. New York: Peter Fenelon Collier, 1848.

_____. *History of the Reign of Ferdinand and Isabella*. 3 vols. Philadelphia: J.B. Lippincott, 1882.

Puga, Vasco de. *Provisiones, cédulas, instrucciones para el gobierno de la Nueva España*. Madrid: Ediciones Cultural Hispánica, 1945.

Purcell, Mary. *The Great Captain, Gonzalo Fernández de Córdoba*. London: Alvin Redman, 1963.

Quevedo, Francisco de. *El buscón*. New York: Doubleday, 1961.

_____. *The Scavenger*. Translated and with an Introduction by Hugh A. Harter. New York: Las Americas Publishing Co., 1962.

Rashdall, H. *The Universities of Europe in the Middle Ages*, 3 vols. Edited by F. M. Powicke and A. B. Emden. Oxford: Clarendon Press, 1936.

Ratekin, Mervyn. "The Early Sugar Industry in Española." *Hispanic American Historical Review* 34 (February, 1954): 1–19.

Reichel-Dolmatoff, Gerardo. *Datos históricos-culturales sobre las tribus de la antigua gobernación de Santa Marta.* Bogotá: Imprenta del Banco de la República, 1951.

Remesal, Antonio de. *Historia general de las Indias Occidentales y particular de la gobernación de Chiapa y Guatemala.* 2 vols. Madrid: Biblioteca de Autores Españoles, 1966.

Restrepo Tirado, Ernesto. *Historia de la provincia de Santa Marta.* 2 vols. Bogotá: Biblioteca de Autores Colombianos, 1953.

Ricard, Robert. "Remarques bibliographiques sur les ouvrages de Fr. Toribio Motolinía." *Journal de la Société des Américanistes* 25 (1933): 139–51.

Riley, G. Michael. *Fernando Cortés and the Marquesado in Morelos, 1522–1547.* Albuquerque: University of New Mexico Press, 1973.

Riva Palacio, Vicente, ed. *México a través de los siglos.* 5 vols. Mexico City: Gustavo S. López, 1940.

Roa y Ursúa, Luis de. *El reyno de Chile, 1535–1810.* Valladolid: Consejo Superior de Investigaciones, 1945.

Robledo, Emilio. *Vida del Mariscal Jorge Robledo.* Bogotá: Biblioteca de Autores Colombianos, 1955.

Rodríguez Becerra, Salvador. *Encomienda y conquista, los inicios de la colonización en Guatemala.* Seville: Publicaciones de la Universidad de Sevilla, 1977.

Rodríguez Villa, Antonio, ed. *Crónicas del Gran Capitán.* Madrid: Nueva Biblioteca de Autores Españoles, 1908.

Rosenblat, Ángel. *La población indígena y el mestizaje en América.* 2 vols. Buenos Aires: Editorial Nova, 1954.

———. "Base del español de América: Nivel social y cultural de los conquistadores y pobladores." *Revista de Indias*, nos. 125–26 (July–December, 1971): 13–75.

Rubio Mañé, J. Ignacio. *Don Luis de Velasco, el virrey popular.* Mexico City: Edicones Xochitl, 1946.

———. *Introducción al estudio de los virreyes de Nueva España, 1535–1746.* 2 vols. Mexico City: Universidad Nacional Autónoma de México, 1959.

Saco, José Antonio. *Historia de la esclavitud de la raza africana en el Nuevo Mundo y en especial en los países américo-hispanos.* 4 vols. Havana: Librería Cervantes, 1938.

Sahagún, Bernardino de. *General History of the Things of New Spain, Florentine Codex.* 13 vols. Translated and edited by A. O. J. Anderson and C. E. Dibble. Santa Fe, N.Mex.: School of American Research and University of Utah, 1982.

Sancho, Hipólito R. "Diego Fernández de Zurita, alcaide de Arcos, embajador en Granada." *Revista de Historia y de Genealogía Espa-*

ñola (Madrid, 1929–31): 1: 1–42; 2: 107–16; 3: 327–37; 4: 178–236.

Sarabia Viejo, María Justina. *Don Luis de Velasco, virrey de Nueva España, 1550–1564.* Seville: La Escuela de Estudios Hispano-Americanos de Sevilla, 1978.

Sauer, Carl O. *The Early Spanish Main.* Berkeley and Los Angeles: University of California Press, 1966.

Schäfer, Ernesto. *El Consejo Real y Supremo de las Indias.* 4 vols. Seville: La Escuela de Estudios Hispano-Americanos, 1935–47.

Schoenrich, Otto. *The Legacy of Christopher Columbus.* 2 vols. Glendale, Calif. Arthur H. Clark, 1949.

Scholes, France V. "The Spanish Conqueror as a Business Man." Offprint from *New Mexico Quarterly* 28 (Spring, 1958): 1–29.

Scholes, France V., and Eleanor B. Adams, eds. *Documentos para la historia del México colonial.* 7 vols. Mexico City: José Porrúa e Hijos, 1955–1961.

Scholes, Walter V. *The Diego Ramírez Visita. University of Missouri Studies* 20, no. 4 (1946).

Seaver, Henry Latimer. *The Great Revolt in Castile: A Study of the Comunero Movement of 1520–1521.* New York: Octagon Books, 1966.

Serrano y Sanz, Manuel, ed. *Autobiografías y Memorias.* Madrid: Librería Editorial de Bailly-Bailliére e Hijos, 1905.

Sherman, William L. "Indian Slavery and the Cerrato Reforms." *Hispanic American Historical Review* 51 (February, 1971): 25–50.

_____. "Tlaxcalans in Post-Conquest Guatemala," Offprint from *Tlalocan* 6 (1970): 124–39.

_____. *Forced Native Labor in Sixteenth-Century Central America.* Lincoln and London: University of Nebraska Press, 1979.

Simón, Pedro. *Historia de la expedición de Pedro de Ursúa al Marañon y de las aventuras de Lope de Aguirre.* Lima: Biblioteca Cultural Peruana, 1942.

_____. *Noticias historiales de las conquistas de Tierra Frime en las Indias Occidentales.* 9 vols. Bogotá: Biblioteca de Autores Colombianos, 1953.

Simpson, Lesley Byrd. *The Encomienda in New Spain: The Beginnings of Spanish Mexico.* Berkeley and Los Angeles: University of California Press, 1966.

Slicher van Bath, B. H. *The Agrarian History of Western Europe, A.D. 500–1850.* New York: St. Martin's Press, 1963.

Smith, Buckingham, ed. *Colección de varios documentos para la historia de Florida y Tierras Adyacentes.* London: Casa de Trubner y Compañía, 1857.

Sordo, Enrique. *Granada.* Barcelona: Editorial Planeta, 1964.

Soustelle, Jacques. *Daily Life of the Aztecs on the Eve of the Spanish Conquest.* New York: Macmillan, 1968.

Spores, Ronald. *The Mixtec Kings and Their People*. Norman: University of Oklahoma Press, 1967.

Suárez de Peralta, Juan. *Tratado del descubrimiento de las Indias: Noticias históricas de Nueva España*. Mexico City: Secretaría de Educación Pública, 1949.

Tannenbaum, Frank. *Slave and Citizen: The Negro in the Americas*. New York: Vintage Books, 1946; copyright, Alfred A. Knopf.

Tawney, R. H. *Religion and the Rise of Capitalism: A Historical Study*. New York and Toronto: New American Library, 1954.

Thayer Ojeda, Tomás, and Carlos J. Larrain. *Valdivia y sus compañeros*. Santiago de Chile: Imprenta Universitaria, 1950.

Thayer Ojeda, Tomás. *Formación de la sociedad chilena y censo de la población de Chile en los años de 1540 a 1565*. 3 vols. Santiago de Chile: Prensas de la Unviersidad de Chile, 1939–43.

Torquemada, Juan de. *Monarquía indiana*. Mexico City: Editorial Porrúa, 1975.

Torre y del Cerro, José de. *Obras de don José de la Torre y del Cerro*. Córdoba: Imprenta Provincial, 1955.

Toynbee, Arnold J. *A Study of History*. 12 vols. London: Oxford University Press, 1934–61.

Ubieto, Antonio, et al. *Introducción a las historia de España*. Barcelona: Editorial Teide, 1966.

Ustarroz, J. F. A. de, and D. J. Dormer. *Progreso de la historia en Aragón y vida de sus cronistas*. Zaragosa: Imprenta del Hospicio, 1878.

Valbuena Prat, Ángel. *La vida española en la edad de oro según sus fuentes literarias*. Barcelona: Editorial Alberto Martín, 1943.

Valle-Arizpe, Artemio de. *La casa de los Ávila*. Mexico City: José Porrúa e Hijos, Sucesores, 1960.

Vance, J. T. *The Background of Hispanic-American Law: Legal Sources and Judicial Literature of Spain*. New York: Central Book, 1943.

Van der Kroef, Justus M. "Francisco de Vitoria and the Nature of Colonial Policy." *Catholic Historical Review* 35 (April, 1949–January, 1950): 129–62.

Vázques de Espinosa, Antonio. *Compendio y descripción de las Indias Occidentales*. Madrid: Biblioteca de Autores Españoles, 1969.

Vicens Vives, Jaime. *An Economic History of Spain*. Translated by Frances M. López-Morillas. Princeton, N.J.: Princeton University Press, 1969.

Vicens Vives, Jaime, ed. *Historia de España y América*. 5 vols. Barcelona: Editorial Vicens-Vives, 1961.

Vigil, Ralph H. "Negro Slaves and Rebels in the Spanish Possessions, 1503–1558." *Historian* 33 (August, 1971): 637–55.

———. "A Reappraisal of the Expedition of Pánfilo de Narváez to Mexico in 1520." *Revista de Historia de América*, nos. 77–78 (1974): 101–25.

_____. "Alonso de Zorita, Early and Last Year." *Americas* 32 (April, 1976): 501–13.

_____. "Bartolomé de Las Casas, Judge Alonso de Zorita, and the Franciscans: A Collaborative Effort for the Spiritual Conquest of the Borderlands." *Americas* 38 (July, 1981): 45–57.

Vitoria, Francisco de. *Relectio de Indis o libertad de los Indios.* Edited by L. Pereña and J. M. Pérez Prendes. Madrid: Consejo Superior de Investigaciones Científicas, 1967.

Wagner, Henry Raup, with Helen Rand Parish. *The Life and Writings of Bartolomé de las Casas.* Albuquerque: University of New Mexico Press, 1967.

Washburn, Wilcomb E. *The Indian in America.* New York: Harper and Row, 1975.

Wauchope, Robert, ed. *Handbook of Middle American Indians.* 15 vols. Austin: University of Texas Press, 1964–75.

Wieruszowski, Helene. *The Medieval University.* New York: D. Van. Nostrand, 1966.

Wolf, Eric. *Sons of the Shaking Earth.* Chicago and London: University of Chicago Press, 1970.

Zavala, Silvio A. *La encomienda indiana.* Madrid: Centro de Estudios Históricos, 1935.

Zorita, Alonso de. *Breve y sumaria relación de los señores de la Nueva España.* Edited by Joaquín Ramírez Cabañas. Mexico City: Ediciones de la Universidad Nacional Autónoma, 1942.

_____. *Historia de la Nueva España.* Edited by Manuel Serrano y Sanz. Madrid: Imprenta de Fortanet, 1909. Vol. 9 of *Colección de libros y documentos referentes a la historia de América.* Madrid, 1904–29.

_____. *Life and Labor in Ancient Mexico: The Brief and Summary Relation of the Lords of New Spain.* Translated and Introduction by Benjamin Keen. New Brunswick, N.J.: Rutgers University Press, 1963.

Index

Arroyo Valdivia, Pedro de: 21
Artisans: of Spain, 9, 13, 16, 243; of
  Española, 60; of Santiago de
  Guatemala, 125; of Mexico City,
  162; of pre-Conquest Mexico, 287–
  88, 290
"Asiatic mode of production": 287,
  342n.
Asistencia: 197
Astudillo, Gaspar de: 53
Atacubaya (encomienda, Mexico): 188
Atitlán (Indian district, Guatemala):
  194–95
Audiencia in New World: 47
Audiencia of Charcas: 20, 226
Audiencia of Granada: 37, 46, 83, 164,
  211, 247, 263; composition of, 255
Audiencia of Guatemala: 46, 74,
  121ff., 130, 214
Audiencia of Lima: 261
Audiencia of Mexico: 46, 127, 134–35,
  140, 150ff., 211ff., 229ff., 283; staff,
  plaintiffs, and defendants of, 163–
  64; and financial need of judges,
  179; and arrogance of judges, 180;
  and differences with viceroy, 181–
  85; weakness of, in 1564, 204
Audiencia of New Galicia: 46, 206,
  211–12, 218, 227
Audiencia of New Granada: 97ff.,
  110, 119–20
Audiencia of Santo Domingo: 41,
  45ff., 56ff., 65ff., 77–80, 96ff., 119,
  122
Audiencia of Valladolid: 28, 36–37,
  112, 164
Augustinian order: 171, 183, 232; and
  dispute with Indians of
  Teotihuacán, 197–200
Avería: 54–55, 74
Ávila, Alonso de (conqueror): 201–
  202
Ávila, Francisco de: 58, 75
Ávila Alvarado, Alonso de: 162, 164,
  172, 174, 202ff., 228; see also
  Cortés-Ávila conspiracy
Ayala, Bernarda de: 175
Ayala, Luis de: 62
Ayala, Pedro de (bishop of
  Guadalajara): 216

Ayala de Espinosa, Cristóbal: 172,
  175, 208
Ayllón, Lucas Vázquez de: 58
Azpilcueta Navarro, Martín de: 36,
  236
Aztecs: 221; pre-Conquest social and
  political organization of, 279–83,
  285–93
Azua, Española: 77

Baeza, Spain: 208
Balamiha, cacique of: 144
Balancolob, cacique of: 144
Baldes, Melchor de: 114
Ballesteros, Alvaro de: 107
Bancroft, Hubert H.: 129, 132, 138,
  156, 204, 208
Bandelier, Adolph F.: 286
Bandits: 9, 14, 243, 251, 253–54; in
  Guatemala, 132–33
Barahona, Sancho de: 194–95
Barcelona, Spain: 49
Barcía, Andrés G.: 276
Barrios, Indian: 189, 290; see also
  calpulli
Barros de San Millán, Manuel: 195
Bartolus of Sassoferrato: 31, 36
Bastidas, Rodrigo de (bishop of San
  Juan): 71ff.
Baudot, Georges: 273
Bayarcal (Morisco settlement): 253
Bazán, Alonso de: 199
Bazán, Alvaro de: 45, 65
Bazán, Luis de: 79–80
Beaumonts (Spanish party, Navarre):
  85ff.
Becerra, Cristóbal de la: 256
Belandia, Francisco de: 95–96
Beltran, Nicolás: 85
Benalcázar, Sebastián de: 32, 84–85,
  91ff., 119, 321n.
Berchul (Morisco settlement): 251
Berja (Morisco settlement): 253
Bermúdez, Licentiate: 47
Bernáldez, Lorenzo: 53
Berrio, Juan de: 80
Betanzos, Pedro: 148
Beteta, Gregorio de: 215, 277, 340n.
Bielsa (villa): 84
Biscay: 242

85, 191–93, 203ff., 222, 228ff., 245;
character of, 223, 230–32; on Las
Casas and Dominicans, 224; on
judges of Audiencia of Mexico,
226–27; accomplishments of, 233;
see also Cortés-Ávila conspiracy;
visita
Valdivia, Pedro de: 21
Valdivieso, Antonio de: 121;
murdered in Nicaragua, 131–32
Valencia, Catalina de: 65
Valencia, Martín de: 273, 340n.
Valencia, Spain: 15
Valera, Cipriano de: 258
Valera, Diego de: 23
Valladolid: 110, 216
Valladolid (Honduras): 121
Valladolid, La Nueva Villa de
(Comayagua): 121
Valladolid, University of: 27, 37
Valle, Juan del: 91, 112, 119
Valle de las Lanzas: 113
Valor, Hernando de: *see* Aben
Humeya
Vara de justicia: 89, 154, 188, 198
Vázquez de Coronado, Francisco:
201, 214, 218, 220
Vázquez de Coronado, Juan: 130, 134
Vázquez de Coronado, Marina: 202
Vecinos: 21, 55, 60, 74, 134–35, 166,
169, 189, 197, 232, 255–56, 263; of
Española, 78; of Guatemala, 147; as
synonymous with "white" and
"Spaniard," 167
Veedor: 95
Vega, Lope de: 61, 199
Vega y Fonseca, Hernando de: 37
Velasco, Francisco de: 168, 181, 206
Velasco, Luis de: 39, 161, 164ff., 189–
90, 192, 200–201, 204, 212–13, 219,
223ff.; recommends exchange
between judges and members of
Council of the Indies, 179; on
appointment of judges in Mexico,
181; differences of, with audiencia,
181–84; on Zorita's appointment to
special Indian court, 183; freeing of
Indian slaves by, 185; death of,
1564, 204; debts of, 329n.
Velasco, Luis de (son of viceroy): 206

Vélez (Colombia): 89
Vélez, Málaga: 211
Vellón: 81; *see also* coinage
Venezuela: 47, 106
Ventas: 43
Vera Cruz: 65, 206
Veraiz, Leonor: 85
Veraiz, Pedro: 85
Vera Paz (Tuzulutlán), Mexico: 144–
45, 213, 217
Verdugo, Francisco (*cacique*): 199
Vergara y Agramont, Isabel: 85
Vetancourt, Agustín de: 278
Vico, Domingo de: 144–45
Vidoy, Juanes de: 66
Villach, Carinthia: 242
Villa del Río: 21
Villadiego, Alonso de: 117
Villafranca: 12
Villagar, Licentiate: 178
Villagrán, Pedro de: 20
Villahermosa, duke of: 67
Villalobos, Pedro de: 179–80, 201,
204, 209, 226, 231
Villanueva, Luis de: 115
Villanueva de Barcarrota: 168
Villanueva Zapata, Luis de: 179, 201,
226–27, 230, 335n.
Villaroel, Alvaro de: 19
Villegas, Isabel de: 178
Villoria, Juan de: 63
Villoria, María de: 63
Virgén de Guadalupe: *see* cult of
Guadalupe
Virgén de Piedad (Nuestra Señora del
Socorro): 124
Visitador: 20
Visitas: 48, 81, 127, 130, 145ff., 153,
182, 185ff., 192, 194–97, 210, 211,
214, 255, 261; of Teotihuacán, 197;
of Valderrama in Mexico, 184–85,
221–34
Vitoria, Francisco de: 30–31

Wagner, Henry Raup: 213, 217–18,
221
Washburn, Wilcomb: 292
Witchcraft: 68
Witte, Nicolás de: 193
Wittfogel, Karl: 287

Wolf, Eric: 284
Wool: 9, 15, 242
Women: of Andalusia, 38; Berber
slave women in Española, 55; of
Moorish Granada, 246

Xalapa: 195
Xaltocan: 202
Xegua: 117
Xeñiz, Gonzalo (bandit): 251, 254
Xeñiz, Lope (bandit): 251
Xicalpa (Indian district): 194
Xilotepec, Mexico: 168, 328n.
Xochimilco, Mexico: 190

Yaguana, La: 77–79, 110
Yucatán: 121, 171, 201

Zabra: 79
Zacatecas, Mexico: 195, 206, 208, 221
Zamora: 26
Zárate, Juan de: 80
Zayas, Gabriel de: 248
Zorita, Alonso de: birth and
background of, 3, 10ff., 305n.;
name, title, and ancestry, 10ff.; at
University of Salamanca, 29–36;
appointed royal judge in Audiencia
of Santo Domingo, 41; *residencia* in
Española, 62, 81–82, 139, 325n.;
and defense of Española, 77–80; on
secular clergy, 109, 135, 171; as
captain of cavalry in Cartagena,
109–10; as reformer in Guatemala,
127; on Cerrato, 129; *visitas* of, in
Guatemala, 145ff.; appointed judge
in Audiencia of Mexico, 158–59;

admitted as doctor in laws to
University of Mexico, 165; and
"demons" of Mexico, 167; on
Indian tribute of Indians of Mexico
City, 189–90; on excessive tribute
paid by Indians, 193–94; infirmities
of, 210–11, 222ff.; and Las Casian
project for spiritual conquest of
borderlands, 213–21; and charges
resulting from Valderrama's *visita*,
230–34; retirement and financial
difficulties of, 233–34, 241, 255–56;
last years and death of, 262–64; and
humanism, 265–66; written works
of, 266–79; and Indian tribute
question, 267–70; first
bibliographer of the New World,
272; and primitivism and
apocalyptic eschatology, 275–76,
340n.; *see also Brief and Summary
Relation of the Lords of New Spain*;
"Discursos de la vida humana";
"Recopilación de las leyes de
Indias"; "Relación de las cosas
notables de la Nueva España...";
"Suma de los tributos"
Zorita, Francisco de: 19, 21
Zorita, Inés de: 19, 21, 256, 263
Zorita, Lucía de: 19, 21, 263
Zorita de los Canes: 11
Zorita de Villavicencio, Ana: 19, 21,
256, 263
Zorita de Villavicencio, Elvira: 19, 21,
263
Zorita de Villavicencio, María: 19, 21
Zumárraga, Juan de: 36, 273
Zúñiga, Inés de: 73
Zurita, Jerónimo de: 10